HIRED GUNS
AND COUPS D'ETAT

About the Author

Anthony Mockler has covered the activities of mercenary soldiers for decades, watching their triumphs, surveying their fiascos and investigating their backgrounds. He probably knows more about mercenaries, dead or alive, past or present, than anyone else in the world.

Educated at Downside and at Cambridge, a classicist (Double First) and a historian by training, a journalist and author by profession, he has himself served in the Queen's Bays, been a war correspondent not only in the Congo and other parts of Africa but also in Central America and Vietnam.

He has written books on a wide variety of topics apart from mercenaries. Among his other publications are:

Lions Under The Throne: the Lives of the Lord Chief Justices of England
Francis of Assisi: The Wandering Years
Graham Greene: Three Lives
Hostage (with Glen Dixon)
Our Enemies the French: The Syrian Campaign 1941

And his massive, much-praised:
Haile Selassie's War

His children's books include:
Sir Yvain the Gold-Green Knight
King Arthur and the Knights

He travels widely; and lives, mainly, in France.

HIRED GUNS
AND COUPS D'ETAT

MERCENARIES: THIRTY YEARS
1976 – 2006

Anthony Mockler

Hunter Mackay
Oxford and Scotland

Cover Illustration: At Camp Kandani in the Comores one of Bob Denard's mercenaries is saluted by a Comorian comrade-in-arms - just before the surrender to overwhelming French Forces. The date is October 1995. (Adil Bradlow Boomerang Presse)

First published in the English language in Great Britain in 2006 by
Hunter Mackay, 140 Upper Road, Oxford OX1 5LW

© Anthony Mockler 2006.

The right of Anthony Mockler to be identified as author of this work has been asserted by him in accordance with the Copyright, Design and Patents Act, 1988.

A Cataloguing in Publication - CIP - Data for this book is available from the British Library.
Mockler, Anthony
Hired Guns and Coups d'Etat
1. *Mercenaries.*
2 *Military History*

ISBN 0-947907-07-6
ISBN 978-0-947907-07-05

Typeset, printed and bound in Great Britain by Oaklands Book Services,
Unit 10, Oldends Lane Industrial Estate, Stonehouse, Gloucestershire, GL10 3RG.

Contents

Dedication

If the Moulin d'Andé had not existed, none of my books would have been written. So this book is dedicated to that inspiring and enchanted place; and to Suzanne Lipinska and Maurice Pons, the benevolent and irreplaceable *genii loci*.

Acknowledgements

Inevitably in the course of writing my books I have come across many mercenaries or ex-mercenaries. The only one to whom I took an instant and intense dislike was a gentleman named Ian Gordon, and that dislike was mutual. He had me chucked into a cell in Stanleyville in the Congo and left me to cool - or rather (it was suffocatingly hot) sweat - my heels there for twenty-four hours before expelling me. Apart from that anti-acknowledgement I have found most mercenaries to be surprisingly like most professional soldiers, helpful within limits, wary of letting their names be known or used or acknowledged, and almost invariably polite - very different in fact from the perceptions I had first had and held against them. So, logically, in a book like this I must first express my general gratitude for their assistance; as also to many other sources who, like them, prefer to remain anonymous.

$$\star \qquad \star \qquad \star$$

Without Kate Fraser's endless patience, total reliability, and up-to-date technical skills this book like so many other books of mine, would never have been finished. For their hospitality and for help in other ways I would like to thank in particular Peter Kemmis Betty, Phyllis Sipahioglu, Irene and Laura Andreae, James Ferguson, Jania Macgillivray, Mark Le Fanu, Yvonne Leclercq, Sylvie Camet, Bill Myers, Patricia Malraux, Leonie Hannan, Ben Kobus, Jane Wilson, Miles Irving, Roland Reeves, Stratford and Leone Caldecott, Kasia and John Greenwood, Philip and Patricia Hawkes, Andrew and Felicity Wedderburn, Alban and Chiara de Bonnecorses-Loubières.

Last but far from least Gwendoline Marsh who has wisely criticised, helpfully corrected and invariably supported throughout.

A Guide to Abbreviations

Initials, like jargon, are a curse; and I have tried to keep them to a minimum in this book. Nevertheless they do have to be used; and though it seems fair to assume that everyone who reads this book will know that the RAF is the Royal Air Force, the UN the United Nations, and the USA the United States of America, it would perhaps be wrong to take much else for granted. Hence this list. In many cases I feel it is less important to know what the initials stand for than what they refer to. I hope baffled readers will find it a useful aid to turn back to when in doubt. It covers almost all the 'initialese' used in this book.

Military Ranks

CO	Commanding Officer (usually a Colonel).
NCO	Non-commissioned officer (eg. Sergeant/ Corporal).
RSM	Regimented Sergeant Manor.
DMI	Director of Military Intelligence.
ADC	Aide-de-Camp; go-fer to a General.

Military Units

1er REP	The 1st Foreign Legion Paratroop Regiment, now disbanded.
2^{e} REP	The 2nd Foreign Legion Paratroop Regiment, still in existence.
SAS	The British Army's semi-secret elite unit. (Also the Rhodesian SAS - white Rhodesia's much smaller equivalent).
RLI	The Rhodesian Light Infantry.
1^{e}, 2^{e}, 6^{e}, RPIMA	French Marine Paratroop Regiments.
13^{e} RDP	French Dragoon Paras.
RIAOIM and 2^{e} RAMA	Other French Units.
SADF / SANDF	South Africa's armed forces.

| SWATF | South West Africa Territorial Forces. |
| FAC | Comores' armed forces. |

Military Vehicles, Weapons, Planes

RPG	Rocket-propelled grenade (and launcher).
AK 47	Folding rifle – Soviet bloc.
SAM	Anti-aircraft missile.
MIG	Soviet plane.
DC (3,4, etc)	Dakotas.
BRDM	Soviet armoured car.
BMP	Soviet troop carrier.
BTR	Soviet amphibious vehicle.

Secret Services

CIA	American.
SIS / MI6	British.
SDECE / DGSE	French.
BOSS / DONS / NIS	South African.
SID	Italian.
KGB	Soviet.

Official Titles

OAU	Organisation of African Unity.
USSR	Union of Soviet Socialist Republics (now defunct).
RSA	Republic of South Africa.
PNG	Papua New Guinea.
HMG	Her Majesty's Government.
FO	Foreign Office.
MP	Member of Parliament (n.b. not used in this book of Military Police).
QC	Queen's Counsel; high-up British lawyer.

Political and Revolutionary Organisations

In Angola

MPLA	The Marxist movement that seized power successfully pre-Independence in the capital Luanda; and still holds it.
UNITA	Jonas Savimbi's; in the centre and south of the country, mainly Ovimbundu.
FNLA	Holden Roberto's; in the north, mainly Bakongo.

In Southern Africa

ANC	Nelson Mandela's; now the ruling party in South Africa.
SWAPO	Sam Nujoma's; now the ruling party in Namibia (formerly South West Africa).
ZIPRA	Joshua Nkomo's; in Rhodesia / Zimbabwe.
ZANLA	Robert Mugabe's; in Rhodesia / Zimbabwe.

Elsewhere

OAS	Represented the French who wanted to stay on in Algeria. Attempted to assassinate De Gaulle.
IRA	Represents the Irish who wish to take over Northern Ireland. Has assassinated, and attempted to assassinate, many English leaders.
PLO	Represents the Palestinians. A political body but involved in many assassinations.
BRA	Represents the inhabitants of Bougainville seeking independence from Papua New Guinea.
RUF	Represents certain tribal factions of the interior of Sierra Leone, in their anarchic struggle against Freetown and the Creoles.

Other Abbreviations

UDI	Originally Ian Smith's 'Unilateral Declaration of Independence' – by Rhodesia from Great Britain – in 1965.
NGO	Non-governmental Organisation. Used particularly of charities (such as Oxfam) active in the Third World.
CFA	Francophone Africa's currency (and now Equatorial Guinea's too) – in francs, whereas France herself has only euros…
NBG	No Bloody Good – colloquial.
ASAP	As Soon As Possible – military.
"O" Group	Order Group – assembled to receive orders – military.

Private Military Companies

PMC	Private Military Company (British usage)
PSC	Private Security Company (American usage)
MPRI	Military and Professional Resources Inc. (of Virginia, USA).
CRG	Control Risks Group (UK).

DSL	Defence Systems Ltd (originally UK; since amalgamated with Armor Holdings of USA to form ArmorGroup).
MTS	Meteoric Tactical Services (of South Africa; Hecky Horn and Jacobus Carlse's outfit).

List of Maps

Foreword

What exactly is a mercenary? A simple question but one surprisingly tricky to answer. *Soldat qui sert à prix d'argent un pouvoir étranger* is the Larousse definition. It covers extremely well the (mostly) hard-bitten young thugs who tended to join the French Foreign Legion, created in 1831. But it covers just as well the (mostly) idealistic young men who volunteered to fight in the International Brigade in the Spanish Civil War of 1936-39. Members of both groups were certainly paid, though in both cases poorly paid – so they both served *à prix d'argent*. Unarguably both were fighting for a *pouvoir étranger,* a foreign power. Yet the coupling of these two groups under a single heading leaves a distinct feeling of queasiness: that something is very wrong.

And it is the same, unfortunately, with all other attempts at definition. Not one is satisfactory in all cases. My conclusion is this: that it is useless to attempt to give a formal and final answer to the question 'What is a mercenary?' because the implications and connotations of the term have varied enormously through-out history. To elaborate a little: – at times of great empires and almost universal citizenship the term is applicable, or not, almost at will. The Kaiser famously condemned the Indians who fought for the British as "an army of mercenaries". Yet by the Larousse definition the Sikhs and Rajputs, who fought in the Indian Army in the First World War, were subjects of the King-Emperor and therefore not mercenaries – though the Gurkhas who fought beside them, being from an independent kingdom, undoubtedly were. At periods of close national unity and limited citizenship when the nation state or the city state is the dominant form of government, 'mercenary' can be more precisely defined. In the feudal age, when loyalties were confused and multitudinous, the term is almost – but far from totally – meaningless. When a rich nation goes to war, its poorer allies (as so often in eighteenth-century Germany) become in effect mercenary states, hiring out their whole armies. The mercenaries who fought for Katanga in the early 1960's called the troops of the United Nations who opposed them – the Swedes, the Irish, the Ethiopians – *les super - mercenaires*. Were they entirely wrong?   This quick gallop through history will, I hope, indicate the complexities of any possible answer.

In the end it is easier to recognise the true mercenary by practise rather than by definition. Take Xenophon's thumbnail sketch of the Greek mercenary leader, his old commander, Clearchus:

> He could have lived in peace without incurring any reproaches or any harm but he chose to make war. He could have lived a life of ease but he preferred a hard life with warfare. He could have had money and security but he chose to make the money he had less by engaging in a war. Indeed he liked spending money on war just as one might spend it on love affairs or any other pleasure. All this shows how devoted he was to war.

This seems to me the mark of the mercenary throughout the ages: a devotion to war for its own sake. The Greeks, lacking the Christian ethos, saw nothing outrageous in this love of war. They were aware of war's miseries too. They considered such devotion exceptional but not morally wrong. Christian society, however, demanded that pleasure in war should be masked, often hypocritically, under the pretence of devotion to duty. But an open devotion to war as an art and a way of life is the distinguishing mark of the mercenary;   and the mercenary's casting aside of a moral attitude to war that is often hypocritical, at best uneasy, both fascinates and repels.

In the chapters that follow there will be several examples of mercenary leaders who, like Clearchus, could have lived in peace or comparative comfort but chose to risk their own money in war - or rather, as modern mechanised war is prohibitively expensive for individuals to finance, in coups d'états. With varying success. This does not however apply to the first coup d' état, the Cotonou Coup, which was 'properly' financed... as readers will, in reading on, shortly discover.

Anthony Mockler.

Prologue

THE MATRIX –
AND THE MASTER

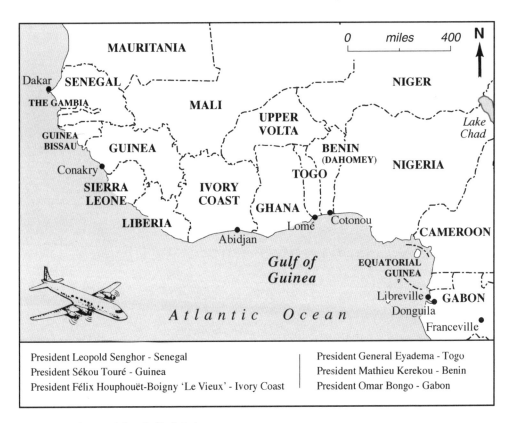

President Leopold Senghor - Senegal

President Sékou Touré - Guinea

President Félix Houphouët-Boigny 'Le Vieux' - Ivory Coast

President General Eyadema - Togo

President Mathieu Kerekou - Benin

President Omar Bongo - Gabon

West Africa and the Gulf of Guinea

I

The First Coup:
Omega to Cotonou

It was just before dawn when an unknown aircraft, all lights extinguished, packed with mercenaries, came skimming in over the Gulf of Guinea to land at Cotonou Airport.

How To Organise A Mercenary Coup?

Easy enough in theory. First select your target. A small West African state with an unpopular régime and a badly-trained army would be ideal. Next line up your backers. You will need money, arms, and a base. Thirdly recruit your men. That always presents problems but if you are an experienced mercenary leader you will have a solid nucleus around which to build.

Then all you need to do is to draw up a plan, recce the target, train your men, stimulate your backers, select a figurehead to replace the wicked tyrant you are planning to overthrow, and above all keep the whole affair under wraps.

How are you going to get your men in? By land, by sea or by air? By land will be slow, by air will be swift, by sea will be silent. It's a major decision. (And if your target happens to be an island state you can, obviously, rule the land option out.) Or are your men to be infiltrated in small groups, perhaps as tourists? And, if so, how are their weapons and ammunition to be sent in; and where do mercenaries and arms meet up? Not so easy.

All the problems have been solved. All the plans have been made. Secrecy, as far as you know, has been preserved. All that remains is to put the plan into action. D-Day has arrived. The *coup* must be swift, decisive, possibly brutal. And once you have seized the Presidential Palace and the Radio Station and broadcast your message (or rather your figurehead's message) of liberation, what then?

The follow-up plan will swing into action. That is assuming of course, - not always a wise assumption, in fact not ever a wise assumption - that things have gone according to plan.

THE FIRST OF THE COUPS: TARGET – KEREKOU OF BENIN

The year was 1976. The target was Benin, an impoverished strip of territory inhabited by three million or so West Africans, bordered on one side by the mighty Nigeria and on the other side by an equally impoverished and even smaller strip of territory, Togo.

Mighty Nigeria was not interested in its comparatively tiny, French-speaking neighbour. There had been, up till independence in 1960, two vast empires in West Africa: the British Empire of which Nigeria was the jewel, and the French Empire which General de Gaulle, on granting independence, had split into no less than fifteen separate states.

Togo, Benin's other neighbour, and like Benin formerly a colony of France, was ruled by General Eyadema. Eyadema was a thug, a burly northern tribesman who had joined the French army in Dahomey (as Benin then was), fought for the French in Indochina and Africa, and had personally (so he boasted) fired the shots that killed the sophisticated southerner, the Marxist-leaning first President of Togo, Sylvanus Olympio. France supported him

In his turn Major Mathieu Kerekou overthrew the government of Dahomey on 26 October 1972, almost ten years after his neighbour Gnassingbe Eyadema had seized power in Togo.

President Kerekou rechristened Dahomey (once famous for its army of Amazons) Benin, and eyed neighbouring Togo (which had once been part of the mediaeval African empire of Benin) avidly. General Eyadema was not happy.

Nor were the old politicians whom Kerekou had exiled happy. In the Ivory Coast, then and for many many years afterwards, the most stable, the most prosperous, the most closely-allied with France of all the former colonies, under the rule of that former black French senator, Félix Houphouet-Boigny *Le Vieux,* had taken refuge many potentially-useful refugees, the detritus of upheavals in more unstable West African states. Among them was Dr Emile Zinzou, a former President of Dahomey; and a former Ambassador to Brussels, his supporter and spokesman, Gratien Pognon.

Nor was the army in Benin all that happy, either. In June 1975 one of its most popular members, Captain Michel Aikpe, was convicted of adultery with Madame Kerekou; and executed.

Nor, above all, was Jacques Foccart happy. Foccart, secretary-general of the French *Communauté* and France's *Monsieur Afrique,* did not care for Marxist-leaning Presidents in her former colonies - any more than did his master, General de Gaulle. And Kerekou was not only a rabid left-winger; he had had the effrontery to nationalise various French-owned companies. France most certainly did *not* support him.

Hence it came about that on 5 November 1976 Gratien Pognon former Ambassador signed a contract on behalf of the 'Dahomey National Liberation Front' with the French mercenary leader Colonel Gilbert Bourgeaud to overthrow the communist-inclined and cuckolded Kerekou and to restore, in the person of Dr Emile Zinzou former President, 'the rightful civilian government'.

FORCE OMEGA'S ALTERNATIVES

The mercenary contract provided for the temporary hire of ninety 'technicians' - sixty, it was specified, white and thirty black. Interesting financial details were included. The pre-operational budget would be $475,000, the post-operational budget $530,000; and it was noted that a project budget of $145,000 had already been paid to the Colonel.

Of this project budget $5000 had already been spent on an 'observation mission' - a trip by one of the Colonel's men, Gérard, in December 1976 to Cotonou, the coastal capital of Benin, to recce the lie of the land. A further $100,000 had been needed for travel and administrative expenses, and then a further $40,000 still. All this had led to the drawing-up of a plan for a two-pronged attack to be launched against Benin on 5 January 1977.

As so often in military operations, the plan lightly veiled the names of the countries concerned; but with slightly more imagination than the traditional NATO style of 'Blue Land will launch an attack on Red Land'.

In this case the plan was for a pre-emptive attack against the non-existent Republic of Banalia - i.e. against Benin. Why? Because Banalia/Benin was itself about to attack the neighbouring Republic of Zangaro. This was pure imagination of course; there is no evidence at all that President Kerekou was planning to attack Togo. But it was a nice touch to christen the neighbouring Republic 'Zangaro'. In Frederick Forsyth's thriller *The Dogs of War* (published two years earlier) - of which much, much more in a later chapter of this book – Zangaro is the fictional West African state that mercenaries do in fact attack, the object of attack there, the object of defence in the Colonel's plan.

For Zangaro/Togo's available forces only numbered 1000 men in all whereas Banalia/Benin had an army of 6000. Fortunately, though, wretched Zangaro had a traditional friend and ally: the Republic of Loana. Or, to put it in more realistic terms, Togo had a traditional friend and ally in Gabon, President Omar Bongo's Gabon, hundreds of miles away to the south, across the Gulf of Guinea. And French-dominated Gabon had a highly professional little army, white-trained, white-officered, the Presidential Guard, of which one combat company was, most fortunately, already in Togo.

The plan therefore was for Bongo's men to launch an attack, a diversionary attack, at the head of the thousand noble Togolese warriors across the frontier. Just as fortunately, Benin's 6,000 men were split into small packets, a company here, a company there, so that the attackers would not immediately be overwhelmed. On the contrary all these scattered companies would be called upon to repel the attack; whereupon the Colonel's group of ninety 'technicians' would assault and seize the capital.

The capital was garrisoned by Benin's 1st Battalion, 600 men strong, at the military camp of Guezo near the Presidential Palace; and there was also a squadron of Ferret armoured scout cars in Cotonou. The attacking force would therefore have to rely on speed and surprise: the seizure of the Presidential Palace, the elimination of Kerekou himself, then the takeover of the radio station and (this was planned with loving detail) the interruption of the morning broadcast of the 'Voice of the Revolution'. There would be a thirty-second pause; then the 'Voice of Dahomey' would take the air. 'The tyrant is dead! *Enfants de Dahomey, debout!*' The National Anthem, 'New Dawn' , would follow in three different versions (one sung by a male choir), then M. Gratien Pognon, President of the Directing Committee of the Liberation Front, would read a Proclamation in French -which would be repeated in Fon, in Dendi, in Yoruba and in four other languages.

In the event of failure the force attacking from Togo would fall back over the frontier. But how, in the event of failure, would the ninety mercenaries fall back? This of course would largely depend on how they came in; and a very interesting 'appreciation of the situation' paper analysed the various possibilities.

★   ★   ★

Cotonou, Benin's capital, had begun life, like so many of the capitals of West African states, as a trading station. It was therefore on the coast and it boasted a harbour. For a West African capital it was very small, with less than 200,000 inhabitants, and therefore very compact: the airport, the Presidential Palace, the 'Voice of the Revolution' radio station, the army camp, the ministries, the embassies - all the obvious coup targets - were within, at most, ten minutes' drive of each other. As Cotonou was on the coast, the attacking force - Force Omega as Bourgeaud now christened it - could come in by sea, by air, by night or by day. There were therefore four alternatives, each with its advantages and disadvantages. In *The Dogs of War* in a similar situation Fredrick Forsyth had had his small group of mercenaries come in by night and by sea, setting off from the mother-ship in near-silent Zodiac black rubber landing craft; and Bourgeaud considered this method. A landfall could be made very near the main target, the Presidential Palace, at 1a.m.- and that was clearly an advantage. On the other hand night operations could very easily go wrong (Forsyth had argued in his book, and possibly in real life too, that European soldiers were excellent at night operations whereas Africans even on their own territory were useless - in its first premise at least, a dubious thesis); it would be impossible to bring in and unload heavy weapons from the Zodiacs; and, above all, if things went wrong, escape would be difficult. The other seaborne possibility was for the mother-ship simply to sail into Cotonou's harbour by day. This, for obvious reasons - it would be too slow and the vital element of surprise would be lost – the Colonel rejected.

The alternative was that Force Omega should arrive, all together, by plane at the airport. The great advantage here was that they could bring their heavy weapons in with them and above all that they would have a ready means of escape. The airport was lightly defended, if at all, and it would be easy to seize control by acting swiftly once the plane had landed. Force Omega would then split into two groups: Group A, fifteen men, would guard the airport, control the road outside and set up a heavy mortar group, ready to shell the army camp if there were any resistance. Group B, forty-five men (the thirty black mercenaries were for operational purposes ignored – they were designed for decorative propaganda, rather than for real action) would themselves split into three groups. Twenty men would assault the Presidential Palace, the seat of the government. Ten men would concentrate on attacking the President's own house, in the Palace grounds, and on eliminating Kerekou himself. Fifteen men would 'neutralise' the nearby army camp. Then the radio station would be seized, and the 'Voice of Dahomey' take the air.

That was Stage A. Stage B would follow: the occupation of the whole western quarter of the capital. Stage C would take longer: extending the new régime's control over the whole of the country; and Stage D would involve taking measures against a possible counter attack launched from abroad.

It now became apparent why the mercenary leader Colonel Bourgeaud had been asking for, and had obtained, such large budgets. In the pre-operational budget each of the sixty white mercenaries would be paid three months' salary (most of it, clearly, a retainer) of $2,000 a month; but in the post-operational budget (Stages C and D) each of the mercenaries would be under contract at the same salary for a further four months, with – a thoughtful touch – no less than one month's paid leave. The 'bill' for salaries alone, therefore, would be $840,000. As for the thirty blacks, they would be paid out of the pre-operational budget a 'salary' of $1,200, plus a $1,000 bonus if all went well – a comparatively minor $66,000. The other major expenses would be the hire of a jet-propelled DC8 and the outright purchase of a propeller-driven DC7, which – with generous payments to the pilots and crew – would come to a total of $95,000. Though the Colonel did not of course mention this in the contract, the DC7 and the DC8 for which he had negotiated were the two planes of Jack Malloch's Affretair, the charter company in which he himself had an interest – and no doubt Malloch was delighted at the thought of getting rid, by outright sale, of the ageing DC7, the aeroplane which would actually be at risk during the *coup* attempt at Cotonou airport.

The question, however, remained: should the aircraft with Force Omega aboard fly by night? Or should it fly in boldly by day? Kerekou's ministers met regularly once a week at the Presidential Palace, on Wednesdays from 10.30 to midday, and there was therefore much to be said for timing the landing boldly at 11.30 am on a Wednesday, seizing cars and taxis at the airport, and – within ten minutes or at most a quarter of an hour after having landed – attacking the Presidential Palace and capturing or killing not only the President but all alternative leaders in one fell swoop. This was the bold

decision taken; and the attack was therefore planned for Wednesday, 8 January.
But three days before it was due to be launched General Eyadema of Togo and
President Bongo of Gabon met secretly; and they insisted on the plan's revision.
The General had developed cold feet. There was to be no second prong, no cross-
border attack - until at any rate the tyrant had been eliminated and the new régime
could legitimately call for aid in 'restoring order'. But the Colonel, the mercenary
leader, though he must have been worried, would not consider abandoning his
plan. A brief postponement at most. For his men had already been assembled and
were training at a military base in Morocco, his pre-operational budget had been
invested, and his post-operational budget was guaranteed - a most important consideration - not only by President Bongo but also by King Hassan of Morocco.

For where had the money, the million-dollars-plus that the *coup* would cost,
come from? Clearly not from the impoverished Liberation Front of the exiles.
Gabon had since 1973 been suddenly transformed by the oil boom from one of
the poorest to one of the richest countries in Africa; and President Bongo would
have been less than human if he had not wanted to speculate politically with some
of Gabon's new-found wealth. The Moroccan interest was more obscure. But
King Hassan had to some extent acted as France's support and indeed substitute
in policing Africa - it was Moroccan troops, airlifted by French planes, that came
to the aid of General Mobutu against the invading Katangese gendarmes in the
'First Shaba War' later this same year - and the King's former minister, the dreaded
General Oufkir, had at the time of the 'Libyan contract' shown great interest in
helping 'James Kent'★¹ to piece together again his thrice-failed scheme. Oufkir
had later tried to assassinate his royal master and had himself died; but the thought
of using white mercenaries to overthrow his ever-more troublesome neighbour,
Gaddafy of Libya, no doubt remained germinating in the King's mind.

Indeed, according to Colonel Bourgeaud's story - hard to check - there was
a long-standing relationship between the Colonel and King Hassan; ever since
1972 when the Colonel after Oufkir's death had flown to Morocco with his
right-hand man Freddie Thieleman and plotted a quick punitive / sabotage raid
on Gaddafy's residence and capital at Tripoli. *That* had involved, in theory, 200
mercenaries disguised as tourists, an ex-US Navy destroyer to be brought down
from Stavanger in Norway; a recruitment bureau in Rue Flandrin in Paris; a
reconnaissance trip by two men and a woman; four landing craft and a quantity
of light vehicles. But Colonel Dlimi, General Oufkir's successor, much more of
a secret policemen than, like his predecessor, a ruthless fighting man, was suspicious, a dampener. And then, unexpectedly and annoyingly, King Hassan made
his peace - at least temporarily - with Gaddafy. Meanwhile, however, the King

---

¹ See the previous volume of this trilogy. Whenever a star ★ appears in this book beside a
reference to some mercenary incident, it will mean exactly the same thing: the full account is
to be found in Volume Two.

had become, almost, a personal friend to the Colonel, phoning personally from the Royal Palace to France when one of the Colonel's many children, Katia, was born, on 24 November 1972, to one of the Colonel's many 'wives', Marie-Elise, his Florence Nightingale (so to speak) in the Congo.*

Besides, President Kerekou had recognized Polisario, King Hassan's real bugbear – far more so than the gadfly Gaddafy. Polisario claimed independence for the ex-Spanish Sahara, rightfully Moroccan land in Morocco's eyes. Reason enough to dispose of the dastardly Kerekou.

And so King Hassan put the military base at Benguerir, sixty miles outside Marrakesh, at the disposal for training purposes of Colonel Maurin and Commandant Mercier.

THE MERCENARIES

Who was Colonel Maurin, Colonel André Maurin? Almost no French mercenary of note has ever written his memoirs. Most, unlike their British or American or South African counterparts, are reluctant to give interviews. Furthermore almost all have the confusing habit of adopting false names.

This is very French. Hardly ever has an Anglo-Saxon mercenary used an alias; and, as will be seen, when they did attempt to disguise their names, as 'Mad Mike' Hoare was to do in the Seychelles, it was in a very amateurish way indeed – though it worked.

Colonel André Maurin was a *nom-de-guerre* for Colonel Gilbert Bourgeaud himself. Who 'Mercier' was I have not been able to discover but I suspect that he may have been André Cau, also known as Carrel, one of the mercenary leader's most loyal lieutenants, who certainly took part in the *coup* attempt.

Two other close associates of the Colonel were involved in the preliminary stages. Roger Bruni had been with him at Paulis in the Congo,* way back in the old days, when the Colonel had broken his leg and acquired his trademark limp. (He had stepped out of a jeep, straight into an elephant trap dug by the Simbas.) Bruni's job was to recruit the sixty white mercenaries needed. He rented an apartment in Paris, then used a publicity agency, Havas, to put advertisements in the press appealing for former soldiers to apply for a post with an overseas security company. The response was astounding: five thousand replies, no less, which were quickly whittled down to a serious five hundred, then to a hundred and fifty, and then, by interview with the Colonel in various Parisian hotels, to the necessary sixty.

Those chosen were sent in small groups, with a month's pay in advance, to Morocco, to Benguerir, where the Colonel's second close associate, René Dulac, known as *Le Grand*, was in charge of training. Training was tough, ten hours a day of physical exercise, commando hand-to-hand combat, plus weapon training. The weapons and ammunition were provided by the Royal Moroccan Army;

which guarded the base and ensured the men were totally isolated. Belgian FAL rifles, and MAG machine-guns, French mortars and anti-tank RPGs, American bazookas and .50s were the weapons provided, and more live rounds were fired in the month the mercenaries were there - from early December 1976 to early January 1977 - than, as one recruit put it, he had ever fired in his whole career in the French Army.

Dulac, a former Legionary himself, used tough and tried Legion methods in an attempt to break and remake his men. Among them, fortunately for him, there were at least a dozen former *Légionnaires*, of whom the older ones - Louis Cabassao alias Carden, Franz Heinemann alias Eugene Francois, Alfons Holzapfel alias Lingen, Werner Kolibius alias Koli and Istvan Wagner (who chose, unusually, to go under his own name) - had all been in the 1er REP, the first regiment of Legion paratroops, whose dissolution in Algeria by General de Gaulle had virtually created the mercenary profession almost twenty years earlier.★

There were plumbers and bar-waiters and indeed youngsters with no military experience among them too but most had seen active service of some sort or another. And now the thirty black Africans began to join them. Half were Benin exiles, from the Ivory Coast or Senegal, under the command of Adjutant 'Montagne' - in fact a former warrant officer in the Benin army, Soglo by name, who had already taken part in a failed attempt to overthrow Kerekou and who had subsequently escaped from jail in Benin. The others were Guineans, recruited by Sy Sawane Umar, an exile like themselves, under the pretext of an attempt to overthrow the hated President Sekou Touré, the one black President who had refused, on independence, to join the French *Communauté*. These were stiffened by three or four out of a dozen Guinean exiles the Colonel himself had been training for a similar purpose in, of all places, a park attached to the Convent of Magesc - the nuns were apparently deeply unworldly and highly incurious - remotely situated in the flat but heavily-wooded Landes near Bordeaux. Indeed as early as 22 November 1970 the Colonel may have been involved in an attempt to overthrow Sekou Touré, as many black Africans have alleged.

The attack on Cotonou had been planned for Wednesday 5 January. It was, following the change of plan, postponed not till the following Wednesday but till the Sunday after that. Tension was mounting at Benguerir, nobody except the Colonel and his few close associates as yet knew the target; but it seemed obvious that it would be one of Foccart's Marxist bug-bears, either Sekou Touré's Guinea or Kerekou's Benin, and the Moroccans feared the whole operation could not be kept under wraps much longer, might be blown.

★   ★   ★

On the night of 10/11 January Colonel André Maurin - Colonel Gilbert Bourgeaud - was in Paris at the Sheraton Hotel where he apparently summoned an 'O' Group of senior officers and NCOs, revealed the target, and issued his operational orders. He would, he announced, lead the assault in person.

The NCOs included such men as Hugues de Chivre alias Sergeant Rucker and Michel de Charette de la Contrie, who chose the very Breton *nom de guerre* of Kermarec. Less imaginatively, a real old hand, a Belgian ex-Para who had fought in the Congo, Van Den Berge, simply called himself Van. The final plans were made. On Saturday 15 January training ended at Benguerir; Force Omega were flown out in the hired DC8 from Marrakesh to El Hadj Omar Bongo Airport at Franceville in Gabon. There they were transferred to the propellor-driven DC7 (like the DC8, a cargo plane without seats). It was piloted by a Swedish pilot, Bjorg Isberg, who had flown for the Red Cross (and very possibly later for Von Rosen) in Biafra.★ The plane had been due to take off at 11.00 that night; but the plane was old, there was a bad oil leak and take-off was delayed for what must have been an agonising two hours. Nevertheless in the first hours of Sunday 16 January the DC7 carrying Force Omega, an ample supply of sten-guns, machine-guns, bazookas and rockets, the Colonel himself and, by his side, with his speech all prepared, M. Gratien Pognon (travelling as M. Jacky) was winging its way through the darkness across the Gulf of Guinea and the Bight of Benin towards Cotonou.

Assault On Cotonou

The assault went in just after dawn, as recounted in the opening sentence of this chapter.

The handful of technicians in the control tower and the scattered airport work-ers and officials were bewildered, for on that sleepy Sunday morning the first flight officially due in was not expected till nearly four hours later. The unknown aircraft taxied up to Piste No. 6, the landing-bay that had been used six years ear-lier for the Red Cross mercy flights to Biafra. It came to a halt at 7.03 precisely, only three minutes - apparently - later than planned. The technicians were even more amazed when the doors were thrown open before any landing steps could be wheeled up and ropes slung out. Their amazement turned to alarm and their alarm to panic as armed men, black and white, slithered down the ropes, touched *terra firma,* fired their weapons noisily but terrifyingly into the air – and started running for the control tower where the said technicians were ensconced.

Within minutes the airport was in Force Omega's hands, and the initial opposi-tion - two Ferret scout cars that appeared on the perimeter of the airport - had been dealt with by the mercenaries' bazookas. Bougeaud's men now split into six mixed groups of black and white mercenaries. The smallest group, the 'command group' that took over the control tower, consisted of six men - three white and three black: Colonel Maurin, alias - for the duration of the operation - *Soleil*; two white officers, Lts Verdier and Tanguy; M. Gratien Pognon, the potential liberator; Sy Sawane Umar and Adjudant 'Montagne'.

A group of twelve - *Pourveyeurs Protection* - acted as close protection to the 'command group'; a group of nine - *Groupe Couverture Ouest* - covered the airport buildings and entrance; and a group of thirteen - *Groupe Appui Couverture* - assured the vital protection of the aircraft in which they had all landed, at the same time setting up a mortar group that could range onto the army camp, less than a mile and a half away. This meant that well over a third - indeed, allowing for last-minute drop-outs, very nearly half - of Force Omega remained at the airport itself. The remainder - and my impression is that these were nearly all whites - were split into two groups, *Groupe Bleu*, twenty-nine strong, and *Groupe Noir*, twenty-four strong. One group immediately set off along the coast road, the esplanade, for the Presidential Palace; the other group headed down Cotonou's central avenue in the same direction.

The original plans had, of course, been changed. The rash project for a landing in broad daylight on a Wednesday at a busy airport had been abandoned [wisely in my view] in favour of a dawn landing on a Sunday at an almost deserted airport. So swift sudden and unexpected had been Force Omega's arrival that it seems that they achieved without difficulty one of their major aims, which was to seize control of the airport's telephones before the alarm could be raised. But, on the other hand, early on a Sunday morning the private cars and taxis, which the two assault groups had planned to seize as transport, were simply not there at the airport entrance; and so Blue Group and Black Group had to double down the esplanade and the central avenue, on foot. At least one of the two groups evidently decided that, with the advantages of concealment that transport would have given obviously lost and their own small numbers only too apparent, terror was now a better tactic than secrecy. They opened fire on the facades of a dozen ministries and embassies as they jogged past, a terrifying awakening indeed for the occupants.

The central avenue group, nearing its target, seized a modern block of flats, Quarante Logements, overlooking the Presidential Palace two hundred yards away. They set up a bazooka group at the entrance and from the fourth floor - whose scared apartment owners had been forcibly woken and hustled out - opened fire. The esplanade group meanwhile had occupied the Palace of Congress, on another side of the Presidential Palace - which was therefore caught in a crossfire. But there was no attempt at an assault. Instead - and this may have been a hasty variation on the original plan - President Kerekou's residence was mortared, and mortared most thoroughly. But momentum, vital for a small attacking force with much inferior numbers, had been lost, the Presidential Guard from inside the Presidential Palace opened up with counterfire, one white mercenary was killed outside Quarante Logements and, worst of all from the attackers' point of view,

President Kerekou was still alive. It was known that Kerekou was always in his residence at 7.30 every morning; but for once - and it seems to have been merely a stroke of fate, though a very fortunate one for Benin's President - this was not true. He had spent the night elsewhere, in a house three miles away; and less than two hours after the DC7 had landed, he was on the air, speaking via 'the Voice of the Revolution' to all the people of Benin, calling on them to seize whatever weapons they might have, report to local party headquarters and set up road blocks everywhere to repel the dastardly counter-revolutionary invaders.

An hour later, by 10 am, the attempted coup was over. Two hours of desultory exchange of fire around the Presidential Palace had led only to a stalemate that was broken, after Kerekou's belligerent broadcast, by the appearance of citizens wielding machetes and two hundred soldiers from the military camp, Camp Guezo. Radio contact between the various mercenary groups - all officers and NCOs carried walkie-talkies - was obviously functioning perfectly; and the two assault companies, called off, withdrew to the airport apparently without difficulty. At 10 am, only three hours after having landed, the DC7 was airborne again, winging its way back to Gabon, leaving behind it on the tarmac an assortment of weapons and equipment, ammunition crates (including one labelled 'Colonel Maurin' that proved to be full of documents), six dead and over fifty wounded Beninois (soon to be proclaimed 'Martyrs of the Revolution'), two dead mercenaries, one white and one black (soon to be exposed for photographers in the local morgue) and one very scared black mercenary, forgotten, in the last minute rush to get away, on top of the control tower building where he had been left as a sentinel.

This was Ba Alpha Umaru, a Guinean, of the Peul tribe, who while working in Senegal had joined an anti-Sekou Touré exile group in 1972 after the execution by Sekou Touré of the former Secretary General of the OAU, Diallo Telli, and the subsequent oppression of the Peuls. Recruited like a dozen other Guineans by 'Monsieur Joseph' - Sy Sawane Umar - he had been flown from Dakar to Casablanca on 30 December and had had less than a fortnight's military training - his first - at the Benguerir base before the coup attempt. As various Commissions of Enquiry - United Nations, OAU, and Benin's own - hastily assembled in Cotonou, Ba Alpha was produced again and again to tell his story. President Bongo meanwhile scornfully and pungently denied any involvement in the whole affair - if indeed there had been any attempted *coup* at all and it was not all a fiction invented by Kerekou - and invited the various commissions to visit Gabon and make as many enquiries there as they might wish: an open invitation which none of them accepted. King Hassan maintained a lofty and impassive silence. Various reports were issued; and the affair was quickly forgotten - except, presumably, by the wretched Ba Alpha Umaru (whose fate is unknown), President Kerekou himself and the disappointed backers who had invested well over half a million dollars in vain.

THE FIRST MERCENARY COUP – A FAILURE?

This may seem an otiose question. Of course the *coup* was a failure. President Kerekou not only remained in power but was still in power, just, almost thirty years later. (So, come to that is President Bongo of Gabon; and so would have been General Eyadema of Togo if he had not died - rather amazingly, of natural causes - in February 2005: a long-enduring trio of small West African dictators, admirable if only for their stubborn longevity.)

On the other hand it was, as far as I am aware, the first attempted mercenary *coup d'état* ever since the re-emergence of the modern mercenary in Katanga in 1960.* Before Cotonou mercenaries had always been employed in the great civil wars - in the Congo,* in the Yemen,* in Biafra,* marginally in the Sudan,* in Angola* and indeed in Rhodesia and Namibia later. (Of course there might have been a civil war in Benin too if the *coup* in Cotonou had been successful, if the invasion from Togo had followed, and if Benin's five thousand remaining troops had decided to resist rather than to yield. But those are the 'ifs' of history.)

But as it was, this was a first, an experiment, almost a matrix. It had been well and carefully planned. The funds were there, the weapons were there, the base was there. Mercenaries had been recruited in numbers believed to be sufficient, training had been intense, transport had worked – just; and, though the *coup* had failed, it had not, from the mercenaries' point of view at least, been disastrous. They had flown in, they had landed, surprise had been achieved, they had seized the capital's airport; and when things had begun to go wrong, their officers had wisely enough called the whole thing off in good time and successfully evacuated almost the whole force.

So what had actually gone wrong? Most *coups* fail. General Oufkir's almost-foolproof *coup* against his master King Hassan had, despite the General's immensely powerful position, failed. It would have been, as King Hassan said, the perfect crime had everything gone as planned. But never, in any *coup*, does anything go exactly as planned. Luck had been against the General – luck, and the King's astounding *sangfroid* when his plane had been attacked by six of his own fighters above the Mediterranean. General Oufkir had paid for his lack of *baraka* with his life.

Luck had been against the mercenaries too. It must have seemed to them hardly conceivable that there were no taxis or private cars or vans for them to commandeer early that morning at Cotonou Airport. True, it was a Sunday. True, with hindsight it should have been checked. The distance was not far from the Airport to the Presidential Palace. But it was far enough, in daytime, to lose the vital element of surprise – and also to demoralize the troops. Mercenaries in the Congo and in Angola had always relied on swift, sudden attacks in their jeeps and landrovers.* They were not ready, nor mentally prepared, to go back to the old ways of jogging miles to the attack, however strenuous their physical training may have been. And of course, compared to the five or six hundred troops opposed to them, they were few in number. Everything depended on shock, surprise, speed: once they had become bogged down in the urban equivalent of trench warfare, they were in a pretty hopeless situation, and they knew it.

Luck had been against them again in the sense that President Kerekou had not been sleeping, as usual, at his residence. Admittedly there had been a lack of punch in the assault and a failure to capture the all-important radio station from which Kerekou had broadcast and rallied his people. But even if the Presidential Palace in Cotonou had been taken by assault, even if the '*Voix de la Revolution*' had been interrupted, as planned, by the '*Voix de Dahomey*', the *coup* would still almost certainly have failed with Kerekou alive, at liberty, and able to rally his supporters. Once he went on the air and his familiar voice proved that he was alive, well, and calling for resistance, the *coup* was doomed. This was a point that future mercenary leaders of future mercenary *coups* were to bear very much in mind.

And there were to be a myriad future mercenary *coups* planned, inspired, I believe, by the near-success of the Cotonou Coup. As in 1981 when a group of ten American mercenaries were detained by the FBI en route to topple Eugenia Charles' left-wing régime in the tiny Caribbean island of Dominica (their leader Michael Perdue was to receive $150,000 and a concession for the backers, Nortic Enterprises Ltd, from the exiled ex-prime minister, Patrick John); or as in 1982 when ex-President Binaisa of Uganda was plotting to overthrow President Milton Obote with a two-pronged landing on Kampala and Entebbe airfield. That was backed by US businessmen from the Southern States; and the five hundred mercenaries involved were to be recruited by Raymond Ingram's International Security Agency in Britain. It too never got off the ground; but this is just one single example that has come to the surface of a whole web of subterranean activity in the Eighties. New names, new faces were continually cropping up in the mercenary business.

Old names too. Probably the greatest single error of the Cotonou attempt, and the most bizarre one, was the abandonment of the ammunition crate at the airport that was labelled 'Colonel Maurin'. For, from the documents it was found to contain, it quickly became clear not only that Colonel André Maurin was the alias of Colonel Gilbert Bourgeaud; but that Colonel Gilbert Bourgeaud was in its turn the alias of Colonel Bob Denard, the most famous French mercenary, and possibly the most famous mercenary leader too, in the whole wide world.

Portrait of a Mercenary Leader

'Mad Mike' Hoare liked journalists. He got on well with them, he gave them interviews, he bought them drinks, he was courteous, charming even. Bob Denard detested and distrusted them. Perhaps that is why he had so many aliases – as much as anything else to throw the hated bloodhounds of the press off the scent. There is a story that in Katanga, or possibly in the Congo, he and his men on a bar-crawl came across a bar full of journalists. Whereupon he fired a burst from his sten-gun into the ceiling and gave them seconds to leave.

They left. But that was in his rough and ready days, his boisterous days, when he was enjoying, rather like an over-excited puppy, his new-found power. In later life he mellowed. In his sixties, at a period when he was lieing low in South Africa, he offered an interview to a delectable young English researcher – in French of course, for, like de Gaulle, as a matter perhaps of principle, he spoke little or no English. She was impressed.

> He was a powerful physical presence, his eyes behind the spectacles were a piercing turquoise.…They were the eyes of a younger man and a hard man.
> "What characteristics make a good mercenary?" she asked.
> "One has to be courageous," Denard replied. "You have to be more than a good soldier. A soldier works within an army structure with logistical support, a pension and social security. A mercenary doesn't have all that. A mercenary is paid, and that's it. He needs to be not only a good soldier and brave but also organised and willing to take risks. One cannot be a good mercenary only for the money, it's not possible. One can't kill oneself for money."

It is worth pausing a moment on that reply, and considering it in the light of the Cotonou Coup. In landing at Cotonou airport Denard and his mercenaries certainly showed they were courageous and willing to take risks. But they were certainly also not prepared to kill themselves for money. When the situation turned tricky, they did not fight to the end. Like the journalists in the bar they decamped. When a *coup* fails there is usually a heavy price to pay in casualties – but in this aspect the Benin *coup* had been exceptional. Though there were rumours of forty mercenaries wounded, they had all been evacuated speedily and successfully. The withdrawal – always the most difficult and dangerous part of any military operation – had been remarkably planned and brilliantly executed. Denard was always realistic. Some of his men were not. Particularly when fighting far away from their leader, they could get caught up in the cause for which they were fighting, and sacrifice their lives heroically - as Jean-Baptiste was so noticeably to do four years later in Chad. But it was not the norm.

Denard was prudent. He was also well-organized. He paid great attention to careful planning. "When he is planning something, he is very meticulous," as one of his men put it. "He rehearses and makes sure that everything is accounted for. There is always a purpose behind what he does; no room is left for improvisation and he is one hundred per cent in control at all times. He is also capable of taking a lot of hardship and he is very, very, very pragmatic."

If the above gives the impression of a hard man, *un dur* as the French say, that would be only half the story. Almost everybody who has had anything to do with Bob Denard likes him personally. "He struck me as a very charming man," said a white South African diplomat who was politically at odds with him. "He always conducted himself in a thoroughly gentlemanly fashion." "He's a nice guy, he has great charisma, and he's capable of attracting loyalty – which is a vital characteristic of a mercenary leader," said Patrick Ollivier, the mercenary quoted above. "Did you know Bob Denard?" Samantha Weinberg, the English reporter, asked an Italian doctor. "Yes, he was a splendid fellow. It was he who found the leprosy camp in a terrible state in 1978. Everyone had forgotten about the lepers. He arranged for funding and for medical assistance. He was definitely a force for good in the Comores."

Of course there was another side to his character, a harsher, more ruthless side. But there can be no doubting his personal charm, his personal magnetism. Without it he could not have become what he undoubtedly was: the longest-lasting mercenary leader in the western world, the man who, despite a string of failures that would have ruined a lesser figure, has dominated mercenary history in the second half of the twentieth century; and is not only still alive but, in the opening years of the twenty-first century, still on the scene – unlike any of his rivals and contemporaries.

HOARE AND DENARD

What a contrast there is between the two mercenary leaders whose stories will dominate the next chapters of this book. Both came to fame in the sixties, in the civil wars that devastated the Congo – Hoare as the leader of 5 Commando, Denard as the leader of 6 Commando. That tangled, almost Shakespearian tale has already, been told;★ and it would be foolish to attempt to summarize it here. But, as men, the two great mercenary leaders – for no-one can deny that this is what, in the heart of darkness, they had become – could hardly have been more different.

Hoare, despite his nickname of 'Mad Mike', was a typical Englishman; or, to be more accurate, a typical Anglo-Irishman – that is to say a gentleman by class, breeding and background, a touch old-fashioned, an Army man, but with the charm and sense of humour that came from his particular background and that so many British Army officers without Celtic blood in their veins by tradition utterly lack. He was a conventional man, living a conventional-enough happily married life with his wife Phyllis (admittedly his second wife) and two strapping sons in The Old Rectory in Natal. And he had a conventional enough Anglo-Irish taste for adventure. Of course there was more to him than that. But no-one anywhere in the world could ever have mistaken him for anything other than what he was: a traditional British gentleman, with the traditional conservative views of his class and time, self-deprecating, fond of understatement, yet with backbone and a certain stern rigidity, respecting hierarchy and authority, disliking intrigue.

Hoare insisted on the mercenaries of 5 Commando attending church parade on Sunday mornings in the Congo.★ One could never, in one's wildest flights of fancy, imagine Denard doing anything remotely like that.

For Bob Denard was a typical Frenchman. More than that, he was a typical Gascon. Just as in Mike Hoare's case, Bob Denard could never have been mistaken, in any context, for being other than what he was, where he came from.

If Mike Hoare's was a figure that in many ways stepped out of the pages of a Boy's Own adventure story, or even an imperial novel by G.A. Henty, Bob Denard's was a figure almost straight from the pages of *The Three Musketeers*. Like D'Artagnan he was a Gascon. Like D'Artagnan, he loved women. Like D'Artagnan, he was a wily planner as well as a courageous fighter. Like D'Artagnan, he was basically amoral. Like D'Artagnan, he trusted no-one, not even his closest companions.

Like D'Artagnan too he was born poor and into a military family. Robert was born on 7 April 1929 in Bordeaux, second and last child of Leonce and Marguerite Denard. The Denard clan owned houses all over the little village of Grayan to the north of Bordeaux. But, unlike D'Artagnan, Bob Denard was not nobly born. Though his mother is said to have had pretensions to an ancestry, and to have married beneath her, his father was an N.C.O. in the French Army, and his father's father a peasant.

His background is important. He himself joined not the army like his father Leonce, but the navy, and trained as a mechanic. "He has a very strong class complex," said Patrick Ollivier. "Remember he never made officer class in the French navy. To understand Denard you have to look at his family. His life has been one long quest for recognition and approval."

Jean Larteguy, the famous French writer of war novels, came to much the same conclusion, though more nuanced in tone. "I personally, as an officer, think Denard had a complex stemming from his days as an under-officer in the navy. He always wanted to make up for this by being the perfect commander." In other words his lowly origins were actually a stimulus to efficiency. "He was capable and honourable and very courageous. He was very meticulous in his planning and organisation and obsessively neat. He could have been an officer, you know. He had great vitality and he was very loyal to his men and his friends."

To understand Denard it is necessary to know Denard's career. After the *Ecole de Mécaniciens de la Marine* – useful practical training that was greatly to help him as a mercenary leader – he almost followed in his father's footsteps. Leonce had been stationed in China, in the French Concession at T'ien-tsin. Bob was stationed in Indochina, from February 1948. As a quartermaster he was in charge of landing craft near Saigon, in the Delta, under Pontchardier, against the Viets. There he had his first child, a daughter by Ti Sao, a village girl. There he spent three months in hospital, blown up by a Vietminh mine, badly burnt. There he spent two months in prison for sacking a Chinese restaurant – a black mark on his naval career. His five years' engagement up he left the navy.

He went out to Morocco, as a mechanic, employed in a vast military base near Casablanca. He met a Moroccan Jewess, Giselle Riboh. Eventually he married her. They had a son, his first son, Philippe. Morocco was in political turmoil. He joined the police in Casablanca, then the centre of both terrorism and counter-terrorism. It was a time of bombs, riots, lynchings, killings of civilians, countless assassinations. It was a dark, filthy period of violence, the sort of spiralling uncontrolled violence that a Mike Hoare, who had served in the Second World War with the London Irish, had never known. From 1956 – 1957 Denard spent fourteen months in detention before a trial that acquitted him of attempting to assassinate (with a trio of companions who were found guilty) the left-wing leader of France, the man who had granted Morocco's independence, Pierre Mendes-France. That too was an experience a conventional officer like Mike Hoare would never have known, could barely have imagined. D'Artagnan on the other hand would totally have understood.

There are periods in the life of Bob Denard when he has lain low, usually in France, taken on ordinary jobs or enterprises, kept out of politics and action. One of those torpid periods now followed. He did *not* get involved in the vast upheavals that brought De Gaulle back to power; nor, fortunately for himself, in the ill-fated attempts to assassinate the general when De Gaulle 'betrayed' the cause of *Algérie Française*. The Mendes-France episode had taught him at least *that* lesson. But in July 1960 this period of inaction ended. He read, in *L'Aurore,* an article about Katanga. At just over thirty years of age his real career, his career as a mercenary, was about to begin.

GABON – THE PRESIDENTIAL GUARD

Eight years later, by 1968, it seemed to have ended in total failure. The extraordinary tale – the most extraordinary in modern mercenary history – of the Mercenaries' Revolt, of its initial failure, subsequent triumph, then disastrous collapse – has already been told.★ With the fall of Bukavu★ and the collapse of the 'Second Front', with Denard's notorious 'bicycle invasion',★ with Schramme's last and bitter radio message " – VOUS ETES DES ASSASSINS – STOP ET FIN",★ with suspicions of double-dealing and accusations of treachery engulfing the mercenary world, it might have been thought that Denard was finished.

He was not. He had been badly wounded (both literally, again in the leg, this time by a stray Congolese bullet – thereafter he always walked with a limp) and morally. But Denard had a certain ferocious obstinacy. He was a resilient man.

In Paris, in those joyously revolutionary days of May 1968, he met a personage who saw his usefulness, and was prepared to use him. The Hôtel de Noirmoutier at 138 Rue de Grenelle was Jacques Foccart's lair; and thither flocked in the heady month of May De Gaulle's toughest supporters, men who were not prepared to see a student revolution taken over by the workers and the communists.

Among them was Colonel Maurice Robert, an important figure in France's Secret Service, the SDECE. Fourteen years earlier he had founded its *Service Afrique*; and almost inevitably he became Foccart's ally in the complex manoeuvrings of French official and semi-clandestine bureaucracy. For Jacques Foccart's spidery webs trailed all over French-speaking black Africa, and Foccart, almost alone of all officials, had instant access to General de Gaulle's majestic presence and attentive ear.

Bob Denard did not meet Foccart in person then; or indeed, according to Foccart, ever. But he was presented to Colonel Maurice Robert, and Colonel Maurice Robert took him up.

The scares of May, the hopes of May, passed. "Nothing will ever be the same again," the young French idealists had proclaimed. A traditional sense of authority had certainly been broken. But with the return of the General to Paris after his mysterious absence in Germany; with the vast Gaullist demonstration on the Champs-Elysées, it seemed as if, in that useful French phrase, *tout était rentré dans l'ordre* –everything had been restored to order.

Jacques Foccart and Colonel Maurice Robert – and indeed to some extent the General himself – could turn their attention back to what had been preoccupying them before the events of May: the civil war in Nigeria, the Biafran secession which the French were supporting.

Supporting from where? Why, from Gabon just across the Gulf of Guinea. In Biafra there were French mercenaries fighting for Ojukwu, at first under the command of Faulques, Denard's initial mercenary commander in Katanga.★ Some of them, like Biaunie (who stayed on when Faulques had left) had been with Denard in the Congo.★ But Bob Denard himself did not get directly involved in the fighting. Jack Malloch, whom Mike Hoare described as the most fearless avia-tor he had ever met, was flying in supplies to Biafra both from Lisbon and, later, from Libreville in Gabon – arms, ammunition, mortar bombs, rockets as well as, when famine struck Biafra, food and supplies. But DC3s and DC4s – which was all Malloch had at the time – could only fly in twenty or thirty tons at a time. Bob Denard was given the funds, by Colonel Maurice Robert, to buy, equip and man a boat that could bring in five or six hundred tons, from France and from South-West Africa. In other words he became, for the time being, not a merce-nary leader as such but a gun runner.

The pivot of the whole operation was Libreville in Gabon. And there, in 1968/9, the Presidential Guard was being formed.

This Presidential Guard was not so much a guard as a miniature army. Formed by one of Colonel Maurice Robert's men, Bob Maloubier of the *Service Action* of the SDECE, it was commanded by the legendary ex-Legionary of the 1er REP, Commandant Yves Le Braz (who was to be succeeded by the still more famous Loulou Martin). It was composed, largely, of former legionaries. It had its own armoured vehicles and air force. It was an elite body, 1200 strong. It kept President Bongo in power. It kept the influence of France, and of Foccart, dominant in Gabon: which at the time, let it be remembered, before the discovery of oil was a very poor, under-populated little state with a small coastal strip of 'civilization' and a vast undeveloped hinterland of swamps and rivers and jungle, inhabited in the north by the savage and superstitious Fang – of whom more, much more, later.

Biafra collapsed. De Gaulle departed, to shadows and silence. But Jacques Foccart stayed on. And in Gabon Bob Denard stayed on. He never joined the Presidential Guard. But Félix Houphouet Boigny, *Le Vieux*, the ruler of the Ivory Coast, apparently persuaded his young protégé Bongo to reward Denard with a farm, Donguila, sixty miles outside Libreville in the tropical jungle. So Denard became, like his grandfather, a peasant farmer of sorts - together with Marie-Elise, his half-Greek half-Congolese 'wife'.

But only of sorts. Denard still had his mercenary contacts; and, though he may not have been *persona grata* at the headquarters of the Presidential Guard in Libreville, many of his friends and acquaintances were members of that semi-offi-cial mercenary army.

Who was Denard working for in these years? President Bongo? Colonel Maurice Robert? Himself? Anyone who would employ him? Probably a com-bination of all four. He was forty now, a man in his prime, with a great deal of experience under his belt, with a vast range of contacts, and quite obviously with a devouring, persistent ambition to win back the position and reputation which he had once held in the military world and of which he had in his own view so unjustly been deprived.

Jack Malloch, who had flown Spitfires with Ian Smith for the RAF during the War, set up Affretair in Gabon and gaily broke the Rhodesian blockade imposed

on his old comrade-in-arms. Tons of Rhodesian beef was flown out, tons of
sanctioned goods flown in, and Bob Denard certainly had his finger in that pie.
But, was he involved in the November 1970 mercenary attempt to overthrow
President Sekou Touré in Guinea? Did such an attempt ever seriously take place?
Was it Denard who with one companion cold-bloodedly murdered in Libreville
a year later one of Bongo's political rivals, Germain M'ba, as Pierre Peán's book,
published in France in 1983 to an immense stir, unchallenged, stated? One would
hesitate to say. But the general opinion is that Denard was not ever, by nature or
inclination, an assassin. As he himself was, later, to put it:

> "A mercenary is a man who fights for a country that is not his own, who fights
> for a wage. He is paid by the country he fights for. He doesn't kill for wages or work
> for individuals – the people who do that are not mercenaries, they are killers."

There had of course been the Mendes-France affair in Morocco, almost twenty
years earlier. But Bob Denard had been a young man, caught up in a sort of
vicious little civil war, influenced by older men than himself – and, on the worst
interpretation, he had agreed to chauffeur the would-be killers' car, not himself to
take a direct part in the assassination. And in any case he was acquitted.

★   ★   ★

So in these years Denard was involved in a profitable little business, flying Rhodesian beef out from, and cosmetics and television sets into, Salisbury.
Affretair's 'fleet' expanded from a single propeller-driven DC7 to a jet-propelled
DC8. But this remained for Denard just a sideline, though a sideline that he was
later - both directly and indirectly – to develop.

Meanwhile, in the shade, so to speak, of Le Braz's Presidential Guard he certainly set up, with President Bongo's blessing (and presumably with Colonel
Maurice Robert's and Jacques Foccart's too) a *Groupement Etrangère d'Intervention*,
a kind of Rapid Deployment Force, the nucleus of a mercenary 'Company'
comprising both blacks and whites, ready to intervene in nearby countries and
conflicts. And not just nearby conflicts, like Angola and Cabinda but in Libya, as
already described, and further afield still in Kurdistan.

Kurdistan – in 1974 Maurice Robert's successor at the SDECE put Denard in
touch with a Kurdish delegation in Paris. (Colonel Maurice Robert went on to
become the security chief for Elf-Total, the dominant French oil company in the
Gulf of Guinea – for oil had now been discovered in Gabon and offshore; and,
later, the French Ambassador in Libreville, Paris' man on the spot). Kurdistan.
Fascinating to think that Bob Denard and his mercenaries might have challenged
Saddam Hussein and the Iraqis. In 1974 he made no less than three trips out to
Kurdistan, via Teheran, Tabriz and Mahabad. Massoud Barzani was the Kurdish

leader of 50,000 *peshmerga,* almost submerged by the tanks and planes of Iraq. Denard could see that it was a totally different situation from that of the Yemen: where he and his men, after Katanga, had been involved in a civil war in which neither side, if possible, came to blows which intrigue and negotiation could delay.★At least the Kurds fought. But when the Shah of Iran and the President of Iraq negotiated a treaty, and the Iranian borders were closed to Kurdish supplies and Kurdish supporters, that was the end of that particular venture.

Angola and Cabinda were looming. Benin was still to come. But meanwhile Bob Denard's aid was sought elsewhere, in a part of the world with which he had previously had no contact at all. It seemed as if it would be a very minor affair. Little did Bob Denard think, in the spring of 1975, when he was once again on the Guinean warpath, and had rented the Park of Magesc in the Landes to train what he described as the "first African mercenaries", a dozen Guinean exiles, that he was about to be enticed into an affair that, one way and another, would dominate the rest of his mercenary career, indeed the rest of his life.

Book One

ISLAND PARADISES

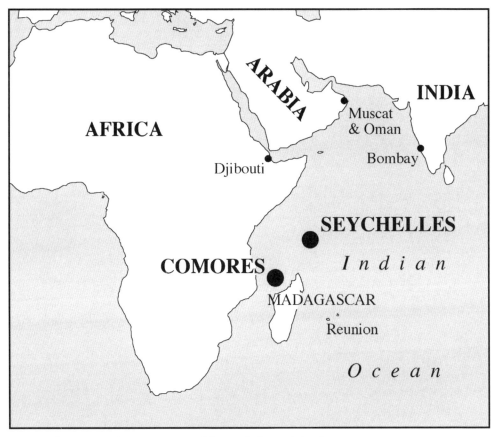

Indian Ocean showing position of the Seychelles and the Comores

III

Paradise Gained –
Coup in the Comores

'I think that, as long as there are people who enjoy adventure, there will be mercenaries. But adventure is like love, it needs to be well done and one needs to have partners.'
Bob Denard to Samantha Weinberg

Bob Denard first set foot in the Comores on 5 September 1975. He came in by plane. He was wearing a full colonel's uniform, with paratroop insignia; and he had 10½ tons of weapons and ammunition in the hold of the plane that flew him in, Jack Malloch's DC3.

He was to leave the Comores for the last time - probably for the last time, who can be absolutely sure? - on 5 October 1995, twenty years and one month later, again in uniform, but this time with a white moustache on his face and handcuffs on his wrists.

He can have had no idea when he first set foot on the Comores for what must have seemed a comparatively minor and comparatively simple task what a web the Fates were about to spin for him, and for so many others whose lives his appearance, his arrival on the scene, was profoundly to affect in the years to come. He can have had no idea that he was fated to overthrow no less than three Presidents.

The Archipelago Of The 'Battling Sultans'
Few people have ever heard of the Comores, fewer yet would be able to lay a fast finger on the map and proclaim with total confidence: *voici!* or *voilà!* Among the obscure little groups of islands that dot the Indian Ocean and were engulfed, at one stage or another, in the womb of the British or French Empires the Comores must be one of the most obscure. Undeservedly so, however. The four islands that make up the archipelago are, though impoverished, beautiful and varied; their history is fascinating, their inhabitants picturesque and their position definitely strategic.

It always has been strategic. In the era of the 'Battling Sultans' the Comores was basically a nest - or rather four nests - of slave-trading Arab, Persian and even Malayan pirates; and pirates have always had a beady eye for strategic positions. The Comores archipelago dominates and controls, at its northern end, that much-used sea-lane known as the Mozambique Canal, the wide stretch of ocean separating Mozambique, on Africa's eastern coast, from the great island of Madagascar. Ever since the Cape was rounded this has been and continues to be a major trading passage, the route up and down which, nowadays, the vast oil tankers pass. The inhabitants of the Comores were, though charming, a ferocious and bloodthirsty lot; and slave-trading continued up to nearly seventy years ago. This even though one hundred years earlier the French had annexed one of the four islands that formed the archipelago - Mayotte. Mayotte was not the biggest or the richest of the islands but it had what was possibly the best natural harbour in the Indian Ocean. Inevitably the 'battling Sultans' in the rest of the archipelago were drawn into alliance with, or opposition to, the French. By the turn of the century Sultan Said Ali, the most liberal and open-minded potentate on the biggest island, Le Grand Comore, had, with the backing of the French, achieved dominance over his rivals. By the time the Sultan Said Ali died, in 1916, the Comores was a French colony, he its leading figure, and Moroni, which he had founded, was on the way to becoming the archipelago's capital. Times changed, and titles varied, but power remained with the ruling family. In 1970, on the verge of Independence, Prince Said Ibrahim, son and heir of Sultan Said Ali, was President of the Government of the Comores: what in a British colony, pre-independence, would have been called Chief Minister.

Politics seem to be even more passionate in small countries than in large. With only a quarter of a million inhabitants the Comores was undeniably a small country; but it was riven, as many archipelagoes are, by inter-island rivalry. The families of Anjouan, one of the two large islands, hated with an ancestral loathing the leading family of Le Grand Comore. Anjouan was rich, a spice island invested in and exploited by French plantation owners: they backed one of the leading Anjouan notables, Ahmed Abdallah. Le Grand Comore was twice as large, contained half the total population but was poor. The people of Mayotte, the third island (the fourth, Maheli, is small and unimportant), used to French rule, employed by French government services, distrusted both of the other larger islands but in particular the French plantation owners of Anjouan who coveted their own land. There were more formal names for the political parties that eventually sprang up, but they were known generally (and simply) as the Parti Vert and the Parti Blanc. The Parti Blanc were Prince Said Ibraham's supporters; the Patri Vert Ahmed Abdallah's. Both those gentlemen, it should be stressed, were robed and dignified Islamic ancients, outwardly on the most friendly terms; but Ahmed Abdallah was, in addition to being an island notable, a French Senator

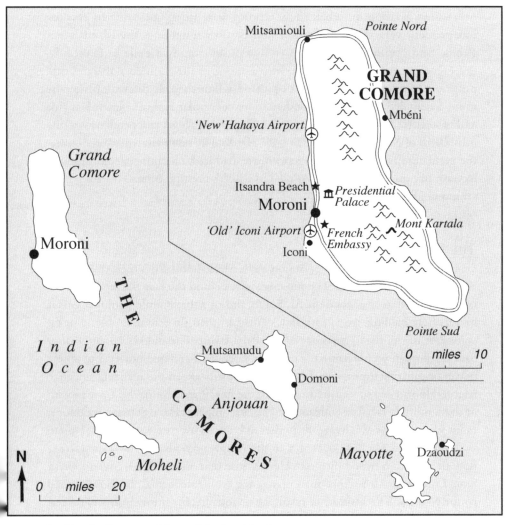

Le Grande Comore and inset of the four islands

with (rather surprisingly in view of his local plantation-owner backers) strong support from the French Socialists. In one of those unforeseen upsets that can happen in any elected assembly, the Prince was in 1972 voted out as President of the Government and Ahmed Abdallah was voted in. Even more unforeseeable was Ahmed Abdallah's next move; he suddenly and unilaterally declared the Comores independent.

It looked like - it probably was - a Mitterand-backed move, designed to embarrass Mitterand's recently triumphant opponent, the newly elected President of France, Valéry Giscard d'Estaing. Certainly Ahmed Abdallah, a. gnome-like figure, would hardly have dared risk such a step without being assured of support in France; and indeed this mini-UDI did embarrass Giscard. He could hardly order French troops in when the Comores were in any case due to become independent very shortly; and he could hardly reimpose as the islands' ruler Prince Said Ibrahim, who retired to live in self-imposed exile in France. So the French government accepted, with a shrug of the shoulders, this political pinprick; but cannot have been displeased when the inhabitants of Mayotte immediately declared that they wished to remain under France's benevolent rule and protection. What was France to do? Impose an illegal independence on the inhabitants of Mayotte against their will? Hardly. The manoeuvre had rebounded; the premature Declaration of Independence had led to a mini-state mutilated of its most important asset, unity; Ahmed Abdallah's prestige, instead of rising high, sank very low.

THE FIRST FORAY

Less than four weeks later, on 3 August 1975, Ahmed Abdallah's régime was overthrown in a bloodless *coup.* The moving spirit behind the *coup* was a young man of a totally different generation, Ali Soilih, and of a totally different kind: genial, prematurely balding, large, with Black African (that is to say slave) blood in his veins, but for all that a member of the Parti Blanc. The old nobleman, Prince Said Ibrahim, in whose name the *coup* was carried out, refused however to accept power originating from a *coup d'état;* he died shortly afterwards on a pilgrimage to Mecca. His son and successor, the third of the line, Prince Kemal Said, a man with an extraordinary facial resemblance to the late Emperor Haile Selassie of Ethiopia in his younger days, was living in another of France's overseas ex-colonies, Djibuti on the Red Sea. He did not return to the islands immediately; he waited to see how the situation would turn out. He was sure that Ali Soilih, his contemporary, would rule well: Ali Soilih was an easy-going semi-intellectual, much influenced by the May 1968 Paris students' revolt, non-violent, joint-smoking, open-shirted, open-minded, and very popular. Meanwhile there remained an immediate problem; the deposed President, the wily Ahmed Abdallah, had fled to his own island of Anjouan and Anjouan was in revolt. Fortunately Ali Soilih had a French friend of his own age, Le Bret, installed on the Grand Comore, a *'gars de bonne famille',* indeed a cousin by marriage of France's President, Valery Giscard d'Estaing. Le Bret had founded the local airline, Air Comores. His chief pilot was a man named Morançay, who had flown relief supplies into Biafra. Morançay had his contacts in Gabon. Le Bret used them. In Gabon, out on his farm, was Bob Denard; and Denard accepted the contract. It did not seem over-complicated.

On 19 August Bob Denard's advance party arrived. There were two of them, Roland Raucoles, a pilot for the Presidential Guard in Gabon, and Thaddeus Surma, a former legionary, a veteran of Indochina and Algeria, a thug but an experienced thug. Le Bret put them up in his own villa at Mitsamiouli on the northern tip of the Grande Comore.

Their report must have been favourable. There were virtually no weapons on the islands since the French had pulled out, since Giscard d'Estaing had withdrawn the garrison of Foreign Legionaries and the French gendarmerie in part to Mayotte and in part to the far bigger French island of Réunion, way out in the Indian Ocean. Ali Soilih's *coup* had been carried out at mid-day on a Sunday with ten young Comoriens in two old Renault 6s, armed only with four shotguns and five pistols. That had been enough to scare the fifty-odd guards at the barracks in Moroni and to set them running. It was not a question of mortars and machine-guns, of armoured cars and bazookas, it was more a question of puncturing car tyres with sharpened umbrella prongs.

True, President Abdallah had got away, and was holed up among his own people, in his own island of Anjouan – from where he was broadcasting urgent appeals to all and sundry to reinstate him, even for French legionaries and gendarmes to be rushed back by kindly France. The appeals were ignored. True, he would have to be winkled out. But it seemed he had less than a hundred armed men on Anjouan and that their arms too were only pistols and shotguns.

It did not sound a Herculean task. Back in Gabon Bob Denard raised $15,000, bought 300 small arms plus ammunition, hired a Dakota from Jack Malloch, loaded up, and, a fortnight after his advance guard, was there at the airport of Moroni, the little capital of the Grand Comore. Next day his men flew in, by the regular Air France flight from Paris. There were five of them to start with, led by Roger Bruni, one of Denard's old guard, a veteran of the Congo and before that of Algeria, Indochina and even Dien Bien Phu, a man who had never been wounded in action - except by his own commander, Bob Denard, in the Congo. But that had been accidental; and he bore no malice.

Two days before Denard's arrival there had been trouble on the Grande Comore, and blood - for the first time since the National Council of the Revolution had taken power - had been split. Ali Soilih and his young guards had gone to the large village of M'beni on the other side of the island, to arrest another recalci-trant notable, Mohammed Taki. Booed and stoned, they had opened fire. Three of Mohammed Taki's loyal supporters had been killed, many wounded. The situation was tense; for, killings apart, there was no money left in the Revolution's coffers. Even rice and sugar were running short.

But Denard got on well, surprisingly well, with Ali Soilih, a man ten years his junior. Together with Le Bret, they concocted a plan. It involved a swift training course up in the mountains at the newly-built military camp of Itsundzu for 250 of Ali's enthusiastic but ragged young supporters. Denard had the arms, he had the mercenaries to train the *Mapinduzi* as they called themselves, and he had the backing of the government such as it was. This was no *coup d'état* he was planning – the *coup d'état* had already taken place.

What it was was a little invasion, an airborne invasion. It took place on September 21, just over a fortnight after Bob Denard had first set foot in this archipelago of flowing white robes, a thousand mosques, tropical scents, intrigue, secrecy and shy sensual women.

Of course there was no element of surprise. The little airport at Anjouan would be expecting a landing, might well be blocked. So the first plane to land, at first light on the 21st, was a tiny Cessna 180, piloted by Le Bret. On board were Thaddeus Surma, a Comorien and a new arrival – René Dulac *Le Grand*, one of the most professional of Denard's mercenaries.

The four jumped out, cleared the runway of obstacles, seized the control tower, fired a few bursts, and promptly scared the ten or so guards into surrendering. Then the two Dakotas, a DC3 and a DC4, carrying Denard himself and the bulk of the invading force, landed. This consisted of five more mercenaries (including another former Legionary, the German Helmut) and a hundred young *Mapinduzi,* looking thoroughly professional, clad in uniforms (supplied by Christian Olhagaray, a Basque adventurer who had much earlier worked out in Gabon for President Bongo's predecessor, Leon M'Ba and now ran an import-export shipping company on the islands) and wielding rifles and sub-machine-guns. But with less than a fortnight's training, Denard was not about to let them run riot. Their presence was a bluff, an astute bluff. No ammunition had been issued. They had guns but no bullets. Only the mercenaries were properly armed.

So it happened that one of the *Mapinduzi* was hacked to bits by the enraged citizens of Mutsamudu, Anjouan's capital, in the confused hours that followed the initial success. For Abdallah had again evaded capture, fleeing across the island to his birthplace, his fortress of Domoni, wily old bird that he was. His residence in Mutsamudu was empty. The dead *Mapinduzi,* caught apparently at a crossroads on the edge of the town, was Moissi by name. And thereafter Ali Soilih, in his honour, rechristened his young guards the *Moissi.* It was to become a name of dread for most of the inhabitants of the Comores.

But that was still in the fairly remote future. For the time being everything went well. Twenty-five of Abdallah's armed guards surrendered. Negotiations were opened. There had only been two deaths in all; and both sides were eager to avoid bloodshed. Ali Soilih flew in. The mercenaries, except for Bob Denard, flew back to the Grande Comore. The Prefect of Anjouan, the French-trained Mohammed Abdillai, negotiated terms. And four days after the invasion President Abdallah gave himself up and 'voluntarily' resigned the Presidency. He was escorted to the airport at Anjouan before being flown to the Grande Comore. And there Bob Denard met him for the first time, a small, turbaned, dignified ancient, with an air of authority and a heavy wrinkled face.

Thus Anjouan returned to the fold. Ahmed Abdallah after four months' house arrest was packed off first as ambassador to Idi Amin in Uganda, then - which must have been much more congenial to the old gentleman - to exile in Paris, with a large cheque signed by Ali Soilih in his pocket as a gesture of goodwill and consolation. As for Bob Denard, within weeks he was back in Gabon with a successful and very discreet little action to his credit, presumably a large cheque from the new government in his pocket too - and the memories of a spice-tanged tropical paradise where manners were perfect and morals most attractively lax lodged firmly (if memories can be lodged in that part of the anatomy) in his heart.

Ali Soilih's Rule

Not that Bob Denard totally disappeared form the Comorian scene. He was always flying back for brief visits, for chats with Ali Soilih, trying to get the new ruler to set up a proper little army – to be trained of course by Bob's men - trying to persuade him to be reconciled with France, trying in effect to set up a new little base of his own.

But Ali Soilih was erratic, impulsive, an idealist - almost everything that Denard was not. His idea of the perfect army had been to enrol four 'Amazons' who guarded President - ex-President - Abdallah when the latter was brought back from Anjouan to Moroni and placed, temporarily, under house arrest. When Denard *à la* Nestor, tried laboriously to insist, Ali quite rightly retorted that the Comores could not afford an army in the French sense, they would make do with a hard-working agricultural people's militia. And when Ali decided to 'invade' Mayotte with an unarmed 'army' of 150 young men, all Denard could do for Franco-Comorian relations was to persuade Ali to call it not the *Marche Rouge* but, less provocatively, the *Marche Rose*. (It took place on 11 November. There could be no doubting Ali Soilih's personal courage. He led it. But it had no popular support in Mayotte, whatever Ali's dreams may have been. It was beaten back at Mayotte airport by a crowd of enraged locals; and the would-be marchers, red, pink or simply yellow had to be re-embark ignominiously under the protection of the French gendarmerie.)

By then, by November, Denard had other and bigger fish to fry. Angola, his old place of refuge, became independent on the very day of the *Marche Rose,* the Portuguese pulled out rapidly and ignominiously, a three-sided civil war flared up, and Denard sent René Dulac *Le Grand* (alias Vincent) with a mercenary team to oil-rich Cabinda in the north. Had that venture succeeded★ it would have dwarfed in interest and importance any little affair on the other side of Africa in the Comores. It came, swiftly, to nothing, and thereafter Denard concentrated his efforts – led by Freddie Thieleman and André Cau - in the south, supporting Jonas Savimbi and UNITA; of which more in its place. When that more heroic episode in its turn ended, there was the Cotonou Coup to plan.

Meanwhile President Kerekou of Benin was not the only West African ruler to have had marital problems. If Pierre Péan is to be believed, a Haitian had seduced *Madame la Présidente*, Madame Bongo; and Denard was given by President Bongo of Gabon the job of punishing the adulterer. The Haitian had fled to Miami;

Denard apparently sent Thaddeus Surma, the former Legionary, to track him down. It is not too clear whether the Haitian was killed or not. It is not too clear what proof there is at all that Denard was in any way involved in this (or in a later, successful murder of another of the amorous Madame Bongo's lovers, carried out in France allegedly by gangsters from Bordeaux on Denard's orders). But what is clear is that Bob Denard does have questions to answer – the sort of questions that would never be put to a Mike Hoare, whose experience of life had been so different and so comparatively limited. On the other hand: "He (Denard) doesn't have the mentality of an executioner, he thinks like a soldier," said one of his mercenaries, by no means entirely favourable to him. And Jean Larteguy agreed: "I don't think he ever really had the mercenary mentality. He was not mad, he didn't like killings."

★   ★   ★

At the beginning of 1976 Ali Soilih, who had been using another aged noble-man, Prince Mohammed Jaffar, as figurehead, arranged to be elected Head of State himself; and from then on the nature of the régime began to change. Curiously, the Comores must have been the only state in the world where the extravagant ideas and ideals of May 1968 were actually tried out and where, in the words of the famous student slogan, '*L'imagination prend le pouvoir*'. In complete contrast to a man like Ayatollah Khomeiny (whose time had of course not yet come) Ali Soilih swept away the veil, and all puritanical Islamic traditions. He tried to abolish too the non-Islamic and distinctly non-puritanical tradition of *le Grand Mariage,* the vast four-day-long wedding feasts with gold jewellery and the dancing for men and the dancing for women and the aphrodisiac lunch for the bridegroom and the grandmother 'hidden' under the bridal bed, and the unbridled extravagance that (as Ali rightly pointed out) ruined so many middle-class families and prevented so many poorer ones from ever marrying their daughters.

More dramatically still he handed over power to the Island's youth. It was not to the Head of State but to a collective of schoolchildren that the flabbergasted American Ambassador in Moroni found himself presenting his credentials. Pot was legalized. Jeans replaced flowing white robes. The people of Mayotte, meanwhile, voted by 99.4% to stay under French rule. However much they may have disliked Ahmed Abdallah and his plantation-owner backers, they disliked even more this extraordinary version of Mao's Cultural Revolution in action that had even the Chinese Ambassador to the Comores jittery with apprehension. In the other islands a certain anti-French tinge for the first time developed. Numerous French *co-opérants* left. At the end of the year Prince Kemal Said, in a sense the natural head of state, flew down to Moroni. 'You can't go on like this, Ali,' was his message to a man for whom he still had great sympathy. '*Tu es un bourgeois,*' retorted Ali Soilih somewhat inaccurately, '*tu n'as rien compris.*'

What most shocked Prince Kemal Said was the sight of a handful of imported Tanzanian troops; he left the islands after three days, convinced he could do nothing to moderate his contemporary's actions and afraid of being arrested. Yet, as Kemal Said always stressed, Ali Soilih's was more of an idealist's than an oppressive régime; only one man was ever executed, and that a sorcerer who (according to the Prince) deserved death. Agriculturally speaking the economy boomed. Politically speaking Ali Soilih was convinced that, provided he kept the Russians at bay - as he did despite all their blandishments, a true child of May '68 in that - the French would make no attempt to overthrow him. He foiled an attempted *coup* on Anjouan; he quarreled with his mighty island neighbour Madagascar (most justifiably —hundreds of Comorians who had settled there were massacred at Majunga); he rechristened the Republic *'democratique, laique et socale'* and he continued to attack religion. He even organised on 28 October 1977 a referendum which showed —-it must have been one of the few true results ever to emerge in a one-party African state - that only 55 per cent of the voters supported him. Yet in a sense it was the honesty of this openly-proclaimed result that led to his downfall. The end of the year was marked by rumours of plots and arrests - as was only to be expected in a country where nearly half the population, and that probably the older, more economically powerful half, was openly against 'the Revolution'. The early spring was marked by riots and deaths on the Grand Comore. And in the late spring, assured of important support for the 'counter-revolution' they proposed to install, the mercenaries struck.

★   ★   ★

This is the only instance I know of in modern mercenary history where a mercenary leader - Denard - acted in the worst traditions of his 'profession', selling his services first to one side and then without scruple to the other. That said, it must be admitted that Ali Soilih had himself changed and that all his French friends - feeling that he was going too far, too fast, too wildly - were deserting him. What is somewhat repugnant is that they did not all do so openly. His friend Le Bret, who had contacted Denard in the first place, was Ali Soilih's semi-official ambassador-at-large; but it seems that even Le Bret was involved in the betrayal - as were his chief pilot Morançay and another acquaintance of Denard already installed on the Grand Comore, Christian Olhagaray. On the other hand, in any coldly calculated analysis it must be admitted that inside aid, which had been lacking in Benin, is probably vital to the success of any sudden coup that involves an invading force. That does not make those who treacherously provide that aid any more attractive as human beings.

THE PLANNING OF THE COUNTER-REVOLUTION

Abdallah, it is said on the Comores, was always conscious of his African origins, his slave blood. But if that may be true, what is certainly even more true is
that, like Stendhal's Julien Sorel, he knew himself to be far more talented than
his superiors by birth, the Arab princes. He was boundlessly ambitious and, like
Julien, almost totally amoral. He had sworn on the Koran that he would take no
further part in politics; and Ali Soilih had believed him. Naively. For to Abdallah
politics was power, and power was money, and money was at the root of the
family fortune. "*Etablissements Abdallah et Fils*" had been built up by him in the
Comores as the foundation – for Abdallah had six sons, and Ali Soilih despite
his lovely and beloved Amazons had (I think) none – of a new dynasty. Exile
in France, even a generously–funded exile, left him deprived of that position of
influence, that atmosphere of intrigue which from his young days had given his
life its spice and its success.

It was not extraordinary, then, that the former President should ignore his
oath on the Koran. And it is perhaps not totally extraordinary that he should,
in his desire to be restored, have turned to the mercenary leader who had been
responsible for having overthrown him. For that mercenary leader had been
swift, resolute, unbloodthirsty – and on the airport at Anjouan had treated him,
Abdallah, with formal courtesy and apparent respect.

Did Abdallah know of the failed *coup* in Benin? Probably. He, as a former
member of the French Senate, had his contacts. And in any case details were
beginning to leak out. Did it put him off? Obviously not. For here was a mercenary leader who could not only fight in civil wars and suppress rebellions but
who could mount a mini-airborne invasion against a capital, a country where
he knew no-one, had only a second-hand idea of the lie of the land. That would
not be the case could Colonel Bourgeaud, Colonel Maurin, Colonel Denard, be
persuaded to mount an invasion of the Comores.

They met in mid- February 1977, either in Enghien in Switzerland or at a
restaurant in Paris. Stories differ. What does not differ is the account of who
was present at the meeting; a French intermediary who brought them together,
on the mercenary side Bob Denard and René Dulac *Le Grand,* only a month
after the failure at Cotonou; and on the Comorien side not only Abdallah but
two other of the principal merchants of the Comores, the round and genial
Mohammad Ahmed and the suspicious Indian wholesaler Kalfane. An agreement was quickly concluded. Ali Soilih had gone too far, was out of control,
was expendable. He was, for the benefit of the people of the Comores, to be
overthrown, and a triumvirate of merchants to be established in his place. Denard
was to do the overthrowing. He would be paid a preliminary fee of three million
French francs; and, if successful, be given the long-term task of reorganizing the
military and the police in the archipelago.

They shook hands on the deal. Denard did not believe in contracts on paper. But he did believe in paper money; and a suitcase containing the agreed sum in 500 franc notes was then, or soon thereafter, handed to him. Planning could begin.

It began with the setting-up of a company based in Rue Bachaumont, Paris, entitled France Outre-Mer Services (later rechristened Horus) which was a barely-concealed mercenary recruiting operation. Colonel Maurice Robert took a share in it, André Cau ran it, and Roger Bruni, another of Denard's old faithfuls, acted as liaison.

The first new mercenaries to be recruited were two French officers who had served briefly in Rhodesia, Jean-Luc Sarron and Hugues de Tappie. And the first plan was for pretty much a repeat of the Benin operation: to fly a force of just over ninety mercenaries in, to land on le Grande Comore, and to take the archipelago over. The base, the point of departure, was to be Salisbury in Rhodesia: and clearly this decision was influenced, if not suggested, by the two new recruits, intelligent and adventurous young men, who had both seen action with Grey's Scouts.

But mercenary operations never go as planned. South Africa, which always had an uneasy relationship with Ian Smith's Rhodesia, refused transit rights, the mercenaries already recruited had to be paid off and dismissed. The next plan involved the Sultanate of Muscat and Oman. Jack Malloch had a company there. There was Moroccan influence. But there was even more British influence, and three months passed in negotiations that came to nothing. Abdallah went on a pilgrimage to Mecca, seemed depressed – understandably so, the money was running out fast – said his prayers. Kalfane, the Indian, more sulphurous, accused the mercenaries of stealing his money and backed out.

A lesser man than Denard might have given up at this stage. But Denard never lacked what mercenary leaders must have, persistence in the face of difficulties. Looked at objectively, his story since the great days of Six Commando★ had been of failure after failure: the failure of the attempt to rescue Munongo★, the enormous failure of the Mercenaries' Revolt★, failure in Cabinda★, in Angola, in Benin. Yet invariably he had picked himself up *à la D'Artagnan,* dusted himself down, and come up with yet another undaunted or ingenious scheme. Now, when his resources were certainly fading fast and his reputation with them, he surpassed himself.

THE VOYAGE OF THE *ANTINEA*

First and foremost Denard decided he would do without a base. Secondly he decided he would do without training. And thirdly he decided he would do without weapons. None of those statements is quite literally true; but that is how it must have appeared to his shocked and dubious subordinates. He had decided to contravene the three basic rules of all mercenary operations.

Of course there were enormous advantages. A base of departure, like Gabon or Rhodesia or Oman, means negotiations with officials and governments, who can always, at the last moment, withdraw their approval and scupper the whole operation. No base, no negotiations with officialdom, meant freedom of action. Therefore, instead of a proper base, use a mother vessel, a boat; and with it the freedom to roam the seven seas. No need on the high seas to request transit rights!

As for training, choose men who are pretty well-trained to begin with, and do your pep-up training on board ship. The same advantages apply. Mutiny on the high seas apart, no-one can scupper your plan.

As for weapons, it was obviously impossible to mount an invasion with no weapons at all. But Denard has seen at Anjouan what seven lightly-armed men and a hundred troops with, in effect, toy guns could achieve. And he knew that any order to any arms dealer for any quantity of weapons would (as later *coup* attempts were again and again to show) alert the various intelligence services, alert via them the local police, and risk raids, interception, arrest and possibly detention. He decided to use sporting weapons: pistols, 12-bore Remington shotguns, Franchi repeating rifles and Winchester elephant guns. All these could be bought, and were bought, with their ammunition – very limited, not more than a hundred rounds a weapon – here and there, in ones and twos, without exciting suspicion. And there would be only 48 guns in all; for there would be only 48 men. So: no machine-guns, no mortars, no RPGs, no grenades. None of the usual paraphernalia of the common or garden mercenary operation. Just the bare minimum – and less than a company of men to seize a state.

What the proposed invasion would depend on was stealth and swiftness in execution; but above all on total secrecy beforehand. Bob Denard became M. Henri-Antoine Thomas, a Swiss citizen with a Swiss bank account, about to undertake an exploratory geoseismic survey in Chilean waters, off Punto Arenas.

The boat he found was at Brest, the *Cap Faguet* by name, a retired Newfoundland fishing boat, 75 metres long. It cost what was left of the initial money, half a million francs. Denard then did what he had never done before. He mortgaged his share of a Citroen garage he had invested in near Bordeaux, for a further two million francs. It was perhaps a sign of increasing desperation that he was ready to risk his own money, and probably his last reserves, to self-finance a mercenary operation. The boat needed extensive refitting – satellite navigation, cranes for the launching operations, storage for half a million litres of fuel which would ensure three months' sailing time without the need to touch dry land, cold storage of 500 square metres for provisions. This all took place at Lorient in Brittany. It was now December 1977.

The first batch of men came aboard in March – Jean-Luc, Hugues, the radio-operator, Gérard, Laurent, Damien, Noel the Belgian, and his black dog Raki, ex-Katanga, put in charge of the galley, Jean-Baptiste the carpenter, Jean-Louis the 32-year-old former paratrooper, the doctor. Van too, the Legionary, Helmut who had stayed on for some time in Moheli, and Carcasse alias Narbonne, the boxer, who had been with Denard in the Congo, Biafra, the Yemen and Benin. Crates were loaded: of weapons and ammunition but also of flares, waders, camouflage kit, black uniforms and green berets. Two Zodiacs were hoisted on board, each capable of carrying twenty-five men. Two mechanics and an electrician had to be hired, and a Captain and Second Officer. Then all was ready.

*   *   *

The *Cap Faguet* weighed anchor on 22 March 1978. The voyage across the Gulf of Gascony towards the Canaries was storm-tossed, nauseating. But it took only five days and the ship was not overcrowded: there were only twenty men on board, plus the crew. At Las Palmas, as agreed, Captain Blanchard was thanked, paid and sent home. 'Monsieur Thomas' himself took charge – just as well Denard had some training in the French Navy to fall back on – but the Second Officer, Faquet, two mechanics and a nervy little electrician were kept on. The boat itself was rechristened. It became the *Antinea*.

In the Canaries, on the eve of departure, 25 more men joined them, recruited by André Cau and Roger Bruni in Paris. The biggest single contingent was the Belgian group led by another old hand, Lt Colonel Roger Bracco. But perhaps the most significant were two who arrived together a few days earlier. Marques, a former Legionary and Mélis, an East European who had been refused by the Legion but accepted by its Spanish equivalent, the *Bandera*. Both had been in Gabon, both had gone out to Rhodesia with Major l'Assomption's ill-fated group (of which more in its place) and there both had briefly made themselves notorious. Mélis' real name I have been unable to discover. Marques was Dominique Malacrino.

The *Antinea* set sail from Las Palmas just before dawn on April 26, making seven to ten knots. Ten days of perfect sailing weather followed. The men were kept busy with physical training. No alcohol was allowed. No telephoning was allowed. Telegrams from the crew were taken for transmission but never transmitted. Once past the Equator Denard called all his men together to announce a change of plan. The contract in Chile had been cancelled. Fortunately a new contract was, he announced, on offer – in the Persian Gulf. They would be rounding the Cape of Good Hope.

The men were hoping for a shore break at Cape Town. Bob was having none of it. They had been guessing at their target – Sao Tomé? Equatorial Guinea? Benin – and revenge? But of course once the Equator had been passed, those were ruled out. And once the Cape was rounded, so was Angola. Seven days short of the Comores the Zodiacs were brought out of storage and tested. Tension began to mount. Four days later, seventy two hours before the assault, Denard at last revealed his target: the Comores. Feverish activity followed. Facing them would be a militia of at most twelve hundred poorly-trained men, armed with Chinese weapons, plus ten Tanzanian instructors. Even though their opponents had had no combat experience, the odds were enormous. But failure, said Denard, could only come from treachery or lack of fighting spirit.

Assault on Moroni

In the early hours of Saturday 13 May, on a dark night, all lights extinguished, the *Antinea* cast anchor two nautical miles off the coast of the Comores.

The target was the sheltered Itsandra beach, a few miles to the north of Moroni. A brief coded radio message had been flashed to Christian Olhagaray. He would, on its reception, arrange for guiding lights to be displayed on Itsandra beach, and for vehicles to be on stand-by ready to transport the mercenary groups to their various destinations.

In the centre of the Grande Comore the vast volcanic bulk of Mt Karthala loomed. But there were no guiding lights on Itsandra beach. The first part of the plan had gone wrong. Denard decided to go ahead all the same.

Two mercenaries – Le Bosco and Philippe – were left behind to guard the *Antinea* and to make sure that the four members of the crew took no initiative of their own, now that they knew what they were willy-nilly involved in.

The rest, 46 mercenaries in all, embarked on the two Zodiacs. Armed, wearing black uniforms, faces blackened, carrying daggers, torches, handcuffs, they embarked behind their two leaders, the Colonel – Bob Denard – and the Lt Colonel – Roger Bracco. The time was 2 a.m. The Zodiacs, their engines silenced, set off over the darkened sea.

No shots rang out. If they had not been assisted, at least they had not been betrayed. They beached. Denard was the first to set foot on the Comores. Still, however, there was no sign of Christian Olhagaray. First no lights, now no vehicles. It began to look ominous - as if it might be Cotonou all over again. But at least there were no inhabitants about, no-one to give the alarm.

Bracco's target was the militia camp at Voidju, two and a half miles to the north. Cardinal and two men stayed on Itsandra beach, guarding the Zodiacs. Noel and another two took up position at the crossroads on the coastal road, where one road led inland towards the Presidential Palace about a mile away from Itsandra beach. Beside it, just below, lay the Kandani guard-house and barracks. In the Comores, even more than in Benin, the whole force of the régime was bound up in one man. Ignoring all other objectives Denard had decided, rightly, to concentrate his own efforts upon seizing the person of this one man, the President, the Head of State, Ali Soilih. The great advantage this time was that with inside information from men in Ali Soilih's immediate trusted circle, he could be absolutely sure where the President was to be located – as it happened, in the Presidential Palace. This was the target of Denard's group. Their task was to occupy the Presidential Palace and seize the President.

The Presidential Palace was not as grand as it sounds. The former residence of France's Delegate General was a double-storied building arranged in a three-sided square around a central courtyard, dominated by a mango tree. It was still dark night. Mélis silently stabbed the sentry at the Kandani guard post. Then a Renault 4, a police car, came out through the gates of the Presidential Palace, lights ablaze. The mercenaries, by now closing in, opened fire with their shotguns, killing all three policemen. A sentry appeared on the balcony and fired a wild shot. Marques fired back. The sentry fell.

A blast from Gérard's elephant gun blew open the main entrance into the building. Mélis, Marques and Jean-Luc raced in, up the stairs to Ali Soilih's bedroom.

There they found Ali Soilih, in his pyjamas, awake but calm – unlike the two 'Amazons' with him. They knew him from the photos Denard had shown them in his briefing aboard the *Antinea*. Jean-Luc put a shotgun to his head and brought him down to the entrance hall. There he had Ali lie face-down on the floor, his hands handcuffed behind him. Mélis and Marques rapidly checked all the fifteen rooms of the palace. There was no-one else there at all.

Two or three hundreds yards below a small group of mercenaries besieged the barracks of Kandani. These were semi-deserted. There was a brief exchange of fire. Within ten minutes the few militiamen firing back surrendered.

The *coup* appeared to be going amazingly well.

Bob Denard limped into the entrance hall. Apparently when he had last seen Ali Soilih two years earlier, furious at being kept waiting in an antechamber, he had stormed in, pretty nearly waved his fist in Ali Soilih's face; and stormed out again, promising that he would be back. And now - the story is perhaps a little too pat to be exactly true - he stood over Ali Soilih in silence before asking him: "Do you remember me?"

Ali Soilih gazed up.

"Only you could have done this," he is said to have replied.

★   ★   ★

In a sense Ali Soilih was exactly right. Denard had learnt the lessons from Cotonou. This time he had plumped for total (rather than merely relative) surprise; and this had meant a discreet landing by sea, at night, rather than the intimidating but inevitably public landing by air, at dawn. In addition of course, a most important factor, he and three others already knew the terrain and knew the 'targets'. They would not be landing at night, always a muddling affair, on unknown soil. And in Denard's case he would not be in search of a president known only by photographs.

So it was just as well that Roger Bracco too had been on the Comores before, in the 'first foray' (indeed he had stayed on in Anjouan for three months after Denard had left, only finally dismissed by Ali Soilih when he had opposed an anti-French demonstration). This meant that he too knew exactly the lie of the land; he knew where the camp Voidju was, and he knew its lay-out.

His group too achieved almost – but not entirely – total surprise. There was a swift exchange of fire with sentries, three were killed, and then, as the black-clad assailants burst into the barracks and bedrooms, firing mainly for effect, total panic and chaos ensued, some of the young Comorian militiamen running, some hiding under their beds, none – in what must have been for them a nightmarish scene –putting up the least resistance. Bracco's men seized the armoury, and re-armed themselves with Chinese Kalachnikovs.

They seized vehicles too. The next objectives, as dawn was breaking, were all in the small capital of Moroni, that, like Cotonou, lies next to the sea: the barracks of the *Moissi,* Radio Comores, and the prison. The *Moissi* ran for it, Radio Comores was seized, and Ali Soilih's political prisoners were freed. People began coming out into the streets, and, believing that the French were back, shouting *Vive la France!* Fifty arrests, mainly of young *Moissi,* swiftly followed. Prince Kemal Said was phoned in Djibuti to be told that the *coup* (of which he had been forewarned by his father's old enemy, Abdallah) had been successful; and that his old friend, Ali Soilih, was a prisoner.

At 11 a.m. Radio Comores came on the air. "The Clandestine Liberation Force has landed. Colonel Said Mustapha M'Hadju speaking. President Ali Soilih is under arrest." And within days the late Democratic, Lay and Social State had become the Federal and Islamic Republic of the Comores, ruled – under the two co-Presidents - by a Politico-Military Directorate. Here in full are the names of the Permanent Members of the New Politico-Military Directorate: Abbas Jadduf, Said Hassan, Said Hachim, Saidi Madi Kaff, Hadji Hassan Ali – and Colonel Said Mustapha M'hadju.

SUCCESS

The Comores are remote, difficult to reach, and free from journalists. It took some time for it to be realized that Colonel Said Mustapha M'hadju, the new Minister of Defence of the Federal and Islamic Republic, was none other than Bob Denard himself in his most elaborate and imaginative disguise yet. By then, by the time the secret of a mercenary rather than an internal *coup* was out, veils were back in, the schoolchildren at their desks, and everything in its place as it had been before.

Or almost. The *coup* took place on 13 May. In the three days that followed Denard and his men worked night and day, literally, with barely a pause. Jean-Louis was sent to Moheli, with three mercenaries; and met no problems there, only relief and an exuberant welcome. Anjouan was another story. There were six hundred men there, Ali Soilih's occupying force, so to speak, on Abdallah's hostile island; and the feeling was that, as soon as they realized how few the mercenaries were in number they would fight. Obviously there could this time be no question of a surprise attack, or of seizing the harbour and airport with a handful of men, and a large amount of bluff, as Denard had done before. For, before, there had only been a handful of Abdallah's retainers to contend with. The situation was very different this time. There was, however, radio contact with the garrison in Anjouan. Denard decided to negotiate.

It was almost a mediaeval situation. Except that Roger Bracco, who volunteered to go in as herald/plenipotentiary unarmed and under a white flag of truce, was flown in on a Cessna rather than riding in on horseback. At Mutsamudu, Anjouan's capital, he and his pilot Lourdet bluffed the military commander into surrendering, with threats of an attack by four hundred newly-armed mercenaries if he refused. The harder nut to crack was in the interior, where half the force, 300 men, Tanzanian–trained, were encamped at M'Remani. Fortunate it was that Bracco had been so long on Anjouan two years earlier, and fortunately he recognized, among those at the camp with their rifles trained on him, young men whom he personally had trained, whose names he remembered. Fortunately too Denard had prearranged that tense moment to fly low but menacingly over the camp in a DC4. The risky manoeuvre, thanks to Bracco's personal bravery, worked. The nut cracked. The main difficulty thereafter was in evacuating the six hundred safely to prevent reprisals by the angry Anjounais against what they had seen as an occupying force.

That was one of the dangers too in the Grande Comore. But Denard managed it. There were no reprisals or, at least, no massacres. And the mercenaries became, swiftly, the administrators of the new régime. Ten were sent to Anjouan, to support Bracco. Security was reorganized, communications were reorganized, hospitals were reorganised, two hundred soldiers were trained, or retrained, at Voidju, and a 'Black Commando' of sixty, under Jean Baptiste, was given the job of guarding the Presidential Palace, and Ali Soilih safely there under house arrest. Captain Charlier collected two hundred and fifty ex-*Moissi*, and put them to work repainting the capital, whitewashing the hospital, the prison, the stadium, public buildings, private houses, even the edges of the pavements. So that when on 21 May Ahmed Abdallah, a prudent person by nature, finally flew back with Mohammed Ahmed to be welcomed by a cheering crowd of no less than 30,000 – three days later the duumvirate declared themselves Co-Presidents – he was overwhelmed to see what in the space of ten short days M'Hadju and his mercenaries had achieved.

THE DEATH OF ALI SOILIH

One week after the return of the *coup*'s two backers, the two Co-Presidents, Ali Soilih died. There are at least three versions of how he met his end. He had been kept, under Jean-Baptiste's guard, for the two weeks since the attack first in the

Presidential Palace where he had been captured, and then at Kandani just below. In somewhat similar circumstances he had not only spared Abdallah's life but had sent him into a most comfortable exile. Now that the tables were turned, it might be thought that Abdallah would spare him.

On the other hand Ali Soilih's revolution had not only offended too many powerful interests, it had also brought violent death to the Comores. And in strictly realistic terms to have spared Abdallah had proved, as Ali Soilih must morosely have reflected, a fatal mistake – one that Abdallah was unlikely to repeat. Prince Kemal, from abroad, favoured a public trial for his former friend. It never happened. There was no trial. Possibly a trial would have opened too many cans of worms, for Ali Soilih had at one time been a minister in Abdallah's own government. The official communiqué announced in time-honoured fashion on May 29 that the deposed President had been killed 'while trying to escape'.

It seems unlikely. It seems almost equally unlikely that Bob Denard, taking pity on Ali Soilih, and knowing that the deposed President was to be faced with a tribunal that would pronounce sentence of death, had offered Ali Soilih the chance to run for it; and that he was shot down by a Comorian sentry as he ran. Readers might look back to the stories – the rumours, perhaps – about Madame Bongo's lovers. There was never any sort of judicial enquiry following Ali Soilih's death, or indeed any enquiry of any sort; so that it is impossible now to establish the truth. But what seems certain is that there was a meeting that night up at the Presidential Palace attended by the two Co-Presidents and all the Politico-Military Directorate. Cars kept going up and down the hill to and from Kandani that evening. A vote was taken; and only Mohammed Taki of M'Beni (where Ali Soilih's *Mapinduzi* had first shed blood) voted, it is said, in favour of Ali's life.

Did Denard attend that meeting? Did Denard vote? Impossible to say. Did Denard personally execute Ali Soilih? I very much doubt it. It was not in his character to be a cold-blooded killer. But did he arrange for the execution, or at least turn a blind eye to it? Probably yes; possibly with regret. One story has it that all the Comoriens of the 'Black Commando' on duty that night were dismissed for the evening, leaving only mercenaries in charge. And that a mercenary called (or probably not called) Vanne, a former legionary, led Ali Soilih out into the open air. There he stood, quietly. Vanne put a gun to his head, and shot him. Ali Soilih sank to his knees, and the mercenary shot him again.

Next morning – and this seems undisputed – Denard personally drove Ali Soilih's body to his home village of Chouani and delivered it to his sister Fatima to be buried. He offered to send some men, if need be, to dig the grave, and they dug the grave in the front garden of Ali's mother's house. Mother and son lie there still, side by side.

So ended Ali Soilih, second President of the Comores.

A Mercenary Paradise

For the mercenaries the Comores become a second Garden of Eden. In the main they stayed on. They formed, on Gabon's lines, a new Presidential Guard (based on the Black Commando that had watched over Ali Soilih) – the only armed force, once the Tanzanians had been expelled, on the islands. It never became as elaborate and powerful as Gabon's; it never had its own tanks or helicopters; and so perhaps it never quite fulfilled Bob Denard's dreams. But he was very proud of his creation.

> "The Guard was organized, the Guard was structured, the Guard had an adminis-tration," as he was later to put it. "When there was a problem in the Comores, the Guard was called. If there was a fire, the Guard was called. If there were bees in the roof, the Guard was called. If there were problems in the village, the Guard was called. If your house was falling down, you called the Guard. *Voilà!*"

The Presidential Guard was smartly turned out in the trademark black uniforms and green berets that the 'Clandestine Liberation Force' had worn. There were two Companies, the 1st and the 2nd, French-officered, with base and headquarters at Kandani. But its commander was not Denard. He was contacted by one of his very old hands, a Belgian from Liege, who had run most successfully the admin-istrative base for Six Commando back at Stan in the old days.* This man's name was Roger Ghys, well-spoken, diplomatic, tall – and very bored with his job as an accountant in Europe. But a tactful accountant was just what was needed to run what very soon, and inevitably, became much more of an administrative than a military machine. In the Comores Roger Ghys became 'Commandant Charles'.

Pay was not high for the mercenaries in the Comores – it went, according to rank, from $1000 to $1500 a month – but life was sweet in the tropical sun, on the beaches, in the Officers' Mess where there was a formal dinner every Friday night, and, eventually, with the shy but submissive, the beautiful and languorous, women of the Comores. The most adventurous of the mercenaries, bored, soon returned to Europe where André Cau, in Paris, continued to keep his recruit-ing office open on Denard's behalf; so that those who left were soon replaced. Others stayed on to become 'men of affairs', in some cases marrying two or three wives, owning two or three houses, effectively filling the void left by the ejected French plantation owners of Anjouan and the temporary French *co-opérants* on the Grande Comore, neo-colonialists on a new but yet (in that pirate archipelago) surprisingly traditional pattern.

As for Denard himself, he was found a villa in Datche, the smart residential area above Moroni where President Abdallah also had, at Djum-Djum, his private res-idence. 'Colonel Mustapha' was often to be seen in and around Moroni in white robes and a Koffia, the embroidered hat of the Comorian gentry. He converted to Islam. He even made the pilgrimage to Mecca and added a Hadj to his already elaborately impressive alias. And he married. He married in a Muslim ceremony, almost immediately, one of Ali Soilih's young conquests, Mazna, a refugee from the Majunga massacres. She was only sixteen. Perhaps he took possession of her in the same spirit as he had taken possession of Ali Soilih's new Citroen – which he drove ostentatiously all around the island.

The *cadi* disapproved of this marriage. He had other plans for 'M'hadju'; and with Mazna falling by the wayside, Denard was married, in style, to one of the *cadi's* relatives, who, the *cadi* assured the Colonel, was the most beautiful young woman in the Comores. (And I in my turn have been assured he was not much exaggerating.) To the victor the spoils! A proper *Grand Mariage* followed; and rapidly Amina, his new wife, was to give Bob Denard two beautiful daughters, Hamza and Kaina.

In the short term however everything was a little too good to be true. The OAU was the serpent at one remove in this little Eden, demi-paradise. The OAU, outraged, refused to accept the Comores back into its ranks while a notorious mercenary figured in its government. On July 22 Colonel Haji Said Mustapha M'hadju resigned from the Political-Military directorate and as Minister of Defence (while still remaining Commander-in-Chief of the armed forces and the gendarmerie). As a consolation prize the Co-Presidents appointed him a Grand Officer of the Star of Anjouan, and pinned on his proud breast the appropriate Cross.

It was not enough. Two months later, on September 25, Ahmed Abdallah, by now sole President, said a public farewell at the stadium to his Commander-in-Chief. It was a moving ceremony. All his former cabinet colleagues were there, and André Cau, specially out from Paris, was at his side. The President described the Colonel as a 'hero' who had saved the Comores, its people, the Muslim religion and 'all that is humane in this country' – an inhabitual accolade for mercenary leaders.

And that, it might have been thought, was that. But such was very far from being the case. It was significant that Denard flew out, quietly, with a single suitcase, leaving Amina behind, on an Air Gabon cargo flight which was collecting Rhodesian beef and had been diverted to pick him up. He was soon, much more discreetly, back again in the Comores where he assumed, once again, a new identity. He became, at least for the outside world, Remy Destrieux, a French citizen of dual nationality, with a Comorian diplomatic passport, and a mission as roving ambassador for President Abdallah's règime. He had a beach house up at Mitsamioudi on what had been Yves Le Bret's property. He set up a meat-importing company, Socavia, that had the monopoly on meat imports from South Africa. And he arranged – most significantly, it was his greatest triumph of all – for white South Africa to fund, via the SADF and South Africa's military intelligence, the Presidential Guard from September 1979 onwards. At his instigation, and with his encouragement, South Africa poured money into the Comores, financing two spanking new hotels and, Denard's pet project, a 1200 acre experimental farm at Sanguina. It was a hectic life at times, a relaxed life at others. Bob Denard had turned fifty now; and had, it seemed, found contentment and his earthly paradise. *Insh Allah!*

ALIAS CLIENT EASTWOOD

There was an enthralling little might-have-been addendum to the story of the voyage of the *Antinea*. Clint Eastwood had read an account of it, and of Denard's adventures, in *Esquire*. He was fascinated, understandably. It was very much in his line; but at the same time unusual, a film project with a difference. He interested Warner Bros. Warner Bros rented a luxurious apartment on Avenue Floquet for Denard and fellow mercenaries in, presumably, their role as script advisers – Roger Bruni, Le Bosco, Jean-Baptiste and others. Three times, no less, Denard was flown out to Hollywood. The proposed budget was in the region of $30 million; and Denard received an advance of $300,000 – the only large sum he ever made in his life, as he was to put it, without having to risk it.

This was all in the spring and summer of 1979 when Denard was lieing very low, and tending to keep away from the Comores. By the autumn the project had collapsed, as so many film projects do. Rather a pity – one can visualize a steely Clint Eastwood as a ruthless mercenary leader, and Denard shooting willy-nilly to worldwide fame, if only at second-hand. For what is undeniable is that the *coup* in the Comores was the most successful mercenary *coup* ever.

But the Comores were not the only set of islands in the Indian Ocean. To their north, hundreds of miles to their north, lay a far more scattered, far less densely inhabited, far more traditionally peaceful archipelago - the Seychelles.

IV

'Mad Mike' and Operation Anvil

'Like most of my plans it had tinsel around the edges.'
Mike Hoare, *Three Years with 'Sylvia"*

When he was a comparatively young man, before he had ever dreamt of becoming a mercenary, Mike Hoare had fallen in love with the Seychelles.

> Let me begin [he later wrote] by telling you something about the Seychelles and why I went there in the first place. There are ninety-three islands in the archipelago and they are formed by the tips of underwater mountains protruding through the sea. Coconut and bread fruit trees grow everywhere and the islands are lush with foliage which grows profusely in a climate drenched twice yearly by the monsoons.
>
> Hot and humid it can certainly be, after all Mahé, the principal island, is practically on the equator – four degrees south if my memory serves me right. Dense mangrove and takamaku trees on the edge of lovely white beaches, with cloves and vanilla high up in the hills and surrounding it all crystal clear water. Sounds enchanting, doesn't it? Well it is - a regular paradise.

In those days, in the 1950s, the Seychelles slumbered in the Indian Ocean, almost untouched by modern civilisation or development. The British India Steamship Line ran two ships between South Africa and Bombay, the *Kampala* and the *Karanje,* and they touched at Mahé on alternate months. Their arrival and their departure, with both passengers and mail, marked the great monthly excitement at Victoria, the tiny capital which boasted in its main square, Gordon Square, the tiniest statue of Queen Victoria on public display in the British Empire, one foot tall. British governors ruled lethargically over this backward dependency with the support, barely needed in view of the general good humour and peacefulness of the population, of a smart and excellent little police force. The official language was, of course, English; but the inhabitants spoke between themselves a form of French dialect, Creole. For the islands, previously uninhabited, had

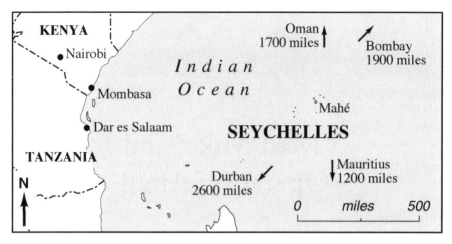

The Seychelles and the East Coast of Africa

been colonised two hundred years earlier from the larger French island-colony of Mauritius far to the south; and the French planters, the *grands blancs,* had brought with them their own slaves. Then, before Napoleon became Emperor, a Royal Navy squadron seized the Seychelles and, at Mahé, had the finest natural harbour for hundreds of miles. Thereafter British governors in Government House lived in general harmony with the *grand blancs,* the Savys, the Michaux, and the rest, with whose language, customs and way of life they interfered as little as possible.

By the middle of the twentieth century when Mike Hoare arrived for a nine-weeks' holiday with a 16 mm Bolex camera - a luxury in those days - and an ambition to make a documentary on island life, the coconut plantations, the main source of revenue for the landowners and of employment for the islands' men, had fallen on bad times.

> The girls were very often beautiful [he wrote] and ranged in colour across a wide spectrum, which was not surprising seeing that their forbears had been drawn from all parts of Africa, Arabia, India and Europe. Many were extremely attractive, and there in very large numbers to boot. Fish were ten a penny, and girls were ten for one fish, went the local and unnecessarily harsh saying, a state of affairs brought about by the economics of the island. To find work it was essential to emigrate to the mainland: on the island it was almost unobtainable. So there were very few men about.

Mike Hoare appears to have had a rounded and engaging personality with a noticeably wry sense of humour. He must still have been married to his first, English, wife at the time; he was obviously however bored with his post-war life as an accountant and a respectable family man in Durban. His passion was for adventure in general and in particular for sailing. His film project came to nothing: but he did hire and sail a wooden dinghy the *Miranda* around the crystal-clear lagoons of the Seychelles. He sunk it too, in twenty foot of water, three miles from shore, capsized by a sudden gust of wind as the sun was setting. His two crewmen, Jean and Pierre, brothers who had served in the British Army in Cyprus in a Seychellois Pioneer Battalion, thrashed around the *Miranda's* mast, one foot of which protruded above the waves, screaming with their terror of *les demoiselles*, the tiger sharks that often swim quite close inshore. Hoare trod water for one hour, two hours, trying not to think of the barracudas and the sixteen other varieties of shark that infest this part of the Indian Ocean. He and his crew, hoping against hope, were rescued, of course, in the end by a lucky chance and three pirogues of young boys; and in gratitude Hoare spent fifty pounds – 'a veritable fortune', the local French priest assured him – on a three-day-long beach party for his rescuers. He went home, to Durban, to take a share in a second-hand car business and to set up, more actively, a safari company. He went to Katanga, separated from his first wife, and married a South African girl, Phyllis Sims, by whom he had two children to add to his original three. He became famous as a mercenary leader. In his mind the Seychelles faded to a happy if spectacular memory of nine weeks in paradise.

THE PRESIDENCY OF JAMES MANCHAM

During his time there Hoare had stayed in a bungalow in the grounds of the Hotel Seychelles, on the most beautiful stretch of beach in the main island, Beauvallon Bay. The owner of the hotel, Gerry Le Grand, had come from South Africa, convinced that there was a vast tourist potential in the Seychelles if only they would open an airport. In the end 'they' – the British authorities – did. But it took a long, long time. Mahé International Airport, as it was grandiosely called, actually opened on 4 July 1971, though it was not officially opened till March the following year when the Queen paid her first and last visit to what was still, just, a part of her Empire.

The opening of the airport changed the whole way of life in the islands. The Seychelles did, almost immediately, undergo a tourist boom. Smart new hotels sprang up in the decade that followed: a cluster of three on Beauvallon Bay: the Coral Strand Hotel, the Beauvallon Bay Hotel, and the Fisherman's Cove Hotel, and, out a mile or so past the little lagoon-style airport, the Reef Hotel, on its own. Roads were built, work increased, tourists, developers and speculators poured in; and politics inevitably reared their head.

The *grands blancs* had seen with regret their old style of life fading away: though a plantation owner like Henri Michaux, a *grand blanc,* could still boast – or rather state without boasting – that he had had over sixty children of his own on his plantation and that his grandchildren could be counted in their hundreds. But though the *grands blancs* retained their social prestige, their economic power base had disappeared. A few by property speculation made new fortunes. The future however obviously lay with the commercial classes rather than the landowners; and from the ranks of the commercial classes sprang the epitome of the islands' *nouveaux riches,* Jimmy Mancham.

Mancham's father had been, in the words of one of the oldest British inhabitants, 'just a grocery store owner'. But the grocery store had prospered, a chain of stores had developed, and Mancham's father set his son on the traditional upward path for intelligent young men in any British colony by sending him to study law in London. In due course Mancham qualified as a barrister-of-law at the Middle Temple. He was a flamboyant, bearded young man of great charm and dynamism, proud of his racial mixture and his streak of Chinese blood, intent on cutting a dash in the great world outside and on bringing prosperity and glamour to the islands. In November 1970 the Seychelles' second-ever elections were held. Shortly afterwards Jimmy, as everyone called him on the islands, became at the age of thirty-one the Seychelles' first Chief Minister. His party won ten out of the fifteen seats in the little local parliament. Next year came the opening of the airport; the year following the visit of the Queen. Mancham loved the pomp and the ceremony, the luxury, the power, the connections with the rich and famous and above all the girls. Heather Jane, his English-found wife, did not last long. Soon it was the turn of a Yugoslav starlet, Olga Bisera, of Helga Von Mayerhofer, a New York jewellery designer, of Michele First, the model, even of Fiona Richmond, 'Britain's nudest dancer'. 'So I'm happy with another woman,' Mancham told journalists. 'Is that a crime? You must remember these are the Seychelles, not stuffy Westminster. I'm only human, a common trait in politicians, despite what people think.' Yet in a way it was the girls that ruined Jimmy; even the easy-going locals said that he ought to have been more discreet. Moreover he always chose what he described, with almost touching snobbery, as 'young ladies of international stature' whereas his political opponents were in his view 'only going out with some village girls'.

The Seychelles is a small place, and this sort of remark wounds. When they came back almost simultaneously from London together, Mancham and another newly qualified Middle Temple barrister, France-Albert René, used to do the rounds of the Seychellois bars together. But that was in the early Sixties, before Mancham could afford to sneer at René's choice of girls. René was four years older, also an extremely handsome and very attractive man, but of a very different cast of features and mind. His father had been a rich Frenchman from France, M. Lanier; René was illegitimate, no disgrace in the Seychelles, and half-French, half-Seychellois, no disgrace either. He too had married an English wife in England, Karen, whom he discarded in favour of, eventually, one of the Savys – hardly a 'village girl' therefore, though certainly no café society girl like Jimmy's preferred set. There were far greater divergences, though, than their attitude towards women between the two fellow barristers and former friends. René had originally trained for the priesthood and always had a more serious turn of mind. The political party which he founded and led, the Seychelles People's United Party, wanted independence from the British, preached social justice and was highly suspicious of capitalist development and of tourism. Mancham and (as the 1974 election proved) just over half the Seychellois population with him, were perfectly happy to remain under British protection as long as they could run their own internal affairs. 'Do we want Independence?' Mancham thrice asked a vast rally (by Seychellois standards) in Victoria's stadium and thrice the answer came roaring back from thousands of throats: 'No, No, No!'

Nevertheless the British government forced Independence on the Seychelles; and on 29 June 1976 Independence came. 'You must know when I move into the Governor's Residence on Tuesday it is going to be the swingingest State House in the whole world,' Mancham told the delighted guests who arrived to celebrate. They included, apart from the Duke and Duchess of Gloucester, a bevy of the international jet set, Adnan Khashoggi's brother, Essam, and a 'friend', a British businessman discreetly anonymous, who presented the new Head of State, President Mancham, with a blue Rolls Royce Corniche in which he left Independence Stadium (he had arrived in a more modest Jaguar) to the cheers of his supporters.

Earlier on Independence Day he had joined hands with his new Prime Minister, Albert René - for the British had insisted on a coalition government - in a more serious gesture.

'In this spirit,' he proclaimed, 'I call upon my Prime Minister to hold my hands as a once and for all demonstration of our mutual respect, as a resolve of our determination and that of the parties we represent to work together for the common good and as a symbol of lasting national unity.'

One year later, while he was in London attending the Commonwealth Leaders' Conference - to be even more precise, while he was, in his own words, in bed with a 'tousled blonde' in the Savoy Hotel - he was telephoned by his Arab friend Khashoggi to be told that there had been a *coup* in Victoria. The President - or rather the ex-President as he had just become - had been overthrown in his absence and that, despite all the hand-holding and proclaimed mutual respect, by none other than his own Prime Minister, Albert René. Swinging time was over.

RENÉ'S RÉGIME

In retrospect it is difficult to blame René too much for this Judas-type conspiracy. The Seychelles are a relaxed place and the Seychellois a relaxed people who were at ease with Mancham's genial style; but many of them felt he had gone too far when he had allowed whole clusters of out-islands to be sold to Arab business men or to members of the Shah's family. They approved when the new President, René, re-appropriated these islands without compensation. They approved when René introduced social security, health clinics and free education. But they approved much less when he instituted a one-party state, censored the rival newspaper, and set about abolishing the religious fee-paying private schools. And they approved not at all when he formed an army and called in the Tanzanians to 'train' it.

The Seychelles of course had never had an army. They had never needed an army. As Mancham had pithily put it, 'the only weapon of the Seychellois people is their laughter'. There was a British-trained police force and police armoury containing the only firearms on the islands, about two hundred rifles, at Montfleury in Victoria. That was why René's *coup* had been so surprisingly easy. Sixty of his supporters had flown in from the out-islands on the Sunday night, 4 June 1977; and in the early hours of the Monday morning, at 2 am on 5 June, they had simply seized the armoury at Montfleury, and all was over. They were armed with ten Kalashnikovs that had been smuggled onto Mahé from Dar-es-Salaam; in the brief struggle one policeman was killed and two men were wounded, one on each side. But once the armoury was in the 'Revolution's' hands that was that: there was simply no possibility of resistance. The Commissioner of Police, Mr Patrick Somerville, and four other British police officers were arrested and expelled. The Chief Justice of the Seychelles, Mr Aidan O'Brien Quinn, who was unwise enough to describe the Prime Minister's 'task-force' to the press as 'people with long criminal records', followed within a few days. The only other casualty appears to have been the brother of the Anglican Minister who was dragged into a courtyard and for obscure reasons shot. But of course the real casualty was the whole way of life in the Seychelles. For the first time murder and violent death had, like the serpent, intruded into the politics of paradise; and it ought never to be forgotten that it was René and his party, not Mancham and his supporters, who were responsible for this ruinous development.

The problem the new government now therefore faced was this: that it would be as easy to overthrow them as it had been for them to overthrow their opponents – unless of course an army was created. So, with the help of President Nyerere of Tanzania, an army was created. Not a large army - it was at most six hundred strong - but still a new and oppressive element that would never have been needed if Britain had not unwisely imposed an unwanted independence. The police force, some 450 strong, kept to their British traditions though their British officers had departed: they despised the ill-disciplined, idle and ragged army and they, like the populace at large, loathed the loutish, aggressive Swahili-speaking Tanzanians who were imported technically to train the new army but in fact as a sort of presidential bodyguard. Ogilvy Berlouis, who had once worked as an office boy for the British-owned company Mahé Shipping, a small man with a big head, generally feared, became Minister of Youth and of Defence in President René's new government.

'MAD MIKE' TAKES A HAND

Mike Hoare had, by the early 1970s, apparently abandoned forever his mercenary ambitions. He had, presumably with what remained of his Congolese money, bought and refurbished a Baltic schooner and for three years fulfilled one of the dreams of his life by sailing her around the Mediterranean, with his second wife Phyllis and various of his children as crew. But by early 1974 he was back in South Africa. The Baltic schooner was sold. He wrote a book about her, a very attractive book called *Three Years with 'Sylvia'*; but books rarely keep a family alive; and by 1975 Hoare was wistfully dreaming of a comeback, with his eye on Angola. He made contact with a young and ambitious operative of BOSS, South Africa's much-feared Bureau of State Security, named Martin Dolinchek. But though Dolinchek was keen to play a part in any intrigue that might increase his own importance, in the end the head of BOSS, General Hendrik Van Der Bergh, warned Hoare off. The former mercenary was not, the general cabled, 'to meddle in State affairs'.

But, as Dolinchek later put it, 'Guys like Mike Hoare - they live for this kind of operation. They go to bed praying that something will turn up!' It is impossible to say whether Hoare immediately thought of the Seychelles as a possible target when the news of Mancham's overthrow and René's coup came through on 5 June 1977; or whether the idea gradually developed. Indeed it may originally, and most ironically, have been put there by René himself. For only five days after the coup the new President was accusing Mancham of recruiting mercenaries for a counter-coup, an allegation which Mancham immediately and almost certainly truthfully, from his London exile, denied. René, he said, was 'a victim of his own over-reactive mind': and he added, with less prophetic truth, 'I have been fighting a diplomatic battle and will continue to do so.'

Less than a year later Denard launched his successful coup in the Comores; and I personally always felt that it was this success by his despised rival of the Congo days★ that induced Mike Hoare to make the Seychelles his target. After all, the similarities were only too evident; both the Seychelles and the Comores were newly independent small archipelagoes in the Indian Ocean; in both the legitimate, elected right-wing government had been overthrown by violence and in both a left-wing régime had been installed. If anything, the Seychelles with only a fifth of the population of the Comores was the easier target; and if Bob Denard could overthrow Ali Soilih's régime with fifty mercenaries in one night, why could not he, Mike Hoare, as easily do the same in the Seychelles?

I still believe that this age-old rivalry with Denard spurred Hoare on. But, more recently, conclusive evidence has come to light that Hoare was already plotting a mercenary *coup* in the Seychelles *before* the success of Denard's *coup* in the Comores. For on 12 May 1978, that is to say *two days before* the Comores' *coup*, Hoare was writing as follows to a prominent Seychellois exile:

Dear Gonzague,

I am enclosing Plan No. 2 which I would like you to consider. It seems a very workable plan to me ... Tender my respects to Mancham and tell him my services are entirely at his disposal if he needs me.

          Mike.

PS Beware of a man named Banks in Britain. He is very dangerous and bad news in our line of country.

Gonzague – Gonzague D'Offay – had been Minister of Internal Affairs under Mancham's short-lived Presidency; and this letter is conclusive proof that less than a year after Mancham's overthrow Hoare was already hard at work preparing plans for a mercenary *coup* in the Seychelles and in close touch directly with leading right-wing exiles and indirectly with Mancham himself. Indeed it seems that Hoare had revisited the Seychelles as a tourist the previous September, that is to say three months only after René's *coup*, and presumably on the strength of that reconnaissance had drawn up not only Plan No. 2 but Plan No. 1 – whatever they may have been. It is not at all clear whether at the time the letter was written Gonzague D'Offay was in Durban, where many Seychellois exiles were gathering, or in Australia or in Paris, other centres of activity (indeed in Paris about this time a Seychelles Liberation Committee was formed) or in London; but the reference to John Banks 'in Britain' and the advice to steer clear of him would seem to imply Paris. As for John Banks, he ought to have been flattered that Hoare deigned to consider him as a rival mercenary leader who was worth warning the Seychellois off.

FIGURES FROM THE PAST: BANKS, TOMKINS, DEMPSTER

Hoare's concern was partly justified in that Banks had been very active in 1976 and 1977, in and out of intrigues with his old cronies from Angola days⋆ Dempster and Tomkins, one more fantastic than the next: a parachute raid and rescue on Luanda prison; blowing up Cabinda oil wells (Gary Van Dyk, a South African living in England, set up a training centre for this abortive venture at Pine Valley Farm near Okehampton in Devon); forming a new anti-communist mercenary recruiting organisation, ACRO. Later he was to become very bad news indeed: involving himself in the terrorist scene: in attempts to trap Carlos for the Israelis (which Tomkins and Dempster, to trap him in his turn, denounced to the PLO): allegedly in activities connected with the IRA; and definitely in unsavoury plots involving assassination in Somoza's Nicaragua. By 1981 he had been on the run for several months from an open prison where his blackmailing activities had landed him. Hoare's diagnosis of three years earlier had proved only too accurate a forecast as far as John Banks was concerned.

Banks was last heard of in 1993, in hiding, protected by Britain's Customs and Excise investigation squads for whom, for years, he had been acting as an informer and agent *provocateur* in murky drug-dealing and arms-selling deals. Prior to that he had been living prosperously with his wife Maggie in Gainsborough in Lincolnshire. Dave Tomkins, much more interestingly, had spent two years in Colombia, trying to assassinate (on whose behalf?) the drug baron Pablo Escobar. This had involved, in 1991, an ambitious attempt to buy a fighter-bomber, no less, an A37 Dragonfly, in America. The attempt, though abandoned, caught up with him. He was arrested in Texas over ten years later on a conspiracy charge, pleaded guilty and landed in an American jail, leaving his wife Mary and three sons to guard the mock-Tudor family home in Basingstoke. Rather unfairly – seeing that Tomkins had been in and out of prison ever since the age of eighteen – his wife seemed to blame Chris Dempster for leading her husband astray (and, which she seemed to resent even more, for calling her 'Doll'). Of the latter there has been, since the late 1970s, no reliable news.

The Wild Geese

Hoare himself was having a busy year in 1978. Apart from preparing plans for a *coup* in the Seychelles, he was hired as technical adviser on far and away the best mercenary film ever yet to be made, *The Wild Geese.* In the film, based on the Irish-born Rhodesian-based Daniel Carney's novel, Richard Burton played the leading role, of a Mike-Hoare-style figure, an ageing mercenary leader called out of retirement for one last venture, a swift mercenary raid (rather on the lines of the abortive Libyan Contract★) to rescue an ex-president from a prison in Albertville in the Congo. Among the actors - the cast included Roger Moore and Richard Harris - was one with whom Hoare struck up a close friendship, a man some twenty years younger than himself named Tullio Moneta. Though born in Yugoslavia - curiously enough like Martin Dolinchek the BOSS opera- tive - Tullio was basically an Italian, an impressive athlete six foot five inches tall, who had been a champion discus thrower in Italy before emigrating to South Africa and becoming, in South Africa, a well-known television actor; he still retained, however, a strong Italian accent. He was also a karate expert and it was via karate that Tullio Moneta knew a man of his own age, in his late thirties, a 5th Dan named William Dunlop Paul who owned a string of health studio clubs and had, more importantly, close connections with South Africa's commando force of which he had once been a member. From playing a mercenary in a film to becoming a mercenary in reality there seems to be only the slightest imaginative jump, particularly in a country like South Africa which was, at that time, awash with rumours of mercenary plots and generally indignant at the state of affairs in what had previously been one of South Africa's favourite tourist destinations, the Seychelles. While Hoare continued in his role as technical adviser, Tullio Moneta and William Dunlop Paul travelled down to Capetown to meet the last com- mander of Five Commando, George Schroeder.★

Schroeder was now a businessman in the Cape; but, like almost all ex-mercenary leaders, he seems to have had a nostalgia for the good old days. He too had a plan for a Seychelles *coup* that involved two Hercules cargo planes with two amphibious troop carriers on standby and he offered Moneta and Dunlop Paul 20,000 rand down and 20,000 rand on successful completion of the 'mission' to join his team. (There were approximately two rand to the pound; at the time a rand was about equal to a dollar. As most of the figures will from this point on be in rands, it is worth bearing these rates in mind. 1,000 rand therefore would be about £500 or $1000.) These were large sums but the two were not impressed with Schroeder or with his plans; they did not like the man, they considered him politically ill-informed and they preferred in the end to work with Hoare - who would almost certainly have talked of *his* plans to Moneta during the shooting of *The Wild Geese*.

The Mystery of the November Plot

Nevertheless all these plans apparently came to nothing until, well on into the following year, in November 1979, President René announced in the Seychelles that he and his government had foiled a plot 'sponsored from abroad with the cooperation of mercenaries standing ready in Durban'. At the time, to the world in general, this seemed a mere invention, a pretext dreamt up by René to crush internal agitation against his régime - even the schoolchildren were demonstrating against the hated National Youth Service that would take them from their families - and to imprison his opponents. Sure enough, over eighty Seychellois were arrested and held, in the main, for nine months without being charged or tried before being exiled. But, with hindsight, it seems more than likely that there was a real plot against René. Whether it was Hoare's Plan No. 1 or Plan No. 2 or even No. 3. or No. 4, I doubt; it seems far more likely that it was French-inspired. France after all had been the original colonial power in the Seychelles, French and Creole were still more widely used as languages than English, France had, with its Indian Ocean fleet and troops at Mayotte and on Réunion, a far stronger position in the area than Britain and, after all, it had almost certainly needed France's approval and complicity for Ali Soilih's régime in the Comores, another left-wing régime on another Indian Ocean archipelago, to have been overthrown so easily only eighteen months earlier. (Indeed it still seems to me just possible that the whole fantastic story of the voyage of the *Antinea* was just that: a fantasy, a total fiction; and that Denard and his commando had assembled, with the French authorities closing their benevolent eyes, in neighbouring Mayotte, so much closer to the target, so much easier a crossing, so much more likely a base. After all, Ahmed Abdallah had flown out before the 'invasion' to the nearby French-owned island of Réunion to await the turn of events. The Foreign Minister, Mouazoir Abdallah, who had also been sounded out, was carefully abroad. The Tanzanian troops, the only real threat, had been sent well away from the scene of the action, to Anjouan. Ali Soilih was a man around whom in May 1978 a void had been created, practically a man alone.)

Furthermore it was a Frenchman, Schroeder had told his visitors, who had first approached him with the suggestion of a mercenary *coup;* it was France which, in early 1979, had gifted the Seychelles the *Topaz,* a heavily-armed fisheries protection vessel complete with crew; and it was a Belgian, Noddyn, who was in charge of President René's close protection squad.

Could the *Topaz* have been France's Trojan horse? On the discovery of the November Plot the twelve Frenchmen (out of the total thirty-man crew of the *Topaz*) were arrested. So was the man in charge of training the Harbour Police, M. Jacques Chevalereau. The thirteen Frenchmen were deported two months later after allegedly admitting preparing a *coup* – which they denied on arrival in Paris.

But the whole thing does rather whiff of the Denard touch. Could he even have been planning – which would have been possible with the help of the Harbour Police and the benevolent neutrality of the *Topaz,* the only armed vessel protecting the harbour at Victoria – to repeat his landing near Moroni? Certainly in early November he was writing to President Abdallah from France, to say that the project for the Clint Eastwood film was no longer timely but that it had provided excellent cover. And certainly too Noddyn, who apparently as a Belgian was viewed without suspicion by President René, stayed on. What President René did not know was the significant fact that Noddyn had been in Bob Denard's Six Commando in the Congo.

Meanwhile, back in the Comores, Bob Denard had sent out his old comrade-in-arms René Dulac *Le Grand* to, so to speak, hold the fort while he, Denard, lay low. Dulac had refused to take part in the Comores expedition; but had since been forgiven. *Le Grand* however had ambitions of his own, as future events were to show, and closer contacts apparently with the French government than Denard himself, particularly since René Journiac had after a bitter power struggle in Paris succeeded Jacques Foccart as France's *Monsieur Alfrique.* Could Dulac have been planning, off his own bat, a *coup* in the Seychelles that would rival Denard's *coup* in the Comores? Dulac of course had known Noddyn, fought alongside him in the Congo too.

Between the Comores and the Seychelles, between Moroni and Victoria, lay barely a thousand nautical miles of almost empty ocean. If a boatload of heavily-armed mercenaries had sailed north-east from the Grande Comore to Mahé in November 1979, if this invasion had been successful – if there is any foundation at all in this speculation – then Denard or Deluc, or possibly both acting in unison, would have become figures of unrivalled prestige and menace in the Indian Ocean.

THE END IN RHODESIA

A month after the failed November Plot in the Seychelles events occurred elsewhere in Africa that were to have a bearing on future mercenary plans. In December 1979 the bitter war in Rhodesia at last came to an end. UDI was terminated, the ceasefire held, Lord Soames flew out from Britain as Governor to preside over the elections that would lead to the independence of what now became Zimbabwe – and hundreds of whites who had fought the black guerrillas of Nkomo and Mugabe in the Rhodesian army were faced with an uncertain future. They began to consider their position. Their position, they knew, would he insecure in a black-ruled Zimbabwe, particularly if they had served in any of the units most reputed for their ferocity and ruthlessness in hunting down the guerrillas who would now almost inevitably become the masters of the new country.

Consider, for example, the case of Mike Webb, an Englishman just turned thirty at the time. Webb was in effect a high-class professional soldier, a man whose life was soldiering. He had joined the British Army and had been commissioned into the 15th/19th The King's Royal Hussars, a regiment that, like all Britain's cavalry regiments, only accepted gentlemen of the traditional breeding and background as officers. Five years later he had resigned his commission and joined, with the rank of captain, the Trucial Oman Scouts. By doing so he had technically become a mercenary but a mercenary of a very official sort, for Sultan Qaboos' army was with British government approval almost entirely British-officered. After only a year, however, in March 1975, Mike Webb again resigned his commission; and this time he took a further step towards becoming a fully fledged mercenary by joining the Rhodesian Light Infantry,

White-ruled Rhodesia lacked white manpower; and as in the mid-Seventies the war against the guerrilla forces of Joshua Nkomo based in Zambia and those of his rival Robert Mugabe based in Mozambique grew more ferocious and more murderous, conscription of the local white settlers proved insufficient to fill the ranks. Therefore, at first discreetly, then much more openly, Ian Smith's régime began to recruit professional white soldiers from all over the Western world. Most, like Mike Webb, were British. They were of course fighting for a country that was technically a British colony in rebellion against the British Crown; but they can hardly be described as traitors. For Rhodesia was quintessentially British in style and way of life, and proud of it. Perhaps that is why so very few South Africans joined the Rhodesian army - there has always been a strong mutual antipathy between the Boers of South Africa and the British of Rhodesia despite their common boundary, shared interests and similar colour of skin.

Indeed worse than that – Vorster's South Africa was, from the point of view of Ian Smith's Rhodesia, about to betray them, to throw them to the twin wolves, Nkomo and Mugabe, to cut off aid, particularly military aid, and insist on a settlement.

Perhaps more typical than Mike Webb was Don Kenny, a Yorkshire man. He too had served in the British Army but not as an officer, as an NCO. What was unusual about Sergeant-Major Kenny however was that he had also served in the Foreign Legion, in the 2ᵉ REP, Colonel Erulin's men, stationed in Corsica. So he spoke pretty good French.

GREY'S SCOUTS: ENTER PATRICK OLLIVIER

Hence when, most unusually, a young Frenchman from Touraine, Patrick Ollivier, flew out to Salisbury in 1976 to 'volunteer' for the Rhodesian Army, he was placed under Kenny's wing. Ollivier had done his military service in the 6ᵉ RPIMA in France. Kenny had been seven years in the Rhodesian Army by then, in one of the four all-white squadrons of the Rhodesian SAS. But he had been seconded under an elderly Captain Steevens, to attempt to form an extraordinary new guerilla-chasing unit – Grey's Scouts.

The more famous Selous Scouts had been formed three years earlier, mainly of 'turned' Zipra or Zanla rebels – blacks therefore who knew that they could expect no mercy at the hands of their former comrades. As a result they became one of the most efficient, ruthless and highly-feared units of the Rhodesian Army – never comprising more than about 500 men. Grey's Scouts were even smaller in numbers, and almost entirely white, bar the trackers. The extraordinary thing with Grey's Scouts were that they were mounted on horses. The theory was that horses could go, particularly in the rainy season, where lorries could not, were obviously more mobile and more suited to pursuit than foot-slogging infantry-men, and above all were silent. The theory worked. 'Sticks' of Grey's Scouts – each 'stick' consisting of five heavily-armed white riders and one black tracker on foot - fought a bitter and successful little war on and across the Mozambique border, tracking, ambushing and generally sowing panic among infiltrating Zanla guerilla groups. Grey's Scouts were officially reformed (the original Mr Grey had raised his own mounted troop to support Frederick Selous in the days of Rhodes' Pioneer Columns and the great Matabele Revolt), given their own smart uniforms and based in refurbished barracks at Inkomu, complete with a smithy run by Master Farrier Bill Lewis, a Scotsman from Falkirk.

By 1977 – the year after Vorster's 'betrayal' – white Rhodesia was desperate for new sources of men. The war in Vietnam had ended, and a certain number of Americans came out recruited indirectly via articles and advertisements in *Soldier of Fortune* and more directly by Major Robert Brown, the magazine's publisher, who came himself to Salisbury in June 1977 to discuss recruiting with Colonel Lamprecht, head of Rhodesia's recruiting office. Hence for example appeared Major Mike Williams, to take over, Captain Steevens announced, as operational commander of the expanding Grey's Scouts. He had been with Special Forces in Korea and at the Bay of Pigs. He hoisted the Confederate flag at the entrance to Inkomu Camp.

Robin Moore, author of *The French Connection*, came out too, to write a sequel to his other famous adventure story *The Green Berets*. He and his wife Susan set up 'The Crippled Eagles Club' at his rented home in Mazoe Street, Salisbury for these expatriate mercenary American Officers. The atmosphere at the time was temporarily euphoric. But the pay for even US mercenaries was not high – a mere £40 a week – and the contract long: three years. As the war against the guerrillas intensified however the pay rose to $800 a month minimum, up to £3000 maximum, and the number of foreigners serving with the Rhodesian Army either as 'volunteers' or as 'immigrants', to no less than fifteen hundred.

And it could have gone up to two thousand. In the summer of 1977 Sergeant Patrick Ollivier of Grey's Scouts and his compatriot, an older man, ex-Katanga, Sergeant Jean-Michel Desblé of the Selous Scouts, were summoned to Army headquarters in Salisbury. There, to their amazement, they were told that no less than five hundred former Foreign Legionaries were being recruited in France; and that on the arrival of this comparatively vast force, they, the two Frenchmen already serving in Rhodesia, would act as liaison officers cum interpreters, to help the newcomers settle in.

Things did not quite work out like that. The original idea had been put by a French industrialist from Lyons with business interests in Rhodesia to the number two of Rhodesia's Armed Forces, General MacLean; and it was enthusiastically welcomed. But the two joint commanders of the French force turned out to be veterans of over fifty, Major Roland de l'Assomption and Major Mario La Viola. Both had had plenty of fighting experience – the former in Indochina and Algeria as an *Adjudant-Chef,* a Sergeant-Major; and the latter, more interestingly, (he was Italian born) with Rommel in the Desert where he had been awarded an Iron Cross. Both had been with the Presidential Guard in Gabon; but L'Assomption had been too much of a Gaullist – Loulou Martin, Le Braz' successor as commander of the Presidential Guard, detested Gaullists – and La Viola, though promoted to Captain there, had also been dismissed. One of them was back in Lyon running the Bar de l'Epi – which had to function as a recruiting centre.

The end result was that not the expected five hundred but a mere fifty Frenchmen landed at Salisbury on 7 October 1977. They were formed into the 7th Independent Company. Patrick Ollivier did not think much of the capabilities or potential of his compatriots, except for the two Majors. They were given three weeks' basic training at Cranborne Camp in Salisbury, the base of the (all-white, very fit, crack, 80% British) Rhodesian Light Infantry, the heliportered RLI. Then they were sent out to Inkomu for weapon practice. On December 5 they transferred to Rushinga, a hundred miles north of Salisbury, for their first eight weeks' stretch of active service as lightly-armed lorry-transported infantry.

Thereafter minor disaster followed minor disaster, if Patrick Ollivier is to be believed (and why not? He was certainly with them till, apparently abandoned in an ambush by his boastful but cowardly new fellow-soldiers, he saw one of his best Rhodesian friends needlessly killed and himself was bayoneted and lucky to get to hospital alive). Major Bessis who had been with Denard's men in Angola was transferred to the Intelligence Corps. Sergeant Butoni, who had been at Benin, was promoted Lieutenant. Toumi le Métis, who sounds like an improbable figure out of a Fifties French gangster movie, also ex-Congo and an ex-Benin, was promoted Captain and proceeded to ambush his own men. Most noticeably of all, Marques who flew in with a second batch of recruits – apparently now recruited by Roger Bruni from the offices in Rue Bachaumont – first complained the pay was too low, and then refused to keep the one minute's silence ordered by Major L'Assomption at the funeral service held for Patrick Ollivier's dead comrade-in-arms. For in general the French made no effort to integrate with the English-speaking Rhodesians. They ended despised as soldiers (apart from the two majors) and disliked, indeed hated, for their appalling attitude. Their second tour of duty, as militarily shambolic as their first, ended in April 1978. Desertions, embezzlement and crime were rife in the unit. On 16 May the 7th Independent Company was formally dissolved; and its former members ignominiously herded by military police to the airport. They must have envied such as Marques who had refused to sign the Rhodesian contract and who, three days earlier, had been involved in so much more successful an operation – in the Comores.

With a sigh of relief Patrick Ollivier went back to his own unit, to Grey's Scouts, with a commission first as Lieutenant then as Captain. But he had earlier been tempted by a letter from his old friend Hugues de Tappie, from the shipyard at Lorient in Brittany where the *Cap Faguet* was being fitted out for – exactly what? Hugues wondered. Probably not for that geoseismic exploration in Chilean waters. But, despite the fascination Denard's name had always had for him, Patrick Ollivier was to stay on in Zimbabwe - Rhodesia, as it had now become under Bishop Muzorewa's interim rule, till the bitter end finally came.

SPECIAL FORCES, THE CITIZEN FORCE, THE RECCE COMMANDOS

As for Mike Webb, he had joined the RLI and then, after three years, switched in 1978 to Rhodesian Special Forces. A certain air of mystery surrounds Special Forces. It was not a guerrilla-hunting unit nor a commando group specialising in cross-border strikes into Mozambique like the Rhodesian SAS, the apple of the commander-in-chief General Peter Wall's eye (he had commanded C Squadron of the Malayan Scouts in the 'emergency' there and had modelled this unit on that). Special Forces continued to function after the ceasefire of November 1979 up to and through the elections of February 1980. On 4 March the victor in the elections, the Marxist-orientated Mugabe, was asked by Lord Soames - his last act of importance as Governor - to form a government. There had been rumours in the interim of a last desperate fling by the still white-commanded army, a *coup* in

Salisbury to preempt Mugabe's installation as Prime Minister. It came to nothing. The white units - the Rhodesian Light Infantry, the Selous Scouts and of course the Special Forces - were dissolved. Mike Webb - one of many - headed south, away from possible reprisals, across the Limpopo into the Republic of South Africa. Rhodesia's C Squadron SAS headed south too, and were immediately enrolled, most of them, in a rather special unit of the South African Defence Force (as the Republic's armed forces were called), the Reconnaissance Regiment, stationed at The Bluff just outside Durban, overlooking the Indian Ocean.

A word of explanation is necessary here about the Citizen Force, South Africa's army. As its name implies, it is not a regular standing army in the traditional European sense but rather an extension of the time-honoured Boer concept by which all male citizens, in time of war or crisis, take up arms to defend the State. In practical terms this meant - and means - that there is a skeleton staff of full-time professional officers and NCOs, the Permanent Force, but that the mass of the army, trained by compulsory military service and by compulsory annual camps, is on stand-by, ready to be called up at a moment's notice for a campaign or for an operation.

Units such as the 'Buffalo Battalion' in the Caprivi strip or the bounty-hunting Koevoet (Crowbar - mainly ex-Selous Scout officered, with, as troops, 'turned' ex-SWAPO guerrillas) in South West Africa, raised for a special purpose and a special theatre, obviously lay outside this system; as did the theoretically independent budding 'armies' of the Bantustan homelands. Ron Reid-Daly, the former commander of the Selous Scouts, found a new mercenary niche as commander of the Transkei Defence Force, with Tim Bax, also ex-Selous Scouts, becoming the CO of the Transkei Regiment - his second-in-command being a thirty-two year-old American.

Also theoretically outside the Citizen Force/Permanent Force system were the traditionally most prestigious units of Afrikanerdom, the Commandos. Training for the Recce Commandos, as the various units of the Reconnaissance Regiment were called, continued on and off for no less than sixteen years. Most of their members were civilians - citizens - with ordinary jobs in or around Durban, but they were not permitted to leave the country or even their homes without the permission of their commanding officer and they were used to being suddenly summoned to report to barracks at The Bluff for short, sharp operations - usually, it seems, cross-border raids into Mozambique or Angola or perhaps even further afield on 'special missions'. As South Africa's otherwise surprisingly free press is muzzled by laws of exceptional severity when it comes to military matters, it was almost impossible to discover what exactly the Recce Commandos did and how and where they were used. But they certainly considered themselves an elite, and an operational elite at that.

THE OLD RHODESIA HANDS

The Rhodesian SAS veterans did not, however, apparently fit in too well with what was very much an Afrikaner-dominated Afrikaner-speaking force; and when their one year's contract came up for renewal in March 1981 , it was not renewed. This meant that Natal in general and Durban in particular, the former centre of British power in South Africa to which the ex-Rhodesians naturally gravitated, was by early 1981 full of disgruntled ex-soldiers who had led an adventurous life in Rhodesia, who had had to become reconciled to the idea that the South Africa army did not want them, and who were trying half-heartedly to reconcile themselves to civilian life and civilian employment. Mike Webb had become, without enthusiasm, an insurance salesman. Others, Rhodesian born and bred like Aubrey Brooks (who had served in the Selous Scouts), had left Zimbabwe a little later with his family and his wife, Di. Brooks had tried to set up a printing business in Durban; but like many of the exiles was under-capitalised, for it was impossible to take money out of independent Zimbabwe. They used to meet, many of these ex-Rhodesians who still retained Zimbabwe citizenship, in the Riviera Hotel on Durban's waterfront. The Riviera was owned by a Briton, Ken Dalgliesh, who had been a policeman in Rhodesia, a Special Branch inspector. Dalgliesh had seen the end coming earlier than most and had emigrated to South Africa in 1975. Rhodesian reunion evenings were, from March 1980 onwards, celebrated nostalgically at the bar of his hotel every week.

HOARE'S PLANS MATURE

It is now time to draw together the various strands that form the complex but fascinating background to the planned Seychelles mercenary *coup* of November 1981. Mike Hoare, from his home in a small village outside Pietermaritzburg, the capital of Natal, was undoubtedly the moving spirit in the whole venture. Undiscouraged by the failure of the November Plot in 1979, he got in touch with the new group of exiles - those Seychellois who were later expelled by René's government after months in prison without trial. They had, in June 1980, formed a far more dynamic exiles' group than the original Paris-based Seychelles Liberation Committee. It was called the *Mouvement pour La Résistance,* and its leading activists were, in London, Paul Chow Singh, a young man in his thirties of - obviously - very mixed blood who had run a bookshop in the Seychelles and acted as stringer for foreign wire services and, in Durban, Gerard Hoareau. Chow acted more as a spokesman and propagandist; Hoareau was the more ambitious. He had been Assistant Secretary for Foreign Affairs under Mancham and Chief Immigration Officer under René till his arrest in November 1979. Exile politics, however small the country involved, are always tricky and riven by personal rivalries; and Jimmy Mancham in his Putney home by the River Thames always kept his distance from the *Mouvement pour La Résistance.* Hoareau for his part appears to have despised Mancham but to have seen that it was vital to use him as a figurehead if René and his left-wing régime were to be overthrown. The situation was further complicated by the existence of a large community of Seychellois exiles in Australia including Robert Frichot, a wealthy young barrister from a 'big family' who represented the *grand blanc* interest. Precisely whom Mike Hoare had most dealings with it is impossible to be sure. But certainly in the months before November 1981 he went out to Perth to meet Frichot, visited London to meet Mancham and kept in constant contact with Gonzague D'Offay, the 'money man', and with Gerard Hoareau and the other Seychellois exiles in Durban. As early as July 1980 Hoare was able to show Tullio Moneta in Johannesburg a letter from 'the exiles' authorising himself, Hoare, to draw up a plan for the overthrow by a mercenary force of President René's régime in the Seychelles. One month later Charles Njonjo, Kenya's Minister for Constitutional Affairs, secretly visited South Africa.

No mercenary *coup* can hope to succeed without at least the tacit complicity of the country in which the mercenary force is recruited and the active complicity of a country bordering the target country, the objective. That at least, I hope, is clear from all that has gone before. The South African government as such – the prime minister and the cabinet – may not have known that a mercenary *coup* was being plotted on their territory against the Seychelles but that may simply have been because they had no desire to know. Certainly their intelligence services, both military and specialised, both knew and were directly involved, as the sequel will show. But the Republic of South Africa could only have a minor interest in what happened in the Seychelles.

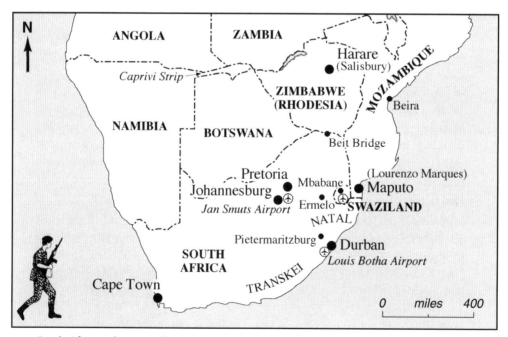

South Africa and its immediate neighbours

Kenya on the other hand had a major interest. The Seychelles were almost equidistant – about six hundred miles – from Mombasa, Kenya's major port on the Indian Ocean and from Dar-es-Salaam, Tanzania's capital, Tanzania had been since independence Kenya's great and annoyingly influential rival in what was formerly British East Africa. Oversimplifying wildly, one might say that Tanzania was socialist verging on Maoist (certainly much-influenced by the Chinese) whereas Kenya was capitalist and pro-Western. Among the most pro-Western of the Mzee's[1] successors was the elegant, suave Kikuyu, Charles Njonjo known – only half-affectionately – among Kenya's elite as 'Sir Charles'. Kenyatta had been succeeded as President by a man who was generally, if wrongly, considered to be a mere stopgap, the inconspicuous Daniel Arap Moi. The colourful Njonjo, invariably to be seen with a carnation in his buttonhole, was thought to be the power behind the throne, the strong man of the régime and a potential president himself. For any black politician to make a trip to the bastion of apartheid, South Africa, particularly at that period, was personally unpleasant and politically full of danger if the 'secret' should leak out. There must have been extraordinarily strong reasons for a man as ambitious as Njonjo to take the risk; as he was later to take the risk of issuing visas for South Africans to enter Kenya. It is almost certain that what induced him to come was the need to meet the leaders in Durban of the *Mouvement pour La Résistance* and very probably Mike Hoare himself to discuss Kenya's part – Kenya's vital part – in the proposed overthrow of President René and his left-wing régime in the Seychelles

Politically the plan finally decided on was this: that Jimmy Mancham, whom Charles Njonjo knew and liked – they were in political outlook much of a muchness, 'men of the world' both – should be restored to his rightful position as President of the Seychelles with Gerard Hoareau as Vice-President and Robert Frichot, from Perth, as Prime Minister – the Vice-President holding, at least in Hoareau's view, the real power in the new régime. The coup would be carried out by mercenaries led by Mike Hoare who would act rapidly and decisively and then withdraw. Kenya would have troops and police standing by ready to fly in and 'restore order' should there by any serious resistance to the new régime or any danger of the Russians or the Tanzanians intervening directly. South Africa would be rewarded with the restoration of landing rights (withdrawn by René) for South African Airways, and with increased trade. Kenya would profit by an extension of the nation's sphere of influence – a matter which, incidentally, could not fail to rebound to the personal prestige and advantage of 'Sir Charles' in his (as it was then thought) looming struggle for power against his fellow Kikuyu and rival, the Vice President Mwai Kibaki. As for Mike Hoare, he would be rewarded with the knowledge that he, like Denard, had made a successful comeback as a

---

[1] Mzee was the title given to President Jomo Kenyatta, the Old One, the father figure of Kenya's Independence, himself a Kikuyu tribesman, who had died in 1978.

mercenary leader; with the prospect of retiring in his old age to the island paradise which he had always loved; and, of course, with money.

It was the question of money, however, that delayed for over a year the imple-
mentation of the plan. Basically the trouble was simple: there was not nearly
enough of it. Hoare's original plan had envisaged a budget of no less than five
million dollars; a sum large enough to equip, arm and transport an impressive mercenary force and to prepare at the same time a popular uprising in the
Seychelles. But the difficulty with exile groups is that by the very fact of being
exiles they are, at least comparatively, impoverished. The Americans, though
mildly alarmed by the size of the new Russian Embassy in Victoria and mildly
annoyed at President René's drastic rent increases for their satellite tracking station installed on a mountain in Mahé, were not prepared to back a *coup* or a
civil war as they had been in Angola. The British and the French, had they been
approached, might well have informed René of the threat - in the case of the
British out of distaste for Mancham, in the case of the French out of distaste for
English-speaking mercenaries rather than their own variety. Neither the Kenyan
nor the South African government nor any of their departments, though prepared
to help in other ways, put up a single penny. It was later rumoured that Adnan
Khashoggi had financed Hoare's plan; if so he seriously under-financed it; and,
according to Hoare, when approached by Mancham his old playmate Khashoggi
courteously refused. Hoare had been to Salisbury – and it was probably there
that he met, and recruited, ex-Sergeant-Major Don Kenny of the late Grey's
Scouts as his personal bodyguard-to-be - and indeed had visited Mazoe Street.
So he even wrote to best-selling Robin Moore in an attempt to raise money; but
Moore was not prepared to follow Frederick Forsyth's possible example and risk
the profits from his own bestsellers on a mercenary adventure. In the end instead
of five million dollars there was less than half a million available: 400,000 rand
apparently, and not all of that at once. With such a comparatively pitiful sum (in
my view probably all contributed by Seychellois exiles and by the *Mouvement pour
La Résistance*), Hoare's options were severely restricted. It would necessarily be an
inexpensive operation, indeed so inexpensive as to be, many would argue, almost
doomed from the start. But Hoare was growing older and he had been planning
his coup in the Seychelles for three years. In June 1981 he and the colleague he
now thought of as his second-in-command, the actor Tullio Moneta, flew out
to the Seychelles, as tourists, on the trip that was to decide whether or not to go
ahead with the planned operation; and, if so, how to put it into effect.

They had chosen June in order to watch the Independence Day parade of
29 June and to gain a first-hand impression of the Seychelles army, its numbers,
weapons, equipment and general appearance. After the parade Hoare, satisfied,
flew back to South Africa. Tullio Moneta stayed on for nine days, holding clandestine meetings with opponents of René on the island, visiting the American
satellite station and the Russian Embassy (no less than 105 strong), returning with

maps of State House – the President's 'Offices' in the centre of Victoria – and of the airport, details of the garrisons and anti-aircraft defences, and an impression of a 'jittery' President René rarely appearing in public and living in what had once been the British Governor's Residence but was now the Presidential Palace way up in the hills above the capital, guarded by Tanzanians.

Tullio Moneta returned to meet Mike Hoare at the mercenary leader's family home outside Pietermaritzburg, the Old Vicarage, and to find Hoare in close contact via Martin Dolinchek with the South African intelligence services. Intelligence services all the world over are a source of confusion if only because of their multiplicity and their rapidly changing names and personnel. The ill-famed BOSS had disappeared in the internal Afrikaner struggle for power that led to the replacement of Vorster as South Africa's Prime Minister by his long-serving Minister of Defence, P.W. Botha. Or rather BOSS had not disappeared; it had simply been twice renamed less gratingly, first as DONS, then as NIS – National Intelligence Service – and its overlord General Hendrik Van Der Bergh replaced by a younger civilian, Dr Neil Barnard. But the organisation's changes of name were as nothing compared to those of its employee Martin Dolinchek – alias Malcolm Donaldson, alias Eddie Smith, alias Martin Van Rensburg, alias Martin Van der Merwe, alias (during Bobby Kennedy's 1966 tour) Frans Zajc – ostensibly representing the Yugoslav news agency Tanyug which in fact had no correspond-ent covering the visit. Dolinchek had been born at Krajn in Yugoslavia in 1948 and of course his ability to speak Serbo-Croat and Russian was, theoretically at any rate, an asset to any 'intelligence operative'. He loved to describe himself as an 'intelligence operative' and to adopt, along with his aliases, mysterious airs. He had long been a bit of a joke among the South African press corps who kept a weather eye well-open for *agents provocateurs* in the government's service; and there was certainly no mystery in Durban or among fellow members of his jog-ging club about which 'government organisation' Dolinchek was working for. It was he who had originally sought out Mike Hoare in 1974, to pose questions about the Congo (and secretly tape-recorded the interview) – presumably off his own initiative as answers about the Congo could have been of little or no interest to BOSS at that stage. But Hoare and he kept in contact; indeed as early as July 1978 Dolinchek was consulting General Hendrik Van Der Bergh about a proposed *coup* in the Seychelles. He was told at the time that BOSS had no inter-est in any such affair; and it seems that for all Dolinchek's attempts to interest the NIS three years later the result was almost exactly the same.

Not quite however. Hoare was invited to meet the Deputy Director of the NIS, N. J. Claasen. They lunched together in a Durban hotel; and Claasen informed Hoare that the NIS could not support the operation, Operation Anvil as Hoare, romantically, had christened it. This was disappointing. What however was far less disappointing, positively encouraging, was Claasen's next remark: that the whole affair had been handed over to South Africa's military intelligence.

Hoare, elated, made his final plans. It was now the month of September. He visited London and met Jimmy Mancham in a London hotel. He was not impressed at the opening remark with which Mancham greeted him: 'Hello Mike, how do you like my jacket?' Mancham, Hoare told Dolinchek on his return, was in his opinion a political disaster, self-indulgent, with an insatiable sexual appetite. He would however be only a figurehead and it would give the coup legitimacy if he were restored. He visited the Seychelles again, briefly, from 12-15 September, and tied up a few last details with Jean Dingwall, a local businessman and organiser on the spot of the *Mouvement pour La Résistance*. And then finally on 26 September he was summoned to Pretoria by Claasen to meet in the Zanza building two representatives of military intelligence, Brigadier Daan Hammam, the Director of Military Intelligence for Special Forces, and Brigadier Martin Knoetze. Hoare's plan was now very simple: with the military co-operating fully all his worries about men and weapons and training programmes would disappear - and with them most of his worries about money. He would use, on 'loan' from the SADF (as he had once proposed doing in the Congo★), 150 South African troops, members, he would suggest, of the Reconnaissance Regiment, who were used to and trained for this sort of rapid in-and-out operation. And they would of course be equipped with weapons supplied on the instructions of military intelligence. Furthermore as a refinement those weapons would all be Eastern bloc weapons from the stockpile of those captured by the South African forces which had been operating in Angola. And Hoare had, ready to hand, together with his own personally observed assessment of the Seychelles army, a list of the weapons required.

The two brigadiers demanded from Claasen a written Minute from the Prime Minister's office which the Deputy Director of the NIS promised to obtain. It should be pointed out that P.W. Botha had not only been Minister of Defence for fourteen years but was at the time in addition to being Prime Minister also Minister of the National Intelligence Service. As such, he presided over the regular meetings of the National Security Council, generally regarded as the Republic's major policy-making body. There is no evidence that the two brigadiers ever obtained the written Minute that would have formally covered their activities, but there is evidence that Hoare had previously been introduced to a gentleman named Alec Van der Wyck who had submitted a Minute describing Hoare's proposals to the cabinet. These are arcane matters, of interest mainly in the sequel when the Prime Minister formally denied before South Africa's House of Assembly any knowledge whatsoever of the proposed Seychelles *coup*. That P.W. Botha distanced himself from it is clear; that he knew nothing of it is, despite his formal denial but in the face of what evidence we have and in the face of his own vast experience in both intelligence and defence matters, barely believable.

The formalities complete, the two brigadiers plied Mike Hoare with questions. How, above all, did the mercenary leader plan to get his attacking force onto the islands? Mike Hoare had clearly been considering very carefully the various alternatives, as Bob Denard had done. Victoria, the capital, was on the sea like both Cotonou in Benin and Moroni in the Comores; and, as there, the airport was a little way outside the capital. The invasion could therefore be launched by sea or by air, by night or by day, with the usual advantages and disadvantages. The difficulty was that Kenya, though prepared to support a successful *coup,* was not prepared to offer itself as a launching-pad for the invading force itself - which would consequently have to set out from distant South Africa. A seaborne invasion would mean therefore a long and difficult voyage, with increasing risk of discovery once the out-isles of the vast archipelago were reached and considerable risk of a breakdown in discipline or morale or both among the cooped-up mercenary force. Hoare must have thought back to his period as technical adviser on the film of *The Wild Geese* and considered the advantages and disadvantages of parachuting in, the method Richard Burton and his fictional mercenaries had used. But even if the South African Air Force had been prepared to lend a plane, which it was not, and even if his proposed troops had all been trained paratroopers, which they were not, Mahé was a mountainous wooded island, not at all suitable terrain for parachuting onto. The other alternative seemed to be, as at Cotonou, a landing at Mahé International Airport. But, unlike Denard, Hoare had no access to a spare DC7 or DC8. Furthermore the distances were so great that refuelling would be necessary. If so, where? Furthermore could one be sure that, in a highly sensitive area like the Indian Ocean, the approach of an unauthorised and unknown aircraft skimming across hundreds of miles of ocean would not be picked up by radar and reported to the Seychelles government long before the aircraft could land? The air approach seemed, though faster, almost as risky and dangerous a proposition as the sea approach.

Hoare had thought it all out, however; and had come up with a highly original scheme that would reduce both the risks and the difficulties to almost zero. The basis of the scheme was this: that the men and the weapons would go in separately and would only combine once both were on the islands. The men would go in by air; and the weapons would go in by sea. The men would go in, in batches, as tourists; and the weapons would go in concealed in the hold or fuel tanks of a motorised ocean-going yacht. In other words there would be no invasion as such but rather an uprising; and all the problems associated with an invasion and a landing would be sidestepped. It was a most ingenious idea and it appealed to the brigadiers, particularly when Hoare explained how little South Africa would be formally involved. First of all the weapons used would be of the sort with which the Seychelles army was already equipped. Secondly, as soon as the coup was successful, the 'tourists' would revert to being tourists - and by the time the emergency was over, the new government installed and the airport open to curious journalists, the 'tourists', their job done, would already be back in South Africa. As far as the outside world was concerned, all the evidence would point to an internal uprising that had overthrown an unpopular government.

Better still, there was to be as little bloodshed as possible. There would be no attempt to kill President René as Ali Soilih had been killed on the Comores. It was known that René would be visiting France in the last week of November and, as Hoare later put it, 'in the best tradition of African *coups* the attempt was to be made when the head of state was away'. There would, as Hoare must have been well aware, be a poetic justice in this: just as Mancham had been overthrown by René in his absence, so René in his turn would be overthrown in his absence by Mancham. It was a very neat plan.

The only thing the brigadiers objected to was the number of men involved. They thought it could be done with half the men, with 75 instead of 150; and Hoare agreed. It would in any case be a far less conspicuous group on an island no longer used to the arrival of South Africans *en masse*. But Hoare stressed the urgency of obtaining the arms. The yacht would need a month to sail to the Seychelles; so, if the *coup* was to be launched in November, he must have the arms by early October.

At 9 am on 6 October one of the most curious scenes in this whole affair occurred, a scene in which cosy domesticity blended with potential menace. A five-ton lorry, driven by Sergeant Van der Merwe in plain clothes, drove into the little drive of the one-storey suburban bungalow-style house called 'The Old Vicarage'. The sergeant presented SADF Form DD 12 to 'Mad Mike', headed Lynwood near Pretoria, the DMI's office, and listing the contents of the lorry: the mercenary leader signed the 'delivery note' and he, his sons, and the sergeant proceeded to unload and store in 'The Old Vicarage's' modest cellar sixty unused Rumanian AK 47 assault rifles with folding butts, fifteen used Hungarian AMDs, very similar, seventeen green ammunition boxes stencilled with yellow paint containing 23,800 rounds, ten RPG rocket launchers with 102 rockets, forty Chinese hand-grenades and fifteen two-way radios. The weapons had, as promised, arrived.

Hoare phoned Martin Dolinchek and invited him to come and test-fire them, which they did on a disused airport outside Durban, together with Hoare's elder sons and his wife's brother. All but one were perfect. Hoare had clearly been warned by military intelligence to steer clear of their rivals, the NIS; he spun Dolinchek a yarn destined as much to impress as to mislead about having obtained the weapons from Adnan Khashoggi. But at the same time he wanted to use Dolinchek, whose abilities and ambition he obviously admired. Would Dolinchek, he asked, act as his intelligence officer on the spot? Would he go to the Seychelles in advance of the main body? Not officially, Dolinchek replied, that would be quite impossible. But he would do so privately. He would concoct a story about going elephant-hunting on the Botswana border and would take leave from 5 November to 17 December. He set about obtaining, to deceive his own superiors, a false passport; and via a personal contact, a secretary in the Department of the Interior, he obtained one in the name of Anton Lubic. He offered to obtain a false passport for Hoare. But Hoare had already twice been in and out of the Seychelles without difficulty on his own passport, lightly doctored. It was an Irish passport - Hoare, like many British post-war expatriates, had never formally become a South African citizen - and Hoare, whose name of course might have awakened suspicious echoes of bygone days, even in the sleepy Seychelles, had himself altered the H to a B and added a final I. Dolinchek a totally humourless man, was horrified at the amateurism, the lack of professionalism of 'Thomas Bernard Michael Boarel'; and certainly it makes a striking contrast to Denard's array of aliases and false identity papers. But it worked.

No mercenary operation, indeed no military operation of any sort, ever proceeds exactly according to plan. The first blow to fall on Operation Anvil was almost a fatal one. Brigadier Hammam telephoned Hoare and warned him not to send the weapons in by boat. Hoare had set aside, and indeed possibly already spent, no less than half his total budget on the ocean-going yacht - 150,000 rand for the yacht itself, 50,000 rand for the captain and crew. But, money considerations apart, the warning - which must have been backed by facts picked up by military intelligence, possibly about Seychellois harbour security - struck at the whole essence of Hoare's scheme. For if the weapons could not go in by sea, separately, how on earth were they to be smuggled in? Hoare mulled over the problem. He came up with a daring half-solution which very wisely he kept for the time being strictly to himself.

Meanwhile equally important was the question of the men. The key figure here was Major Willie Ward, of the Permanent Force, formerly Sergeant Major of No. 2 Recce Commando, then a major in the 1st Recce Regiment. A meeting was set up at the Kyalami Ranch Hotel near Johannesburg. The two brigadiers seem to have left this part of the operation entirely to the mercenary leader, though they may well have dropped a preliminary word in the right ear. Dunlop Paul, the health studio club owner, Tullio Moneta's friend, approached his contact in No. 2 Commando, Sergeant Brian Walls, a Johannesburg jeweller. Walls contacted Ward. Tullio Moneta arranged the actual meeting. Hoare expounded his plan and his needs. Ward enthusiastically offered to raise seventy of his men for the operation. Pieter Dooreward, a Citizen Force staff sergeant in No. 2 Recce Commando and, though aged only twenty-eight, a veteran of over twenty 'special operations', was also present, and also enthusiastic. No. 2, incidentally, specialised in the use of communist weapons. The system Hoare proposed was that the men should under his own overall control be divided into two groups, one under the command of Tullio Moneta, the other under the command of Willie Ward with Pieter Dooreward to back him up. Ward would, like Moneta, receive 40,000 rand; Dooreward less, 20 or 30,000 - payable of course on successful completion, with one tenth down in advance. Other 'officers' would be paid on the Dooreward scale, whereas the men would be offered, on the same terms, 10,000 rand each. Furthermore, Hoare announced, Brigadier Knoetze of Military Intelligence, had offered them a training ground in north Transvaal. Training for Operation Anvil could begin therefore within the next two weeks, on 7 November.

At first everything appeared to be going swimmingly. Willie Ward, accompanied by an ambitious local Nationalist politician named Norman Reeves, visited in Durban Gerard Hoareau, the future Vice-President of the new régime. But then – *post hoc? propter hoc?* – the second blow fell. On the pretext, which was true, that no arrangements had been made for evacuating the mercenary force if the operation went wrong Ward backed out. And so, with only four weeks to go till D Day, Mike Hoare was faced with a major crisis: the need to put together, rapidly, a purely mercenary team. A lesser man might at this stage have been inclined to throw up his hands in despair and abandon the whole project. Not so 'Mad Mike' Hoare. He was determined, come what might, whatever the obstacles, whatever the difficulties, that Operation Anvil should go ahead.

V

Paradise Lost — Coup in the Seychelles

'I should have taken Richard Burton and Roger Moore along with me and we'd have had a happy ending.'

Mike Hoare

On the last day of October three apparently innocuous tourists flew into the Seychelles - Mike Hoare's advance guard. Two were men, one was a woman. The woman was frail, grey-haired, British-born, a mother of four - and at the time the girlfriend or, as the authorities later more pompously put it, the common-law wife of the older man. She called herself Sue Sims but in fact the name on her passport was Susan Ingle. Her 'husband', Bob Sims, was the brother of Phyllis Hoare, Mike Hoare's wife. He was aged 49, by profession a jockey and trainer as his father had been before him. Hoare clearly believed in keeping his affairs as much as possible within the family. The Sims had rented, for a month's holiday in the Seychelles, via Colin Whiting, a Durban associate of Gerard Hoareau, a small villa in a remote mountain village named La Misere high up in the centre of the island of Mahé. 'Remote' is of course a very comparative term in an island of the size of Mahé which is at its widest point less than three miles wide and only twenty miles long. 'Fairview', the villa, was at most half an hour's drive from the airport. But it was certainly not easy to find, inconspicuous, though with splendid views down towards the airport and the capital, Victoria - just the place for a quiet holiday and a quiet couple.

The third tourist, Barney Carey, was a much more conspicuous figure, a publican from London - for years he had been the landlord of The Gloucester Arms - a big man, aged thirty-eight, twice married, who had come out in 1980 to Pietermaritzburg to join his father in a small repairs business. But there was much more to Carey's background than this, much more to Carey's contacts with Hoare than the mere coincidence of address. Certainly he had spent years of his early life in Africa, certainly he spoke Swahili. He was rumoured to have been in the Congo at the age of nineteen and then in the Yemen. His own accounts of his

past, and his friends' too, have, to say the least, varied. But the dates fit: Barney
Carey may very well have been in Five Commando and, like Hoare himself,
come back to the mercenary business after a gap of almost twenty years.

The two men, in addition to their ordinary luggage, each carried a tan-col-
oured cricket bag, full of clothes and personal effects. The cricket bags had false
bottoms five or six inches deep. In each bag was concealed an AK 47 with folding
butt and two ammunition chargers each holding 30 rounds. Mahé International
Airport welcomed 2,500 South African tourists every year. It is - or rather was
at the time - a small, relaxed airport despite its grandiose name. Tourists' visas are
stamped on passports with a smile and a word of greeting; tourists' baggage is
waved through, the only prohibition being on spear-guns which are illegal for
fishing in the Seychelles. Within minutes Mike Hoare's ingenious plan for smuggling arms and ammunition into the Seychelles had been tested and been found
to be workable. The 'dummy run' had been successful.

Barney Carey stayed only a week, at the Reef Hotel on the coast to the south of
the airport, before flying back to South Africa and reporting to Mike Hoare. The
Sims stayed on, quietly, barely seen by their neighbours at La Misere, the owners
of 'Fairview', the Savys. The two cricket bags, with their contents, were stored
carefully away. Sue Sims - Susan Ingle - went down to Victoria, to the Standard
Bank and there played her part in the affair by opening a bank account in her own
name. The Swiss Bank Corporation in Geneva had telexed $10,000 to be held at
her disposal on the instructions of their client M. Thomas Hoare. Dolinchek,
the self-styled professional, later condemned this as he had condemned Hoare's
technique of altering passports as 'childish'. 'You should use cash,' said Dolinchek,
'not bank accounts. It's contrary to ground rules. It's like leaving fingerprints on
the scene of the crime. It's just not done.' But, as in the case of the passport, Hoare
had one retort - the best: it worked.

Next to appear in the Seychelles, on Saturday, 14 November was Dolinchek
himself, travelling as 'Anton Lubic' on a South African passport, No. D631473
issued on 12 October by Mrs Van Heerden, his contact in the Department of the
Interior in Durban. His task was, in his own typically overblown phrase, 'to evalu-
ate the political, social-economic and military situation for Mike Hoare'. He had
been booked via Budget Tours in South Africa on a two-week package holiday,
the first week to be spent at the Reef Hotel, the next on the other side of the
island at the Beauvallon Bay Hotel. The *coup* was less than a fortnight away. Hoare
had seen him off at Louis Botha Airport, Durban's airport; and had handed him a
letter for Bob Sims plus a bag, a heavy bag containing, Hoare said, 'communications equipment'. 'I realised Hoare had crossed me once more,' said Dolinchek
later, 'and I was carrying my personal weapon. But it was Hobson's choice.' Mike
Hoare had indeed decided on his technique; were he to warn his men that they
would have to smuggle in their own weapons, they would undoubtedly – and
understandably –have cold feet. In this, the second trial run, he was experimenting

as much with psychology as with the system. If even the uppity Dolinchek rather than pull out at the last minute would accept an added risk, then there was little danger that the rest of his men would baulk.

On arrival at Mahé airport Dolinchek took an extraordinary risk. He went through the red 'something to declare' channel, to declare the cigarettes and liquor he had bought duty-free; and the customs-officers not only mentioned spear-guns and the need to deposit them but searched his bags. They failed to find the concealed weapon. Hoare must have been jubilant when he telephoned Seychelles 23591, his brother-in-law's number at 'Fairview', and heard of this double success. Not only had a third weapon passed in successfully but, even when searched for, it had not been found. Outside the airport Sims was waiting. He had met Dolinchek before, both at the racecourse and at the deserted aerodrome near Durban where together they had test-fired the AK 47s in the company of Hoare and his sons. Dolinchek handed over the bag and the letter - which instructed Sims to pay Dolinchek's car hire and personal expenses. Understandably, with the tension, Sims was a bit drunk - much, however, to Dolinchek's disapproval. He called Dolinchek 'my little boy'. 'I firmly believe,' noted Dolinchek, 'there is a time to work and a time to drink.' But however much he might disapprove of Sims' behaviour and Hoare's methods, Dolinchek accepted two cheques from Sue Ingle - one for a thousand rupees for personal expenses, one for 1,600 rupees for car hire. He began his investigation of social-economic conditions by swimming and refusing American tourists' offer of an all-night party. On his second day he made contact with the native population. 'Local boy grabbed me by my balls,' he noted in his diary. 'Asked me if I was queer. Name Gee. All is normal; beautiful place, beautiful people.'

Back in Natal Mike Hoare, meanwhile, was drawing the strands of his operation rapidly together. He had established a safe house and an inconspicuous paymaster on the Seychelles. He had an operative in position. He had, above all, twice tested a method of passing in arms and ammunition that was, compared to his original more grandiose ideas, both simple and inexpensive. It could of course never be applied to RPG rocket launchers and their shells; the strike force would simply have to make do with AK 47s, a minimum of ammunition - sixty rounds only per man - and a few hand-grenades. But if the *coup* could be organised swiftly and bloodlessly, that would be more than enough. It would be a 'pushover', Hoare had assured Dolinchek; and so he continued to assure the other members of the 'team' that, despite his earlier difficulties, he was now successfully assembling.

HOARE'S TEAM

That team divided, roughly, into three very different groups of men. First and most naturally of all Mike Hoare turned to the 'old hands', men who had served under him in the Congo and of whom Barney Carey was probably one. There were surprisingly few of them[1] so many years later, who were still in the mercenary market. One, the oldest of all, at fifty-seven not much Hoare's junior, was Jeremiah Puren. Puren was still in the secondhand car business, running a 'repossession centre' in Durban's Smith Street. My guess, though Puren always denied it, was that he had been in continual contact with Hoare ever since Hoare's return to South Africa; indeed there is evidence that Puren too had visited the Seychelles, with radio equipment, in 1979, though whether before or after the November Plot is not clear. But in his late middle age Puren had become both respectable and a maverick. He was the father of three sons, still married to his Belgian wife Julia, and chairman of The Bluff Ratepayers Association – The Bluff where the Reconnaissance Regiment had its headquarters. But he had also been a local candidate for the marginal, extreme right-wing, British-style, New Republic Party. 'You can't take an old crazy like Jerry Puren on this,' Dolinchek had told Hoare and Hoare per Dolinchek had replied: 'Only over my dead body will he go in.' Whatever Hoare may or may not have told Dolinchek, Puren was definitely in, once again to play – as always throughout his mercenary career – a somewhat mysterious role.

Another ex-Congo mercenary was Peter Duffy, a news photographer described as 'the best sneak pics man in the business', who worked mainly for Durban's *Sunday Tribune*. He had in fact served a contract in Five Commando not under Hoare but under Peters; so had Peter Rohwein, whom Duffy contacted on his coffee farm in Zimbabwe – a German, born in Minsk, who had left Five Commando at the same time as Duffy and apparently, curiously, in Hoare's company when 'Colonel Peters shot a man just for no reason, just to impress people' – a reference most probably to the never-forgotten affair of Captain Hugh Van Oppens.★ Kurt Priefert – another German, a crossbow champion in South Africa – was almost certainly in the Congo too, though it is not clear who recruited him. Des Botes, at fifty-two the oldest bar Hoare himself and Puren, had another traditionally useful combat speciality: Botes ran his own karate school in Johannesburg and had once been South Africa's karate champion. Peter Duffy, Gordonstoun educated, was not only a bouncy photographer but a physical fitness fanatic too, who had studied karate under Shigero Kimuru and was a leading expert of the Shokokai style. Not that he was an ascetic, far from it. He loved people and girls and parties. He 'seemed to be the man', Hoare wryly decided, 'most able to carry conviction as the leader of a beer-drinking group.'

For that was the cover under which Hoare planned that his main group should go in. Forty-five men plus himself and Puren – that was to be the strength of the main group; and forty to fifty men arriving all together, mainly young and fit, would be bound to arouse suspicion even in the easy-going Seychelles. It may have been, as he later claimed, Dolinchek's idea or it may have been Duffy's – they were planning to work together on the island – but whoever it was it was

---

[1] Tullio Moneta, Hoare' second–in-command, may have been in Five Commando himself. If so he kept rather quiet about it. According to one account he was the mercenaries' cook there.

a brilliant refinement, the scheme that the forty-five men - rugger players, hence young and fit, three teams, hence forty-five strong, plus their two older 'managers' -should be spending a fortnight in the Seychelles on a package tour as a beer-drinking group. It was probably Duffy in any case who came up with the further twist that the beer-drinking group should have a jokily formal and impressive title, one that must have appealed to himself as an associate of journalists and that would appeal in due course to journalists throughout the world: Ye Ancient Order of Frothblowers.

So the 'Frothblowers' were born. It remained to fill their ranks. Major Willie Ward might have backed our but that did not mean that all was lost on the side of the Recce Commandoes. Tullio Moneta and William Dunlop Paul approached Ward's potential number two, Pieter Dooreward, directly; and Dooreward agreed to sound our a dozen men, mainly - like himself - Afrikaans-speaking. His friend Vic de Beer, a lieutenant in One Recce Commando, issued the call-up papers which its Citizen Force members were accustomed to getting before going on a special operation that, so they thought, would cover them; Two Recce Commando's commanding officer, Commandant Davie Van Der Spuy, was bypassed on, as De Beer later put it (thereby presumably doing his future military career no good at all) 'the need to know' principle. Half a dozen men from Two Recce Commando were enlisted plus two ex-Parabats, bored with civilian life, Patrick Henrick and Johan Fritz, plus no less than three young doctors, all connected with the Recce Commandos, Steyn de Wet, Chris de Jager and Theodorus Van Huysteen. These, with one or two others, formed what I would roughly describe as the Afrikaner group: all trained soldiers, most of them used to working together

The third and numerically the most important group were the ex-Rhodesians. It was Puren who first approached Ken Dalgliesh, the owner of the Riviera Hotel where many of them met every Thursday for 'Rhodesia Night'; and it was Dalgliesh and Mike Webb, the former British cavalry officer, bored out of his mind with selling insurance, who recruited almost all the others: Rhodesians like Aubrey Brooks, formerly of the Selous Scouts, Englishmen like Roger England, formerly of the Rhodesian SAS and before that - a throwback, the only throwback, to the Angola mercenary era - a long-serving member of the 3rd Paras,★ and even Americans like Charley Dukes, ex-Rhodesian SAS too, ex-One Recce Commando for a year but at the time a bouncer (he was well over six foot tall and had hoped to be a professional boxer but had failed, knocked out in the second round of his first major fight by a black in Bulawayo) at 'Father's Moustache', the night-club bar in Durban's Malibu Hotel.

For the ex-Rhodesians Mike Webb's participation and enthusiasm was almost a guarantee of success. Among many others he recruited Peter Hean and Richard Stannard. Hean, aged thirty, 'a fearless resolute soldier', had as a major commanded a battalion of the RLI; he was at the time manager of a Pretoria textile firm. Stannard, though two years younger, had an interesting career already behind him, first with the British special press and propaganda operation in Ulster, then as a captain in the Selous Scouts and a much-decorated hero of the Rhodesian war, finally as an officer with South African forces in Angola, service for which he was later to be awarded the Honoris Crux, the Republic's Victoria Cross. He immediately resigned his job as the manager of a retail store in Durban. Simon Willar, Scots born, had like Stannard been a captain in the Selous Scouts; his father, Colonel Mac Willar, was a senior intelligence officer in Rhodesia. These were all experienced fighting men, indeed more experienced than the Afrikaner group, and what will immediately be noticed is the number of obviously excellent officers enrolled. With such men as these in his team Hoare could be satisfied that there would be no risk at all of a repeat of the disorders and ill-discipline that had turned the Angola affair into bloody chaos. On Wednesday, 18 November he gathered the 'old hands' and the new officers together at the Riviera Hotel for a meeting. His most important announcement was that they would be flying to the Seychelles precisely one week later, on Wednesday, 25 November, on the weekly Air Swazi flight from Matsapa airport, across the border in Swaziland.

The Advance Party

But first Hoare had decided – though he did not of course announce it to the assembled mercenaries – that he needed not one but two more trial runs yet to test his weapon-infiltrating system; and, incidentally, to get more men onto Mahé and acquainted, in advance of the main group's arrival, with the layout of the island.

So on Saturday, 21 November Barney Carey flew back in for the second time, taking with him a list of instructions from Mike Hoare and no less than three fellow mercenaries: Des Botes (who at fifty-two would have been, however fit, decidedly old to pretend to be a rugby player), Ken Dalgliesh, and Aubrey Brooks. Dalgliesh and Botes had this in common, that they had both been in the Rhodesian Police (Special Branch); Brooks was in a sense the odd-man out, though he was Dalgliesh's friend. But he had a very important technical skill; he had worked, after demobilisation, as master controller at Salisbury's broadcasting station, and he knew exactly how broadcasting stations functioned.

Mike Hoare had told them to be sure to take cricket bags with them. He himself arrived at the airport with four brand-new cricket bags which he substituted for theirs. Once again everything at the other end went smoothly; even though with four of them the odds of something going wrong, of discovery, were four times as high. Nothing went wrong. The only thing the newcomers did not appreciate was Dolinchek's disapproval when he joined them at the Reef Hotel later. 'Not my type of people,' he described them as, 'very undisciplined, on the loose side: not that I'm a moralist'. Even less did they appreciate Dolinchek's attempt to stop their drinking. Barney Carey, whose livelihood drink had, after all, for many years been, apparently warned Dolinchek that if he pushed it he would get a bullet in the back once action started; and Dolinchek beat a strategic retreat.

Not that Dolinchek should be underestimated. He had made contact with the local soldiers over a drink or two, he had while at the Reef located the Tanzanian mini-barracks at Pointe La Rue, the main army camp lying between the airport and the Reef Hotel, and most important he had studied the Russian Embassy in Victoria and its occupants. This was where his ability to understand Russian was helpful; and he listened in to Russian officials at a football match as well as getting the general Seychellois opinion – highly unfavourable – of the Russians; 'they even accuse them of stealing their fish,' he noted. What he and Duffy apparently planned to do was, during the confusion of the *coup*, to bluff their way behind the high walls of the Soviet compound and photograph whatever documents they could find – a highly risky venture but with Duffy an expert photographer and Dolinchek speaking Russian, a possible one. Hoare presumably approved and saw this as a way of improving his position with the South African authorities. Indeed the general suggestion may have been made by military intelligence. For it is impossible to believe that the various branches of South Africa's intelligence services were ignorant of or totally uninvolved in Hoare's *coup*. Dolinchek apart, there were at least three mercenaries who finally came in with Hoare who were thought by the others to have some intelligence connections: 'Blue' Kelly, a burly Australian, generally suspected of being an NIS agent, Kevin Beck who had certainly been in intelligence, and, almost inexplicably, Jan Olaf Sydow of military intelligence – inexplicably because he spoke only Swedish – though many Swedes, it must be added, speak fluent Russian as well.

Another somewhat inexplicable event was the next and final trial run. On the Sunday, the day after his own return onto Mahé, Barney Carey went out to the airport to meet two more incoming mercenaries, the tall American Charley Dukes and the stocky English ex-paratrooper Roger England – the pair had served in the Rhodesian SAS together. The minor mystery is this: why did they fly in, as they did, via the French-owned island of Réunion, France's major military base in the Indian Ocean? There seems no reason why they should not have come in the day before with Carey and his three. In any case there were, once again, no difficulties with customs. On four separate occasions now, arms and ammunition had been successfully smuggled in in false-bottomed bags; and there were now nine AK 47s, each with sixty rounds, on the island – four up at 'Fairview' with the Sims (for Barney Carey had passed his second trip's bag to Bob Sims) and five at the Reef Hotel. There were nine members of Hoare's advance guard on Mahé too – the middle-aged couple in the safe house at La Misere, Barney Carey and the five mercenaries under his command at the strategically located Reef Hotel, and Dolinchek all on his own at the Beauvallon Bay.

Carey however at some stage seems to have moved to the Coral Strand Hotel, next door to the Beauvallon Bay, on the other side of the island.

MAHE ISLAND

North Point

Northolme Hotel

Beauvallon Bay

Coral Strand Hotel
Beauvallon Bay Hotel

Union Vale

Victoria

Sainte Anne
Island

Long Island

Cerf Island

Presidential Palace

The Auberge

La Misère

Cascade Police Station

Mahé International
Airport

US satellite
tracking
station

Pointe la Rue
Barracks

Boileau
Bay

Reef Hotel

Anse aux Pins

Indian
Ocean

Anse Forbans

Cap Malheureux

N

0   miles   4

Mahé

He had more to do than drink and reconnoitre. The list of instructions Hoare
had written out for him at the airport before departure mainly concerned his
own and Sims' role in welcoming Hoare the following Wednesday: 'Barney take
me Auberge – Bob to draw funds 18,000 rupees – Bob to arrange car for me
– Bob to bring all arms to meet plane.' But at least three of the items were both
more cryptic and, almost certainly, more significant 'Movement Blue not White';
'Bob to introduce Anton'; and thirdly a list of names; 'Rollye Marie, Raymond
Bronté, Claude Vidot, Philip Lucas, Macdonald Marengo.' This list was far and
away the most significant entry; it was a list of the five majors who commanded

the Seychellois army under the Minister of Defence, Colonel Ogilvy Berlouis.

'Movement Blue not White' had certainly to do with the local support to be expected from clandestine members of the *Mouvement pour La Résistance,* and the significance of the colour change will become apparent. 'Bob to introduce Anton' – Sims to introduce 'Anton Lubic', Dolinchek - but to whom? Not, obviously, to his fellow mercenaries in any case. As for the names of the five majors, this proves at least that Hoare's local intelligence service was functioning well. But it indicates much more than that. Either it indicates that these were the five men who would have to be arrested or eliminated if the *coup* was to be successful; but in that case it would have been enough to specify 'the five majors' without spelling out (and most accurately) their names. Or, much more probably, it indicates that these were the men who either were to be discreetly approached or had already been discreetly approached for their support, active or passive, in the *coup* attempt itself. The five majors were the men who would physically be issuing orders to the Seychellois troops -if they could he bribed, flattered or threatened into reacting slowly or not at all, then the chances of the *coup*'s success would be enormously enhanced. What this list does not show is how exactly a local uprising was to be organised or local resistance to the *coup* sabotaged. But what it does prove beyond any shadow of doubt is that Mad Mike's *coup* was a carefully planned affair in which all factors had been taken into consideration. It was not (as so many of his critics have implied) an ill-prepared improvisation.

The Detailed Plan

On Monday 23 November a second meeting was held in South Africa to which all the mercenaries not already in the Seychelles were summoned. Here, with the aid of a papier-mâché model of the island of Mahé, Hoare expounded the final plan. The main group, the Frothblowers, were booked into the Reef Hotel for a pre-paid fortnight's package tour. They would be not only a drinking-cum-rugger club but also a charitable group, doing their bit for South Africa's public relations by taking in toys, advance Christmas presents, for the black kids in the Seychelles - an ingenious new touch, extra 'cover', an extra excuse for their presence. Peter Duffy would be the tour leader; Hoare himself was booked into the Auberge, a remote inn in the hills, not far from La Misere. For a few days they would simply enjoy themselves in the sun as tourists. Then at zero hour on D day they would strike. The *coup* would probably be all over in an hour or two. The airport would immediately be closed - except to the new government which would fly in from Kenya and be followed, if necessary, by a planeload of Kenyan troops and a planeload of Kenyan police. The mercenaries meanwhile would have reverted immediately to their role as tourists. They would enjoy another week's relaxation in the sun. Then, when the airport was reopened, they would fly out as they had flown in, as simple tourists, back to South Africa where they would, within fourteen days, be paid the 10,000 rand still owing to them. They would return therefore bronzed and relaxed after a fortnight's paid holiday on an island paradise, interrupted only by a short sharp spell of 'work', to a considerably richer life. There was a hint that a few, like Hoare's personal bodyguard, Don Kenny, the forty-five-year-old Yorkshireman, Patrick Ollivier's Sergeant-Major in Grey's Scouts, might be used to stay on and train a 'reformed' Seychellois Army *à la Denard*. It was an alluring prospect.

Hoare emphasised that there was to be, if possible, no bloodshed. They were there to liberate the Seychellois from an unpopular government and to restore the rightful President; and they could count on the support of most of the local people. They would therefore be using light weapons, assault rifles and hand-grenades, only; and these mainly as 'frighteners'. An advance party was already on the island. That advance party, under Carey's command, would seize the Seychelles Radio station that lay just a mile to the north of the capital, Victoria, at Union Vale. It was guarded by sixteen soldiers at Union Vale barracks; but Carey and his men had already carefully reconnoitred the surroundings and were confident they could easily seize both the radio station and the barracks just above it. Once the station was secured, Aubrey Brooks would play over the air a tape-recording that he, Hoare, now had with him: it would announce that René's régime had been overthrown by a popular rising; and then Jimmy Mancham himself, the former President, would be heard proclaiming that he was back on the island - a white lie, insofar as he would in fact still be in Kenya at this point - and appealing for calm.

Meanwhile Group II, commanded by Mike Webb, eighteen men strong, would have seized the airport and the main army barracks at Pointe La Rue, just to the south of the airport and to the north of the Reef Hotel. Richard Stannard would be Webb's second-in-command; and his team would be divided into three sub-groups. The main sub-group, twelve men under Peter Hean, would neutralise the Seychellois army barracks and secure the airport perimeter. A stick of four men, commanded by Simon Willar, would assault the two houses inside the Pointe La Rue camp where the Tanzanian soldiers were lodged: they would be the most dangerous opponents but it was hoped that, at zero hour, noon in the heat of the day, they would be caught off their guard, dozing. Finally two men, both formerly in the Rhodesian airforce, Vernon Prinsloo who had been a captain and Charles Goatley who had been a helicopter pilot, would seize the control tower and allow only those planes which they authorised to land. Numbers were small but with speed, surprise and, no doubt Hoare hinted, with local complicity, as well as with the expertise of soldiers trained in the Rhodesia war, success should not be difficult.

Tullio Moneta would be commanding Group III which would attack targets in Victoria itself; essentially army headquarters, the barracks in the capital, State House and a mile and a half outside, the Presidential Palace, guarded by, per Dolinchek, 'ten guards, not too awake'. The Presidential Palace however would be a secondary target; for the attack would probably be launched while President René was abroad. The most important objective by far was State House, which would be the target for the sub-group of Recce Commando men led by Pieter Dooreward. The aim would be to seize, at one fell swoop, the entire Cabinet which would be there in session at midday on the Friday. They were to be taken prisoner unharmed - unless of course they resisted. At this stage Hoare passed around photos of President René and the Cabinet members. Apparently he pointed out two who were particularly dangerous, probably Ogilvy Berlouis, the Minister of Youth and Defence, and James Michel who combined the post of Minister of Education and Information with that of the army's Chief of Staff. It is interesting that Hoare passed round René's photograph too; there was of course always the danger that René might cancel his trip abroad or that the *coup* would have to be launched before his departure. But there must be a suspicion that talk of a bloodless *coup* was merely window-dressing, and that René and the two 'dangerous' ministers were to be killed, no doubt 'while attempting to escape'. According to Kevin Beck, they were told that all three would have to be 'taken out, eliminated or spirited away' - for if not, Mancham would refuse to return to the islands. Beck admittedly is hardly the most reliable of witnesses; but later, chillingly, Bob Jones-Davies confirmed that he would have killed Seychelles Cabinet ministers if ordered to do so.

Once the three groups had successfully seized their targets, Mike Hoare would establish his own headquarters in Victoria, in the Cable and Wireless offices that controlled all overseas phone-calls and telex messages. His own HQ Group was to consist of three men: Kenny for close protection, Sydow the Swede for undisclosed reasons, and an Austrian named Sven Forsell, who can only in the most remote sense be called a mercenary at all. Forsell, an ex-opera singer, was a would-be film director who for years had been planning a documentary on mercenaries; an old friend of Tullio Moneta's, and like Moneta living in South Africa and working on South African television series. Hoare, who always had a not totally-disinterested sympathy for journalists and film producers, invited him along for the ride. He was to carry no weapon; and Hoare himself was to carry no weapon either. Once headquarters was established in the Cable and Wireless Office (manned - if that is the word - almost exclusively by young and attractive Seychellois girls as I can personally testify), then Hoare would take personal control, of the entire operation and in particular would flash the success signal across the Indian Ocean to Kenya. There had been last-minute difficulties with the Kenyan side of the operation; the two turbo-jet-propelled aircraft originally scheduled had been stood down and at least one of the Kenyan 'backers' had pulled out. But Njonjo had paid another rapid visit to South Africa, Hoare allegedly one to Nairobi (he stayed, if the story is true, at the Hotel Fransea in Moktar Daddah St.), and apparently two weeks before the *coup* all had been sorted out.

The new government would be standing by at Nairobi ready to board a Beechcraft Super King 200, call sign Caroline Alpha, leased from Captain Peter Lucas of Sunbird Charters. Hoare would send through the codeword for success, 'Cloudburst' - which would be acknowledged by 'Fairy Bell'. The Beechcraft would then take off and disgorge at Mahé airport, now securely held by Webb's men with Prinsloo in the control tower, the returning President Mancham, his ambitious Vice-President Hoareau and most if not all of the proposed new cabinet. Meanwhile Kenyan troops and police would be at Mombasa ready to fly in if and when formally requested to do so by the new government - the 'ace in the pack' Dolinchek rightly called Kenya. No-one bar the mercenaries and the cabinet would know that Mancham had not actually been on the island when his voice was heard over the air; but as the gap between the broadcast and his actual arrival would only be a few hours, no-one would in any case much care. It was a carefully prepared operation, with targets and the sequence of events, the chain of command and expected enemy reaction all meticulously defined. Hoare added one further encouraging touch: local support could be expected as soon as the *coup* succeeded, with members of the *Mouvement pour La Résistance* taking over such duties as the guarding of prisoners from the mercenaries. In order to avoid confusion the Resistance members would have been instructed to wear blue shirts; and just in case they had forgotten to do so, Peter Duffy and Jeremiah Puren would be bringing suitcases full of blue shirts with the 'team'. (Hence the message to Barney Carey to inform him that Blue would be substituted for White for the 'Movement'.) The briefing was over.

THE FROTHBLOWERS FLY IN

Hoare had organised the whole Frothblowers' package tour through Budget Tours of Johannesburg and had paid them 14,000 rand in advance to cover the round trip and the hotel bookings. The men met, on Tuesday, the day after the briefing, at 2 pm at Louis Botha airport on the outskirts of Durban. From there they were taken by coach to the Ermelo Holiday Inn about sixty miles outside Swaziland where they were to stay for the night. At 8 pm Peter Duffy as 'tour leader' called them together to explain the procedure next day, with Jeremiah Puren in the chair. At 10 pm the men were dismissed while group leaders and sub-group leaders were held behind for an 'O' group. At 4 am the next morning, in the early hours of Wednesday, 25 November they were woken up, bleary-eyed; and then and only then, at a time when psychological resistance is notoriously low, they were issued with new cricket bags - on the side of each one of which was inscribed the initials A.O.F.B. (Ancient Order of Frothblowers) - and told that they would be carrying their own weapons through the customs. At this stage, one - but only one - of the mercenaries backed out, Sergeant Chris de Jager of No. 2 Recce Commando. 'A nasty surprise,' he called it. But as he was one of the three doctors, and doctors are not expected to be physically brave, and as the other two in any case stayed on, the defection was not too serious. The remainder - now forty-four men in all - were driven across the border into Swaziland, crossing, unsearched, at Oshoek; and at 9 am local time Royal Swazi Airlines' one and only plane, a Fokker Friendship, took off from Matsapa Airport, Manzini on its regular scheduled flight to the Seychelles, stopping off at the Comores. The Frothblowers were on their way.

Swaziland lies roughly two hundred miles north of Durban and is separated by only a narrow strip of Mozambique from the Indian Ocean. But it is still a long haul north of almost a thousand miles to the Comores and at least half that distance again from the Comores north-east to the Seychelles. The Royal Air Swazi flight was not due in at Mahé International Airport till shortly before sunset that evening. Earlier Dolinchek had telephoned the airport, to be told that only two flights were expected, Air Swazi and Air India, and that Air Swazi was due to arrive as scheduled at 5.30 pm. Long before that he was out at the airport, sitting in his hired car, reading *Punch* and the local Seychellois daily paper, *The Nation*. The other members of the advance party were there too, tense, apart. So was Bob Sims, down from La Misere with four AK 47s and their chargers in his boot. There was always the risk that the whole plot might have been betrayed to the government - in which case a 'welcoming party' of troops would certainly arrive to surround the incoming plane as it landed. If this were to happen, the task of the mercenaries already on the island was to create, by gunfire, a diversion at the moment of landing. Dolinchek's particular role would be to act as the Colonel's bodyguard and escort. Three times he asked Sims for his 'personal weapon' without result. 'I think he was numbed with fright,' said Dolinchek later. 'He didn't say nothing.'

No lorryloads of troops however swung suddenly across the tarmac as, exactly on time, the orange and white Fokker Friendship came in to land and taxied to a halt. Less than a quarter of an hour later 'a fairly short gentleman, a bit aged, with light hair and a small goatee beard' came striding cheerfully out to meet his brother-in-law and friends. This was 'the Colonel', 'Mad Mike' Hoare himself, or (to the Seychellois official who stamped his visa) Mr Thomas Boarel. The first stage of the plan had succeeded, without a hitch.

While Hoare chatted to a much-relieved Bob Sims and to Barney Carey and while Dolinchek, who had mentally allotted himself the role of the Colonel's chauffeur, tried officiously to present his 'intelligence report' only to be waved aside till the following morning, the mercenaries laughing and joking, marshalled by Jeremiah Puren, came out into the open airport concourse carrying their over-heavy grips. Three minibuses were waiting to take the whole group (bar the Colonel whom Sims was going to drive to the Auberge) to the Reef Hotel, less than two miles down the road. They started loading their grips, with the drivers' help, onto the minibuses. The manager of the Reef Hotel had (he later informed

me) laid on a cocktail party especially to welcome so large a group; indeed, ironically, the Seychelles' Minister of Tourism was due himself to show them round
the following day. Everything appeared to have gone exceptionally smoothly.

But the gods must have been jealous. Neither the Colonel nor any staff officer
preparing any contingency plan could possibly have foreseen what happened
next. One of the mercenaries, one of the last off the plane, Kevin Beck, came
safely through Passport Control. But he then turned through the red channel of
Customs, the 'Something to Declare' channel rather than, as all the rest had done,
the green channel, with 'Nothing to Declare'. Why did he do it? It has never been
made clear. There are two possible explanations. The first is that the mercenaries
had had too much to drink on board the flight; in other words that Beck, and others, were, to say the least, merry and liable to make mistakes. Certainly there had
been an incident the night before in the Ermelo Holiday Inn where a drunken
mercenary had challenged another guest to a fight despite all their officers' previous injunctions to keep a low profile. According to Dolinchek the Colonel
himself had said on arrival: 'Martin, I don't think the guys will last till Friday.
We'll have to do it tomorrow. I've got a load of drunkards on board' - to which
Dolinchek had retorted, 'You've got more drunkards here in the Seychelles.' But
this hardly sounds like Hoare's authentic tone. It may very well have been just
Dolinchek airing his pet prejudice after the event. For the mercenary officers on
board have always denied that their men had been allowed to drink.

The other possible explanation was in a way more unforeseeable still. It is that
Beck, like many South Africans, had never left South Africa and had therefore
never in his life gone through a Passport or Customs control; so he simply drifted,
unaware of what he was doing, of the ghastliness of his mistake, into the wrong
channel. Furthermore, like many South Africans, he may not have been able to
read English very well and so simply may not have been able to interpret what
the signs said. In any event there he was with (he apparently insisted) nothing to
declare - a suspicious insistence in the circumstance - on the wrong side of the
customs desks. Despite his protestations the young Indian customs officer, Vincent
Pillay, who had reported for duty one hour earlier that afternoon, insisted politely
on searching his grip.

Two or three other passengers, Peter Hean and Sven Forsell among them, had
been following Kevin Beck and waited, aghast, to see what would happen. Peter
Duffy, as tour leader, did more. He pulled toys from his own bag and attempted to
divert Pillay's attention by pressing a squeaky rubber duck. The diversion did not
succeed. Beneath the socks in the grip which he was examining, six inches from
its bottom, Vincent Pillay's fingers felt the hard outline of a weapon. He hesitated,
apparently, and looked nervously round. Then, plucking up courage, he asked
Beck to accompany him to the guardroom.

Even then, even in the guardroom, all was not lost and Beck might still have
bluffed his way out. The polystyrene was pulled out revealing the dismantled AK

47. But - and this is nearly the most incredible incident of this whole incredible tale of the discovery - the woman police constable in charge, WPC Flavia Potin, took the weapon simply for a spear gun and was in the process of writing out a receipt whereby Beck could reclaim it on leaving the islands when her more observant superior, Sergeant Esparon, took a closer look and presumably did not at all like the look of what he saw.

'What is this?' he asked Beck.

'I told him quite honestly,' said Beck with utter accuracy later, 'I had not seen it before.' Then Beck added - was he trying to joke? was he drunk? was he simply scared? - 'I don't know what it is but there are forty-four more with bags like mine outside.'

That was how, through a combination of bad luck and one man's stupidity, the whole carefully laid plan, that seemed to have had such a promising start and might so easily have succeeded, was, by an utterly unforeseeable event that even a Frederick Forsyth would hardly have dared to imagine, prematurely and, from the mercenaries' point of view, disastrously exposed.

Mahé: Dusk to Midnight

Sergeant Esparon, holding the AK 47 muzzle downwards in his hand, came running through the front of the airport shouting that the buses must not leave, that 'they' had guns. It was Jeremiah Puren, a 'tall white-haired man with sideburns and a moustache, wearing a hat, jacket and tie', who reacted most quickly. 'Come on, boys. Move it, boys,' he shouted. He must already have been alarmed at the delay and had his own AK 47 almost assembled. As the mercenaries dived for their grips and their guns, Puren, leaning against the second minibus, at a range of sixteen feet shot Sergeant Esparon in the shoulder, four inches above the heart. That, the first shot - or rather the first two shots - 'Yah, Yah' it sounded like to the sergeant - was fired at about ten past six, forty minutes only after the Air Swazi flight had landed. Night falls quickly in the tropics and by this time the sun was sinking below the horizon and the light was fading. The confusion and chaos that followed was made many times worse by the growing dark.

'Don't shoot civilians!' Puren shouted. But in the panic that followed as airport staff and passers-by ran here and there screaming; as more and more mercenaries in their shorts and tennis shoes appeared with guns in their hands; and as shooting broke out, not against any target as such but simply in order to frighten, to assert control, one of the mercenaries, Johan Fritz, was shot by accident by his own side - possibly because he stumbled. He was twenty-four years old, the eldest son of the head of General Mining's Gold and Uranium Division, from 'Millionaire's Row' in Westcliff, Johannesburg's richest suburb. His friend Patrick Henrick, who had done his military service in the Parabats with Fritz, saw him lying there bleeding. He yelled for Steyn de Wet, the doctor. But when the doctor came, there was nothing he could do. 'Is he okay?' asked Dunlop Paul. 'No,' replied Steyn de Wet. Johan Fritz, a 'model child', who had been bored with farming the family farm near Rustenberg in the Orange Free State and who had longed for a little excitement, was dead.

That was the only casualty, bar the wounded Sergeant Esparon, there at the airport. The mercenaries quickly herded staff and passers-by, about sixty Seychellois in all, into one of the passenger lounges and disconnected all telephones bar one. Vincent Pillay slipped away onto the road, stopped a passing car, dropped off at nearby Cascade Police Station to tell the police what was happening and then, after his historic day, unlikely ever to be equalled again in his career as a customs officer, wisely went home. Dolinchek sat in his car for five or ten minutes and then drove off. 'I'd realised people in Hoare's party didn't know me,' he explained, unconvincingly, later, 'and they might shoot me, so I drove away... If I had had my personal weapon,' he added in an attempt to put a better face on it, 'I would have stayed with Hoare.' But Sims had apparently already driven off, back to La Misere in the hills. And, like Sims, but with less excuse - he had no woman to look after - Dolinchek retired from the fray, driving south to the Reef Hotel where he 'had a few beers', awaiting, in safety, as a spectator, the turn of events.

For now, of course, all Hoare's carefully laid plans had been ruined and the element of surprise had been totally lost. The cocktails at the Reef Hotel remained unserved, the rooms reserved for the Frothblowers were never occupied. There was now no chance, from Hoare's point of view, of familiarising the men with the island and of launching the *coup* a day or two later. Indeed the question of launching the *coup* - impossible in any case in the dark - now became secondary to ensuring his men's immediate survival. Hoare had no way of knowing that Sergeant Esparon's colleagues had attempted (before the guardroom phone was disconnected) to phone Army HQ and Police HQ only to find all lines engaged so that Pillay's alarm at Cascade Police Station was therefore the first to be raised. He had to assume that the army, at Pointe La Rue, at the southern end of the airport, had been alerted and would shortly be moving in to attack his men. So he immediately ordered four of the advance party (who of course in their days on the island had studied the camp's layout) to drive to the gates of Pointe La Rue camp and there 'seize the barracks'. Ken Dalgliesh, Charley Dukes, Roger England and Aubrey Brooks, all four now with their AK 47s assembled and ready, drove out fast in their hired car. The Colonel paused to organise Mike Webb and Richard Stannard, with the dozen or so Rhodesians in their group, to follow in the commandeered minibuses and then himself set out, chauffeured by Barney Carey (who, like Hoare, was unarmed) and accompanied by the Austrian film-maker, Sven Forsell. But he was delayed, apparently, by the appearance of Jean Dingwall and possibly one or two others of the local *Mouvement pour La Résistance* supporters with whom consultations, in the new situation, were immediately necessary. Meanwhile Webb and Stannard heard an exchange of gunfire ahead as they drove the mile and a half that separated the airport entrance from the Pointe La Rue gates. They debussed their men 150 yards away and advanced in extended line, hesitantly, spreading out across the unknown lush tropical countryside.

The bearded Brooks, Dukes, England and Dalgliesh had leapt out of their car inside the Pointe La Rue entrance gates, firing in approved mercenary style from the hip. In Dukes' expressive phrase there were about 50-100 Seychellois soldiers running around inside 'like chickens with their heads cut off'. A few were wounded; none seriously. They did not run around disorganised for long, however. Within minutes the mercenaries were in their turn under heavy fire. They fled, scattering into the deep grass and trees on the hillside opposite, leaving their yellow Colt the main target of the concentrated barrage. By the time the Colonel and Barney Carey drove up, it was to find Dukes wounded in the arm and bleeding badly, supported by a shaken Ken Dalgliesh. Of the other two, of Roger England and Aubrey Brooks, there was in the gathering dark no sign. These were Barney Carey's men, and Carey decided to stay behind and look for them while Hoare drove Dalgliesh and the wounded Dukes back to the airport. The attack on the army barracks had obviously failed: indeed the revving-up of engines inside could be heard. Further back Webb had identified a heavy 12.7 mm firing from inside the camp. Rather than risk an assault on far superior numbers now clearly ready to riposte, he wisely decided to retreat: to pull back to the airport and 'consolidate'. It was now the turn of the Seychelles Army to counterattack.

Their counterattack took the form of a sortie by an armoured car, a Soviet BRDM, that eventually roared out of Pointe La Rue with soldiers sitting on top. Timings become very confused, and reports of movements too, now that night had fallen. Some mercenaries later claimed that two armoured cars attacked them. In fact it seems that there was only one, roaring around the airport entrance, then reversing, then back again onto the tarmac of the runway, in and out, the soldiers on top dropping off and taking apparently to their heels as they were fired upon, but the armoured car itself firing its cannon utterly impervious to AK 47 bullets. Without RPG rocket launchers - which Hoare had had to leave behind - there was no way it could be destroyed.

While Webb and Stannard deployed their men on the southern airport perimeter and exchanged desultory fire with what they later claimed to be infiltrating Tanzanians, Bob Jones-Davies with five or six other mercenaries had set up a roadblock, of cars and granite blocks, on the main road outside the airport. It was when the armoured car tried to breech this that it finally came to grief. It reversed away, and one wheel stuck in the roadside gutter. Armoured cars are not tanks. They are almost as vulnerable to ditches as ordinary cars - certainly as Landrovers. Despite revving up the BRDM would not budge. It was there - still dangerous but immobile - and potentially most useful if only the mercenaries could now capture it.

Patrick Henrick, with Tullio Moneta, had been trying, unsuccessfully, to make Molotov cocktails from the bottles in the airport bar to deal with the BRDM.

Now that it was immobilised, hatch down, he and other mercenaries surrounded it, banging on the outside with their guns, shouting at the crew to come out and surrender, promising them they would not be harmed. Not surprisingly the crew preferred to stay safe inside rather than trust their lives to the promises of a murderous gang (as no doubt they believed) of white mercenaries. Then Henrick and Alex Deacon climbed on top, poured petrol over the vision ports and set it alight. From inside the vision must have been frightful. What happened next is obscure. But what I deduce happened, from hints dropped on various sides (though both parties officially prefer to gloss over the incident), is that the mercenaries threatened to pour petrol down the gun barrel and set it alight, thus incinerating all inside. Still the commander, Lt. David Antat, refused to surrender. Then one of his own crew, terrified at the thought of being burnt alive, shot him; and the rest surrendered. Certainly Antat (and Antat alone) was killed: and certainly neither the Seychellois authorities nor the mercenaries have ever explained precisely how he met his death. It is tragically ironic, if this account is correct, that of the two men who died in the Seychelles *coup* attempt – one on each side – both were killed not by the enemy but by their own men. The mercenaries set the dazed crew members free.

Despite all the efforts, however, to push, haul or tow the armoured car out of the gutter and give Hoare's men some much-needed mobility, it remained obstinately stuck and immobile. Furthermore, though six rockets were found in the armoured car, there was no rocket launcher; no protection therefore against further attacks by other armoured cars. Not that that came. After this first furious flurry of action, that may have been over by eight or half-past-eight (nobody on either side appears to have been keeping a time-check) there was a total lull. In a sense the military situation was a temporary stalemate. The mercenaries controlled the airport. The army controlled the barracks to its south. Neither was prepared, in the night, to move against the other. To the north of the airport, the government, by now fully alerted, controlled the capital and the radio station and had already imposed a total ban on all movement. Further to the south Dolinchek was still drinking at the Reef Hotel, and Roger England, isolated, had decided to save himself by swimming back to his hotel, also the Reef, from the beach near the barracks. In the jungle above Pointe La Rue, Barney Carey was to spend the night searching without success for both England and Brooks; meanwhile Aubrey Brooks was lying in the bush, semi-conscious, badly wounded with a bullet through his right thigh. Back in the airport Hoare had set up his command post at the Aviation Seychelles Traffic Office near the Transit Lounge where the hostages and prisoners were being held.

Outside the airport, from a phone cabin at the Shell Station across the road, Jeremiah Puren - without informing Hoare - was trying to get in touch with the British pilots of the Air Swazi Fokker Friendship, Captain James Farquharson and Flying Officer Bob Kerr. They and the three Swazi airhostesses, Nanette

Dhlamini, Pinkie Mpungose, and Liz Dludlo had left the airport before firing broke out. They too were at the Reef Hotel. Understandably bemused, the pilots were not willing - even if they had been able - to return to the airport and at the risk of their own lives rescue the stranded mercenaries by flying them out. Nor did the government, whom Farquharson contacted, want them flown out. For President René and his hardline supporters were by now rightly convinced that the attempted *coup* had aborted, that the mercenaries who had landed were neither numerous nor well-armed, that no local uprising had taken place or was now likely to take place in their support, and that in effect the invading rats were caught in a trap.

A certain lassitude, indeed almost a certain apathy, was by now beginning to overtake the mercenaries. They had been up since 4 am. Their initial exhilaration had faded. They could see that their position was poor, though by no means desperate. It was at this stage that differences began to surface between the professional soldiers and the old hands. Professional soldiers, like Mike Webb, were worried by the low stocks of ammunition left and the lack of a plan. Old hands, like Peter Duffy, knew from Congo days how opportunities might always turn up and how improvisation had so often succeeded in mercenary operations when plans had failed. In any case there was, it seemed, nothing more to be done that night: the morning might bring new counsel.

Vernon Prinsloo had, as planned, 'captured' the control tower as soon as firing had broken out by the simple expedient of announcing his presence via the microphone outside to the three terrified women inside. They had told him there was nothing to control in any case till four hours later when the incoming Air India flight would land; but all the same he had the decency to dig out the very nervy young Director of Civil Aviation, Maurice Lousteau-Lalanne, from the crowd of hostages and dispatch him to the control tower to replace the girls. Shortly before ten o'clock Prinsloo suddenly remembered that the Air India flight would soon be approaching. He, his 'second-in-command' Charles Goatley and David Greenhalgh (who had been a lieutenant in the RLI) found the door to the control tower firmly locked and barred. Greenhalgh and Goatley climbed onto the roof; and as they skimmed down through the windows (thoughtfully shot out earlier by Patrick Henrick) a very curious sight met their eyes. The Director of Civil Aviation was cowering under a table, holding - as well - a dustbin lid over his head; apparently he had been in that posture ever since the armoured car in its perambulations had loosed off a round at the control tower. They persuaded him to emerge and to tell them the Air India call sign..

Captain Umesh Saxena, the pilot of Air India Flight 224 from Salisbury to Bombay, had been calling up the Mahé control tower frantically but (in view of Lousteau-Lalanne's posture) without success; a hundred miles out and at 9.57 pm he had decided to divert his Boeing 727 to Mauritius when the Seychelles at last came on the air. Goatley was experienced enough in air traffic control to reassure the worried captain that all was well. Breaking contact, he told Prinsloo that the Boeing - it was a big plane, a Boeing 727, with a crew of fourteen but, with only sixty-five passengers, half-empty - would be coming in to land shortly. Lousteau Lalanne protested strongly: it must not, he argued, be allowed to land - the lives of the crew and passengers would be endangered. Prinsloo contacted 'headquarters' on his walkie-talkie and was told to bring the plane in. This is where the story becomes confused. Prinsloo thought he spoke to Hoare and that these were Hoare's orders. Over the radio of course Prinsloo could only guess that he was talking to Hoare. In fact the 'Sunray' - the commanding officer - with the British accent who was on the receiving end of Prinsloo's message and who gave the order to talk the Air India Flight down was almost certainly Mike Webb. The significance of the order was, of course, this: that the Boeing with its enormous range could, once refuelled, be used as a means of escape. Therefore whoever gave the order for the Boeing to be talked down must already - which was certainly not the case with Hoare - have given up the *coup* for lost and been planning to quit. The Boeing would be the golden, the only, indeed almost the heaven-sent opportunity. In reply to Lousteau-Lalanne's renewed almost hysterical protests Goatley simply retorted, 'The flight must land.'

The landing lights were switched on in the control tower - to reveal a new obstacle, two landrovers and a small truck driven out there earlier by the Tanzanians and still blocking the runway. Goatley radioed the pilot to 'land deep'. The port wing of the Boeing just scraped the second landrover as, at 10.45 pm, Captain Saxena touched down. Peter Duffy was sent out by Hoare with a couple of companions to board the aircraft and explain the situation.

The aircraft's lights were switched off, the blinds drawn, and the passengers, only mildly aware that something was a little wrong, were told to remain quietly in their seats. Saxena and his co-pilot, Captain Misra, were shortly afterwards escorted by Dunlop Paul to the Aviation Seychelles Traffic Office in the airport building while Alan Mann and Kurt Priefert cleared the runway. Hoare had set up his headquarters at the Traffic Office for the simple reason that it had the only working telephone connection with the outside world - the 'hot line' as it was soon to become. He introduced himself as 'Mr Tom'- a mild attempt at disguise. 'You have arrived at a very unfortunate time,' he told the two pilots. 'The flight should never have landed. We are in the middle of a revolution.'

Saxena had been an airforce pilot himself and was not a man to panic, as his cool control in the unusual circumstances of the landing had shown. This was just as well because now, unexpectedly, the Seychellois Army re-entered the fray, even though at (from their point of view) a distance. A .75 mm recoilless rifle, apparently situated north of the airport, on the outskirts of the capital, sent shells crashing around the terminal buildings. As the mercenaries dived for cover from the flying glass, it was Hoare who panicked. Not that he panicked for his own safety; he panicked - and he was right to panic - over the risk of a shell hitting the stationary Boeing. He sent for Lousteau-Lalanne and he sent for Patrick Elizabeth, the Airport Duty Officer, and, having seen them both, he ordered Patrick Elizabeth to telephone the Commissioner of Police in Victoria and demand a truce. For, as Hoare shakily confided in an aside to Tullio Moneta, if the Boeing 727 exploded, he would be blamed for every man, woman and child burnt alive. 'There will not be a place on earth I could go,' he said. He was absolutely right. Had that disaster happened - and it did not - Hoare, who had allowed the plane to land, not the Seychellois Army, the actual direct agents of its potential destruction, would have been held up to universal obloquy. It is yet another reason for believing that Hoare himself never gave the order for the plane to land, the order that placed him in so fearful a dilemma. It is also a reason for thinking that by this stage the Seychelles authorities - possibly President René himself, possibly the more ruthless Ogilvy Berlouis - were very well aware of the precise situation at the airport and were content, once the Boeing had landed, to play a game of cat-and-mice with the mercenaries by carefully continuing the shelling.

The precise details of what happened next are unclear. Even Hoare claims to be uncertain whether he spoke over the 'hot line' to the Commissioner of Police, James Pillay, or to President René himself. At any rate by 11.30 pm, three-quarters of an hour after the Boeing's touchdown, a ceasefire had been agreed. The Boeing would be allowed to take off - provided there were no mercenaries on board. But as a *quid pro quo* Hoare himself would have to stay by the telephone and phone the President in person at the moment of take-off, thus proving that he and his men were still on the ground. If not, the shelling, even at the risk of the innocent lives of all the passengers, would be resumed. That was the deal. It showed a surprising confidence in their military abilities on the part of the Seychellois. It might have been thought that they would have been delighted simply to be rid of the mercenaries in this comparatively harmless way of a flight out - honour satisfied on both sides. On the contrary the Seychellois now seemed intent on keeping the mercenaries on the island for their imminent destruction.

Hoare himself was perfectly prepared, once rid of the incubus of the Boeing, to stay on and fight it out. 'The Old Man wants the plane out and at first light we will attack,' the word spread among the 'old hands'. The plan was for an all-out assault at dawn on the Pointe La Rue camp. The 'old hands', such as Peter Duffy, were all in favour of giving this a try; after all, the mercenaries had not seriously joined battle yet, and all the experience of the Congo days led them to believe that dash and noise would always carry them through - particularly against an army such as that of the Seychelles, no members of which had ever seen any military action at all. Many of the rank-and-file mercenaries too were against any sort of a deal with René. As Nick Wilson later said, 'the position was far from hopeless'. But the 'old hands' were outnumbered by the ex-Rhodesian and Afrikaner Recce officers, men who had always been used, even in in-and-out cross-border raids, to the back-up of a regular army, to helicopters to lift them out when in a tight spot, above all to the knowledge, so reassuring psychologically, that they were backed by the superior weapons of superior forces. Here, by contrast, at Mahé Airport they were under-armed, outnumbered, backed by no-one and – if the Boeing were allowed to depart – literally without a means of escape, with their backs to the wall. They would be forced in the morning to fight and against all odds to win; or to die; or to surrender. Their conventional military mentality, all their training, held them back from so stark a choice.

'We should have issued the Recce boys with a pair of flippers each to keep them happy,' said one of the 'old hands' later, derisively. But no mercenary leader can impose his will against the general wishes of his sub-commanders – particularly when he is ageing and has not himself been in action, unlike them, for many years. His sub-commanders talked of the Tanzanians, of the possible arrival of a Russian gunboat. Wearily, bitterly disappointed, Hoare agreed to an evacuation. Nick Wilson had positively to be forced to withdraw. But others were convinced that the Air India flight had been laid on specially to rescue them. Patrick Eurelle had been told that Kenya would provide an escape aircraft if things went wrong; and assumed that this was it. John Mackay thought it was a South African Airways flight in disguise, laid on by Botha himself. Kevin Beck claimed afterwards, more reasonably, that he had been assured that Air India would be paid 175,000 rand by the South African government to fly Hoare's men off in an emergency. Ideas, to say the least, were at this stage very confused.

THE FLIGHT OUT

Afterwards the mercenary leaders always maintained that the two Indian pilots agreed almost cordially to fly them out to whatever destination they might choose. 'If you save us, we will save you,' Peter Hean heard Saxena say. It seems very likely he did say it – and meant it. It seems probable enough that in their relief at the thought of getting away alive and safe from a very sticky situation that was no concern at all of theirs, with their crew, plane and passengers intact, the price to pay – giving fifty white men a lift – must have seemed very low indeed. Indeed Misra even told Hoare: 'Mr Tom, you are a lovely man.' On the other hand Saxena was later to testify that he had been warned: 'Follow our orders and you will not be harmed. Disobey and you will lose your life.' Here again it seems probable enough that one of the mercenary leaders should have used this sort of language; and the threat was of course, even if not stated so brutally, in any case implied.

Two questions remained to be settled: weapons and destination. Hoare ordered that weapons were not to be taken aboard; but Hoare was beginning by now to lose his authority. Mike Webb and Tullio Moneta countermanded his orders: weapons *were* to be taken aboard; else as Tullio Moneta graphically put it 'we would have been sitting ducks' if attacked at the moment of take-off. There were contradictory reports of how Captain Saxena reacted to this; but it seems most likely that he agreed to the mercenaries bringing their AK 47s on board provided all explosives were left behind.

The question of destination was debatable. Saxena for obvious reasons suggesting continuing the flight to Bombay. Kenya? Very dubious. Sir Seewosagur Ramgoolam's Mauritius? A possibility. Oman? Mike Webb vetoed that: the Sultan would not welcome the arrival of a group of mercenaries and in any case the RAF base there would send up fighters to intercept the flight before landing. In the end the obvious decision was made: to head for home, to return to South Africa.

Peter Duffy had been supervising the refuelling. Lousteau-Lalanne found a car to take Misra out to inspect the runway and check that it had been cleared. There remained only the problem of the take-off itself, of the ceasefire condition that no mercenaries would be aboard the departing plane, and of Hoare's guarantee that he would be standing by the phone and would speak to René at the moment of take-off. It was Saxena who suggested that 'Mr Tom' make the phone-call and sprint across the tarmac, and he would have a rope-ladder hanging down ready for him to clamber up into the cockpit. But Hoare would have none of it. 'Mad Mike' insisted that he would stay behind as pledged. All his plans had crumbled. The past years were wasted. The future for Hoare himself, the failed leader, must at that midnight have seemed bleak indeed. What thoughts ran through his head at that moment it is impossible even to surmise. Rohwein, the former Congo mercenary, offered him a hand-grenade.

'What's this?' said Hoare.

'Well, maybe you need it.'

'What the hell would I need it for?'

Neither a lone last stand nor suicide appear to have been in the Colonel's mind. Nevertheless Tullio Moneta told Kurt Priefert to watch him 'in case he runs off into the bush'. But at the moment of departure, with all the mercenaries aboard, 'Two of my men', as Hoare later and with dignity put it, 'would not hear of my staying and obliged me to return with the group'. In fact Moneta ('Colonel, you are coming with us,' he declared) and Priefert simply frogmarched Hoare to the plane. He ordered Kenny to burn the tapes he was carrying. He seems at the last moment to have remembered his 'documents' ; and Puren ordered Botes to go and fetch them. Too late. When the Boeing finally safely took off, without landing lights, some time after midnight, much to the relief of the passengers who found the seats beside them occupied by jovial young men, and to the relief of the crew – 'My goodness gracious me,' said Stannard, backslapping the captain when Saxena came to check that all was well while Dalgliesh boisterously ordered champagne – a roll-call was held. Forty-five live mercenaries were on board, including the badly wounded Dukes, and one dead body, that of Johan Fritz. But the 'documents' were missing - and so, more mysteriously, was Jeremiah Puren.

Hoare relapsed into understandable depression on the long flight south. Webb, sitting beside him, summoned Charles Goatley and sent him forward to the cockpit, with instructions to make sure that Saxena and Misra were in fact flying towards South Africa. For if by any chance it had treacherously entered their heads to divert back to their airport of origin, Salisbury in Rhodesia, that would have been 'disastrous'. No-one needed reminding twice of how Mugabe and his men would deal with a 'gift' of forty-five white mercenaries, descending from the skies: the very thought was enough to send shudders down the strongest ex-Rhodesian spine.

The thought may fleetingly have crossed Captain Saxena's mind; a successful hijack of fleeing mercenaries would after all, apart from turning the immediate tables, have made him one of the Third World's heroic figures. But, if so, wisely he did nothing about it. In the early hours of the morning he contacted Jan Smuts airport, at Johannesburg, to announce minor engine trouble and request permission to land. He was ordered to head for Durban's Louis Botha airport. It was only when approaching Durban that, apparently with Goatley's agreement, he pressed the transponder that is fitted to all international flights and is used as an alarm signal to signify that the aircraft emitting has been hijacked. From the mercenaries' point of view this may have seemed a wise move to make: it would mean that the airport would be closed and that they would have to deal not with the civilian authorities but directly with the military. From Saxena's point of view only the fact that he was being hijacked, that he was acting under constraint, would, he explained to Goatley, protect his reputation as an Indian accepting assistance from the outcast régime of South Africa. The pilots were 'nice fellows', said Hoare – 'with', it was noticed, 'tears in his eyes'. According to Dalgliesh he 'looked like a broken man'.

At 4.57 am local time the Boeing touched down in thick mist, at Durban. The plane was isolated by armed railway police (traditionally responsible in the Republic for all public transport security operations) under Colonel Mouton; and Dalgliesh and Duffy, on Mike Webb's orders, took charge of negotiations that, to their amazed chagrin, were both long-drawn-out and difficult. Long before the 'siege' was over, local pressmen, alerted to a potential hijack, were pressing around the airport buildings. The police refused them permission to go near the isolated aircraft. 'What's Duffy doing down there?' cried one of the photographers in anguish, having spotted a rival. 'Who authorised him to get in?'

The passengers and crew were after two hours allowed out. 'Mr Tom,' Captain Saxena said, 'I do hope we meet again.' Outside, he talked briefly but in a very friendly way to newsmen, playing down all questions of hijack - later he claimed that he was uncertain how long he, his crew, his passengers and his plane might be detained in what was for him hostile territory unless he was very careful as to what he said. In the plane Pieter Rohwein emptied a whole bottle of whisky as the mercenaries waited. At 11.30 am they emerged, handcuffed, and were imme-

diately flown to Waterfloof Air Base near Pretoria. From there they were driven
in two trucks to Zonderwater Prison outside Cullinan.

★   ★   ★

Meanwhile, at about the same time, back in the Seychelles, from the mountain-
side covered by deep jungle overlooking the airport, Barney Carey was watching
the Seychellois Army brush aside a posse of police waving large white flags to put
in 'a very good commando raid' on the empty airport terminal - empty, that is, of
all but the sixty terrified 'hostages', still cowering in the transit lounge, uncertain
what was happening and not yet daring to come out. 'They must have put about
thirty to forty shells into the building,' said Carey with awe later. 'They shot the
hell out of it. They really tore the place to pieces.' The hostages, including poor
Lousteau Lalanne (whose nerves months later had still not recovered from the
whole episode; he could not bear - shades perhaps of 'Mr Tom's' frantic appeals for
a ceasefire - even to look at a telephone) were released, miraculously unharmed
by this last assault. But at least one fisherman out at sea was killed by the uncontrolled gunfire - his boat according to terrified eyewitnesses cut in two.

The soldiery, having successfully launched a classic two-pronged attack preceded
by the textbook artillery softening-up against a building whose only unfortunate
defect was that it had been evacuated many hours earlier by all enemy forces,
proceeded to relieve their understandable frustrations by breaking into and looting the duty-free liquor shop. 'A bit of a shambles,' commented another spectator
watching from more comfort, Dolinchek. 'You had a good manoeuvre there,' he
later, patronisingly, told a Seychelles officer, 'but that was the real McCoy.'

By now - though the magic name of 'Mad Mike' Hoare had not yet sur-
faced - news of a failed mercenary raid on the Seychelles was flashing around
the world. The wire services reported 'heavy fighting' around the airport that
morning as - apparently - the cornered mercenaries desperately resisted the
determined Seychellois attacks. There was as yet no link-up with the reports of
a hijacked Air India plane that had landed in Durban. Then in the afternoon
news came that the Mahé terminal had been 'stormed'. A group of Seychellois
journalists were escorted out to the airport after its 'fall' to inspect for themselves the heavy damage caused; and the destruction and looting, for which, they
were told, the mercenaries were directly responsible. As their jobs depended
on the Seychelles government - the Ministry of Information controlled all
means of communication on the islands - they had little incentive to question
this information. However one journalist stumbled across - in the ladies' toilet
which he was all the same 'investigating' - an interesting find: two reels of tape,
one completely burnt, one half-burnt, with various strips and shreds lying on
the floor tiles. Within hours these tapes were in the hands of M. Baudouin, the
Seychelles' Director of Information, and being carefully pieced together by his

technicians. Kenny, Hoare's bodyguard, had in the rush of the departure botched his job; and Jimmy Mancham's complicity in the attempted *coup* was about to be proved.

Meanwhile, in London, Mancham was that Thursday denying all involvement to the journalists who phoned him for his comments. He admitted only that he had been contacted two days earlier by an anonymous caller who had told him, in Creole, that: 'The Movement is on the march.' But how did it come that Mancham was in London that Thursday when by rights he ought to have been already in Nairobi, waiting for the success signal to be flashed that would bring him and his new government flying back in triumph to the Seychelles? There is here another minor mystery to add to the list of unanswered questions still surrounding the attempted *coup* in the Seychelles. It is complicated by the fact that a Daily Express reporter claimed to have talked that same Thursday to Mancham not in London but in a remote hideaway in, of all places, Majorca.

So was Mancham in London at all? Modern communications being what they are and journalists being, despite their reputation for cynicism, generally trusting creatures, one can imagine Mancham returning calls perhaps taken minutes before by his secretary in Putney as if from London - but in fact from very considerably farther away, indeed from another continent. One can imagine the Daily Express reporter, probably with a photographer in tow, being turned away from his door with a hastily devised holiday story and the promise of a call back. Or one can even imagine that Mancham was telling the truth, the whole truth and nothing but the truth. If so, he was the only governmental figure - of all the many governmental figures involved in the affair - to be doing so, as the next chapter will tend to demonstrate.

VI

Trials and Tribulations

'You tell me what laws the mercenaries broke in South Africa. They only shot out some windows and ran around in the bush.'

Louis Le Grange, Minister of Law and Order in South Africa

Those who plan a mercenary *coup* and fail pay a stiff penalty. Hoare and his men were held without charge at Zonderwater Prison for almost a week. Conditions were not pleasant in South African jails, even for white detainees. They were stripped on arrival, kept in tiny cells, in solitary confinement, 'like common criminals', commented Hoare afterwards, 'and given the most disgusting food I have ever seen in my life', washed down with Roiboos tea. At the end of the regulation forty-eight hours Major General Zietsman, head of the detective branch of the South African police, summoned Hoare. 'Mike,' he said, 'get your men together and tell them to cooperate on statements. In return we will allow you thirty minutes a day in the open air and later perhaps we will give you your boots back.'

What must have hurt the mercenaries far more, though, than the bad food and the lack of exercise or boots was the fact that they, who, had they succeeded, would undoubtedly have been treated as heroes, were being held as terrorists, under Section 6 of the Terrorism Act - and that not in the country that they had attacked (which would have been understandable) but in the country that had half-instigated the *coup*. They were totally disowned. On the Friday the Prime Minister, P. W. Botha, denounced the 'adventure'. On the Saturday the US State Department demanded 'prompt and severe punishment' for the instigators of the hijack. For the hijack rather than the failed *coup* itself was by now the point at issue; South Africa had severe laws against hijacking and behind the scenes the seven nations who had signed the Bonn Agreement of 1978 were threatening, as that Agreement laid down, to cease all flights to any country that did not punish hijackers. These seven nations were the United States, France, Britain, West Germany, Italy, Japan and Canada . Had all flights from these countries ceased, the effect would have been almost catastrophic.

But had there been in any real sense a hijack at all? By Sunday, though Hoare's name had still not come out (and Mrs Puren was telling inquisitive reporters that her missing husband was on a business trip in Europe) the general sequence of events had become known. Admittedly *Le Monde* in Paris was still referring to ten hours of battle on the island and *The Observer* in London, more specifically and even more inaccurately, was describing how after the defence forces had 'ringed the airport', it was 'not till 4 a.m. that fierce fighting broke out which lasted till 1 p.m'. But back in Bombay Captain James Martin, the spokesman for Air India (whose famous Flight 224 had finally reached its destination on the Friday evening, only a day and a half late) poured scorn on the idea that there had been any 'collusion' between the crew and the mercenaries. 'As far as we are concerned this is a straightforward hijacking,' he said.

The South African government was faced with a dilemma. Under their own severe laws hijacking carried a minimum five years' mandatory sentence. Clearly something had to be done to satisfy international opinion. On the other hand South African opinion (exemplified by the immediate reaction, as quoted at the head of this chapter, of the Minister of Law and Order when first questioned by journalists about the events in the Seychelles) was swinging more and more in favour of the mercenaries, as it became clear how very little damage the attempted *coup* had actually done, particularly when compared to so many of South Africa's covert but official cross-border raids. It was generally considered a sporting attempt that had failed. There was great sympathy for Mr and Mrs Fritz, who buried their son Johan with dignity, and considerable sympathy for the mercenary leader who had taken pains to ensure that his body was brought safely back - particularly when it came out that the mercenary leader was Hoare himself, the ageing folk-hero of what had almost become part of South African mythology, the Congo adventure.*

By Wednesday, 2 December the South African government had resolved its dilemma. The doors of Zonderwater Prison were opened. The mass of the mercenaries were sneaked out without being charged; but with orders to keep their mouths shut - or else. Hoare and four others were released on bail (in Hoare's case 10,000 rand, guaranteed by his nephew, Leo Baxter of Denton Hall, to where he was immediately whisked by private helicopter, thus avoiding the press). They were charged with the offence of 'manstealing' - which carried no mandatory jail sentence. Honour appeared to be satisfied; and diplomatic niceties too. Next day the Prime Minister formally denied that he had in any way authorised, or that the Cabinet had been informed of, the *coup* attempt. He added - for rumours were abounding - that laws would be passed to stop South Africa's part-time soldiers from taking part in any future mercenary operations. Hoare and the other four were ordered to answer to their bail on 7 January. It looked as if their six nights in Zonderwater, unpleasant though these had been, would be the first and last period they would spend in a South African prison; as if, therefore, they could breathe a sigh of comparative relief.

IN THE SEYCHELLES

The same could not be said for the mercenaries who had remained behind in the Seychelles. A week after the attempted *coup* they would have considered a spell in Zonderwater Prison as comparative paradise.

Barney Carey, unarmed – he had never been armed – was picked up as the police and army swept through the dense tropical bush overlooking the airport on the afternoon of their 'commando assault' on the Terminal buildings. An hour and a half later they arrested Aubrey Brooks at Anse Aux Pins. He had lain up for the night and most of the day; then, weak with loss of blood from a badly bandaged wound, had staggered into the hut of a Seychellois named Lionel who had – as soon as he had recovered from his fright and managed to get Brooks' weapon away – informed the authorities. A twenty-four-hour curfew was still in force, the Seychelles government had announced that Tanzanian reinforcements had flown in to help them with 'mopping-up' operations; and the four remaining members of the 'advance party', who had (successfully as they thought) resumed their identity as harmless tourists, lay low in their hotels or at La Misere.

Both Brooks and Carey were badly beaten up by the soldiers who arrested them. Brooks was kicked, punched and stripped, beaten with rifle butts, threatened with having his eyes plucked out and his genitals cut off. Two soldiers bound and tied his legs behind him and kept kicking him on his wounds. Later, he was told he was to be executed. 'It was very quiet,' he said, 'and I wondered if this was death.' On Friday night after a day and a half of beatings he was transferred to Victoria Hospital, where his arms and legs were manacled to the bed frame. There on the Saturday Carey joined him. Understandably the weaponless Carey had been less badly beaten; but he was still suffering from multiple bruises and abrasions and broken ribs, as the doctor who examined him indignantly diagnosed. The Seychelles were not used to official violence or to hospital patients manacled and held under armed guard. Dr Desmond Fosbery, in addition to being a Fellow of the Royal College of Surgeons and the former government surgeon on St Kitts, was a Buddhist, an earring-wearing individualist and a famous character on the islands. That night Barney Carey, who understood Swahili, heard the Tanzanians guarding them talking of killing them. He asked their nurse Betsy to call the doctor – and Fosbery came in and stayed, to protect them, till the early hours of the morning. Next evening the same thing occurred. 'The soldiers prepared six bullets for each of us,' recounted Carey. Once again their lives were saved by the doctor, 'who after having many words with the soldiers told them they would have to shoot him first, if they wanted to shoot us'.

On the Monday, at noon, though Dr Fosbery insisted that his patients were in no fit state to be discharged, he was tricked into phoning Army HQ and, while he phoned, their guards abducted the two mercenaries. They were driven to Pointe La Rue and there they found Roger England. It was England's car, left at the airport, hired in his name, that had led to his interrogation. He was arrested by the police in his room at the Reef Hotel on Friday afternoon and handed over to the army, on their insistence, on the Saturday. He was not beaten badly, as the other two had been. But he was handcuffed, kept in a tiny cell, without a toilet, two foot square; and then when the other two arrived, all three were hooded, hand-cuffed, occasionally beaten, kept for long periods without water and told at least twice that they would be shot at dawn. It was not till the following Thursday, that is to say Thursday, 3 December, the day after their ex-comrades had been released from Zonderwater Prison in South Africa, that they were finally handed over to the police; and their sufferings ended. There was no love lost at all between the long-established British-trained police in the Seychelles and the newly created Tanzanian-influenced army. There was to be no suggestion at any time that the police ever maltreated any of their prisoners.

The police had already rounded up, the previous Saturday, the day after England's arrest, the remaining three mercenaries on the island - Dolinchek back at the Beauvallon Bay Hotel and the Sims up at La Misere. Probably it was England who revealed, under questioning, their names and whereabouts; though any single male South African still on the island, like Dolinchek, would have been automatically suspect. The curfew was still in force day and night. The airport was closed, the Seychelles virtually cut off from the outside world, and the two thousand-odd tourists in the islands prisoners in their hotels, not even allowed to go down to the beach. For the Seychelles authorities were convinced that there were at least three mercenaries still at large on the island, no doubt trying to lose themselves among the tourists. The authorities by this time even knew their names – Dalgliesh, Dukes and Botes, the three still uncaptured members of the advance party. What they did not know was that these three had escaped on the Air India flight. What they never suspected, however, what only the mercenaries back in South Africa knew, was that one mercenary, not a member of the advance party, had deliberately missed the return flight and was in fact still on the island: Jeremiah Puren.

So the curfew remained in force. The tourists however had to be allowed out. Many of them were unable to pay their hotel bills for this unwillingly-prolonged stay and the situation was becoming for the authorities, besieged by frantic hotel managers, highly embarrassing. So the airport was opened and on Wednesday 4 December a thousand tourists flew out in a vast 'rescue operation' organised by the international airlines. They may hardly have noticed, in their relief at escaping from the 'island paradise', the wretched orange and white Fokker Friendship standing, its cockpit and fuselage wrecked by shells, on the tarmac at the airport. For the real material casualty of the whole affair had been Royal Swazi Airlines, now out of business, their sole plane shot up – though neither the Swazis nor the Seychellois were to emphasise this point – by a heavy weapon that could not have been fired (for they did not possess any) by the mercenaries but only by the Seychellois themselves.

By the weekend the authorities were convinced that the threat to their security was over and that no more 'mopping-up' operations were needed. It was the moment to rejoice, to celebrate the Revolution's triumph over the infamous forces of evil. That Sunday a vast demonstration was organised in the stadium where a little over five years earlier Independence had been celebrated with a handshake between President Mancham and Prime Minister René. This time the crowd, 10,000 strong, one in three of every man, woman and child on Mahé island, roared, 'Get us Mancham! Give the mercenaries to us!' 'Capitalist Imperialist Racist Traitor Killer', ran the placards, 'You Must Die!' It looked like Angola all over again.★ It looked like Angola even more when President René announced to deafening applause that 'The mercenaries we have captured will be tried before a People's Court. We will do with them what the people tell us to do!' Next morning *The Nation* of Monday, 7 December carried the headline 'Death For Paid Foreign Killers, Cry The People'; and over the headline, with more wit than was usual, ran its daily slogan revised for the occasion: 'The only good mercenary is a dead mercenary. Let us make them all good ones.'

But the Seychelles is not - could never be - an Angola. It seems that not only did the British High Commission, the Seychelles Bar and the Judiciary protest at the idea of a People's Court but also - which may have carried more weight - both the islands' Bishops. René himself, as a barrister-at-law and Member of the Honourable Society of the Middle Temple, may have felt a qualm at the impulse that had driven him towards 'revolutionary justice', and towards a wild claim that in view of the killing of Lieutenant Antat the charges would be murder. Antat had been named, posthumously, a Hero of the Revolution - but even in a People's Court there was a danger that the whole story of his killing might emerge and the whole charge therefore backfire. The idea was quietly discarded. The mercenaries were not seen again for almost a month. Then on Tuesday, 5 January 1982, barefoot and handcuffed, thin and in certain cases still bruised, they appeared in court, to be charged, banally, with importing arms contrary to the laws established, and to be remanded in custody for a fortnight. The one point of interest in their first appearance in early January was the presence among them of a seventh mercenary, Jeremiah Puren, finally captured.

Puren had not in fact been arrested. He had presented himself at Cascade Police Station near the airport on the Thursday following the mass demonstration. According to his own story he had taken to the hills when firing had begun. 'I am not a fighting man and am afraid of shooting,' he had told the police - and had wandered around lost and in hiding till near-starvation had forced him to give himself up. 'I am not at my best,' he said pathetically when M. Baudouin presented him, clad in blue shorts, desert boots and no socks, to local journalists, 'I have just spent fourteen days in the bush.'

'I understand he was very hungry,' added the Seychelles' Director of Information, keeping an apparently serious face.

Amazingly neither then nor at any time later did the Seychelles authorities question, officially at least, this very tall tale. Tullio Moneta was later to say that Puren told him that he, Puren, had a good cover in the Seychelles; and Des Botes that he had deliberately decided to leave his weapon behind. My personal belief is that he was sheltered by supporters of the *Mouvement pour La Résistance*. There is some evidence that one of the reasons Hoare was reluctant to leave was because he was still hoping for a local uprising the morning after if only the mercenaries had stayed on. Was Puren dispatched by Hoare to attempt to organise that local uprising? Or did he simply think that he would have a better chance of escaping by himself, later, when the hue and cry had died down? If so, why did he give himself up at all?

The only thing that is certain in this still-mysterious business is that the Seychelles authorities were at the time playing down any idea that the *coup* might have had any support on the islands. Jean Dingwall, the local 'resistance leader', was arrested; but contrary to all expectations he was never brought to trial. He appears to have been long detained, then quietly released. Two hundred other suspected supporters of the *Mouvement pour La Résistance* had also been rounded up, but only for a matter of hours. It seems therefore that it simply did not suit the book of the Seychelles authorities to enquire too closely into where Puren had been, whom he had contacted, and how he had survived - nor indeed to enquire too closely into Puren's background at all. They had after all in Puren a prisoner with a notorious mercenary past: an historic catch. But his past, and his background, were never brought up publicly either then or later. He was simply treated like the other mercenaries and indeed, being a white-haired old man, as rather less dangerous - this despite the evidence that it was a white-haired old man who had fired the first shot at the airport and nearly killed Sergeant Esparon. It is all very perplexing.

Puren was mildly maltreated after being handed over to the military, and told he would be executed on Christmas Eve. By Christmas the military had won back control from the police of all the mercenaries bar the 'woman mercenary'. Sue Ingle was held at the Central Police Station in Victoria, and well treated. The rest, the six men, were held in solitary confinement, in bad conditions but at least free from beatings, at Union Vale Camp up in the hills above the radio station which they had planned to seize, while the case against them, and its conduct, was being prepared. One of the 'five Majors', Macdonald Marengo, commanded the camp.

On 4 February, however, all seven, on their third appearance in court, were charged with treason only to be once again remanded in custody. Dolinchek when asked by the presiding magistrate if it would be 'convenient' for him to reappear in court on 19 February burst into loud laughter. But, despite his attempts at joking, his - and their - situation had changed drastically for the worse. Treason is the only crime for which the death penalty, under Seychelles law, can be imposed.

The hardliners had won a delayed victory. The mercenaries were to be tried, not indeed by a People's Court but by the Chief Justice of the Seychelles, for their lives.

FORTY-FIVE IN PIETERMARITZBURG

In South Africa meanwhile the tables had once again drastically been turned, and this time to the escaped mercenaries' disadvantage. On 1 January the Attorney General of Natal, Mr Cecil Rees, issued warrants for the arrest of all the forty-five mercenaries who had landed at Durban's airport within his jurisdiction on the morning of Thursday, 26 November. It took several days to track them down and serve the warrants, in all parts of the Republic; for the thirty-nine who had been released from Zonderwater without charge a month earlier had naturally assumed that the whole misadventure was, for them, over. They had scattered. But none had left the country. All were now charged with serious offences against the Civil Aviation Act of 1972; and all were released on bail ranging from 500 rand to, for Hoare, an increase to 20,000 rand. All were ordered to appear before Durban's magistrates' court on 18 January, to be served with the detailed charges and to be informed of the date and venue of their trial. The previous minor charges of 'man stealing' against Hoare and the four others were dropped.

Why this sudden switch of legal policy? What was behind this decision to prosecute, and prosecute severely, not only the ringleaders but all the mercenaries involved? South Africa is a complex society, constantly – like Heracleitus' river – in a state of flux, and there is no simple, single answer to these questions. Partly no doubt it was the result of continuing international pressure to have the mercenaries 'properly' punished. The United Nations had dispatched a Commission of Enquiry to the Seychelles the previous month, December; its members had interrogated the imprisoned seven mercenaries and witnesses on the island (and had incidentally endorsed the Seychellois government's 'bill' for damage to the airport totalling 7,693,000 rupees which with extraordinary effrontery – in view of the fact that the damage had been almost entirely caused by his own forces – President René was attempting to present to 'the West' in general and Britain in particular). Normally the South African government paid little attention to the United Nations and its enquiries ('I have great respect for the United Nations as an impartial body,' said their imprisoned agent, the shameless Dolinchek); but the implication that they themselves (as well as the Kenya government) had been directly behind the attempted *coup* could only be scotched by severity against its actual executants. Furthermore undoubtedly the South African government wanted to crack the whip not only at unauthorised adventurers but also at its own forces' reservists.

Then there had been the internal pressures. The English-speaking press, led by the *Rand Daily Mail,* had professed itself shocked at the decision to let the mercenaries off so lightly, in the face of world opinion. Even *The Citizen,* which generally supported all official decisions, headed its editorial 'What a Poor Show' and implored Botha to 'throw the book' at Hoare and his men. Mr Kobie Coetsee, the Minister of Justice, had in early December fired, in response, a warning shot. The charges of 'man stealing', he said, were merely provisional and might be replaced; and other charges might still be brought against the thirty-nine released; as in fact happened.

Finally there was the position of the Natal authorities themselves. Whatever the central government of the Republic might advise or warn, Natal's attorney-general was absolutely free, at least in theory, to reject its advice and warnings and to proceed as he and his colleagues in Natal's provincial government might consider best. If they thought it wise, or right, to bring charges against all the mercenaries, there was nothing that the Prime Minister could do, whatever his own reservations, to prevent them. Natal was ruled by a very British-style elite, respectable, rich and long-established, and there was among them a distinct vindictiveness against the various social classes from which the mercenaries were drawn - lower-class Afrikaners, newly arrived and impoverished Rhodesians, and mavericks such as Hoare himself who had never been fully accepted into Natal society. My impression is that there was a remarkable desire among these people to teach Hoare and his associates a lesson which they would never forget, and that they little cared what embarrassment they might in the process cause to the Republic's Afrikaner-dominated government and Afrikaner-officered military forces, for which they felt neither affection nor responsibility.

On 18 January the forty-five accused, dressed mainly (bar the self-styled poet Kurt Priefert) in dark suits, and far more subdued than they had been on previous occasions in court, heard the four charges – which carried sentences ranging from five to thirty years' imprisonment – read out to them, after which the State prosecution summarised the background. Some of them, according to observers, 'visibly blanched'. They were not asked at this stage to plead. They were once again remanded on bail for summary trial before Natal's Supreme Court seven weeks later.

Pietermaritzburg, not Durban, is the judicial and administrative capital of the Province of Natal. It lies up in the hills in the hinterland, about fifty miles from the coast. By contrast to the sprawling, dynamic, humid conglomeration of Durban, Pietermaritzburg is small, cool, 'historic' and discreet. It has the reputation of being the most English town in the Republic, with its red-brick Gothic town hall, its cobbled lanes, its Woolworths and its old-fashioned War Memorials to 'Our Glorious Dead'. In Longmarket Street a Union Jack flies outside the Victoria Club: 'Good God, no,' I was informed 'we would never have had that fellow Hoare as a member here.' Hoare and his family lived only a few miles outside Pietermaritzburg, in a small village, Hilton, set in Home-Counties-style countryside.

The Supreme Court, where the trial began on 10 March, is a small building on College Road on the outskirts of the town, looking rather like a Victorian school outside and like a church, with its high ceiling and oak benches, inside. South Africa does not have the jury system. The accused were tried by the Judge President of Natal, Neville James, and two assessors. Before they were asked to plead guilty or not guilty, the Attorney General announced that charges against two of the accused had been dropped; they would, instead, be added to the list of the State's witnesses. These two were the two doctors, Steyn De Wet and Theodorus Van Huysteen. There was a certain justice in this; they had done nothing violent, nothing morally wrong bar the initial decision to become involved at all, and they were the only two with professional careers at stake that could have been ruined by a jail sentence. They were not in the end called upon to give evidence against their former comrades. Yet the preferential treatment given to them must have rankled with the remaining forty-three. Those forty-three all pleaded not guilty on all four counts.

I do not propose to recount step by step the trial that followed. It lasted for over four months, it was both confused and monotonous, it contained little high drama, and it was fundamentally vitiated by the refusal of the Indian government to allow the Air India crew, and in particular Captains Saxena and Misra, to appear in South Africa as witnesses for the prosecution. Yet their evidence, their confrontation with Hoare and the others, was absolutely vital. For of the four charges laid against all the mercenaries three concerned matters for which, in the absence of Saxena and Misra, the prosecution could produce no real evidence at all bar hearsay. The fourth charge was that of 'jeopardising good order and discipline at Louis Botha airport'; and here the prosecution made much – a string of State witnesses to the fore – of the long-drawn-out 'surrender' negotiations and the fact that Durban's airport had had to be closed to all other traffic for five whole hours. But it was a very legalistic charge; and in the end only Hoare and Duffy were to be found guilty of it. Peter Duffy must have regretted the moment when he volunteered (because he, as a journalist, knew most of them) to negotiate with the airport authorities. Hoare of course was by this stage virtually out of the game. I doubt whether any fair-minded jury would have found either of them guilty on this particular count. The appalling weakness of South Africa's proudly independent judicial system is that it gives legalistically-trained minds the ultimate power.

The other three charges were both more interesting and more debatable. Hijacking strictly as such was not included among them. The general view among South Africa's legal experts was that hijacking could only take place 'in flight'; and that 'in flight' was to be defined as from the moment when an aircraft's outer doors were closed prior to take-off. If therefore an agreement were made, even under the threat of force, while on the ground, this would not technically constitute a hijack.

But legal texts can be twisted to cover most eventualities. The first count alleged that the accused had 'unlawfully by threat of force or intimidation' seized or exercised control of Air India Flight 224 during a stopover in the Seychelles. The second count alleged that they had endangered the safety of the aircraft and of its crew and passengers, its good order and discipline, by boarding it at Mahé Airport; and the third that they had possessed weapons on the plane without permission – to wit, thirty-eight AK 47s, 2,345 rounds of ammunition and three Chinese hand-grenades.

To consider the last of these charges first: it seems clear that the AK 47s were taken on board with, in the end, Saxena's permission – and in any case neither they nor the three hand-grenades (which may easily have been taken on board by mistake) were used to threaten or endanger either passengers or crew. It was a totally different case from that of the normal armed hijack, where smuggled arms are suddenly produced and crew and passengers menaced with death unless the plane is diverted. In this case the diversion had already been agreed; the arms were arguably for the aircraft's protection only.

On the second count the prosecution's general argument was that by the very act of boarding the plane the mercenaries endangered its safety; for a fight with 'the Tanzanians' could have followed. This, while theoretically true, was a very hypothetical argument – based on what might have happened, always disputable, never disprovable, rather than on what actually *did* happen: nothing.

The first count however, was the real crux of the whole affair; and here, in a sense, it was simply Hoare's word against Saxena's. For Saxena did give evidence, though in a very unsatisfactory way. The whole trial in Pietermaritzburg was suspended for most of April while the three-man prosecuting team, led by Cecil Rees, and the three defence lawyers flew out to the Seychelles to hear evidence given 'on commission'. By this bizarre legal device the Judge President of Natal empowered one of the Seychelles' three judges, Judge Frank Wood, to conduct, as it were, a hearing on his behalf, almost a trial within a trial. The Indian government allowed Saxena and Misra to come to the Seychelles for this, not so much accompanied as guarded by their Indian lawyer, Mr Madon Gujadhuri and after confusions and diplomatic 'illnesses', after Judge Wood had heard certain Scychellois witnesses like Lousteau-Lalanne again tell their tale, at last at the end of April Saxena gave his evidence. To no-one's surprise he denied any collusion or agreement at all with the mercenaries. It would have been, evidently, the end of his professional career with Air India if he had done otherwise. But a trial where the main, essential prosecution witness is heard at a distance, never seen by the Judge presiding, never confronted directly with the defendants, is a botched trial. Back in South Africa, Sven Forsell, himself the son of an Austrian high court judge, was to give evidence of his conversation with Saxena and Misra in the airport terminal. 'So you could take us?' he asked. 'No problem if you get us out of here,' they replied. He had reported this to Hoare. 'Thank you, Sven,' Hoare had said.

Forsell's evidence has the ring of truth to it. The mercenaries can hardly be said to have 'seized control' of the aircraft 'by threat of force or intimidation' if the pilots themselves had voluntarily agreed to fly them out. The only 'threat of force' around at the time was that emanating from the 75 mm recoilless rifle shells fired from the outskirts of Victoria, and very 'intimidating' they must have been too. But this was a threat not by the mercenaries against the passengers and crew but to mercenaries, passengers and crew alike. The whole situation may have been – obviously was – provoked by the mercenaries' arrival: but that is a very different matter; and they were not being tried, as the South African authorities always insisted, for having attempted to organise a *coup* in a foreign country. There was no law under which they could have been tried. *Coup* plotters are normally only legally at risk if caught by the country against which the *coup* was being plotted – and then, of course, only if it has failed.

By early May Michael Hannon, a smart Johannesburg lawyer who had been hired by most of the mercenaries to lead their defence, had retired from the case. He had not distinguished himself and had often appeared confused, particularly in the Seychelles; it was something of a waste of the 40.000 rand that Hoare, according to certain accounts, had paid him on behalf of them all. But what formally occasioned his withdrawal was not so much a lack of further money to pay his very high fees as a 'conflict of interest' among his clients. To begin with, the forty-three remaining accused had presented a united front, filing into court in almost military fashion, respectfully behind their leader. But by the time Hoare himself came to give evidence in early May, cleavages had occurred among the defendants. Many, most vociferous among them Kevin Beck, were claiming that Hoare had totally misled them, that he had told them that the *coup* was officially backed, and that therefore they had nothing to fear. 'I am sure I would have said,' nuanced Hoare in mid-May, 'that if the operation went wrong, we were not friendless and our friends in high places would help us.' He was by now, like Kurt Priefert, defending himself – and that rather unskillfully, for Hoare was legally naive and still apparently believed that he and his men were bound to be acquitted. With his own total legal expenses rumoured to be nearing 80,000 rand he could no longer afford a lawyer. He had had to sell the family Rover. But his wife Phyllis still continued to bring the accused mercenaries flasks of tea and necessary sympathy. Local counsel, Piet Oosthuizen and Steve Janson, replacing Hannon and his junior Eddie Stafford, continued to defend the rest.

'With great reluctance' Hoare told the story of his meetings with N.J. Claasen of NIS and with Brigadiers Hammam and Knoetze. He even announced that he would sub-poena them as his witnesses but later dropped this move. It would certainly have embarrassed the South African government. Was he threatened with a heavier sentence if he did so or promised a lighter one if he did not? He can by this stage of the trial have had few illusions about its eventual outcome. He was according to some accounts growing both frightened and angry. He had already had several snappy exchanges with the Attorney General.

'Mr Hoare, you have several catchphrases you continually use,' said Rees at one stage.

'You, sir,' retorted the normally courteous Hoare, 'have pitifully few'. In his final summing-up the Attorney General, by many accounts an unpleasant man, described Hoare as a 'cunning schemer', and, without giving any instances, as 'an unmitigated selective liar with a smooth and persuasive tongue'. It was too much for the Colonel. He protested passionately, when his turn came to speak, at having to sit there listening to a string of personal insults which, he added, Rees would never have had the courage to voice except under the protection of a courtroom. He virtually challenged Rees to step outside and settle their differences as gentlemen should. Then on 16 July he launched into his own carefully prepared but embarrassingly overblown final plea.

> I see South Africa as the bastion of civilisation in an Africa subjected to a total communist onslaught. In the last twenty-two years I have watched – in many cases physically battled against – its inexorable encroachment into free Africa and its conquests by default.
> The enemy is at the gates. I prophesy that this country of ours will fall a prey to Marxist doctrine before the end of the century unless South Africans of all races become actively engaged in the fight against communism.
> I see myself in the forefront of this fight for our very existence. I see my men as a noble band of patriots motivated by the same desires.

One hopes that some of the 'noble band' had the grace to look a little ashamed of themselves. The trial was adjourned on 18 July. On 29 July the Judge President summed up. He accepted that Colonel Hoare was a dedicated anti-Marxist. But he was no knight in shining armour. He had expected to be well paid for what he did. He would have received 100,000 rand if the *coup* had been successful and 'his reputation as a mercenary would have reached new heights'.

But the *coup* had been miserably botched. Colonel Hoare had gambled with the lives and safety of his men by asking them to smuggle rifles through customs at Mahé airport and by having no contingency escape plans if they should be discovered, as in fact happened.

'You are an experienced soldier and commander,' concluded the Judge President, 'and you obviously realised that although the prizes for victory may be high, the penalties for defeat are even higher.' He proceeded to find Hoare guilty on three of the four charges and to ask him what if anything he had to say in mitigation - before those ominous and 'higher' penalties for defeat were imposed.

The Judge President's summing-up calls for various comments. First it was hardly his role to say that the *coup* had been 'miserably botched' - a point totally irrelevant to the charges. But a comment not easily forgotten, designed, it seems, only to wound the pride of a man already downcast and defeated. It was in any case the only point that Hoare took up in his brief and dignified plea in mitigation. 'My Lord,' he said, 'I did my duty as I saw it. I brought my men home safely and I am proud of that. I have nothing further to say.'

Yet Hoare might well have taken up, more directly, other points. He had in fact been paid as his personal fee only 15,000 rand, though he expected, he had told the court, the new government once installed to 'show its appreciation' with 100,000 rand for himself and 50,000 for his second-in command, Tullio Moneta - the rewards of three years' planning and very possibly less, he might have added, than the Judge President received for only one year's work. Fifteen thousand rand, the actual fee, was by no-one's standard, certainly not by the standards of mercenaries such as Denard, a fortune; Hoare was not, and would not have been, even if he had earned the whole 100,000, a rich man. Did he offer to pay Air India, Rees had asked him? No.

'Do you think Air India is a charitable organisation?' pursued the Attorney General.

'No,' Hoare had retorted. 'They are not a charitable organisation and I am not a millionaire.'

It was only too true. As for the smuggling of the AK 47s through Customs, that had been a carefully prepared gamble, the success of which all the odds favoured. The lack of any contingency escape plan was arguably a major weakness; yet on the other hand many famous military commanders have deliberately sabotaged their means of escape in order to force their men to stay on and fight without thought of fleeing. This may not, however, have been Hoare's case at all. In one curious, overlooked, statement in the witness box he had mentioned that he had $55,000 set aside to fly his men off the Seychelles if something went wrong. This was not as much as the 175,000 rand that Kevin Beck suspected the South African government had paid Air India to do the same: but it is a curious half-confirmation of Beck's suspicion. What is even more curious is the information contained on Hoare's passport, an Irish passport issued on 6 March 1973 in Berne and extended in 1978 for a further five years in London: it gives his occupation as: 'Chartered Accountant with Air India in Calcutta'. This was a point never brought up either by Air India or by himself. There may have been much more to the contingency escape plan. much more collusion, than has ever yet come to light.

When Steve Janson, speaking in mitigation for thirty of the other accused, pointed out quite rightly that the crime was unique in the annals of aviation history and unlikely to be repeated, the Judge President interrupted. 'This was a case of being in the frying pan and finding it too hot and jumping into the fire. They were in a mess and they had to get out,' he commented dismissively. But earlier, he had half-praised most of the mercenaries as impressive, decent young men, led astray by a desire for adventure as well as easy money. He reserved his rancour for Hoare and for Peter Duffy, whom he described as 'a most unreliable witness' who 'in essential matters was untruthful'. Hoare and Duffy were each sentenced to five years' imprisonment on the first charge, of endangering good order and discipline at Durban airport. The rest were, on this charge, acquitted.

They were also acquitted, all of them including Hoare and Duffy, on the charge of bringing weapons without permission aboard the plane. But they were all found guilty, all of them, of endangering the safety of the plane, its passengers and crew at Mahé Airport. For this offence they were all sentenced to six months' imprisonment.

On the main count, that most equivalent to hijacking strictly speaking, unlawfully seizing and controlling the plane, seven including Hoare were found guilty, and the rest were acquitted. Hoare was sentenced to no less than twenty years' imprisonment, to run concurrently with his other sentences and with half suspended on account of his age – ten years in all, then, a fearsome sentence for a man aged sixty-three whose only real 'crime' from the South African point of view was failure. Mike Webb and Tullio Moneta were sentenced to five years. Arguably, they had actually 'controlled' the plane more than Hoare. And in accordance with this scale of diminishing control, Ken Dalgliesh was sentenced to two and a half years and Vernon Prinsloo, who had given the order for the Boeing to be talked down, to one year. Charles Goatley was sentenced to two and a half years, mainly on the grounds that he had sat in the pilots' cockpit, with his gun and wearing headphones (which he denied) and thus 'controlled' the flight . Most surprisingly of all, Pieter Dooreward was sentenced to five years too, though it is hard to see for what. The Afrikaners had in the event played a very small part indeed in the whole affair. The real reason no doubt was government pressure, this time yielded to, to crack down on the ten Recce Commando reservists by severe punishment of the senior among them; that no more unauthorised ventures were ever to be lightheartedly undertaken was the implied message.

The condemned men began their prison sentences the following day, on 30 July – the majority mightily relieved that they would have to serve (with remission for good behaviour, available in sentences of under two years only) a mere four months, the minority depressed and bitter, but all – one supposes – with a certain sympathy for their leader, faced with twice the price inflicted on any others to pay, and with little or no future left not only as a mercenary leader but indeed as a human being. The Judge President, Neville James, went into retirement shortly afterwards, able to boast – had he wished to do so – of a spectacular and possibly fitting climax to an otherwise undistinguished career that would merit him at least a minor place in South Africa's history. He had preferred to accept as true the evidence of an absent witness, objectively most unlikely to be truthful, to that of defendants whose stories in general agreed. He had ignored the presumption of innocence and the reasonable doubts that in an English court of law would almost certainly have saved the accused. He had tempered a questionable verdict with gratuitous insults and a pitilessly harsh sentence. He had, in fact, presided not over a fair trial but over a dubious and disorganised one that did no credit at all to South Africa's often vaunted legal system. On 6 August he himself heard and dismissed Hoare's application for leave to appeal, on the grounds of a biased trial, against his own judgement.

One man, however, stepped lightheartedly from Pietermaritzburg's Supreme Court, acquitted - quite rightly - on all charges. Charley Dukes must that day have blessed the bullet that incapacitated him from disturbing 'good order and discipline' at any airport or aboard any plane, and that had indeed led indirectly to his safe return to South Africa. For if, like most of the 'advance party' he had stayed on in the Seychelles, he would have been in a far, far worse position.

SEVEN IN VICTORIA

To temper the confusion caused by two separate trials that most newspaper-readers understandably felt at the time, particularly over numbers and places, it may help briefly to recap here the whole affair. Fifty-four mercenaries in all were involved in the attempted *coup* in the Seychelles. Of these nine were already on the island on the evening of Wednesday, 25 November 1981; and one, De Jager, had backed out at the last moment in Swaziland. Forty-four therefore landed at Mahé Airport; of these, one, Johan Fritz, was almost immediately killed. Fifty-two mercenaries in all were, as dusk fell, still involved. Forty-five flew back to South Africa on the Air India flight and were tried, by the South African authorities, basically for hijacking. Seven remained on the Seychelles and were tried, by the Seychelles authorities, basically for treason. The two trials occurred simultaneously, and it was this that caused most confusion; but the trial in South Africa overlapped the trial in the Seychelles at both ends. The Seychelles trial was far, far shorter, It began in mid-June when the Pietermaritzburg trial had already been under way for several months and it ended three weeks later in early July, before the final pleas in the Pietermaritzburg trial had even begun. What with weekends, Independence Day on 29 June, and adjournments, the Seychelles court sat for only thirteen days and many of those were very short sessions indeed. But, though shorter, it was also far more dramatic than the trial in South Africa – a legal battle, the result uncertain till the very end, with men's lives at stake.

Bar this one major similarity nothing could have been, on the surface, more unlike the trial of the mercenaries in Angola than the trial of the mercenaries in the Seychelles. The Angola trial before the Popular Tribunal had been revolutionary in tone and intent.★ The Seychelles trial, before judge and jury, was traditionalist to an almost caricatural extent. Where in Luanda the People's Prosecutor had ranted and roared, in the Seychelles the Attorney General, Bernard Rassool, was invariably calm, unrhetorical and utterly without aggression. The trial was presided over by the Chief Justice of the Seychelles, Mr Justice Earle Seaton, a courteous elderly Jamaican with a mild American accent[1] resplendent as

---

[1] Seaton had practised in Bermuda – hence the accent. He had been imported as Chief Justice by René from Tanzania after a 2½ year vacancy following the expulsion of the previous Chief Justice, O'Brien Quinn. He was therefore very much the President's man.

a cardinal in his scarlet robes. The defence was conducted by a Queen's Counsel from the United Kingdom specially imported for the occasion, begowned and bewigged, a gentleman named Nicholas Fairbairn with, as his junior, a local advocate, Mr Kieran Shah. The trial was held not in the tiny Supreme Court but in the larger Assembly Chamber in National House, on Victoria's outskirts, which had galleries for both press and public. The prisoners were dressed in dark suits. The only obvious similarity with the Luanda trial was that they too arrived and departed under heavy military escort; and during the hearings were handcuffed by their left hands to the dock rail in front.

This trial opened on Wednesday 16 June 1982; and quickly resolved itself into a duel of wits between the Counsel for the Defence and the Chief Justice. Nicholas Fairbairn was of a very different calibre from the British barristers who had flown out to Luanda.★ For a start he was older and far, far more experienced. 'I have defended all sorts of people accused of all sorts of major crimes,' he confided unworriedly, 'including hundreds of cases of murder and one of piracy, but this is the first time I will be defending people accused of high treason.' He opened his attack on the first day of the trial, arguing strongly, forcefully - and to observers it seemed most logically - that there was no case for the accused to answer: whatever else they might be guilty of, they were not and could not be guilty of high treason in the Seychelles because they were aliens and hence owed no duty of allegiance to the Seychelles state. He quoted Archibald, he quoted Halsey, he quoted Russell. The Chief Justice meticulously noted the references. 'Well, what have you to say to that, Mr Attorney General?' he asked courteously.

Mr Rassool had come prepared. Section 39A of the Seychelles Penal Code defined as guilty of treason any person–without stipulating their nationality–'who levied war against the Seychelles or did certain acts preparatory to levying war against the Seychelles'. For two and a half hours the legal arguments continued, lawbooks and penal codes to hand, far over the heads of most of the spectators (some sixty or seventy of the hundreds queuing had been squeezed into the public gallery), of the press, and indeed of the seven accused. Down among the lawyers the official observer from the OAU, an opulent lady with a variegated wardrobe and shapely arms, Madame Esther Tchoora Moussa of the Cameroons, began leafing through illustrated French magazines. There would clearly be no vitriolic denunciations of *mercenarismo*★ to be expected in this courtroom. Mr Fairbairn orated on the 'jurisprudential understanding of the crime of treason'. The Chief Justice nodded sagely, announced that he would consult the authorities and give a ruling next day, and adjourned the court.

That first session set the slow, almost stately tone that the trial was, despite sudden leaps and bounds, generally to follow. The first three days, the Wednesday, Thursday and Friday, were all devoted to legal arguments. Every lunchtime Nicholas Fairbairn, clad despite the sweltering heat in dark jacket, striped trousers, waistcoat and watchchain, held court on the terrace of the Pirates' Arms, the social club of Victoria, astounding even the brash South African press corps with his scabrous stories, his condemnations of 'this ghastly Socialist paradise' and his pitiless mimicry of both his political friends and enemies at Westminster. For Fairbairn was not merely a lawyer; in his own entry in *Who's Who* he described himself as 'Author, farmer, painter, poet, T.V. and Radio broadcaster, dress designer, landscape gardener, bon viveur and wit'. In that impressive list he omitted only 'politician'. He was in fact the Tory MP for what had previously been the ultra-respectable Alex Douglas-Home's constituency in Scotland – Kinross and West Perthshire, a constituency which, Fairbairn was fond of pointing out, had more inhabitants than the Seychelles but no international airport, embassies abroad, or other costly extravaganza. He had bought a ruined castle with a title attached – Baron Fairbairn of Fordell he was entitled to call himself, and thereupon embossed his luggage with the initials F.OFF – had married the daughter of the 13th Chieftain of Clan Mackay, and subsequently divorced her; had become Her Majesty's Solicitor General for Scotland – Mrs Thatcher liked him; and then early that year had lost the post, partly because of his controversial decision not to prosecute in a notorious Scottish rape case, partly because his private life had become too embarrassing even for the Tories: his secretary Pamela had for love of him draped a rope around her neck (without any permanent ill effects) outside his London home. Almost exuberantly indiscreet on most personalities and topics, Fair-bairn was not so about one: how and why he had come to be briefed for the Seychelles defence at all. He had, he said somewhat mysteriously, 'important contacts' in South Africa. He had certainly seen Mike Hoare earlier that month, for Hoare had dedicated a copy of *Three Years with 'Sylvia'*:

> For Nicholas Fairbairn, Q.C.
> with everlasting gratitude and admiration for a man of courage: from Mike Hoare, Col.
> Hilton, RSA.
> June, 1982.

An interesting and unexplained inscription. He was certainly in close contact with a firm of Durban attorneys; but the mercenaries' families had little or no money and he appears to have been paid, no doubt via these attorneys, by a South African popular magazine in return for 'exclusive rights' to his clients' inside story. He was also, and probably much more profitably in the long run, acting for the Lloyds insurance syndicate in London that wanted to reclaim the still-stranded Fokker Friendship belonging to Royal Swazi Airlines – a knotty legal negotiation. Money apart, however, I believe he saw the Seychelles trial as both a challenge and an opportunity: a challenge to fight and win a sensational case, an opportunity both to save the lives of men with whose views he sympathised, and by doing so to redeem his own slightly shaky legal and political reputation.

He lost the first round. Courteously but predictably, quoting two Lord Chancellors of England, Loreburn and Jowitt, the Chief Justice ruled that the charge of treason could stand. Fairbairn immediately put forward a second, probably less expected objection: that a fair trial would be impossible because no impartial jury could be empanelled. What with all the publicity on the radio and in *The Nation* condemning the mercenaries, and what with - a telling point - the mass 'kill them, kill them' demonstration of 7 December which one in three of the island's inhabitants had attended, the jury - any jury - would already be automatically conditioned to believe that the mercenaries were guilty - particularly, added Fairbairn, in a country with only one party where the members of the government had already publicly announced what they expected the verdict to be. But on the Friday the Chief Justice overruled that argument too; and, the preliminary legal fencing over, the court adjourned for the weekend.

Fairbairn, however, had won, behind the scenes, a partial victory. Journalists from overseas had been eagerly awaiting the appearance of the 'woman mercenary' in the dock; imagining a sort of glamorous gun-slinging Pasionaria - in any case a dramatic story on which to fasten. The Seychelles authorities had hamhandedly never let it be known that the 'woman mercenary' was frail, middle-aged, grey-haired and obviously frightened. They would have exposed themselves to worldwide mockery and derision if they had allowed her trial as a dangerous enemy of the state to proceed. On the second day therefore the Attorney General announced that all charges against Sue Ingle had been dropped. She remained one night more in the Central Police Station, with her pet cat, 'protected' from journalists; and was then discreetly flown back to South Africa. It had to be done. But the hardliners in the Seychelles government were not pleased; and they became even less pleased with Mr Rassool when it became apparent, on the Monday, that a certain amount of behind-the-scenes wheeling and dealing, a certain amount of plea-bargaining. must have taken place over the weekend.

For on the Monday Fairbairn played his trump card. The court assembled to hear the six remaining accused plead; and it was naturally expected that they would plead not guilty to the charge of high treason and that then the trial proper could begin. Instead, to general amazement, one after the other they pleaded guilty – all except Bob Sims, who pleaded not guilty to high treason but guilty to importing arms illegally into the Seychelles. It seemed suicidal; and it must have seemed suicidal to many of the accused too when Fairbairn, in his visits to them at the army camp, had persuaded them to follow this course. For by pleading guilty they were, on the face of it, condemning themselves to death. But then, on reflection, the subtlety of Fairbairn's manoeuvre became apparent. With the pleas of guilty the whole process was virtually over and done with: all that would remain was a speech by Fairbairn in mitigation, and then sentencing. There would be no show trial at all, no witnesses describing the landing at the airport, no evidence of Kenya's or Mancham's involvement, no gradual working up of passions against the accused as day succeeded day. Nothing. The whole purpose of the trial, from the point of view of the Seychelles government, would be defeated. It would be a non-event politically and internationally. Furthermore how would it look abroad if the Chief Justice were to impose the death sentence on shadowy figures whose particular misdeeds were unknown because never recounted? It would look brutal. Indeed it would look barbarous. It was a gamble that Nicholas Fairbairn took, and that he persuaded his clients to take: to play it low key. But it was a brilliantly calculated gamble; and it very nearly came off.

That it failed was due to one man: Dolinchek. Dolinchek had refused to be represented by any lawyer, maintaining at first that the South African government, his employers, ought to provide a lawyer to defend him; and later refusing even a local one. 'I don't need a lawyer to lie on my behalf,' he said, 'I don't lie.' So he, the odd man out to the very last, was defending the - by implication - only honest man of the seven accused: himself. Confusingly he pleaded guilty - but not really guilty. This confusion gave the Chief Justice the pretext he needed to adjourn the hearing and to consider, overnight, Dolinchek's position. There were rumours, later, that as soon as a day's proceedings were concluded the Chief Justice immediately sidled off to report to President René at State House and received his instructions for the next day. These rumours were certainly never confirmed, and probably purely malicious. But it is hard to imagine, equally, that that night passed without any consultation between the highest legal and political authorities. Certainly next morning, Tuesday morning, the Chief Justice announced that after due consideration he had decided to rule that Mr Dolinchek had entered a plea of Not Guilty. The trial therefore would proceed - the trial admittedly of Dolinchek alone. But in Dolinchek the court and the country had, it seemed, the ideal sacrificial victim: a self-confessed spy from a country theoretically at least loathed and feared. At this stage few would have put much money on Dolinchek's prospects of survival.

But, before the other mercenaries were dismissed, temporarily, from the dock and the courtroom and Fairbairn (except as an observer) with them, the Attorney General announced that the charge of treason against Sims had been withdrawn. It would have been difficult to do otherwise after allowing his companion, Sue Ingle, to go scot free. On the other hand his plea of guilty to importing arms - four AK 47s had been found hidden in the grounds of La Misere -was registered. For Sims, therefore, there was no longer any risk at all of the death penalty - another client saved by Fairbairn. On the other hand this very fact served only to infuriate the hardliners even more against the suspiciously unforceful attorney-general whose father had been a personal friend of the Mancham family. And the hardliners were not only to be found in the party or the military. 'Kill them, kill them, kill them,' a fierce young Seychellois, matching his gestures to his words, told me. 'If they do not kill them, I tell you this: I will personally demonstrate against the government.' That, though uncommon, was certainly reminiscent of Angola.★

The Chief Justice having outmanoeuvred his most dangerous opponent, the much-desired show trial could now proceed. But with Nicholas Fairbairn reduced to a frustrated and impuissant silence and with Martin Dolinchek more or less clay in the court's hands, the Chief Justice could afford to show himself most meticulously concerned for the defendant's rights. The days that followed were punctuated by continual courteous murmurs of 'if this is agreeable to you, Mr Dolinchek,' or 'I wonder if you have quite taken this point, Mr Dolinchek,' or 'pray interrupt me if there is anything here you do not follow, Mr Dolinchek'. And in indirect response to Fairbairn's views on the obvious bias of any jury, the Chief Justice spent no less than a whole day quibbling over their selection. First he disqualified two jurors because they were related to witnesses or policemen; then, on his 'advice', no less than three more disqualified themselves as being already convinced in advance that the accused was guilty; and finally, at the very last moment, the foreman of the jury was ignominiously dismissed for having failed to tell the Chief Justice that he was a member of the local militia. As if to make impartiality doubly sure, the Chief Justice ordered that for the duration of the trial the jury finally selected - six men and three women - should live together, without any contact with the public or indeed members of their families (this reduced one jurywoman to tears). In fact they were put up in the government-owned Northolme Hotel, near Beauvallon Bay. It was all something of a charade. Free from casual outside pressure they may have been. But they lived under the watchful eye of an army officer and escort; and there could be little doubt of what the army's view was: they wanted Dolinchek found guilty and the mercenaries executed.

Not that the army can by any means have been happy with the six days of Dolinchek's trial - an opportunity for the police, far more experienced, naturally, in legal procedure than the army, to produce not only a succession of far more coherent witnesses than the few rather incoherent soldiers who were called, but also to bring into the open the 'list of the five Majors' in Hoare's notes to Carey. Significantly, the list was given in full, without comments, in the following day's issue of *The Nation,* though *The Nation* often censored in its daily reports on the trial the more embarrassing aspects of, for instance, Dolinchek's own evidence. It was almost as if President René was issuing an open warning to the five majors that they were under suspicion and that he preferred to rely on Commissioner James Pillay's officers and men. One of these five, Major Rollye Marie, appeared in court to give evidence of the finding of the arms at La Misere - a large, capable man. He made no reference to the list, nor did the Chief Justice nor did the Attorney General. It just lay there, as it were, on the table, a silent indictment, a legal weapon that might, in the infighting of Seychelles political life, one later day be used.

The trial organisers had their moments of triumph: the evidence of Vincent Pillay and Sergeant Esparon, for example, with their graphic descriptions of how the Frothblowers had been uncovered; and the production of seventeen AK 47s, complete with ammunition and the grips in which they had been abandoned or hidden, more out of place and sinister perhaps in the courtroom, almost within reach of the handcuffed mercenaries in the dock, than they would have been in action. Mike Hoare's passport was produced too, plus written indications of Kenya's involvement - the 'documents' which had, in the rush of departure, not been recovered. But undoubtedly the most spectacular moment, the moment around which in a sense the whole show trial had been planned, was the play-ing-over of the tape-recordings reconstructed from the burnt and torn spools that, if the *coup* had been successful, would have been played over the seized radio station. The words and phrases, in French, English and Creole, were very jum-bled and bitty; but there were three distinct male voices there. The first a radio technician gave evidence as recognising: 'That voice is very familiar,' he said. 'I've recorded him on several occasions before.' It was the voice of Gerard Hoareau. The second was 'a friend of mine. We have talked on many occasions before.' Paul Chow. The third - its most audible phrase was 'today a free nation' - the techni-cian also immediately recognised.

'How can you recognise it?' asked the Attorney General.

'I think anyone who hears that voice can recognise it,' replied the technician, 'I've recorded things for him, heard his voice, a lot of times.'

'Whose voice is it?'

'Mr James Mancham.'

For all those listening, for everyone in the Seychelles, there could be no fur-ther reasonable doubt possible: the former President, despite his denials at the time, must have been directly implicated in the preparation of the *coup* attempt. The government had proved its major political point; Mancham was a dangerous 'enemy of the people'; and in that sense the whole setting-up of the trial had been worthwhile.

All this of course was basically irrelevant to Dolinchek's own trial. Witnesses and evidence were introduced on the pretext that it had to be proved that war was levied, on the night of Wednesday, 25 November, against the Seychelles. Fairbairn, had he been defending Dolinchek, would no doubt forcefully have objected. But the Chief Justice, with his deadpan explanations to the jury of how Item A should now after identification be listed as Exhibit B, and with his silky courtesy towards the defendant, preempted all possible criticism. The only moment in the whole trial which occasioned a display of judicial peevishness came (if I remem-ber rightly) during the poor Lousteau-Lalanne's once-again repeated story. 'The Colonel?' said the Chief Justice. 'Who is this Colonel to whom these continual references are being made? What Colonel is this?' Had Hoare remained behind in the Seychelles and been captured, his trial there would have been in every sense a historic trial. He was what the French call *le grand absent* in the whole proceedings, and the rest were poor substitutes. But in the Colonel's absence

Dolinchek undoubtedly became the star turn. He answered in his own way the Chief Justice's rhetorical question. Hoare, he said, was 'an overglorified soldier who got his Colonel title from Mobutu Sese Seko'. 'For a conspiracy-type operation,' he added dismissively, 'he was not up to standard.'

Dolinchek's whole attitude to Hoare resembled that of a rejected and embittered suitor towards a once-admired, now-lost, object of love. It had been very different before when he had cast himself in the role of the Colonel's right-hand-man. As he said of his first meetings with Hoare, and his own part in the conspiracy, 'Of course it takes two to tango'. He had added in his diary: 'If my government knew I was discussing this with him, they would chew my balls.' The diary, hidden by Dolinchek on the island before his arrest, then produced by him as a sop to the authorities, was a source of considerable light relief when extracts were read out in court. Dolinchek asked that a part of it should not be read out, because it would be 'embarrassing for my family' and the Attorney General gravely, to the vocal disappointment of all the South African journalists in the press gallery, agreed.

Had his fellow-prisoners been in the dock, but they were not, they would hardly have appreciated Dolinchek dismissing them in his evidence as 'rubble' or referring to Sims as 'a stupid man called Bob'. When he came to describe how he had, in the Reef Hotel, criticised Carey and his men - 'Drunkards only interested in birds. I told them there were lots on the trees' - and how they had responded, both the court and the translators (for the sake of certain members of the jury everything had to be translated into Creole) were left far, far behind. 'Those guys,' explained Dolinchek, 'who were threatening me with a zap-off, they were skimmering – a good Afrikaans word.' That occasion the Chief Justice let pass; but on others he had to intervene, to ask Dolinchek for an explanation of his language. For instance: Chicoms? 'An intelligence abbreviation, my Lord,' the accused gravely explained, 'for Chinese Communists.' Dolinchek was extremely insistent on his status. 'I am not a mercenary,' he told a somewhat flabbergasted courtroom, 'and I will never be one because it is below my dignity. I am a professional intelligence officer.'

The drama was not only in the dock. Among the spectators attending the trial every day was a grey-haired Englishwoman who had come out specially from South Africa to see Dolinchek condemned. She was convinced, rightly or wrongly, that he had been involved in the assassination of her son, Dr Richard Turner, a banned liberal lecturer at Natal University, shot down mysteriously at his home in January 1978. She was not the only woman specially there. Di Brooks, a dark-haired woman of twenty-eight always fashionably dressed, usually smiling, had flown out, alone of the wives or relations, to be present at her husband Aubrey's trial. On leaving Rhodesia they had together tried to set up a printing business in South Africa. But 'the debts piled up', she told me, 'and that's probably why he got involved in all this'. Her opinion of Hoare is worth giving, if only as a contrast to

Dolinchek's: 'a gentleman, an absolute gentleman'. She was allowed most days to pay a brief visit to her husband at Union Vale Camp, usually escorted by Nicholas Fairbairn. She found him resigned to his fate, whatever that might be, and reading the bible – a sort of religious conversion, bordering occasionally on exaltation, that Fairbairn worriedly confirmed. Alone in their solitary cells, in what Fairbairn described as 'abominable conditions' – handcuffed day and night, without light and with little air, having to scrabble on the floor for their food, jeered at and promised death by their captors – the other mercenaries, knowing that one way or another their fate was sealed, had to wait out with growing mental tension the long days of Dolinchek's trial.

This came to an end with the final pleas on Thursday, 1 July. The Attorney General for the prosecution was brief, civil, but firm in calling for the death penalty. Dolinchek, addressing the jury, grovelled. He had been misled.

> I know I committed a ghastly wrong to all of you [he said]. I can only hang my head and say I'm truly sorry. I now believe Mancham's government harboured a lazy and crooked bunch of parasites who wallowed in super luxury and opulence and gallivanted the world of high jinks where corruption was rampant. What a catastrophe, what a calamity for your gentle nation if Mancham and his accomplices were to return! I'm glad we were foiled in our plan to impose this bunch on your liberated people.

A recantation of the sort that by Gus Grillo★ before the People's Tribunal in Luanda had seemed astutely machiavellian appeared in the much calmer atmosphere of the Seychelles merely faintly ridiculous. The press gallery could barely stifle their indignant guffaws at the hypocrisy of Dolinchek's peroration.

> In conclusion, [he said] I humbly ask your Lordship to allow me to offer my hand of brotherly friendship. There is a time in every man's life to stand up and be counted, to take sides. From now on my place will be in the ranks of anti-apartheid forces to save Africa from a certain holocaust.

This must have been the most surprising recantation since St Paul's conversion on the road to Damascus. The Chief Justice, unblinkingly, announced that he would, if Mr Dolinchek were agreeable, adjourn the case till the Monday following to consider and prepare his judicial summing-up. 'Indeed, my Lord,' said Dolinchek with unctuous deference, 'your wish is my command.'

The court reconvened, after a long and sunny weekend, on the afternoon of Monday 5 July. The Chief Justice ran briefly through all the evidence, pointing out that Dolinchek had not taken part, like most of the rest of the accused, in the fighting around the airport or the barracks but that he was, by his own admission, a party to the conspiracy to overthrow the Seychelles government. He concluded his summing-up shortly after three o'clock. The jury retired. Exactly half an hour later, they returned.

'Mr Foreman, have you reached a verdict?'

'Yes, Your Lordship.'

'What is it?'

'We find the accused guilty as charged.'

'Is that a unanimous verdict?'

'Yes, Your Lordship.'

Dolinchek, previously standing, was asked to sit. 'Now then, Mr Dolinchek,' said the Chief Justice, 'I do not propose to sentence you this afternoon - though I know that in your situation I would like this to be over with one way or the other.' Pleas in mitigation for the other accused were still to be heard; then all the five now found guilty of treason would be sentenced together. The court would reconvene the following day for the final act.

This was Nicholas Fairbairn's chance to redeem the situation. He rose to address the court on Tuesday afternoon, conscious that he was the cynosure, both in the courtroom and outside, of all eyes and ears. He skated lightly over the careers, characters and family situations of Brooks, England, Carey and Puren, and even more lightly over their motives and their past military careers, emphasising their humanity. Then he drew breath. 'The matter to which I must now turn,' he said, 'is equally relevant but perhaps more distasteful'; and for the first time the court, and the press, heard the details of how the mercenaries had been beaten up and maltreated after capture. As the long recital continued, the Seychellois in the public gallery began to show signs of protest. But none of the account of the army's brutality - Fairbairn carefully made the point that the police had always behaved impeccably - was to be reported over the radio or repeated in *The Nation* next morning; this time discretion ruled, As for outsiders, the non-Seychellois press, they found it difficult to be too shocked by what in a sense is a risk that must be accepted by any mercenary if captured, or to be too impressed by Fairbairn's legalistic point that 'if the State claims allegiance, then the State must also offer protection'.

Finally, Fairbairn, step by step, and with caution, turned to the offence of treason itself . 'Those who gain power by tainted hands,' he concluded amidst a profound and attentive silence, 'must show mercy to those who attempt to regain it.' But he went no further than that. He named no names and he made no precise comparisons. He did not point out, as he could have done, that René himself was guilty of treason against Mancham and that only by 'levying war' and by bloodshed - the exact crime of which the mercenaries were accused - had René and his supporters come to power. A Cicero or a Demosthenes would have made immense play with the open secret on the islands that René, under Mancham's presidency, had used his own position as Prime Minister to smuggle weapons into the islands - the ten Kalashnikovs with which his supporters were armed

- via the airport, in almost exactly the same way, *mutatis mutandis,* as Hoare had attempted to do, but with greater success. British lawyers of modern times are not used however, unlike their Roman and Greek predecessors, to attacking men of state head on. Fairbairn did not dare to be specific. He was already worried, as he confided afterwards, that he had gone too far in the detail of his descriptions of the army's brutality when his clients would, that very evening, be back under Major Macdonald Marengo's untender control. But that, he felt, was a risk that had had to be taken. It would of course have made a far greater impact on both the courtroom itself, on the Seychelles, and on world opinion if he had come out with an open and detailed denunciation of the hypocrisy of René's régime, itself installed by a *coup,* instigating a trial of any sort against those who had attempted - in the name moreover of the legitimately elected President - to do the same thing. But he did not. He left it unfortunately merely as a hint and an allusion, hanging in the air. He ended with an unremarkable plea for leniency.

Dolinchek on the other hand, who now again had his turn to speak, ended with one of the most remarkable pleas that a man of his type may ever have addressed to a court of law. 'Lastly, my lord,' he said, 'if the death sentence is passed on me I appeal to your Lordship to direct that I should be executed by a military firing squad as befits an officer or gentleman.' At this last request even the Chief Justice appeared to wince. He adjourned the court briefly before pronouncing sentence. At 4.30 in the afternoon he returned to the courtroom. All rose, then sat. The five found guilty of treason, unhandcuffed, remained standing.

'The accused,' said the Chief Justice, 'allowed themselves to become involved in levying war against a small country that was not their own. All of them must have known that what they planned would have risked the lives of hundreds of people.' This seemed to me at the time, and still seems on reflection, a remarkable exaggeration. 'I take into account,' added the Chief Justice, 'the eloquence of their learned counsel.' He did not however, answer, refute or indeed take into account at all the arguments, whether express and implied, that Fairbairn had put forward in mitigation. It was an empty phrase.

'I believe however,' he continued without any change of pace or tone, 'this type of crime calls for deterrent sentences. If people engage in these kind of activities because they are lucrative the penalties must be as heavy as they possibly can be.'

He paused; and eyes turned surreptitiously towards Di Brooks, apparently calm, flanked by a Seychellois policewoman and the impassive British Consul.

'Aubrey Vincent Brooks,' said the Chief Justice, 'I hereby sentence you on Count 5 to suffer death in the manner authorised by law.' Sentences of death on Carey, England and Puren followed. There was no awful solemnity, no black cap, no reference to 'being taken from this place and hanged by the neck until you are dead', no appeal to God to have mercy on their souls. It was all spoken in a conversational tone of voice; almost like a word of advice from an older man to a young friend. The only surprise, to many unpleasant, was that Dolinchek, 'because he has shown a spirit of contrition', was sentenced not to death but merely to twenty years' imprisonment – rather as if a hypocritical sinner had half succeeded in hoodwinking a somewhat naive father confessor. The convicted men, pale but showing no emotion, were escorted out of the courtroom into the bright sunlight and, constantly photographed, into the waiting military vehicle. Di Brooks was taken out that evening by a shocked Nicholas Fairbairn and her South African lawyer, newly arrived; Fairbairn fulminating against the duplicity of the Chief Justice and openly worried that he had himself chosen the wrong tactics. My opinion (never confirmed by him) is that he had fixed up a behind-the-scenes deal with the authorities and had been given some sort of guarantee, probably by Bernard Rassool, the Attorney General, that if his clients pleaded guilty, they would not be sentenced to death. But if the Attorney General did give a guarantee of this sort (and clearly for reasons of legal etiquette even Fairbairn would never have had the gall to approach the Chief Justice directly), he was in no position to enforce it. Indeed Mr Rassool did not survive as Attorney General very much longer. In view of his unconvincing performance in the trial he was dismissed in the autumn, and later, I believe, went voluntarily into exile and joined the ranks of the opposition.

For the passing of the death sentence was not of course the end of the affair in the Seychelles. The question remained, posing much more of a long-term dilemma than in Angola; would the sentences ever be carried out ? 'Now it's all over,' said one Seychellois, 'we wish they would just send them back to South Africa and forget all about it.' Such was the general attitude of the ordinary people. On the other hand President René had to consider that a pardon of any sort would inevitably encourage his exiled opponents to try again whereas executions actually carried out would certainly act as a deterrent to would-be mercenaries in the future. He had to balance the interests of tourism and aid and trade, and the islands' reputation as a tropical paradise, which would be almost irretrievably scarred by executions of white men, against the pressures of his own party hardliners, of the army, of the Tanzanians on the islands (now rein-forced to a strength of perhaps five hundred), of President Nyerere, his ally, and of the OAU in general: all favouring death. A further complication was that the Seychellois authorities were faced with rather a macabre practical problem if the executions were to go ahead. For the accused had been sentenced to die in 'the manner authorised by law': hanging. But no executions had been carried out on the islands within living memory and not only had the gallows rotted but there was no-one remotely capable of acting as a hangman on the islands. A foreign 'professional' would therefore have to be imported, a distasteful procedure and one likely to lead to a bad press.

Perhaps fortunately for the President the legal system itself imposed a delay and solved his immediate dilemma. Fairbairn had before leaving the Seychelles lodged an appeal against both conviction and sentence. The appeal would have to be heard by the three peripatetic judges of the Appeal Court, one Irishman and two Mauritians, but it could not be heard until the autumn. No immediate political decision on whether to go ahead with the executions or not was therefore either necessary or possible. Fairbairn set great store by the appeal, believing that on strictly legal grounds he would win his argument that there had been a mistrial. Others however were much more sceptical and did not see how the Appeal judges could do anything but support, with whatever qualms, the Chief Justice of the Seychelles, his conduct of the trial, his summing-up, the verdict and his sentence. The date for the appeal hearing was set: 20 September.

The appeal however was never heard. Two events intervened - one minor and one major. The minor event, but one that at first must have been most nerve wracking for the condemned mercenaries, was this: shortly after the trial had ended they were without explanation taken from their prison camp to the office of the President himself. This was the first time the mercenaries and the man they had planned to overthrow but who now held virtually the power of life or death over them had come face to face. It seems that René waved at them - it must have been the last thing they were expecting - an article in London's most renowned political weekly, *The Spectator,* which of course none of them had ever set eyes on before.

The article was entitled 'Fairbairn in the Tropics' and gave a detailed account of Fairbairn's views on the Socialist régime in the Seychelles in general and on the army's brutality in particular. It was an accurate article, if anything understating Fairbairn's views on the 'depraved conditions' imposed on his clients by a 'depraved government'. I should know; I wrote it, little imagining it would have repercussions. But it made René see red. He would never, he apparently said, allow Fairbairn to set foot again on the islands - a man who after all in order to appear for the defence had had to be admitted to the Seychelles Bar and so had had, most ironically, to take a formal oath of allegiance to the President of the Seychelles Republic, to himself, President René. The mercenaries must, he insisted, drop their appeal and sack Fairbairn. They must also hold a press conference and deny that they had been beaten up by the army. In return he would spare their lives.

The four condemned men were of course in a horribly unenviable position. The implication was that if they went ahead with the appeal, with Fairbairn as their lawyer, as was their undoubted legal right, and if they lost, then the President would not exercise the prerogative of mercy. No-one would have wished to be in their shoes, unadvised and friendless, at this particular moment. They had no real choice: they fell in with the President's wishes. Fairbairn, to his fury and frustration, was dismissed, the appeal was dropped, and the prisoners held a press conference (attended mainly by local Seychellois journalists and so not widely reported) denying that they had ever been maltreated. No official Presidential announcement followed, however. to the effect that their lives would be spared and their sentences commuted to terms of imprisonment. They simply had to hope that René would keep his word.

The second and major event helped the mercenaries much more directly than my article had done indirectly. There had been unrest in the army for some time; and on 17 August 1982 the soldiers guarding the mercenaries at Union Vale mutinied. They seized, at 6 am, the radio station and broadcast over it an appeal to the President, 'as Commander in Chief of the Army and as the Father of the Seychelles' to help them. They were sick, they said, of being treated 'like pigs' by their officers; and in particular they demanded the dismissal and punishment of two of the 'five majors'. René was in the out-islands at the time, on Almirante, and the mutinous soldiers, as a means of pressure, seized over two hundred hostages at the radio station and threatened to kill them and blow up the petrol storage tanks outside Victoria unless their demands were met. For they had also demanded the dismissal and punishment of two of the ministers, including their own official commander 'Colonel' Ogilvy Berlouis, the Minister of Youth and of Defence. He of course being on the main island summoned his Tanzanian 'allies' to suppress the mutiny.

The mutineers had not only released the mercenaries they had been guarding but had actually asked them to take the lead in the mutiny as their officers. Strangely enough very much the same sort of thing had happened in Angola a year after the trial there, when in the so-called Nito Alves *coup* attempt Sao Paolo prison in Luanda had been 'liberated' and the surviving mercenaries there offered their freedom, and arms. Wisely they had refused both, stayed in their cells, and sat the failed *coup* (later bloodily punished) out.★ But in the Seychelles the opportunities were far greater. By taking the lead in the mutiny the mercenaries might at last have sparked off a popular uprising and been in a position to overthrow – as had been their aim only nine months earlier – the whole régime. It would have been a gamble but a reasonable one: except of course for the fact that the penalty for losing would without a shadow of doubt have been immediate death, and that most of the mutineers appear to have been drunk most of the time. So they too declined. Not only did they decline but it seems that Dolinchek and Carey slipped out from Union Vale and gave information on conditions inside to the advancing 'loyalists'. Shells were falling on the barracks and the prison and by midday the fighting was over, at the cost of nine killed: no hostages, but five mutineers and four loyalists. Not a major rebellion then nor a vast loss of life but still a further dramatic increase in the scale of deadly violence originally inaugurated by René himself. How the surviving mutineers – and there may have been as few as thirty of them in all – were treated I do not know and hate to imagine. But the mercenaries of course had proved their 'loyalty' to President René and his regime. 'You'll never hang as long as I'm here,' René told the prisoners on his return. And Aubrey Brooks apparently replied: 'May I make a suggestion, Sir? We dig in outside your grounds.'

There were even rumours that Dolinchek might be asked to take over the island's security services. René, however, did not go as far as to employ the mercenaries hired to overthrow him on his own behalf. Indeed he did not ever formally commute the death sentences. For there were still, even despite the failure the previous November, exiles and mercenaries actively involved in threatening his régime. In London that September Hoareau and Chow and other exiles were meeting to try again with a plan involving three hundred mercenaries to be sent in by ship . As an advance guard they did send in one, Mike Asher, with five kilos of high explosive concealed apparently in an imported van. The plan was for members of the *Mouvement pour la Résistance* to destabilise the régime, already shaken by the August mutiny, still further by a terrorist bombing campaign for which Asher would train local underground supporters. Asher, instead, blew himself up at the remote beach of Anse Forbans with one of the underground, Simon Denousse, on 20 October. Asher had not only come from South Africa but had been one of those originally considered for enrolment in Hoare's team. Despite everything, therefore, would-be mercenaries in South Africa were still actively involved in plots against René's government, and René, though kept abreast of these plots (Hoareau and Chow's telephone calls in the Carlton House Towers in London were all taped and recorded, very possibly by the Italian Secret Service, the SID) could not afford to be too trusting towards 'his' mercenaries. He seems, though, to have become and to have remained on good personal terms with them. 'Barney', he said, having summoned Carey personally, 'I'm afraid I've got bad news for you. Your wife is divorcing you.' This cannot have been entirely unexpected; Sandra Carey had been close to a breakdown during her husband's trial and imprisonment and was bitter against him for ever having involved himself in the venture. It was, however, a very humane touch on René's part to take the trouble to break the news in person.

So though the threat of execution no longer seriously loomed over the mercenaries, they were neither pardoned nor released. Instead they were sent that October, all six of them – Sims, incidentally, had been sentenced to ten years for importing arms – to an imprisonment that more resembled exile on the remote Platte Island where there was already an army training camp. They were locked in their hut every night – but at dawn every day the doors were unbarred and they were free to wander. They lived on fish six days a week. They swam in the tropical seas – not far, though, for fear of their most effective guards, the sharks. It was a very different sort of life from that of their 'colleagues' who had been suffering for years in Angolan prisons or for months in South African jails. For the mercenaries in the Seychelles, trials, and tribulations were – except for the greatest tribulation of all, the loss of liberty – over.

HOARE INCARCERATED

Shortly afterwards the releases began. On 17 November 1982 thirty-four of the mercenaries imprisoned in South Africa were freed - those sentenced to six months at Pietermaritzburg, released after four. Next Vernon Prinsloo, having served eight months of his one-year sentence, was released. That was in April 1983. Then, in the summer, as an act of clemency by René, all the six mercenaries on Platte Island were told that they were to be freed. 'Aubrey,' said the President to Brooks - it seems almost incredible but I am assured that he did say it - 'you can always come back here, you'll always be welcome. But next time I hope you'll come as a genuine tourist.' The only one who expressed, understandably, a certain alarm was Dolinchek. 'I will have to face the music - or a concert - down there after my trial here,' was how he put it. He must have been remembering how in his peroration he had claimed that the enemy was Apartheid, and that 'back home the people are crying out to be liberated'. But once he was back home himself, he seems to have totally forgotten about his proud boast - that henceforward he would be in the forefront of the struggle side by side with the anti-Apartheid forces. He was ten years out in his timing, the ever-unfortunate Dolinchek. He had been dismissed, Prime Minister Botha himself had confirmed in July 1982, from his post as - in his own favourite phrase - an 'active duty officer' with NIS for absence without leave, as well as for 'action contrary to' state security. But white South Africans seem on his return to have treated him with amazing tolerance. Even members of his jogging club did not boycott him; indeed they generally believed that he was back once again in favour with his old employers.

In November Ken Dalgliesh, Mike Webb and Charles Goatley were released on parole after having served only just over half of their two and a half year sentences.

In December came a curious little incident in South Africa obviously designed to show that the South African government was as a matter of long-term policy rather than short-term expediency clamping down on all mercenary activities – an omen of what was to come under a government of a very different hue a decade and a half later. Five 'foreigners', British and Rhodesian, were detained and interrogated by security police after reports that they were trying to organise another Seychelles mercenary venture. This was on the orders of the Minister, Louis Le Grange, who had certainly changed his tune from the days when he could indignantly ask the press what South African laws the Seychelles mercenaries had broken. He did not allege that these five had broken any laws as such; but his government, he said, took a serious view of the alleged plans and 'were not prepared to allow any such developments to take place within this country'. The five were subsequently expelled. I have been told that three of them were ex-RLI, but I very much doubt whether Dalgliesh, Webb or Goatley were even marginally involved. Being released on parole, as they had been, is a double-edged state of affairs; any transgression, or suspicion of transgression, and the parolee is smartly back inside to serve the rest of his sentence. It was far more relaxing for the six from the Seychelles who ran no such risk of any further imprisonment. That Christmas Aubrey and Di Brooks, earlier reunited, exchanged Christmas cards with President René and considered returning to the Seychelles for a 'second honeymoon'.

Finally in May in South Africa Peter Duffy, Tullio Moneta and Pieter Dooreward were released also on parole. They had served just under two years of their five-year sentences. All the many mercenaries who had been in prison in so many different parts of the world had now been released - some escaping the death penalty, others, – those in Angola★ - freed after only a fraction of the thirty years which they had been condemned to serve, all with their sentences so notably reduced as to indicate that society had in private and in practice pardoned them the 'crimes' which society had raged against in theory and in public.

All, that is to say, except one man, one mercenary, the oldest, the most famous and the least likely to be in a position ever again to repeat his 'offence'. When I visited South Africa in the middle of 1984, Mike Hoare and Mike Hoare alone was still in jail. I walked around the white-washed walls of Pietermaritzburg Central Prison, set at the end of Pine Road, on the outskirts of the town, looking for all the world like a large misplaced Foreign Legion fort. The notice outside the heavy gate mentioned visiting hours. I wondered whether it would be wise to apply direct to the prison governor for permission to visit and talk to his best-known prisoner or whether, first, to approach his wife. In the end I drove out to the Old Vicarage and introduced myself to Phyllis Hoare. She was a friendly, likeable woman, obviously younger than her ageing husband imprisoned only a few miles away, the mother of two good-looking boys; neither of them showed the slightest sign of being ashamed of or reluctant to talk about their father. But there was no chance, Phyllis Hoare assured me, of my visiting her husband. She herself had only two authorised visits of half an hour each month.

I had imagined naively that prison conditions might be relaxed for an elderly white prisoner of distinctly right-wing views in a South African jail. I was quickly disabused. The prison régime, I was told, was certainly less harsh than that of Zonderwater Gaol or of the dreaded Pretoria Central, with its thousand prisoners, where Hoare had spent his first twenty months; and the governor, a colonel, was helpful where he could be. Hoare, who had developed a bad heart and might need open surgery, had been moved down to Pietermaritzburg from Pretoria a few months earlier for compassionate reasons. But all the same whereas political prisoners, black or white, belonged to a distinct category and had certain privileges, Hoare was technically a common criminal and was treated as such.

'Mike wanted to do a degree,' said his wife, 'anything to keep his mind occupied. But it's not permitted.' Indeed he was not permitted books or papers or reading or writing matter of any sort, only the Bible.

'But what does he do all day long?' I asked, horrified at what seemed to me, as a writer and reader, a greater deprivation even than that of liberty itself.

Phyllis Hoare found it hard to say. 'Fortunately he managed to smuggle Shakespeare into the prison at Pretoria,' she mentioned. 'He learnt lots of it by heart. He recites. He says it's the only thing that keeps him going. The warders think there's a madman around when they hear Mike reciting Hamlet to himself in his cell.'

What about other conditions, food for instance?

'We're not allowed to discuss prison conditions. We usually spend our half hours talking about legal things and the hopes of getting Mike out of there.' This seemed almost as saddening an answer as the response to my first question, and a veritable clutching at straws. But why had Mike Hoare not been released too like the forty-two found guilty at the Pietermaritzburg trial? Why were the South African government insisting on keeping her husband behind bars when all the other mercenaries had been released, long before expiry of their sentence, and when his was, in view of his age and health, an obvious case for compassion?

★   ★   ★

I have made no secret of my feeling that a Seychelles coup was morally justified, given the means by which René had risen to power himself; that it might – though this is more debatable – have positively benefited the Seychellois people, that Hoare wanted no bloodshed if it could possibly be avoided, that his plan was indeed designed to avoid bloodshed; that he had acted as a responsible commander throughout; that his trial in South Africa was as much a show trial for political purposes as the trial in the Seychelles had been; that the accusation of hijacking was an unjustified misuse of a term normally applied to a very different context involving demands for money, the release of terrorists, or the diffusion of propaganda statements – of a different order in any case from a mere demand for a ride; and that on the evidence of the actual accusations with which he was faced he should never have been found guilty. I hold no special brief for Hoare or any other mercenary – except the feeling that they too are human beings and should be treated with justice. In this particular case of the Seychelles coup and after having studied it as carefully and from as many sides as possible, I felt most strongly – and imagine that my readers will feel – that the punishment was disproportionate to the 'crime', pitiless in view of Hoare's age if imposed to anything like the full extent, and above all hypocritical in view of the nature and known activities of the government that was imposing it. For what could be more ironic than that President René had pardoned the mercenaries whom he caught though they were trying to overthrow and possibly to kill him while South Africa continued to imprison the mercenary leader who posed no threat to them at all, whom indeed their military minions had encouraged?

The authorities, as it turned out, must have felt a little of the same logic. For, a few months later, after his third Christmas in prison, Mike Hoare was informed that he was going to be released on 28 January 1985. On the occasion of the announcement of the new State President's accession an amnesty was to be declared for elderly prisoners.

The appointed day came and went. Hoare was not released. Instead, a week later, he was suddenly stripped of all privileges and placed in solitary confinement. This was apparently on the State President's direct orders. Why? There was some confused tale about an insulting letter to President Mobutu having been smuggled out of jail; but it is much more likely that it was a shot across the bows – to warn Hoare not, if released, to rock the boat.

Those hopeless days in solitary confinement appears almost to have broken his spirit. He was suicidally depressed. Then, suddenly, unexpectedly on Monday 6 May 1985 Phyllis became a happy woman again. Mike Hoare having served over a quarter of his sentence and being over sixty-five years of age was released under a General Presidential Pardon.

On his release he showed both a sense of humour and of panache. Prison, he declared, had revitalized his soul and refreshed his liver. As for his Seychelles venture, he was totally unrepentant both about the attempt itself and in particular about his decision to bring his men back 'at whatever cost'.

A Final Death

A few months later death came to Gerald Hoareau, the moving spirit among the exiled plotters. He was assassinated in London on 30 November 1985. He was shot several times in the drive of his house in Greencourt Avenue, Edgware by an automatic pistol at a range of 7 feet and fell dying to the ground. His assassin escaped and has neither been found nor identified   The exiles laid the blame on a hitman hired by the Seychellois government; the Seychellois government laid the blame on bitter rivalry among exile groups. So ended, at the age of 34, President René's most bitter and energetic opponent and the man who would probably have benefited most if the mercenary coup had succeeded – a victim of the most vicious and cowardly form of political warfare, secret assassination.

VII

Venture into the Interior

Denard was in the Comores on the night that Hoare and the Frothblowers landed in the Seychelles. He is described as pacing like a caged lion around Commandant Charles' office at Kandani camp; full of expectation and excitement; ordering his men to be put on immediate alert, ready for immediate departure. There was fighting at Mahé airport! But the only news coming through was apparently coming via news reports over transistor radios. The situation was confused. Denard took the decision to 'wait and see'.

That detail about transistor radios is odd. There were no reporters at all at Mahé airport that night, and Radio Seychelles made no mention till the morning of what was going on. Was it Noddyn, Denard's old associate, in direct radio contact with Moroni – Noddyn himself possibly at State House in Victoria, at or near President René's side, getting confused reports of what was happening on that most confused of nights? And then passing them on over the radio to his former and possibly his current boss?

In one sense it would have been amazing if there had been *no* plans at all for a 'second wave'. There was certainly talk on Mahé of a planeload of French mercenaries standing by and, alternatively, a 'second wave' of mercenaries due to come in by sea, by French launch. Remember that the *coup* was planned for a week *after* the safe landing of the Frothblowers; so Denard, if he was involved, would understandably have been upset and bewildered, uncertain how to react, on hearing that there was premature fighting, and that out at the airport, not, as planned, in and around the capital.

Later Hoare himself made one, though only one significant remark, or perhaps slip, at his own trial. He was explaining that there was in any case no need for him to have taken the Air India Boeing because he could, instead, have used the Air Swazi Fokker Friendship piloted by his own men to escape. "I could always," he said, most significantly, "have refuelled in the Comores."

Certainly there were several hints of a Comores connection in the evidence given at the Pietermaritzburg Trial; including a never-explained tale of two women who stayed overnight at the Ermelo Holiday Inn and caught the same flight as the Frothblowers next day, disembarking at the Comores. And certainly there were personal links between both sets of mercenaries, and very recent ones at that. Patrick Ollivier, after the end in white Rhodesia, had flown out to the Comores and joined the Presidential Guard as 'Capitaine Stofflet'. And his old sergeant-major in Grey's Scouts, the man who had first befriended him in the Rhodesian Army, was the French-speaking Don Kenny, Hoare's personal bodyguard on Mahé. Were they still in contact? Very possibly. But even more significant is the still-mysterious role of Jerry Puren. Fifteen years earlier it was Puren who, landing at Bukavu to join Schramme★, had clearly been liaising with Denard in Angola. Puren was always Denard's link-man. I have a feeling in my bones, backed by these hints and premises, that the reason Puren stayed on and Hoare wished to stay on, after everything had gone wrong at Mahé Airport on that November night in 1981, had to do with their expectation, concealed from all others, of a reinforcement by French mercenaries which, in the circumstances, was called off. Had such an elaboration to the Seychelles scheme existed, it would have given the proposed *coup* an even greater chance of success. And, if successful, it would have given Denard a boost that, in November 1981, he certainly needed.

Comores: Uncrowned King

For six months earlier, in May, Mitterand had been elected President of France; and a new left-wing broom was sweeping through the ministries and civil service, and indeed the judiciary too, eliminating Bob Denard's shadowy semi-official backing. A month only after Mitterand's election, the Cotonou Coup came back to haunt Bob Denard. Six Beninois had been killed in that attempt; and, unfortunately for Denard, three of them had dual French-Benin citizenship. The families of these three had, two years earlier, begun a lawsuit in Paris against Denard (and curiously, one other mercenary, Philippe Boyer). It had dragged slowly on; but now it was revived. Denard was advised not to come back to France or he would be arrested; and he was also warned by his now-powerless 'friends' that his various French passports would not be renewed. Later Mitterand was to write that the situation in the Comores was 'intolerable', 'morally and politically unacceptable for France' and that it was necessary for the mercenaries who upheld the régime to be gone. The truth was that Mitterand had never forgiven his old comrade-in-arms Abdallah for failing to get him elected President in the previous Presidential election when the votes of the Comorians, pre-Independence, had been 'delivered' by Abdallah to Mitterand's rival — almost 100,000 of them, enough in Mitterand's view to have swayed the result. But the truth also appears to have been that, in one of those murky affairs that bedevil French politics, the *affaire de l'Observatoire* years and years earlier (where Mitterand had in 1959 arranged for a phoney assassination attempt against himself in the centre of Paris, apparently to give his career a heroic tinge), Abdallah had been in on the set-up, had helped, knew too much. The truth certainly is that both Mitterand and Abdallah were wily old political foxes, who enjoyed complicated political manoeuvrings. But neither wanted an unpredictable showdown.

And in any case President Abdallah relied on the Presidential Guard to keep him in power. And with all the more gratitude to Bob Denard because the Guard cost him nothing. The SADF subsidised it to the extent of 1½ million rand in 1979, 4½ million in 1985, 6 million in 1987; and this was all thanks to Bob Denard's efforts, and his links with Pretoria - Freddie Thieleman ran his office there. And South Africa, keen to try out on a small, experimental scale its new policy of having friendly relations with black states, invested heavily, again thanks to Denard, in new hotels – the Itsandra Beach, the Galawa – and experimental farms. Of course there were certain advantages for themselves: the clandestine supply of arms to Renamo, the rebel movement in Mozambique, a political matter, and the embargo-breaking crates of weapons that were flown out to Iraq, a commercial matter. Meanwhile President Abdallah rubbed his hands, played off France against South Africa, and concentrated on increasing his and his cronies' vast fortunes. Personally he appears to have been genuinely fond of Bob Deanrd, and Bob Denard of him. He had to create a little Comorian army to satisfy the French new look, and indeed as an alternative power base should ever he be forced to dismiss 'his' mercenaries. But the *Forces Armées Comoriennes,* despite their grandiose title, were a fairly ragged and poorly-trained lot, commanded by a fellow Anjouanais, Commandant Ahmed Mohammed, a former French Army NCO, and in any case only a few hundred strong.

In semi-exile from France Bob Denard saw the Comores more and more as his real home. So did the mercenaries. Commandant Charles married a Comorienne; André Cau did the same. It was a pleasant relaxed life, with the scent of the ylang-ylang, the famed perfume of the Comores, pervading the tropical air. By his force of personality, by his contacts, by his wife , children, by the fact that everybody seemed to like and admire him personally Denard was, in a sense, the uncrowned King of the Comores. He was loyal to his men, and he expected his men to be loyal to him. He made his business deals particularly in the meat business, but he also seems genuinely to have tried to do his best for the archipelago. When he interviewed Patrick Ollivier, in early 1981 in Paris, he offered him the same rank as he had held in the Rhodesian Army, that of Captain, a salary of 15,000 francs a month, and the command of a 3rd Company of the Presidential Guard – a new company of 150 Comorians to be raised and trained by Ollivier himself, out in the mountains at Itsundzu, a company of 'pioneers', whose task would be not law and order or military but engineering, building, and development.

But Denard also saw the Comores as a base. The motto he originally chose for the Presidential Guard indicates his ambition: *Orbs Patria Nostra*, the Whole World

Our Country. That was of course in the first flush of success when he clearly dreamt of rivalling, indeed improving upon, the Presidential Guard of Gabon, not realizing how difficult the problems of finance would become, and how in the Comores tropical lethargy would gradually undermine so many apparently fine schemes.

But *Orbs Patria Nostra* was not an idle slogan, exaggerated though it may have been. Denard remained an adventurer and an idealist of sorts. And when in September 1981 the chance for a new venture came out of the blue, he, as ever, was keen to respond.

CHAD: LAND OF WARRIORS AND OF MILITARY CHIEFS

The deal was simple. The land was not. The rebel leader, the hatchet-faced Hissein Habré, had been chased out of his own country across the border into Sudan with 2000 men, women and children. He had, he explained to Denard, no money. But once restored to power he would pay the mercenary leader generously. All he needed were experts to train his men, weapons and ammunition – provided free and, for the moment at least, for nothing. It was the sort of deal that any experienced mercenary leader would normally have turned down flat. *Point d'argent, point de Suisse*[1] ★★ was one of Denard's favourite traditional sayings – no money, no mercenaries. But this time he accepted it: provided that, if successful, he and his men would form and train and command the eventual Presidential Guard.

He would never have accepted if the man had not been Hissein Habré and the country had not been Chad. Look at any map of Africa, at the top half, and you will see almost in its centre what appears to be an inland sea. That is Lake Chad. It pretty much marked – and marks – the junction of black Africa and Arab Africa. No wonder the French explorers and adventurers and soldiers saw its possession as key to the control of the interior of the continent. On 22 April 1900 Captain François Lamy was killed, fighting against the warrior tribes of the region. That same year the French founded Fort Lamy, and set about conquering the governorate, the colony they were to call Chad.

They had a hard time of it in the North. It was a vast land of deserts broken up by spectacular, bleak mountainous ranges, a land of Emirs and Sultans and fierce mounted tribesmen, of oases and raids and feuds, sparsely populated, incredibly romantic. The French won out in the end; but the French military class came to admire the wild courage of the nomads who opposed them in 'military Chad' – the whole of the North – and despise, as the Northerners who for centuries had raided them for slaves had always despised, the amiable black settled population of the fertile South: 'useful Chad'.

---

[1] The Swiss were, at one time, the most feared and fearful mercenaries in Europe. See the first volume of this trilogy. Whenever two asterix ★★ appear in this book, the reference is back to the full account in Volume One.

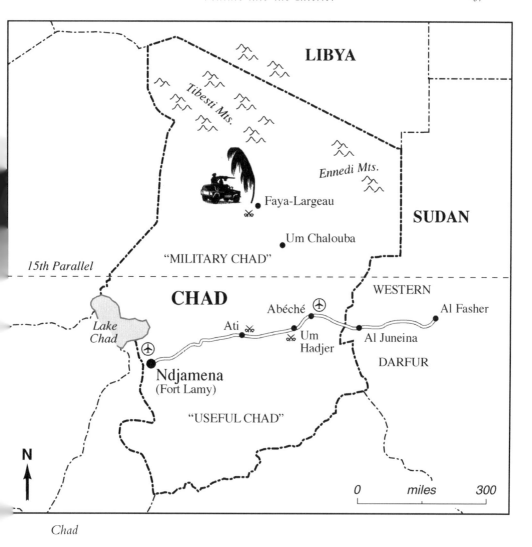

Chad

Came Independence; and the black Southerners, far far more populous, took their revenge. Five years into independence the first civil war broke out, the first of a whole series of civil wars that soon, amazingly, had the Toubous, cousins so to speak of the Touareg, even though there were only tens of thousands of them, dominating the two or three million black Africans in the South. 'Military Chad' had triumphed, once again, over 'useful Chad'. Hissein Habré was a Toubou; a great fighter and, by lineage, an hereditary ally of the French. But the Toubous were split. The other branch were led by the Derdei, a fighting religious chieftain, traditionally anti-French, and the Derdei of the day, by name Goukuni, was alternately Hissein Habré's closest ally and next his most bitter enemy. The two coalesced and they split; they became Ministers of Defence and Prime Ministers and even on occasion President, in the capital Ndjamena – as Fort Lamy had by now been renamed. It was a bewildering kaleidoscope – till Colonel Gaddafy of Libya intervened. The revolutionary Colonel had thrown his weight, and his troops, behind Goukuni; and Hissein Habré had been driven out of the capital, out of power, with his miserable few men across the border into the Sudan. But Bob Denard knew – all Frenchmen knew – that in Chad in particular a man who was a rebel leader one week might, so to speak, be President the next; and that Hissein Habré was not just your common or garden exile and refugee.

In September 1981 Denard met Hissein Habré's representative in Switzerland. He persuaded President Abdallah to agree to initial expenses coming out of the Presidential Guard budget. In mid-October 1981 two of Denard's mercenaries were in Khartoum, under light cover as aid workers. These were Jean-Baptiste and Laurent, both young men who had voyaged on the *Antinea* – Jean-Baptiste, a law graduate from Aix, had become 'head of security' at Anjouan, Roger Bracco's right-hand-man there till Bracco left; Lieutenant Laurent had more military experience – he was a reservist officer in the French Army.

THE LEGEND OF 'AHMED LUCKY'

It was a thousand-mile four-day drive by Toyota out to Hissein Habré's camp at Al Juneina, just inside the Sudanese province of Darfur. Laurent stayed two weeks, then went back to report to Denard on what was needed: radios, and mortars above all.

Jean-Baptiste stayed on; and the real adventure began. For the ever unpredictable Colonel Gaddafy suddenly and unexpectedly withdrew his troops from Chad; and hordes of Gorane warriors flocked to the banners of Hissein Habré. The only white man among them all, Jean-Baptiste must have seen himself as Lawrence to Hissein Habré's Emir Feisal. Except that in this era the wild tribesmen were mounted not on horses or camels but on dilapidated Landrovers and aged Peugeot pick-ups – with Jean-Baptiste at their head in his smart, new Toyota.

In mid-November four columns of vehicles crossed the border from Darfur into Chad. The first little villages fell easily; and Hissein Habré gave the young Frenchman – who had now been rebaptized (if one can call it that) Ahmed – the task of recapturing the capital of Chad's eastern province, Abeche. Twenty pick-ups now rearmed with Soviet machine-guns captured in the previous skirmishes were given to 'Ahmed'. At dawn on 29 November 1981 he attacked. By midday Abeche had changed hands. And in the evening the charging Gorane warriors rechristened him – they must have been trilingual – Ahmed Lucky.

There was a pause. The promised C130 full of radios and mortars, daily expected, never flew out from Moroni. Denard had been unable to persuade the South Africans that Chad was – or could ever be – of the slightest interest to them; and of course President Abdallah was not prepared to finance such a shipment out of his own or the State's – not that there appears to have been much difference between the two - pocket. So all that the mercenary leader could do was to send out two more of his best mercenaries: Hugues de Tappie (alias Mustapha) and the commander of No. 2 Company, Capitaine Rio (who became Abdul). They arrived early in the New Year, in 1982. No wonder that, without the promised shipment of arms, they got a cool welcome from Hissein Habré. But they did wonders. Hugues, who had been Denard's Radio Operator throughout the Comores *coup*, inventorised and repaired all the radio equipment available in Abeche, trained thirty young tribesmen as Morse operators, and organised a communications network between every group of moving vehicles. Rio, a heavy-weapons man, set up recoilless rifles on the Landrovers, machine-guns on the Peugeots, and 23mm rocket launchers on the armoured scout cars captured at Abeche. The Toyota fleet, so to speak the battleships, were fitted out with 81mm mortars or RPG7 Soviet rocket-launchers or SAM 7 missiles – all also captured at Abeche. By the end of January, with on the northern front Hissein Habré's Toubous having already recaptured the oasis-fortress of Faya-Largeau, his own birthplace, all was ready for the dash from Abeche west to retake the capital. First, though, it would be necessary to take the village of Um Hadjer, then the little town of Ati.

At Ati 'President' Goukuni had established his advance headquarters. Um Hadjer was heavily defended with artillery and a battery of Stalin's organs. But Hugues had broken 'President' Goukuni's wireless codes, such as they were, and was listening in, from Abeche, to all the enemy's messages. That helped immensely. On February 20 a triumphant report arrived from the front: it was signed Ahmed Lucky. Um-Hadjer had fallen after fierce fighting – but a counter-attack was expected.

It came at dawn. Goukuni himself brought up his guns, and directed, as Napoleon would have done, an artillery bombardment. Jean-Baptiste with Hugues (who had moved up to the front) abandoned Um Hadjer, swung west in a wide circle, and cut Goukuni's artillery off in the rear. Rio's mortars, thanks to Hugues' knowledge of the precise enemy positions, could deluge, themselves unseen, the enemy guns and transports. Chaos and panic spread among Goukuni's men. They retreated, leaving 500 dead. It had been a famous victory. But it had cost Jean-Baptiste 150 dead on his side. Never mind - the road to Ndjamena, the capital, seemed open.

But Hissein Habré hesitated. He did not take his chance. There was a complication. An OAU 'peace-keeping' force had been sent in, and was theoretically separating the combatants by occupying Ati.

Nonetheless, flushed with victory, Hissein Habré decided to bypass Ati. He detached a hundred Gorane warriors to head south-west and capture the little post of Omm. But Goukuni had foreseen this move. His defenders wiped out the attacking force. Wild with rage, Hissein Habré came in person to Um Hadjer and in person ordered Jean-Baptiste to capture the post of Omm – whatever the cost.

It cost the young mercenary his life. He led 150 vehicles in a four-column attack. He was killed standing on his Toyota by a bullet through the head. The attack was successful. The post was destroyed, the garrison massacred. Rio burnt Jean-Baptiste's body and brought the ashes back.

And by the first days of June, almost without further serious fighting, Hissein Habré had entered the capital. It is said suitcases of dollars persuaded the OAU peacekeepers to open the road. In his turn Goukuni became a fugitive, taking refuge in his own native mountains, in Tibesti in the north. But for Ahmed Lucky, the young French mercenary, it had been a tragically unfortunate campaign.

THE INGRATITUDE OF HISSEIN HABRÉ

Ndjamena had fallen to Hissein Habré's forces, on June 6, after only two hours of fighting. By June 11 Denard in person was in the capital, keen to hold the new President to his pledge. I imagine he was seriously considering switching his base of operations from the languorous Comores to the more bracing, and far more central shores of Lake Chad. A Presidential Guard formed of Goranes or Toubous, officered by mercenaries of his own choice, would have been a far more influential and powerful body, potentially, than even the famed Presidential Guard of Gabon. But Hissein Habré was of a very different mettle to Abdallah. He had studied in Paris but he distrusted the French. It was mutual. The French, and with good reason, distrusted him. Back in power, he showed no gratitude; money was paid but promises were forgotten. For a time he took one of Denard's men, Lieutenant Suresne, as a bodyguard. But Denard was soon back in the Comores, crestfallen; and his men seem gradually to have been frozen out as the new President, never an easy companion like Abdallah, became more remote, more frigid, much more inaccessible. Suresne returned, eventually, to Moroni, but neither Capitaine Rio nor Hugues de Tappie appear to have done so. And by January 1983 Patrick Ollivier, Hugues' friend, had quietly left the Comores too. The Presidential Guard was short of funds – understandably – and the 3rd Company, the Pioneers, had been abolished after a short few months of promising existence.

★   ★   ★

It is not, therefore, surprising that a rival to Denard now emerged. What is surprising is that in Bob Denard's variegated career, Mike Hoare's too, so few real rivals challenged their leadership seriously. But, if anyone, René Dulac *Le Grand* was the man to do so; and he did. He and Denard had fought together, campaigned together, mounted *coups* together for twenty years or more. Everyone acknowledged that René Dulac was a good soldier. But he had always had to play second fiddle. In the Comores he and Denard had finally and apparently irrevocably split up. Denard stayed. He went back to France.

And in France, in the early summer of 1983, Alain Biet and Thierry Villanova caught up with Patrick Ollivier at something of a loose end. A new mercenary operation was being prepared in Africa. Was he interested? Biet had been in Ollivier's 3rd Company out at Itsundzu; Villanova was less well known to him. But Ollivier immediately guessed where the operation would be. For after a few months of relative calm Chad was all aflame with war again. Colonel Gaddafy had formed an Islamic Legion and was back supporting his own protegé, the Derdei of the Toubous, the former President, Goukuni. And not only with an Islamic Legion of Touaregs but with tanks and planes of the regular Libyan army too. From his lair in the desolate lava-strewn mountains of Tibesti Goukuni, like a Nazgul from the Mountains of Mordor, was casting his shadow, and that of his Master, over the land of Chad once again. On June 24 the oasis-fortress of Faya-Largeau fell to his forces. Hissein Habré's position seemed suddenly desperate.

But who, Patrick Ollivier wanted to know, was in charge of the operation? Denard? No, he was told, the *patron*, the new boss, was Dulac; and *Le Grand* would be delighted to have Ollivier as one of his lieutenants. Ollivier refused haughtily, and let Denard know what was in the wind. For a solid hour, according to Ollivier's account, Denard raged against Dulac, a man he had formed, a man who without him would have been teaching the tango or had, at best, a career as a lifeguard at the public swimming baths. He re-enrolled Ollivier on the spot, ordered him to take the first plane out to Chad, remind Hissein Habré of who had put him in power, of his debt of honour and debt of blood; and, basically, insist that if Hissein Habré were going to re-employ any mercenaries, they had better be his, Denard's, not his rival upstart's – that *matamore*, that windbag – Dulac's.

It was a weird but fascinating situation. Two rival groups of mercenaries who knew one another only too well were in effect angling for the same contract. Ollivier seems to have persuaded Villanova to return to his old allegiance; for he, Villanova and Suresne landed at Ndjamena together, on 8 July. The plan they proposed - for by then Abeche had fallen to the enemy – was for a sweep through Darfur, through the neutral Sudan, by three motorized groups of Gorane warriors *à la Jean-Baptiste*, led by fifteen of Denard's men. Moving north fast, the three columns would then swing round in the Libyan Desert and take the invaders in the rear. It sounds a pretty wild plan. But Ollivier in the Rhodesian Army had been used to rapid cross-border strikes; and I suppose with luck, dash and immediate execution (which was what Denard was proposing, providing Ollivier got Hissein Habré's own signature to a proper contract this time) it might have worked.

But the trio of emissaries never even got to see the President. They were kept kicking their heels for a week in Ndjamena waiting for a reaction that never came. For what they did not realize was that *Le Grand* had stolen a march on them. He, Dulac, had already signed a contract; and not with Hissein Habré but with a much more reliable paymaster, the French State; or, to be more pedantically accurate, with the Ministry of Cooperation via its subsidiary, the blandly-named *Carrefour du developpement*.

This was a foretaste of things to come. Little though he realized it at the time, little though anyone realised it, René Dulac had formed the first private military firm – *Saxo*. It had been approved, given the green light, by President Mitterand himself, in a secret meeting on June 21 with his Minister of Cooperation, Christian Nucci, and his own son, his special adviser on African affairs, Jean-Christophe. And no less than 1500 tons of armament were at the same time to be flown out to Hissein Habré. President Mitterand had decided to halt the Libyan Colonel's vast ambitions, and, whatever his own moral reservations, (which in Mitterand's case were more philosophical than actual) to justify the means by the end; to ignore his own declared principles and to use a band of mercenaries to achieve this aim.

Not Denard, though. That would have been too bitter a pill for Mitterand to swallow. So Denard was out, sidelined, relegated to his passive role in the Comores. And René Dulac now had, in mercenary terms, his chance of glory, his great opportunity. The question now was: would be succeed, would he eclipse, as the young lion challenges the old for the leadership of the pack, his mentor, the great, the renowned, the ageing Denard?

The Battle for Faya Largeau

Thirty-three mercenaries flew out from Le Bourget via Cairo to Ndjamena airport on 13 July, on a Hercules C130 of SFAIR – a successor of Affretair. (But during Mike Hoare's trial Jack Malloch had disappeared in the Rhodesian - now Zimbabwean - skies, flying his beloved Spitfire; the wreck of which was found next day.) From the Hercules were unloaded two scout cars, one Panhard armoured car and two containers of Milan anti-tank missiles. After a couple of days' training at Camp Dubut, on the outskirts of Ndjamena, the men of *Saxo* were flown to Abeche, which Hissein Habré had recaptured. There they added to their armament three containers of SAM 7 anti-aircraft missiles, Russian-made, abandoned by Goukuni's men. René Dulac was not with them, he had gone ahead to Um-Chalouba. There he was laid low with a bad attack of malaria. There the *Saxo* column, under the temporary command of Charles and Alain, rejoined him on Monday 18 July. Um-Chalouba was the jumping-off point for the planned attack on, and recapture of, the oasis-fortress of Faya-Largeau, control of which was key to control to the whole Military North. At Um-Chalouba the mercenaries found their pay; and the Gorane whiling away the time with lethal Toyota-versus-Landrover races.

Four days later the attacking column set off. 2500 men strong, in 200 vehicles, World War II Willis jeeps and Mercedes lorries added to the usual Toyotas and Land-rovers and Peugeot pick-ups, plus a dozen light French armoured cars commanded by a Chad officer trained at the French cavalry school of Saumur;

code-name *Poisson*. They must have looked like something out of the Mad Max films as they rumbled and raced north through the desert, travelling first by day and night, then as they approached their target by night only. Like Feisal's Arabs sleeping or resting in the shade of their camels, they slept or rested in the shade of their lorries and jeeps and armoured cars. Before dawn on Saturday 30 July they were in position, ready for the assault on the oasis-fortress.

Fifty Land-rovers and Toyotas, manned by Gorane, led the dawn attack, guns blazing, at a hundred kilometres an hour. But despite surprise, speed and a fortunate sandstorm, a battery of Goukuni's anti-tank guns opened up, and Toyota after Toyota exploded. *Poisson's* armoured car squadron finally took the battery in the rear, and the Gorane massacred the surviving gunners.

It was now mid-morning; and there was an even harder nut to crack, the aerodrome defended by a fortified blockhouse and by dug-in Soviet T54 and T55 tanks. Hissein Habré called on the mercenaries; and this was where the enormous value of the Milan anti-tank missiles proved decisive. No such weapon had ever been used, had ever appeared, on Chad's battlefields before. A mercenary named René fired the first Milan. It rose slowly, arched into the sky, and guided by his remote-control screen slowly descended on the blockhouse. The blockhouse disintegrated. An awed silence thereupon descended on both sides of the battlefield. A second missile was fired, its target a T55. When the tank exploded and burst into flames, the defenders' morale was, understandably, totally shattered. By early afternoon Faya-Largeau, with 1000 prisoners (and a Twin Otter, captured on the aerodrome which Hoffman, who had been with Denard in the Comores, immediately flew back to the capital) was in Hissein Habré's hands. *Saxo* and Deluc had played a crucial part in this amazing success – thanks to their expertise and thanks of course to the amazing weapons which (without the backing of the French State) a Denard could not possibly have afforded.

But the victors hardly had time to relax before at dusk two Libyan MIGs appeared over Faya and strafed and rocketed their positions. On the Sunday, the Monday, the Tuesday, the Wednesday air attacks continued; and Sukhoi bombers joined in. The Libyans had complete control of the air; the SAM 7 missiles were only useful against low-flying single aircraft, became confused by formations, and only managed on the Wednesday to shoot down one bomber. Morning and evening the strafing and rocketing continued, with the horror of phosphorus bombs added, and no defence possible. By the Thursday Goukuni's men, reinforced by the Islamic Legion and by Libyan tanks and artillery - which opened up once within range - had almost surrounded the oasis-fortress. That evening Hissein Habré flew out. From Paris the Ministry of Defence let Hissein Habré know that no special effort should be made to evacuate *Saxo*. Traditionally mercenaries are expendable; and it was only thanks to the greater loyalty of Idriss Deby, Hissein Habré's field commander (and eventual overthrower and successor) that a camouflaged Transail landed and picked them up.

That was on Saturday 6 August. On the Sunday Faya-Largeau fell. But not before, in a final and pretty heroic act, on Hissein Habré's express request Le Blond and four other mercenaries had flown back in to Faya-Largeau aboard the Twin Otter with a load of Milan missiles to cover an attempted break-out and retreat to the east. For Libyan troops were being landed by helicopter and parachute to the north and west of the oasis, ready for a final assault.

There was no news till the Friday following. Then news came that a column of Gorane had, thanks to the four mercenaries and their Milan missiles, broken through the surrounding cordon of enemy tanks and, despite two days of aerial pursuit, of heavy losses and strafing, finally escaped. On that same day René Dulac *Le Grand* was summoned to the French Embassy in Ndjamena. There he was informed that the situation had radically changed. *Saxo's* mission was over, terminated. France had decided, totally at odds with Mitterand's original policy of a hands-off policy in Africa, to draw almost literally a line in the sand. That very day 400 troops of the 1^e RPIMA debarked at Ndjamena – the forerunners of Operation Manta, the arrival as a permanent deterrent force of no less than 3000 men of the French armed forces. Colonel Gaddafy was warned that the *Ligne Rouge* – the Red Line – was the 15th Parallel: almost exactly the borderline between 'military Chad' and 'useful Chad'. The whole operation – later rechristened Operation Epervier – was on a totally different scale to the surreptitious use of 33 French mercenaries. They were paid off, and dribbled back to France. Their 'careers' were over. And so was that of René Dulac *Le Grand*. It was more bad luck than bad management. But he did not have the persistence nor inspire the loyalty of a Bob Denard. It had all been a flash in the mercenary pan, though a rather memorable, indeed in many ways an epic, one.

VIII

A President Dies

'I hate the traffic jams of Paris but I adore the scent of the ylang-ylang'
Bob Denard

In the Comores, that perfumed archipelago, life for the mercenaries was by way of contrast neither adventurous nor heroic. It was not always idyllic, either, in the years that followed. There was the occasional squall or storm, but they were usually of the teacup dimension. Prince Kemal Said, for instance, had been fobbed off with the post of Ambassador to France; but resigned to plan, of all things, an Australian-based mercenary counter-attack that would replace Denard's mercenaries with his own and, of course, President Abdallah with himself. This first attempt ended in an ignominious failure. On 13 November 1983 John Pilgrim, of Southend-on-Sea in Essex, and two others were charged in Perth in Australia with offences under the War Crimes (Foreign Incursions and Recruitment) Act. Years later, with due solemnity Prince Kemal was to tell the delectable Samantha Weinberg that Southend-on-Sea was the undoubted centre of all mercenary activity in England.

President Abdallah of course remained President (and the Prince a plotter in exile). A year later, in September 1984, Abdallah was re-elected with an interesting 99.4% of the votes cast. The following spring there was a more serious and much more ominous an attempt. Sergeant Anouar – 'small but very strong' as he described himself – had been Patrick Ollivier's right-hand-man in forming and training a special group of Senior NCOs after Ollivier's Pioneer Company had been dissolved. It was Ollivier's last gift to the Presidential Guard – and it turned out to be a pretty poisoned one. Almost inevitably the new senior NCOs clashed with their white officers. Almost inevitably they decided to replace them. The whites – the *mzungu* – were to be attacked and wiped out at their weekly regimental dinner at the Kandani officers' mess on Friday 8 March. But there was an informer among the conspirators. Marques, who more and more was becoming Denard's right-hand-man on the Grande Comore, carried out the arrests; and though Sergeant Anouar escaped and for three months became the Robin Hood (or, as he preferred to call it, the Rambo) of the archipelago, twenty-five of the Presidential Guard – including Rambo – ended up in Itsundzu in the hills, now transformed into a military jail. As the Presidential Guard was never more than 500 strong, and more usually 3-400, this was a high proportion of its members, one that left mistrust in its wake. On the other hand minor mutinies, usually far more brutally suppressed, are almost normal from time to time in all new or new-ish African armies, one of the hazards of the profession. And the more significant thing was the efficient reaction: Captain Marques obviously had 'the situation' well under control.

As was proved eighteen months later when an attempt was made to rescue the Prisoners of Itsundzu. Marques, by now Commandant Marques, commanding the guard – for Commandant Charles had long been planning to return to Liege and had finally left, despite Denard's pleas, the year before - was informed of this rescue attempt well in advance. He set an ambush on the road to the interior, and in the night three (or, according to some reports seven) of the would-be rescuers were killed. There were rumours, unsubstantiated stories, of delayed deaths and tortures. They may have been true. Marques appears to have been a ruthless and brutal man.

As he showed himself to be in the Veillard affair. Max Veillard, a former lieuten-ant trained at St Cyr, a cut therefore above the usual style of mercenary recruit – 'small, polite, intelligent, extremely brave' but with 'a definite Machiavellian streak' - joined the Presidential Guard, under the alias of 'Servadac', in 1985. Though an admirer of Denard's he apparently came to feel, and to say, that Denard had the mentality of an under-officer, not a real officer. Unlike, of course, himself. He stayed only two years, resigning in 1987. But fifteen days after he had resigned he was – to the surprise of his former comrades – back in the Comores for, he claimed, a scuba-diving holiday. In fact he was back to lay the foundations for a mercenary *coup* of his own that would oust the current set of mercenaries (and, presumably, President Abdallah) and replace them with a new set, commanded of course by a proper officer – in the event himself.

The plan was to mimic Denard's invasion of almost ten years previously, with a landing of armed men on Itsandra Beach; but to reinforce it by combining this with a second simultaneous invasion by air – a transport plane landing at the airport and pouring out a stream of heavily-armed jeeps. This could (if it was not all fantasy, which it might have been) have been successful – provided of course that it had the unofficial backing of the French government. It could have been a repeat, in a different key, of the René Dulac challenge, and much more dangerous for Denard.

It needed however co-operation on the spot; and that was why Veillard had returned to Moroni. 'Servadac' enrolled – tried to enrol – the three members of the Presidential Guard whom no doubt he knew best and trusted most: two

fellow mercenaries and a sergeant. Apparently there was an indiscreet conversation, a leak. A report was made to Commandant Marques. 'Servadac' had always
detested Marques; and the feeling was mutual. Marques had Veillard picked up,
confronted him and then ordered his immediate execution - he was to be taken
out to sea, shot, and his body dumped in the Indian Ocean - when Bob Denard,
informed of what was about to happen, hurried up to Kandani and immediately
put a stop to it. 'Servadac' was merely held and expelled.

It would be fascinating to know more about this murky affair; but for reasons
which will become obvious later it is unlikely one ever will. What seems sure is
first that it was not just an idle fantasy, as the sequel will indicate; and secondly that
it was not yet another attempt by Prince Kemal. This time the man who would
be President was Mohammed Taki - once a friend and supporter of Abdallah (at
whose village of M'beni indeed Ali Soilih's young thugs had first spilt blood) but
who had since fallen out with him and was now, like so many Comorians, living
in exile in Marseilles.

Was President Abdallah a fixture? He himself obviously thought so. Like so
many long-established African rulers, as he grew older and greedier, he considered himself - and himself alone - indispensable. The Constitution forbade any
President of the Comores from seeking a third term of office. Abdallah proposed
a referendum to change the Constitution. The archipelago was full of secret
mutterings, of discontent at the blatant corruption, of intrigue. The head of the
Forces Armées Comoriennes, the FAC, the little 'native' army, Commandant Ahmed
Mohammed, was involved in a smuggling scandal and offered to resign. Mitterand
had been elected Presidnet of France for a second seven-year term. And South
Africa, the new South Africa, had in principle decided to withdraw its vital funding for the Presidential Guard.

So when Paul Barril appeared on the scene, a general subterranean panic about
the future began to spread, particularly among the mercenaries. Paul Barril was a
smooth suave type, what the French call *mediatique*. He had helped Commandant
Prouteau, of *Rainbow Warrior* fame, found the GIGN, a special unit of the *gendarmerie,* a cross between Britain's SAS and a close protection squad for President
Mitterand. After the *affaire* of *les Irlandais de Vincennes* – yet another murky politico-military French double-crossing set-up – he had been forced to resign. But
no-one really believed him when he approached President Abdallah and offered
his services to reorganize the Presidential Guard as a purely private individual
now running his own security firm, *Groupe Barril Securité*. Everyone was sure,
particularly Bob Denard, that Barril had the backing of the French State and of
President Mitterand. Wily old Abdallah was not quite so sure what to make of it
all. He attempted to keep all options open, to play off South Africa against France,
Barril against Denard, to temporize as he had almost always done. On the one
hand he trusted Denard, his old, loyal, companion-in-arms, and enjoyed their
evening sessions together under the mango tree. On the other hand, if South

Africa was really going to stop paying for his, for Denard's, Presidential Guard, was France offering to take over? On condition obviously, that France's unofficial emissary Paul Barril and his *Groupe* replace Denard and his men? From December 1988 onwards there were secret and not-so-secret meetings in Paris, swarms of them. Barril met Abdallah at 5 Rue Alphand. Neil Van Heerden of the South African Ministry of Foreign Affairs lunched with Jean-Christophe Mitterand at Avenue Pierre I de Serbie. And so on and so forth. It was agreed – almost agreed – that Bob Denard should be gently edged off the chequer board; and a deadline was fixed – almost fixed : 15 December 1989. For of course it was by no means certain that, gently or not, Denard would agree to be edged out.

THE NIGHT OF SUNDAY 26 NOVEMBER 1989

A vast mystery still surrounds the events of that fatal night. What exactly happened, when, where and why? I will try to describe as best as I can the sequence of events.

President Abdallah had sent to Paris two important emissaries. He was playing his cards close to his chest but everyone knew they were going and everyone knew of their importance. Their names were Said Kafé and Dr M'tara Maecha. They had delivered, by hand, a letter from President Abdallah to President Mitterand. They returned from Paris on Thursday - Thursday 23 November – and reported to the Presidential Palace, to Abdallah. That same evening Denard had a long meeting with Marques. It went on till 1 a.m. – and Denard usually went to bed at 10 p.m.

Next day, the Friday, Abdallah flew to Anjouan. He had a long talk at his house in Domoni with Commandant Ahmed Mohammed. He talked him into – it may not have been all that difficult – withdrawing his resignation as commander of the FAC.

Saturday was a quiet day. Abdallah stayed with his family at Domoni. He was there for Sunday lunch too. After lunch he and his son Salim, who ran the business empire of *Abdallah et Fils* from a vast base conveniently close to the Presidential Palace, flew back to the Grande Comore. In the early afternoon the President, escorted by lieutenants Favier and Frederick of the Presidential Guard, went for a drive around the countryside.

At 7 o'clock Salim and his father dined together at the Palace. Just after 9 p.m. Salim left. The guard on duty at the gate, Sergeant-Chef Jaffar, a relative of the President's, explained to Salim that the gate should not be locked. For his father was expecting a visitor – a woman in a red car. Salim had no worries about that. He knew very well who this would be – a Frenchwoman, Monique Terrasse, a maths teacher at the Lycée. She was thirty-eight, thought to be President Abdallah's mistress. It seems an odd time to receive a mistress. She drove in just after 9 p.m. and drove out just after 10 p.m. She had no family of her own. She was 'very proper, very correct' – and also 'very neurotic'. Neither she nor Abdallah realized, of course, that this was to be the last time they were to meet. Or did she? Perhaps she did.

Meanwhile, while Monique Terrasse was with Abdallah, there was great activity among the Presidential Guard. At Kandani second-lieutenants Etienne and Thierry woke Adjudant Ali with orders to report at once to the camp commandant, Lieutenant Fouquet. Fouquet dispatched him and his men into the hills to Itsundzu for 'night manoeuvres'. At about the same time Sergeant-Chef Jaffar phoned Kandani down below from the Police gatehouse to find out why the Close Security Unit hadn't reported for duty, as was normal. He was told they had been sent out on manoeuvres at mid-day the previous day. At about the same time a group of the Presidential Guard who had been on leave reported back – presumably to Kandani barracks. They were told by Captain Jean-Pierre to replace the Close Security Unit.

Meanwhile the mass of the Presidential Guard had assembled for these famous 'night manoeuvres' at Itsundzu Camp. There Captain Hoffman split them into six separate groups, each motorized, and ordered them all to head south, through Moroni, and reassemble at the premises of a company called Socomeia.

It was by now, roughly, ten o'clock at night, and Monique Terrasse was about to drive away from the Palace. The next hour and a half passed, it seems, without incident – except of course that the Presidential Guard moved *en masse* from Itsundzu camp through the sleepy streets of the little capital to their assembly point. There they were given new orders, which they must have been half expecting. The 'night manoeuvres' were a cover. They were to disarm, immediately, the only other armed force on the archipelago, the FAC.

At almost exactly the same time – a quarter of an hour short of midnight – Sergeant Hassan of the Presidential Guard, on duty at the Palace gatehouse, was woken up – he had been dozing off – by rifle shots, what seemed to be an exchange of fire, somewhere to the north of the palace. He saw, first, Sergeant-Chef Jaffar running half-dressed to his room. Five minutes later Commandant Marques arrived, with Captain Siam and their driver, Lieutenant Joel. They parked. "What's happening?" yelled Marques. "Who is bodyguard of the day?" "It's Sergeant-Chef Jaffar. He's gone to change into military uniform." Marques and Siam ran into the Palace; and Sergeant Hassan saw Jaffar, now in uniform, armed with an AK47, charge up to the first floor where the President lived and worked. Five minutes later Denard arrived, driven by Lieutenant Tony. He parked in the same place, hurried into the Palace. It was now midnight. The sporadic fusillades which some of the guards at the gate had responded to, firing wildly into the night, briefly continued.

For exactly what happened next we have only Denard's version of events. Denard had been alerted, like Marques, by a telephone call from the duty officer (but who was the 'duty officer'?) informing him that there was shooting at the Palace. On arrival he found President Abdallah in the entrance hall, in his pyjamas, with Marques and Siam. There was understandable confusion. Was it a night manoeuvre? Abdallah asked. No, he was told, the Palace was under attack by members of the FAC. He was bustled back up to the first floor, to his study and presented with a written order authorizing the Guard to disarm the FAC. It only needed his, the President's, signature.

A brief discussion followed. Was there a heated argument? Was there table-thumping and references to Paul Barril? Very possibly. The shooting had died away, but the discussion was interrupted by a telephone call. Captain Siam took it. 'Siam' – real name Jean-Paul Guerrier – was a comparatively recent recruit to the guard, immediately put in charge of intelligence. The phone call, Siam told the President, was from a woman. Tell her I'll call back, said Abdallah. At ten minutes past midnight he signed the order; and Sergeant-Chef Jaffar, who had been given a roasting by Marques for being half-dressed when he should have been alert and on duty, was sent out with the signed document to photocopy it.

Then - if Denard is to be believed - everyone relaxed, moved from the President's study to the ante-chamber next door, where Denard and Abdallah sat down side by side on a pair of armchairs and chatted amicably for the next few minutes. Relaxed, that is, until at about twenty past midnight firing broke out again, apparently from a different side of the Palace, more intense, closer and of course with the guards on the *qui vive*, responding much more rapidly and violently.

The windows shook. There was automatic fire, bazookas. Abdallah was terrified. He moaned, groaned, started babbling, possibly praying, in Anjouanese. Denard knelt down in front of him, took Abdallah's hands in his own and attempted to calm him. At that moment Jaffar burst back into the room, eyes ablaze, gun in hand. He saw Denard crouching over the President, possibly attacking him. Denard stood up, Jaffar raised his gun. Denard reacted instinctively. He hurled himself flat on the floor as Jaffar opened fire. Siam, behind Jaffar, reacted almost as quickly but just too late. Jaffar's burst tore into the sitting President's chest moments before he himself was shot down by Siam. It was all over in a matter of seconds. Seconds before five men had been alive. Seconds later there were three white mercenaries alive, and two Comoriens stone dead.

Thus – or, at least, there – ended Abdallah, founding father of the Comorian Republic, its first and third President, in his turn shot to death in the presence of the man who had possibly aided him to have the previous President, the second President, the wretched Ali Soilih, shot to death. Twice therefore Bob Denard had been in at the kill. He had helped Ali Soilih to depose Abdallah. He had helped Abdallah to depose Ali Soilih. Now both Presidents had died, violently. Whereas the mercenary leader was still alive. Was it his *baraka,* his lucky star? It was certainly an extraordinary, almost an unheard-of, chain of historical events .

Monday 27 November – the Early Hours

Meanwhile, on the outside of the palace, the shooting had again died away, as the 2nd Company of the Presidential Guard drove up in full force, like the American Cavalry riding to the rescue. But it rather seems as if most of the fire had been between the gendarmerie, on the outer perimeter, and the gatehouse guards at the Palace. In other words everyone had, in the dark and the confusion, been shooting at each other – leaving, in the end, one member of the Guard wounded and, some say (but it is by no means clear), two Comorien gendarmes dead. But the story was quickly concocted that the FAC, knowing they were about to be disarmed, had launched a pre-emptive strike on the Presidential Palace. We can tell how quickly decisions had been made because, less than half an hour after the President's death Captain Siam was setting out to raid Commandant Ahmed Mohammed's house in Moroni. The plan was to pin the blame on him. But his house was empty. They realized he was on Anjouan. And by 2 a.m. sixty soldiers of the Presidential Guard were at the airport, having commandeered a plane and a pilot, and were planning to fly across to Anjouan. However there were mechanical problems, and they landed not half an hour but two and a half hours later. There they split into six groups: two went to the Commandant's house at Mutsamudu. He was not there either. But the other four went to the military camp at Patsy and there they found him. Jean-Pierre was leading these forty men. They bluffed their way into the camp, and attacked the Commandant's house. They shot two rockets into his bedroom, others onto the roof, then opened fire with Kalashnikovs. Or such at least was Commandant Ahmed Mohammed's later story. For, *mirabile dictu,* he survived. Though wounded in eighteen places, he crawled out of the wreckage of the house, then walked to the military camp 200 yards away – where he found his men disarmed and cowering on the floor; and Jean-Pierre.

A most bizarre conversation occurred, and was to continue with Marques when later in the morning the Commandant was flown over under guard to the Grande Comore. The mercenaries almost apologized, told the Commandant they had been ordered to arrest him, and when he didn't answer their knocking on his door, felt obliged to take 'preventative measures' in case he tried to stop them disarming 'his' FAC. It was only back at Kandani that the Commandant learnt that President Abdallah was dead. Marques offered to shake his hand, Ahmed Mohammed proudly refused. But his main display of indignation seems to have been, both then and later, not over the ruin of 'his' house, or the disarming of 'his' men or the death of 'his' president but over the loss of a thousand of 'his' chickens. Even more bizarrely Marques then told him he was free to leave, to go home. Which he did.

★   ★   ★

Meanwhile Bob Denard and Bob Denard alone had stayed on at the Palace. He telephoned the members of the government, and important figures in the administration. This was towards 1 a.m. He summoned them to the Palace. By now telephone lines were buzzing all over Moroni, awash with rumour and counter-rumour. Colonel Abdou Rezac, head of the gendarmerie, arrived at about 2 a.m. to find – another extraordinary scene – members of the government sitting around in silence in a solemn semi-circle, Denard among them. It was half an hour before Ahmed Abdou, Abdallah's right-hand-man, asked how the President was. Denard shrugged his shoulders. How was the President's morale? 'Very low.' Denard went on to explain that there had been an attack on the Presidential Palace, that Sergeant-Chef Jaffar had burst in, that Denard had thrown himself on the ground as Jaffar opened fire, that the Captain had shot Jaffar and Jaffar was dead.

"And the President?"

"Dead also."

At this point pandemonium broke out. Possibly this is the roundabout way in which bad news is traditionally announced in the Comores. But no-one asked to see the body; and the head of the gendarmerie took no steps at all to institute an inquiry. In the hours before dawn they turned to the Constitution. This stated that in the event of the President's death or incapacity elections should be held within 40 days, and in the interim the President of the Supreme Court should take over. This was another ancient, by name Said Djohar. Colonel Abdou Rezac was sent to fetch him; and a communiqué was devised for Said Djohar to read for Radio Comores, also summoned to the Palace to record the message. Said Djohar arrived, did as he was told, possibly swore himself in (who else could have done?) as an interim President; and then everyone seems to have dispersed – possibly reassured that there was not about to be a general massacre, as they had probably feared.

Everyone except Denard. At 4 a.m. he called Salim, Abdallah's son, told him of his father's death, summoned him to the Palace, and there gave him his, Denard's, version of what had happened. There was of course the question of the bodies and the burials. In fact both the bodies were flown to Anjouan within hours, where very cursory autopsies were to be performed on them by a young French doctor at the hospital at Domoni; and the burial took place next day in the presence of the entire government. Abdallah's body at Domoni is now encased in a marble tomb; over the marble tomb rises an immense mausoleum. Four tall gold-leafed minarets stand as supporters to the vast gold central dome. His sons have done their father proud. It is an extraordinary contrast to Ali Soilih's humble grave.

But what is fascinating is that just after 4 a.m., just after Salim had left for the palace, Salim's wife claims to have received a panicky phone-call from Monique Terrasse. She, Monique, had to speak to Salim urgently. But of course Salim was not there.

In the morning, sometime that Monday morning, Monique Terrasse was found dead in her apartment at Moroni. She had apparently committed suicide – the third somewhat mysterious death that day. Though she was a French citizen, there does not seem to have been an autopsy, an inquest, not even an inquiry. She apparently left a will asking to be buried on the Comores. Was she buried there? If so, where – and by whom? Of course she was known to be neurotic. One assumes she was the woman who phoned Abdallah at midnight – if indeed such a phone call ever took place. She may indeed, on learning of the President's death, have taken an overdose of sleeping pills and alcohol. But inevitably rumours began to circulate: that she too, an inconvenient witness, had been killed at the Palace.

At 8.30 a.m. the official communiqué was broadcast over Radio Comores. It was laconic.

> 'The Presidency was attacked last night by unknown elements. The Presidential Guard, who assure the President's protection, riposted. There was an exchange of shots and the President was mortally wounded.'

The streets were at first deserted. The Presidential Guard patrolled. Telephone lines to the outside world were cut. The first stories to circulate blamed the murder on Commandant Ahmed Mohammed. But within hours it became known that the Commandant had been on Anjouan the previous night. By dusk groups were circulating in the streets, muttering "Denard *Assassin!*"

A Farewell to Arms

What really happened that Sunday night? Only three men know; and of those three two, Marques and Siam, have never, ever made the slightest comment or given the slightest explanation. And the third, Bob Denard, has always stuck to his story. And, as he has always added, what possible motive would he have had to murder the President? The general consensus of almost everybody who knew him, Comorien and French alike, was that the cries of "Denard *Assassin!*" were baseless. Denard did not fire the bullets that killed President Abdallah, Denard did not want the President dead, Denard was horrified at what had happened.

But Marques? Marques, almost alone of those on the *Antinea,* had stayed on and on and on. It is said that he once spent over three years without ever leaving the archipelago. He had risen, by persistence and staying-power, from junior officer to Commandant of the Guard. His whole career, his whole life, was bound up in the Comores. He was by reputation impulsive and brutal. A scenario that almost everyone who has closely studied the events of that improbable night seems to agree on is that Abdallah announced that he would have to dissolve, to put an end to, the Presidential Guard. An argument followed, voices raised, threats, guns drawn, guns waved. Marques shot the President. Jaffar burst in, Siam knifed him. Denard always at his best when things had gone very wrong, imposed a Trappist silence on the other two; and, after a brief but failed attempt to blame it all on Commandant Ahmed Mohammed, came up, to Salim that very same night, with what was at least a possible explanation of events; and thereafter never wavered. Why did he do it? Because he saw it as a matter of honour to protect his men, particularly followers such as Marques who had always been loyal to him. Such, at any rate, is one possible version of events.

★　　　　　　　★　　　　　　　★

It was not however till Tuesday, 12 December, that is to say over a fortnight later, that Bob Denard was to hold a press conference and make his version of events publicly known. Before that, though journalists and television reporters had been swarming into the Comores, he had made only a brief statement, refused to elaborate, refused to answer questions. He held the press conference at Kandani barracks, flanked by officers of the Guard in full uniform. '*J'en ai marre de faire figure d'assassin*' – 'I have had enough of being taken for a murderer,' – he said, with genuine indignation. By then however things had moved dramatically on.

At first it had seemed as if things might blow over. The interim President, Said Djohar, declared forty days of official mourning. The islands virtually closed down, impertinent journalists, arriving without visas, were expelled. There were no riots, no mass demonstrations, a few graffiti, a few murmurs. But then, a week after the President's death, there was an ominous occurrence. Denard had asked his wife's relative, the Qadi, to organize a *Hitima*, a cleansing ceremony, at the great Friday Mosque on Moroni's waterfront. He arrived with on his head a *koffia* embroidered with the words 'In the name of Allah the merciful.' He took his shoes off, and entered the Mosque. But onlookers were hostile to what some openly called a 'masquerade', the mosque was empty, the Grand Mufti appeared only to say that the *Hitima* would not take place; and it became apparent that Denard had for once totally miscalculated. His name had not been cleared. Instead, he had been publicly humiliated.

Demonstrations did follow then; and appeals for calm. But, much more importantly, South Africa's Minister for Foreign Affairs, Pik Botha, declared publicly that "in the light of the recent tragic events" all assistance to the Presidential Guard would be immediately suspended: and went on to demand, in the name of his government the "immediate departure of all expatriate elements". And France was preparing an armada. France's Minister of Defence, Jean-Pierre Chevenement, ordered up the flagship of France's Indian Ocean fleet, *La Marne*, the frigate *Protet,* the rapid patrol boat, *La Boudeuse*, and the landing craft, *La Grandiere* with on board the Commando de Marine Jaubert. In addition 150 legionaries of the 2ᵉ REP were placed on stand-by at Mayotte, and a battalion of paratroops, the 1ᵉ RPIMA with a squadron of Puma helicopters and seven Transail cargo transports ready on Réunion.

Was this just President Mitterand's righteous indignation at the death of an old colleague from his senate days? Or was there something much more personal involved? Readers will remember the oddness of Monique Terrasse's death, and the subsequent obscurity that enfolded her end. As a young man François Mitterand had fallen desperately in love with a beautiful young Frenchwoman. They had become formally engaged on 3 March 1940, in the days of the phoney war. Off to the real war, captured in the *débâcle,* a prisoner of the Germans escaping on his third attempt, Mitterand had returned to France to learn that his fiancée had fallen for a Polish officer. Subsequently of course he married the almost equally beautiful, and much more Socialist, Danielle. But, though heartbroken by his original fiancée's decision to break off their engagement he still romantically sent her a red rose on March 3, the anniversary of their engagement, every year.

Her name was Marie-Louise Terrasse. I have no notion whether she was related in any way to Monique Terrasse. I write these words on almost exactly the tenth anniversary of President Mitterand's death; so it is impossible to ask him if sentiment played any part in his decision – and, of course, even if he were alive, and it had, he would hardly have been inclined to admit it. But Terrasse is not a common name in France.

★   ★   ★

At any rate, faced with an almost Chad-style display of France's military might, all Bob Denard could do was negotiate. Two days after his press conference he held a parade of the Presidential Guard at Kandani. Under the rain three hundred members of the Guard presented arms; and various Comorian NCOs were promoted to the rank of officer – including one big burly jovial sergeant, who now became Captain Ayouba Combo. Denard, in a safari suit, stood at the end of the line. The press had been invited; and, the ceremony over, he stated his conditions for an orderly transfer of power.

These included an official parade with flags flying, bands playing, a farewell address to his men, and an official salute from the French military. He was prepared to leave, he said; but "if we depart we must go with our heads held high". It was an astute move to put these demands in public to the press and via the press to the French people in particular. There was a certain mediaeval panache that was bound to appeal to all those folk memories of surrenders of castles or fortified towns, where the garrison was granted the honours of war, marching out under their own officers, colours flying, drums and bugles playing, weapons not surrendered. And on this occasion it would not be at the end of a siege, with fratricidal bloodshed, but before, aborting a siege, with no blood shed whatsoever.

That afternoon, Thursday December 14, half a dozen mercenaries and their families flew out to France via Nairobi. So did Amina, Denard's wife, and their two daughters. The next day, the Friday, as the French armada appeared over the horizon, the Presidential Guard again paraded, this time at 9 a.m. at the airport. Denard, again in his safari suit, stood a little to one side. Five Puma helicopters landed, and red-bereted paras of the 1ᵉ RPIMA debouched, guns at the ready. The Guard presented arms. But there was no farewell address, no bands playing. The French military attaché refused to shake Denard's proffered hand. A few brief words were exchanged between those commanding the new arrivals and the white officers of the Guard. Then the mercenaries marched off, the men of the RPIMA took over, and the Guard was dismissed.

Three hours later, at mid day, Denard was back at the airport, with the remaining mercenaries now dressed less smartly in camouflage uniforms but still carrying their personal weapons. There had of course been negotiations behind the scenes. Denard had obtained an amnesty for himself and his men, with the promise of no charges being brought against those against whom no charges were already outstanding in France (which amnesty did not of course include himself, the Benin charges were still outstanding and had recently had new life injected into them by the French authorities). He had also obtained six months' severance pay for his officers, and a guarantee that all Comorian members of the Presidential Guard would be absorbed into the new combined force – to be set up under French supervision – that would be formed from the gendarmerie, Commandant Ahmed Mohammed's FAC, and Commandant Marques' Presidential Guard. He had also obtained a Hercules C.130 laid on by South Africa – into which he and his men now loaded twenty-eight metal trunks of archives plus a case of champagne, and then themselves – to fly them to Pretoria; plus temporary residence rights in the Republic for himself. He had also obtained compensation, for himself and at least some of his fellow mercenaries, for the loss of their 'moral and material investments' in the Comores. This was believed to be as much as thirty million francs, put up a little by France, mainly by South Africa. So despite the dejecting and distinctly unchivalrous scene at the airport, Denard could congratulate himself on having avoided bloodshed and negotiated pretty good terms for his and his men's withdrawal.

Nevertheless it was the end of a dream; a farewell to arms, a farewell to Paradise. "How do you feel?" he was asked as he boarded the Hercules. "How do you think I feel?" he snapped. "Like dancing? Now get out. I want to sleep a little."

DENARD IN EXILE, SAID DJOHAR IN POWER, 'SERVADAC' DEAD

And in effect for roughly three years Denard hibernated. He and his armed men flew into Jan Smuts airport at Johannesburg on the very day, 15 December 1989 – attentive readers will have noticed – that had previously in Paris been agreed on as the date by which he was to have been edged out of the Comores. His men flew back to France on the 17; he stayed on. His temporary residence permit was renewed. He bought an old red Renault. He leased a long low honey-coloured house on the outskirts of Pretoria, very similar to his house on the hills above Moroni. And there he lived quietly and inoffensively, taking time out, time off, as he had so often done before in his mercenary career when things had turned sour.

But the Comores did not hibernate. France did not hibernate. And above all Said Djohar did not hibernate. The interim President, the inconspicuous judge who had been expected to step down quietly after his forty days of temporary impor-tance, acquired, like so many old men, a taste for power. The Presidential elections to replace the late Abdallah were held in two rounds in March 1990. In the first round Mohammed Taki, the obvious candidate, came ahead as expected of all the rival contenders. But in the second round, when all but the final two contenders had been eliminated, Said Djohar was elected by 55.02% to Mohammed Taki's 44.98%. Mohammed Taki and his supporters were not pleased.

Said Djohar was generally considered a foolish greedy old man. Indeed one of his former legal colleagues tried to have him thrown out on the grounds of mental incapability – that he was just not up to being President. But it was the former colleague, Ali Salim, who ended up relieved of his position and in jail. Said Djohar was not such a cretin as he apparently seemed. Astutely enough, he rallied support from all sides – except of course from the aggrieved Mohammed Taki. He appointed Dr M'tare Maecha, Abdallah's famous envoy to Paris, his Foreign Minister. He appointed Commandant Ahmed Mohammed, once recovered from his wounds, Governor of Anjouan. He appointed Prince Kemal's brother, Prince Nasruddin, his chef-de-cabinet. And he devoted flattering attentions to the late President's family. Indeed only a fortnight after Said Djohar's election the Abdallah family instigated a private lawsuit in Paris, under the French system whereby information was laid against X, for *homicide volontaire et vol aggravé* – deliberate homicide and meditated theft. The homicide of course was of their father and brother, President Abdallah, the theft was of the Presidential and military archives contained in those twenty-eight metal cases that had been whisked off to South Africa, and the X was the triple-headed hydra of Denard, Marques and Siam.

In Moroni and M'Beni Mohammed Taki's supporters rioted. They were severely repressed by the new red-beretted Comorian Defence Force, amalgamated from all the rest and virtually at the orders of the French Embassy, in particular of the military attaché. The red berets opened fire. No-one was killed but there were many wounded; and when President Mitterand paid his long-awaited visit to the Grand Comore in June, the island was clearly tense and Mitterand gave only a partial, conditional blessing to the new régime. He did not go over to Anjouan to incline over President Abdallah's tomb. And Monique Terrasse's? Who can now be sure? But one thing was sure: that France, reluctantly perhaps, at one remove certainly, was in control of the Comores, and above all of the purse-strings. Aid from now on would be conditional.

So, on the face of it, it seems extraordinary that there was another attempted mercenary *coup* that August, only weeks after President Mitterand's visit. The plan was to overthrow Djohar and put Mohammed Taki in what many thought was his rightful, elected place; so the mercenaries could count on a great deal of local support. Perhaps it was not therefore as rash as it seems. But it was nothing to do with Denard, or Marques, or Siam. It was devised and organized and put into practise by Max Veillard, 'Servadac'. I wish I knew more about it. Apparently Veillard thought he could do with four white mercenaries what Denard had done with forty. He knew the islands well, he was a former officer, he considered himself to be of a different class to Denard and the detested Marques, both more intelligent and more capable than they. He was younger too, at thirty-eight in his military prime. But it all went wrong, totally wrong. "He was extremely brave but completely mad," said a Parisian who had known him well; though he said it only *after* the event. What happened to the other three mercenaries I do not know. But Veillard fled from the Grande Comore to Anjouan; and there, on 19 August he was shot dead by the red berets on the beach.

Inevitably, as 'Servadac' had been an officer in the Presidential Guard, there were repercussions. Not in South Africa; Denard must have persuaded the authorities that whatever the press might suggest he was totally innocent of any involvement. But in France it was a good enough pretext for the authorities to forget all about their promises of immunity made when the mercenaries had left peacefully; and to arrest, on 14 September and 26 September respectively, Siam and Marques, in connection with the *plainte,* the impending lawsuit, against X. Later they were to be released on bail – quite a considerable time later. As regards Denard, he was of course outside French jurisdiction. But it cannot have been a happy time for him; and particularly not when, almost exactly a year later, on 16 October 1991 he was condemned in his absence to 5 years' imprisonment in connection with the Benin affair by the 14^e *Chambre Correctionnelle* of the Tribunal of Paris. That 14^e *Chambre Correctionelle* and its investigating magistrate, the enchantingly-named *Juge d'instruction* Chantal Perdrix, were to be his bugbear. But not quite yet.

For in 1992, a year later on still, there was yet more trouble in the Comores. This time it was far more serious. As one Comorian businessman had answered, when asked what had been wrong with the late President Abdallah; "He was very corrupt. But I must say that I'd prefer him to Djohar any day. At least Abdallah brought projects and financing into the country. He was very corrupt but, humanly speaking, he was a good politician. Now Djohar is altogether different." And yet Djohar, corrupt, remote, apparently ineffective, managed to cling on to power as the archipelago sank closer and closer to economic ruin. So, on 26 September 1992, when the President was out of the country, on a visit to Paris, he was overthrown. He was overthrown by two of Abdallah's sons, the twins Cheik and Abdurrahman, both of whom had been trained at St Cyr; by Captain Ayouba Combo, whom Denard, before leaving, had promoted to the position of senior

officer in the Presidential Guard; and by Dr M'tara Maecha, his own Foreign
Minister. With a hundred rebel members of the Defence Force, led by Captain
Combo – one imagines these were ex-Presidential Guard members and that the
amalgamation with ex-FAC and ex-gendarmerie had not gone as smoothly as
it might have done but as amalgamations so rarely do – the radio station was
captured and a broadcast announcing the ousting of Said Djofar went out over
the air. But by 11 a.m. the Radio Station was back in the hands of the government, and a second broadcast announcing the reinstatement of the President and
the surrender of the rebels followed. All very confusing. But disastrous for the
Abdallah twins, for the genial Captain Combo, and for Dr Maecha and several
other of Abdallah's old cronies when there was an attempt, a fortnight later, to
rescue the imprisoned rebel soldiers from Kandani camp. This took place on
October 10. Guards were killed, weapons stolen. But again it all went wrong.[1]
Next week fifteen people were killed. All even more confusing. But President
Djohar – and this *must* have been with French support – remained in power; and,
perhaps understandably, he turned vindictive. The twin sons of Abdallah were
put on trial for their lives. In Pretoria Bob Denard gave interviews by telephone,
indignant, stamping with frustrated impatience, almost begging to be recalled.
But there was nothing he could do. He had been reduced to impotence.

In the Dock

A new breeze was blowing in South Africa. Nelson Mandela, the world's most
admired political prisoner, had been freed in February 1990. Four months later he
was *Madame la Présidente's* guest of honour in Paris. It would be four years yet before
the Mitterands in their turn were to attend Mandela's inauguration as President
– black President – of a black-dominated South Africa. But by '91, '92 it was pretty
obvious which way that wind, that hurricane of change, was veering.

At the beginning of 1993 Bob Denard decided that the 'new' South Africa now
shaping up was no place for him. On February 1 he flew, with a certain *amertume,*
back to *la douce* France. Officially at least he had not set foot on French soil for
twelve long years. He knew who was awaiting him at Charles de Gaulle airport:
his wife Amina, his daughters Hamza and Kaina, and his only other legitimate
child, his son by his first marriage, Philippe. But also his nemesis, Chantal Perdrix,
handcuffs almost literally at the ready. No sooner was he on the tarmac than
a welcoming party of gendarmes whisked him off to an airport cell before he
had even seen his family. He had of course been sentenced in his absence to five

---

[1] One imagines both the *coup* and the rescue attempt went wrong because the mass of the
Defence Force followed not the genial Captain Combo and the two sons of Abdallah but the
instructions of the French Embassy, their paymaster, and in particular of Colonel Leonard, the
French military attaché and the power behind the President's throne, otherwise the double
failure seems inexplicable. It was certainly not for love of Djohar.

years' imprisonment on the Benin charges. His lawyers immediately appealed; but when a date was set for the hearing, Chantal opposed bail on the utterly ridiculous grounds that Denard represented 'a threat to national and international peace'. She won. He lost. But at least he was transferred to a proper prison, Paris' best-known, *La Santé* just off Denfert-Rochereau. There he was to remain for almost six weeks before his trial began.

Nevertheless he had timed his return astutely enough. All France knew that parliamentary elections were approaching, and all France knew that the Socialist government was heading for an utterly crushing defeat at the hands of the Right. So when his trial finally opened at the Palais de Justice on March 10, with the first round of the elections less than a fortnight away, Denard had, so to speak, the political wind in his sails.

He was tried before the 14ᵉ *Chambre Correctionelle.* And for what? Basically for his part in the Cotonou *coup* over fifteen years earlier, on a charge of '*association des malfaiteurs*' – rather as if he had been part of a gang planning a bank raid. It was a pretty ridiculous charge. Denard's defence counsel, *Mâitre* Soulez-Larivière, made great and justifiable play with the legal difficulties of attempting to judge a *coup d'état* in a foreign country. Even the prosecution only asked for a suspended sentence. Only the lawyer representing the families of the three Benin soldiers killed in the *coup* attempt made a scorching denunciation of mercenaries as '*tout simplement malfaiteurs*' ('quite simply evil doers'). But that was more than countered by the letters and statements that poured in in support of Denard – from General Lacaze, who insisted that the government must have been well aware of the planned *coup*, from General Aussaresses whose morale-boosting three-page tribute made Denard feel, he later said, as if he were receiving the *Légion d'Honneur*; and, above all from Jacques Foccart himself. "I have never had any personal contact with Monsieur Denard," he wrote (hard to believe) "but I have always been kept informed of his activities. He is no mercenary but an honest man and a patriot."

Definitions please, Monsieur Foccart, one would have been tempted to say. The *Mâitre* had a field day with the case, describing the prosecution as '*acrobatie juridique*' and, even more elegantly, Denard himself as being 'a prosthetic limb of the State, an instrument for accomplishing that which States cannot openly do'. Or, in a more populist phrase, a '*Corsaire de la Republique*'.

Colonel Maurice Robert, now retired, took the stand in person. He described how he had first recruited Bob Denard for the *Service Afrique* of the SDECE; and went on to say that he was sure that his successor had been kept informed of the Benin operation. "I am a man of honour," added the Colonel. "What I have said with reference to the *Service* I have been authorized to say." After which solid testimony it would have been difficult to continue to say that Bob Denard was associated with evil doers, unless the judge were to conclude that a whole branch of the French State was itself an association of scoundrels.

The judge, the president of the tribunal, Jean-Claude Antonetti, had opened proceedings by announcing that it would be necessary to review the last thirty years of the history of Africa, and had proceeded to do so at great and solemn length. As *Maître* Soulez-Lariviere rather acidly pointed out, the ensuing session had been more like a university lecture than a criminal trial. For by what criteria was it to be decided whether a *coup d'état* was legitimate or illegitimate? Legitimate only if it succeeded? Illegitimate only if it failed? In any case ,the *Maître* pointed out, no such crime as that of preparing a *coup d'état* existed in French law. And the serious press was equally scathing: what exactly they wondered, was Denard being accused of?

The hearings ended. The judge took time - several days - to reflect. It was not till the morning of Monday 5 April that he delivered his verdict. It was in effect more political than legal.

> "It cannot be tolerated," he pontificated, "that a private person should place himself at the service of a foreign State in order to sow disorder in a different country. If the contrary were to be permitted, then every attempt to destabilize a State or a régime by mercenaries would be legitimate."

The more one considers this ruling, the more incoherent it appears to be. I, a Frenchman, cannot be hired by the Republic of Banalia to sow disorder in the Republic of Zangaro. *Soit.* However, by implication, it would be legitimate for me, a Frenchman, to be hired by France to sow disorder in the Republic of Zangaro; or by a dissident Zangaran to do exactly the same. Only the fact (if I have followed the wretched judge's reasoning correctly) that Bob Denard was paid by Gabon or Morocco, or both, to interfere in the affairs of Benin condemned him. Had he been paid by France or by a Benin citizen, he would have been blameless.

Perhaps Antonetti recognized the feebleness of his judgement. Perhaps he only laid down this principle as a sop to the prosecution, and , indirectly, the politicians behind the prosecution. For, though he proceeded to find Bob Denard guilty, and the sentence of five years' imprisonment was confirmed, it was in practice almost meaningless, a suspended sentence.

In other words Denard, though technically guilty, was in fact freed. He gave some moving television interviews, appearing to be a harmless ageing man who wanted only to retire to his native Gascony and live in pastoral peace, like Cincinnatus, with his family around him.

Or so it seemed.

THE LAST ROAR OF BOB DENARD

Time and again journalists, reporters, columnists, and political commentators have decisively announced that the era of mercenaries is over. It happened after the Congo. It happened after Angola. It happened after Benin, after the Seychelles, after the expulsion of Denard and his men from the Comores. Time and again all these fine minds have been proved wrong. So the heading above is tempting fate a little. Who is to say that Denard has roared his last till he is finally laid to eternal rest? Certainly when the burly bespectacled prisoner left *La Santé* on the afternoon of Monday 5 April and was tearfully embraced – tears in the eyes of all three – by his two beautiful daughters as he walked out of the gates after ten trying weeks in jail, a free man at last – for Chantal Perdrix had, no doubt with enormous reluctance, suspended the Comores charge against him on the Saturday – just in time to go down to Grayan and celebrate his sixty-fourth birthday with his sister Georgette, it would have seemed absurd, inconceivable almost, to imagine that he would ever set foot again on the Comores.

But he did.

IX

The Last Coup – Kaskari Versus Azalée

'Bob Denard, it is growing late in your life. It is time to settle down in your native Médoc, among your own people…..The beauty of your daughters will remind you of what you have once loved, on other continents, on other oceans, under more azure skies.'

Mâitre Jean-Marie Varaut

In the same month as Denard was given his suspended sentence and walked free, in the same month as a right-wing government took over the running of France in uneasy cohabitation with a left-wing President of the Republic, Abdallah's twin sons, together with seven others, were condemned to death in the Comores for the treasonable attempt to oust President Djohar six months earlier. Their French lawyer reported that they were being held in terrible conditions at Kandani. Even when their death sentences were commuted, apparently as a result of pressure applied both by President Mitterand and by King Hassan of Morocco, Commander of the Faithful, they were far worse off, far far and away worse off than Denard had ever been. Maybe compassion stirred, maybe that love of adventure which Denard had once described so vividly to Samantha Weinberg, maybe ambition, maybe nostalgia, perhaps a combination of all four. Or was it boredom? "I was an old crocodile," he explained to Samantha when it was all over, "who believed he could retire to his native *terroir*. But I got bored. To be retired is not a job."

So he snapped.

THE GATHERING OF THE CLAN

In the South of France lived a small, round, fat, balding former sailor, Michel Gouge. He had once been a petty officer in a naval diving group stationed at Brest and Cherbourg. He had been on the voyage of the *Antinea,* then in Chad, at Faya Largeau. (And, in between in 1980, he had been out in Burundi too.) So he was perhaps not surprised in early 1995 to get a telephone call from Bob Denard.

The proposed adventure, this time, was an underwater treasure hunt in the Philippines, where three Spanish galleons and their treasure lay sunk (no doubt at a point marked X) and Michel Gouge's old skills as a diver - and he dived regularly off the Côte d'Azur to keep these skills up - would be vital. His other hobby, Denard knew, was arms collecting. And of course in those dangerous waters off the Philippines where piracy was rampant, arms would be needed to protect the teams of divers and the mother ship herself - let alone the eventual gold doubloons salvaged from the deep.

So a delighted Michael Gouge was handed 12,000 francs to buy diving equipment, 4000 francs to buy weapons - small 'sporting' weapons, Remingtons, shotguns, nothing heavy - and promised a monthly salary of 22,500 once the expedition started, and a bonus of 50,000 at the end if all went well. (That was to be more or less the pattern: depending on their skills and seniority recruits for the 'treasure hunt' were offered between 17,500 and 30,000 a month, with the lure of 50,000 always dangled like a carrot on top of the regular salary. And as it was Bob Denard, they pretty well knew that, come what may, they would be paid.)

Dany Forrer had been in Chad with Michel Gouge; they must both have been in René Dulac's 'rival' group. He was younger, a big, tough, bearded fellow. He too was at a loose end. So Michel recruited him. And, more interestingly, the expedition needed a cook; and Michel Gouge had just the girl: a charming 26-year-old, almost his adopted daughter, so he explained, good-looking and adventurous: Sandrine Poirier. So, as 'Charlotte', Michel's protégée was hired, for 25,000, as the ship's cook.

★   ★   ★

And that was how, more or less, recruitment proceeded - by personal contact and word of mouth. Naturally enough the first people Bob Denard turned to were the two most closely linked both to himself and to the fate of the Comores: the two who had been in the Presidential Palace at his side when the fatal shots were fired that killed President Abdallah: Dominique Malacrino - Commandant Marques - and Jean-Paul Guerrier - Capitaine Siam.

All three of them were still due to be tried, officially, some day, for the assassination of the President; and though the trial had been postponed, their Recording Angel, their *Juge d'instruction* Chantal Perdrix had the right, meanwhile, to be kept informed of their movements. Indeed none of the trio were permitted to leave metropolitan France without her permission.

Which is why, no doubt, Bob Denard waited till he judged the political moment right before he moved into action.

That moment came on 17 May 1995 when at the Elysée Palace President Mitterand officially handed over his power to his successor, the newly-elected President Chirac. The ageing Jacques Foccart was reinstated as Chirac's adviser on African affairs; and what may have seemed almost as significant to Bob Denard was that the new Foreign Minister was named Hervé de Charette; for Hervé's brother Michel de Charette had taken part in the Benin Coup almost twenty years earlier, under the *nom de guerre* of Kermarec.

Which is why, also, as a measure of prudence, it was not Denard himself but his right-hand-man Malacrino who went out of France in the last week of May, and why Malacrino/Marques travelled north under the alias of 'Guy Garcia'. He went to Bergen in Norway to take possession of a boat, a 62-metre-long freighter MVS *Vulcain* - the deal had already been arranged by a Dutch shipbroker named Vandercom, and the price was $400,000.

'Garcia' did not go alone. With him, north to Norway, went Captain Faquet, who had been on the *Antinea*, and another old hand, Le Bosco, who had stayed on the *Antinea* to keep an eye on Captain Faquet and the crew. And with them too went a very new hand, 'Charlotte', plus Daniel Marteau, a new recruit, an ex-para, both as a 'security guard' and general handyman.

They kept on the Norwegian chief engineer; leased the boat out to the newly-set-up Virgin-Islands-registered Neptune International Shipping Company, raised the flag of Panama, and sailed the *Vulcain* down to Rotterdam. There in Rotterdam the *Vulcain* was to stay, being refitted and re-equipped, and loaded with supplies, very much as the *Antinea* before her was refitted and re-equipped, from 10 June through most of the summer till 14 August.

'Commandant Guy' - Malacrino - took charge at the Rotterdam end, Captain Faquet supervised the nautical side, 'Charlotte' cooked and smiled, Daniel Marteau worked, and Le Bosco perhaps went home - for Le Bosco's real name was Michel Oiseau and he was in fact a Belgian, by now in his fifties, with the Comores and Angola behind him, with plenty of experience therefore and no doubt very well aware of what was being planned. As certainly was Dominique Malacrino. As for Captain Faquet, he was later to claim that he had always believed it was a genuine underwater treasure expedition, and had been vastly indignant when the truth came out. Maybe.

Meanwhile Denard had contacted, and enlisted, another of his former officers, another who knew the Comores and Moroni and Kandani Camp and the Presidential Palace like the back of his hand. This was Capitaine Jean-Pierre who had played such an active part first at Kandani and then at Patsy Camp in Anjouan on that fatal night. 'Jean-Pierre's' real name was Jean-Marie Dessalles. He too was a para by training. He too had been early in the Comores; and he too, like both Bob Denard and Dominique Malacrino, had married a Comorian wife and produced beautiful children. He had been in Chad too; and more recently, only the year before, had returned from Rwanda. He was a a man with many contacts and he now, apparently, ordered crates of arms from Riga in Lithuania via Geneva; not in his own name, but using that of an old school friend.

Geneva was becoming, by this time, the hub of the whole operation. There another tough ex-para, a certain Sanchez, had for ten years been running a security operation, basically providing bodyguards for rich Arabs. Jean-Claude Sanchez was a pretty well-known figure in the mercenary world. He too had been in Chad. He had met Bob Denard in South Africa - presumably in the early Nineties - and they seem to have formed quite a friendship. He and Bob set up a bank account in Geneva into which large sums of cash were paid; and it was from this bank account that the whole operation (including the biggest single expense, the purchase of the *Vulcain*) was financed.

Bob travelled to Geneva under the alias of 'Bernard Martin'. Even the eagle eye of Chantal Perdrix would probably have overlooked a crossing to a place so near the French border; but, it being Switzerland, no doubt her suspicions would rightly have been aroused if French Customs had reported a 'Monsieur Bob Denard' at that particular frontier. So 'Bernard Martin' played safe. In packets of 200,000 and 300,000 he put 7 million French francs into this joint account. The sinews of war.

For war of course it was; though Michel Gouge bought ten full sets of divers' equipment, plus small arms, hired a lorry, and drove them up to Rotterdam; from where on August 14, by now refitted, victualled, equipped with Zodiacs, officially under the command of Captain Faquet, in fact under the orders of 'Commandant Guy', the *Vulcain* finally set sail.

THE VOYAGE OF THE *VULCAIN*

Bob Denard was not aboard the *Vulcain* when it weighed anchor in Rotterdam. But there were at least twenty persons on board; including two - or rather three - who are worth mentioning. The first, Francois Xavier Sidos, was a graduate in history and an officer of the reserve, who had commanded a section of the Presidential Guard in the Comores for the last two years of its existence. Sidos was intelligent, sporting, well-educated, politically astute, argumentative in that intellectual French way, and highly presentable. Before embarking he went out to Geneva; where presumably Denard and Sanchez briefed him on his rôle, and their own.

Secondly, Olivier Feneteau, a professional soldier, once of the paras and of the *Fusiliers Marins*; but for the previous five years, much more significantly, of the *ll^e Choc*. There is no equivalent (as far as I know) of the *ll^e Choc* in any other army in the world. In the French Army it has a very special rôle. It is the military arm of the French Secret Service, the DGSE. Indeed it is somewhat difficult to believe that Feneteau was not *still* a member of the *ll^e Choc* when he was recruited (by an 'unknown person', he was later to claim, without specifying where when or how); and indeed that the *ll^e Choc* had not given him special leave of absence to play the role of an ordinary mercenary in this extraordinary affair.

The third passenger worth mentioning is even more extraordinary, even more mysterious. His name was (possibly) Staub or (possibly) Stumm; and he appears to have been, of all things unlikely, a lieutenant-colonel in the Swedish army. If so, what on earth he was doing aboard the *Vulcain* (and why he seems to have taken no part at all in the subsequent actions but simply disappeared from the scene) is a total mystery. Some sort of special neutral semi-official Nordic observer perhaps? If his presence on board were not attested by several different witnesses, it would be hard to believe in its truth or indeed his existence.

★   ★   ★

The *Vulcain* sailed, traditionally enough, to the Canaries; and docked at Tenerife on 21 August. There seventeen more men joined; officially *les plongeurs*, the divers. They included Michel Gouge, of course and his recruit, Dany Forrer; the two former officers of the Presidential Guard Jean-Paul Guerrier and Jean-Marie Dessalles; a group of mercenaries who had fought for the Karen forces in Burma and had got to know each other well there, of whom the most conspicuous was Thierry Si Bong Cheng Chun. But the contact with Denard was Emmanuel Pochet, a reserve officer in the paras, who had been out with the Karen rebels three years after the end in the Comores. Back from Rwanda in 1994, temporarily unemployed, Emmanuel had contacted Bob to see if there were any likely contracts; and Denard had spoken not of a fictitious treasure hunt but of a *promenade maritime* - a sea voyage. Pochet had rightly guessed that the aim would be to liberate the prisoners in the Comores. He recruited another Burma veteran, Pascal Clin; and had been up to Rotterdam to buy food and stores from ship's chandlers. On the voyage of the *Vulcain* he was to be the administrator, with his own little office on board.

Two of the newcomers seemed somewhat out of place; the hesitant, shy, bespectacled, bourgeois Olivier Frassnier. But in fact he was the obligatory doctor. The other was odder: a long-haired, narrow-faced, black-jacketed bearded young man who looked more like a tramp than a mercenary, who had always wanted to be a mercenary, he later claimed. He had written a fan letter to Denard a year earlier asking for a job, any job; and Denard, (so he said) had replied a year later, telling the young man: "*Tenez-vous prêt et on verra*" - to stay ready and one will see. Then he had received, out of the blue almost, an air ticket to Tenerife.

On the face of it this is a most unlikely story. But the clue, I believe, lies in the young man's name: Georges Cau. He was almost certainly the son of André Cau, alias Carrel, one of Denard's oldest comrade in arms; and, to do a favour to the father, Denard was ready to take this verbose, unlikely recruit along for the ride.

★   ★   ★

And finally on Friday August 25 ' Monsieur Martin ' himself flew out to Tenerife - like all the rest from Brussels rather than from Paris - and joined the crew. Next morning the *Vulcain* headed south. And the voyage followed almost exactly the rhythm of the voyage of the *Antinea* so many years earlier, except that it was later in the year, the weather was better, the sea calmer, the journey quicker. About a week out the course was changed, away from Panama, towards the Cape, in order it was said, to pick up a 'compressor unit'. For a week or so more the pretence of the Philippines treasure hunt, which must have been wearing very thin, was officially at least kept up. But no landfall was made at the Cape. Bob called all his men (and presumably Charlotte too) together; and 'revealed' his true identity and their destination.

It was - surely to no-one's surprise by now - the Comores. Their mission: to liberate the prisoners held in Kandani Camp since 1992, and in particular the twin sons of the late President Abdallah and the man Denard had left in charge of the Presidential Guard, Capitaine Ayouba Combo. It was, Denard insisted, a matter of honour. And incidentally he added, it would be necessary to restore morale in the Comores.

Everyone knew what that implied. Everyone knew that Denard and many of the men aboard had carried out very much the same operation, successfully, years before; and everyone knew that, once established on the Comores, Denard and his men had stayed on, for over ten years. Was it not possible - probable even - that *Le Vieux* - the Old One - intended to re-establish himself on the Comores and stay there, under those more azure skies, for as long as he could, the Old Mercenary in contented retirement, till at last the gentle wings of peaceful Death wafted him away?

THE ADVANCE GUARD

Way back in June Denard had introduced Marie Hélène Sedran, a 33-year-old artist and photographer from Souillac in the Dordogne, to Sanchez. It seems to have been a highly successful introduction. Marie Hélène had already been despatched to the Comores a month or two earlier to take photographs - presumably in order to reassure Denard that the Presidential Palace was still in the same place, that Kandani Camp had not had its fortifications tripled, that the beaches had not recently been swamped by bungalows built all around, that sort of thing. At any rate on 12 September she and Sanchez flew out again, this time together, and took rooms, or a room, at the Galawa Hotel. Four days later, on 16 September, another couple of 'tourists' arrived: Gilles Rochard, formerly a *caporal chef* in the paras, one of Sanchez' men, plus a Belgian (male) named Jean-Charles Hervé, known as 'Pierre le Belge'.

It will be remembered that in the previous coup Christian Olhagaray had failed miserably to have red lanterns on the beach to guide the Zodiacs in from the *Antinea* anchored offshore; and failed also to have transport waiting for the mercenaries when they had landed. This time Bob Denard was taking no chances of the same thing going wrong again. This time he would rely on his own people sent out specifically for that purpose rather than on a local 'ally' with no doubt a lot else on his mind (primarily, one suspects, in the case of Olhagaray – who had by now in any case emigrated to Japan – worries about what his position would be if the *Antinea coup* had failed and he, remaining on the island, had been impli-cated). Foremost among his own people this time round was Sanchez, the man whom Denard trusted implicitly; and who, of course, like the other two men of the advance guard, had never set foot in the Comores before; so that their faces were totally unknown to the locals.

Sanchez also had the task of standing by, early every evening, for a signal from the *Vulcain*. He was later to claim that he went down regularly to a public phone box by the beach to await a call. This seems risky, unreliable – what if the cabin was out of order? Or vandalised? Or occupied? – indeed inherently improb-able. We know that the *Vulcain* had a call-sign: – 'Karthala'; and my guess is that Sanchez had a radio set up in a nearby villa on the 'Karthala' wavelength; which he listened in to every evening. But in whose villa, where, with whose conniv-ance? He would later have invented the story of the phone box to protect his local accomplice or accomplices.

At any rate on the evening of Tuesday 26 September the call came. Four weeks after weighing anchor in Tenerife, the *Vulcain* had dropped anchor offshore. On shore the cars had been hired; the beach had been chosen; the landing beacons prepared. Nerves of course were taut. Could a *coup* a second time round pos-sibly go as easily and successfully as the first *coup* against Ali Soilih had done? Was not some totally unexpected hitch bound to occur? This time was it not almost inevitable that, for the mercenaries and their chief, things should go dramatically wrong?

OPERATION KASKARI

At 1.30 am on Wednesday 27 September the Zodiacs, loaded with mercenaries, set out from the silent mother-ship. On board remained Le Bosco, as he had done on the *Antinea*, plus the Captain, the Norwegian chief engineer, Serge the French engineer, and Charlotte the cook. The beach chosen for landing lay half-way between the capital Moroni and the new airport of Hahaya to its north. It was isolated but rocky; and with the swell of the sea and the dark of the night land-ing proved difficult. But the lights were there to guide them in. Denard, limping badly, insisted on being the first man to step ashore. The whole operation how-ever took an hour and a half, much longer than planned.

The cars were waiting there, that was the main thing, with Sanchez, Rochard and Pierre le Belge. Malacrino took command of Groupe Alpha, five men. Their target was the police post at the entrance to Kandani Camp. Jean-Paul Guerrier was in command of Groupe Bravo, a further five men. His target was Kandani

Armoury inside the Camp. Both group commanders of course, and several of those with them, knew the lay-out of the Camp intimately: after all they had been living there, running the Camp, only seven years earlier. The two groups, twelve armed men in all, piled into the cars. It was now somewhere between 3.30 a.m. and 4 a.m. – the dead of night; but dawn was not too far away.

The 'assault' on Kandani Camp went like clockwork. Indeed there was no 'assault' to speak of. To the startled, sleepy gendarmes and soldiers the simplest reaction must have seemed the safest. The *Mzungu* were back. Commandant Marques and Capitaine Siam were back. Not a shot was fired; there was no resist- ance. Speedily and efficiently the two small groups of mercenaries took control of the entrance to the camp, the police post, and then the armoury. The next step was to release the prisoners. There were about thirty of them, including the twin sons of President Abdallah, Omar Tamou a former Minister of the Interior, and the genial bearded giant, Capitaine Ayouba Combo. It was almost three years to the day since their failed *coup*; and just under three years since the first attempt to rescue them had gone so miserably wrong. After three years' confinement in Kandani Camp they must have been as astounded as they were delighted to see the unexpected but familiar faces - heavily camouflaged though they were - of their liberators.

And so, it seems, were many if not most of the soldiers there. Before dawn therefore Kandani Camp, with its arms, vehicles, stores, occupants, plus its com- munications network, was firmly and without any bloodshed back in the hands of what had once been the Presidential Guard; of Denard's tiny detachment of a mere twelve mercenaries. Truly an amazing result.

★   ★   ★

At the Presidential Palace things were proceeding more slowly, more cautiously. Jean-Marie Dessalles was the officer commanding Groupe Charly, and Charly was double the strength of the others, ten men strong. For resistance was to be expected at the Palace. There were French officers, 'military advisers', in charge of what was in effect a reformed presidential guard.

The side gate to the Palace was open, Dessalles and his men slipped in. There were no lights at all; indeed the electricity seemed to have been cut off. In his pack of ten Dessalles held one ace: Olivier Feneteau. Feneteau had never set foot on the Comores before; so unlike the former 'Capitaine Jean-Pierre' he did not know the Presidential Palace and its approaches and its sentry posts like the back of his hand. But he had a far greater advantage, he had been in the 11^e *Choc*; and there Capitaine Rubis, the French 'military adviser' commanding President Djohar's guard, had been his own commanding officer. He knew Rubis' code-name, 'Stanislas'.

"*Stanislas, c'est nous*" whispered Feneteau as Dessalles, finger to his lips, edged the group past a startled, bewildered sentry. Once his men were in position,

Dessalles ordered his right-hand-man, Richard Fuhrman, another old hand, one of his former section commanders in the Presidential Guard, to fire a shot into the air. Fuhrman, armed with a shotgun, fired. The noise woke President Djohar asleep in his bedroom upstairs; and brought Capitaine Rubis out at the double. It seems that the guard at the Palace under Rubis' command consisted of twenty-five men on duty at any one time (with another fifty in reserve). And those on duty were heavily armed, with Kalashnikovs and hand-grenades. It was obviously an extraordinarily tense moment. Anything might have happened. But "*Stanislas, c'est nous*" repeated Feneteau; and once Capitaine Rubis saw and recognised his former subordinate, he immediately surrendered his own weapon and gave orders not to resist. He phoned the guardroom where most of the men on duty were and told them to come out peacefully. He then apparently - the sequence of events is a bit hazy here - dashed up to the President's bedroom to announce "*On est attaqué*", and to advise the President to lie low - unnecessary advice as the old man was already cowering under his bed. And there it seems Capitaine Rubis, who had been in charge of his security for two years, locked him 'safely' in.

So, with only one shot fired, and that not in anger, the Presidential Palace too had fallen to the mercenaries. Everything had gone dramatically right.

★   ★   ★

Calm descended around the Presidential Palace. In his bedroom President Djohar brought out his prayer mat, and knelt in prayer. What thoughts, what apprehensions, went through his no-doubt befuddled brain Allah only knows. As dawn was breaking, the door was unlocked; and five armed, uniformed men came in - four heavily camouflaged. The fifth, whom Djohar instantly recognised, was his least favourite political prisoner, one of the trio he had had condemned to death, Capitaine Ayouba Combo. "Do you recognise me?" asked one of the other four. And by his limp Djohar did. "I warned you I would be back to liberate *mes enfants*," proclaimed Bob Denard.

Denard, and Groupe Delta, a headquarters group in effect, had been holding back a little, near the Zodiacs on the beach, till the situation had become clear. He had given strict orders that above all no Comorian was to be killed. President Djohar was not to know this of course; and he must have remembered how his predecessor President Abdallah had been shot dead in that very Palace and in the presence of the man now standing before him.

It was only when his wife was brought in to reassure him that, it seems, the President could be induced to move. *Madame la Présidente* was in hysterics, under-standably, but Denard's doctor calmed her down. The couple were given a few minutes to pack personal belongings; then, escorted out past disarmed and appar-ently disuniformed members of what had been his guard (Capitaine Rubis had been allowed to drive off, to report no doubt to his superior officer at the French Embassy, Colonel Fister). They were plonked in the Presidential car and driven by the mercenaries - without, President Djohar sorrowfully noted, the Presidential flag being flown from its bonnet - to Kandani Camp. There, guarded by Pierre le Belge, they were installed in the Chief of Staff's little villa, next door to that in which Bob Denard had set up his operational headquarters. A little later his wife was escorted to one of her children's houses in the capital. Perhaps her now isolated husband remembered how his predecessor-bar-one, President Ali Soilih, also detained by Bob Denard at Kandani Camp, had been shot 'while trying to escape'. President Djohar was an old man of eighty. He had no intention of trying to escape. Understandably - it had been a disturbed night - the President decided to have a little nap. He slept most of the day away.

WEDNESDAY 27 SEPTEMBER - TUESDAY 2 OCTOBER

It was probably just as well the President - the deposed President - slept; and it was probably just as well he was tucked safely away inside Kandani. Because, even apparently as he was being driven there, there had been an attempt by a large over-excited crowd to lynch him; and in Moroni, that Wednesday morning, the atmosphere was described by Gilles Cadio as "a sort of popular festival" with (per Serge Burie) "spontaneous manifestations of joy" comparable, thought Olivier Feneteau, to "Paris on the Day of Liberation". Clearly it had not taken long for the news to spread. In Kandani Camp 240 of the soldiers immediately enlisted under Capitaine Ayouba Combo in the revived Presidential Guard; which was joined by all but ten of those at the Palace. Never was a *coup* so popular with the masses.

But not with everyone. Next day, on the Thursday, it became apparent that the radio station, Radio Comores, would not be surrendered without a fight. Despite various telephone calls from Denard, Capitaine Soiliye and ten armed soldiers refused to hand it over. The Radio Building, in the centre of Moroni, was 'besieged' from half-past seven in the morning till half-past two in the afternoon, but Soiliye and his boss Colonel Azali hated Capitaine Combo; and no doubt vice-versa. A couple of hundred Comoriens appear to have joined in the siege, with a handful of mercenaries doing their best to restrain them. It ended with one Comorien dead on each side, and Capitaine Soiliye wounded. Dominique Malacrino found the captain lieing on the ground, thought he was dead, found he was wounded, held back the locals who wanted to finish him off - and immediately arranged to have him transferred to the nearby French island of Réunion for hospital treatment. Clearly there was, if not to-ing and fro-ing, at least considerable radio contact between Kandani Camp and the French Embassy, with Bob Denard talking directly to 'Codename *Bleu*', Colonel Fister, his opposite number, so to speak.

On Thursday evening Capitaine Combo broadcast on 'liberated' Radio Comores, to announce the deposition of President Djohar and the formation of a Transitional Military Government with himself at its head; and the neighbouring islands of Anjouan and Moheli appeared to accept the news from the capital as good. Hardly anyone loved the deposed President.

Except his wife and daughter who brought meals to his villa in Kandani (he had by now woken up). In the week that followed the doctor, Olivier Frassnier, gave him a check-up every day. Bob Denard dropped by from time to time for a chat. The only fly in the ointment was that Djohar's Prime Minister, and several of his other Ministers, and no doubt Colonel Azali too, had sought asylum in the French Embassy, out by the old airport at Iconi, on the southern edge of the capital; and from there the refugee Prime Minister had appealed for aid in 'restoring democracy' directly to the government of France.

★   ★   ★

The following evening France responded reassuringly - reassuringly, that is to say, for Denard and his mercenaries - via the voice of *her* Prime Minister. From Paris Alain Juppé declared that, though France deplored *coups d'état* in her former colonies and in independent states with which she was closely bound by treaty, and would welcome the restoration of the rightful President, yet there could be no question of French military intervention.

Meanwhile, however, rumours were spreading. In South Africa there was talk of South African mercenaries being involved and of appeals being made to President Mandela to intervene.[1] In France of course coups in the Comores signified only one thing: Bob Denard. Where was Bob Denard? Was he not meant to be under *contrôle judiciaire*? What was happening in the Comores and who was behind it? Communications with the islands had been cut and the new airport at Hahaya closed - the old one at Iconi by the French Embassy was disused. But France's press agencies and photographic agencies and newspapers sent their correspondents flying out to Nairobi. From there most of them clubbed together to hire a private plane to fly across thousands of miles of ocean to the Comores - only to be informed by the control tower when they requested permission to land at Hahaya that permission was refused. Whereupon they had, of course, much to the annoyance of those paying their expenses, to turn round and fly back again, thousands of miles back, to their point of departure.

---

[1] Executive Outcomes (see Chapter Eleven) denied any involvement. Nevertheless ANC members began discussing anti-mercenary legislation; and there were rumours, over the weekend strong rumours, that Nelson Mandela had threatened to intervene militarily as France had refused. The Comores, after all, had been till fairly recently a client state of both countries…

Except for one reporter and one photographer from the Parisian magazine VSD. These two young men, both named Christophe, found there was a flight from Nairobi to Mayotte. They took it, imagining that Mayotte was just a stone's throw distant from the Grand Comore. Instead, it turned out to be a 24-hour boat journey away. But luck was with them; they and one other local reporter, a hippy stringer for Radio Mayotte, managed to hitch a lift on a small biplane. By the Saturday morning, installed in a hotel in the centre of Moroni, they learnt that their colleagues had been turned away and that they, the three of them, were the only journalists on the island. But it took them a day of pleading to get permission to visit Camp Kandani and interview and photograph Bob Denard; and then only on condition that they held back publication till he gave the go-ahead. For Denard was still hoping for a discreet little change of régime, with minimum publicity and fuss.

Vain hope - when an 'historic' mercenary like Bob Denard was involved.

★   ★   ★

Two important political figures now emerged onto the scene: Prince Kemal Said and Mohammed Taki. The transitional military government was, for once, exactly that, very transitional indeed. The genial and photogenic Capitaine Combo went on the radio again to announce that power was being handed over to a civilian government; of whom the joint Co-Presidents would be Prince Kemal Said, heir of the Sultans, and Mohammed Taki, the man who should have won the 1990 elections. Both had been in and out of power and jail and exile in the interim. Both are said to have signed contracts with Bob Denard back in France. Both were respectable politicians and leaders; both far more popular than the deposed Djohar.

It looked as if the situation was getting back to normal. Life on the Comores resumed its rhythm on the Monday. There had been a small demonstration of 500 people in favour of the two new leaders outside Radio Comores on the Sunday; and the new Co-President, the Prince, went on the air to call for a massive popular demonstration of support in the capital on Wednesday afternoon. The airport was opened; and journalists flocked in.

Some say that it was the arrival of scores of journalists that led to a sudden increase in tension on the Monday afternoon. People asked why they had come if everything was over. What were they there to report? Were they the harbingers of trouble, birds of bad omen?

Others say that Bob Denard only reopened the airport and allowed the world's press in because he already knew that things were about to take a dramatic turn for the worse.

★   ★   ★

The *Vulcain* had steamed into Moroni harbour. Bob Denard had visited, and made his peace with, President Abdallah's widow; though, curiously, little was heard of her released twins and nothing at all of the eldest son, Salim, who is said to have had several meetings pre-*coup* with Denard in Paris. Probably Abdallah's family discreetly retired to the family home (and their father's mausoleum) at Domoni in Anjouan, to await the turn of events.

Meanwhile the mercenaries remained, for the most part, out of sight if not out of mind in Kandani Camp. Queues of young Comorians lined up at its entrance every day, hoping to be enlisted. Roger Fatah trained the new recruits who were taken on; as for Georges Cau, that hapless young man, it seems that Denard had not trusted him with any weapon or joined him to any Groupe on the night of the 'invasion'. He was allotted the rather vague assignment of training young Comorians at 'sport': jogging, swimming, sailing.

But the more serious and experienced of the mercenaries were given the task of strengthening the defences of the two airports, Hahaya and the disused landing ground at Iconi. For there were rumours swirling around that the Iranians might invade and attempt to dislodge them. But I think Denard knew these were just rumours; indeed he may himself have started them. For the invading forces he had to deter were not the Iranians or the Libyans (though President Djohar had indeed been in contact with both) but, most unfortunately for him, once again (as in 1989) his own countrymen, the French.

THE CURIOUS CASE OF PATRICK OLLIVIER

When he was a mere Capitaine, ten years earlier, Jean-Luc Kister had been the leader of one of the two teams of divers that had been involved in the blowing-up of the *Rainbow Warrior*, the Greenpeace ship that was protesting against French nuclear tests in the Pacific. He was working for the DGSE, France's Secret Service, then; and as a Colonel and head of the French military team in the Comores, he was, like his subordinate Capitaine Rubis, working for the DGSE still.

Why had Capitaine Rubis surrendered to Groupe Charly so easily and indeed, for a military man, so pathetically at the Presidential Palace? Here is where things get complicated. The explanation may be that Rubis was half-expecting a *coup*; but a *coup* led not by Bob Denard but by Patrick Ollivier - a fellow member of the DGSE.

For Patrick Ollivier had certainly had training from the DGSE; and if not exactly a full-time employee, was suspected, all during his time on the Comores, of being the DGSE's 'mole' inside the Presidential Guard. Indeed it was reported that in December 1989 when President Mitterand had given the order for a French armada to expel Bob Denard and the Presidential Guard, Patrick Ollivier was with the 1ᵉ RPIMA on Réunion and had given the DGSE and thus France's Ministry of Defence precise details of the 20mm anti-aircraft guns in place at

Iconi airport. And then he had flown in on one of the five Puma helicopters that had landed before the assembled Presidential Guard on that Friday December 14, to witness in person the unchivalrous expulsion of his former boss, Bob Denard. As Dessalles - Capitaine 'Jean-Pierre', on parade at the time - was to put it:"*Patrick Ollivier, je n'apprecie pas du tout*":- Patrick Ollivier was definitely *not* his favourite person.

★   ★   ★

What had turned Patrick Ollivier against Denard? Nothing probably except the sense that he, Ollivier, was superior to Denard in training, ability to command, social standing and intelligence. That, and the fact that his overriding loyalty was to the DGSE, to France's Secret Service, and therefore in a sense at least to official France.

The first of these reasons will explain why he, Ollivier, considered himself to be a better mercenary leader, potentially, than Bob Denard; and the second (if I am right) why he himself had planned a mercenary *coup* before Denard's - also directed against President Djohar in the Comores but with the approval, indeed the backing of the DGSE.

And this hypothesis alone explains why Capitaine Rubis, at the Presidential Palace, on hearing the magic phrase "*Stanislas, c'est nous*" – "Stanislas, it's us" – had so tamely surrendered his revolver, his guards, 'his' Palace and 'his' President. He looked, one of Groupe Charly observed, startled – but startled because he was expecting someone else. And the person he was expecting was Patrick Ollivier, backed by a mercenary troop of fifty Croats and five Frenchmen.

All this implies of course that the French government was keen to get rid of President Djohar. This seems indisputable. There were three reasons why it was keen: first President Mitterand, aware of Djohar's corruption, was unwilling to pay his régime subsidies indefinitely; second President Mitterand, disturbed by the 1992 failed *coup* and the evidence of Djohar's bloodthirstiness, was unwilling to allow an ageing tyrant to stay in power; and thirdly, and more immediately, President Mitterand was shocked by Djohar's visit to Libya and North Africa the preceding winter, and particularly unwilling to risk the Comores becoming a base for Libyan or Iranian expansion in the Indian Ocean.

Mitterand's son, Jean Christophe, had been running 'African affairs' for the *cellule de L'Elysée*, for his father the President. Among his most trusted collaborators in this 'parallel diplomacy' was a discreet negotiator of vast experience named Jean-Yves Ollivier. Was Jean-Yves a relative of Patrick? A close relative? Ollivier, spelt with two 'l's', is not a common surname. Perhaps that was the immediate connection. At any rate in December Patrick Ollivier was given the 'green light' to go ahead, to set himself up as a mercenary leader, to prove himself better than a Denard, to recruit Croats as infantry and Frenchmen as officers; and, with the tacit connivance of the DGSE on the spot in the Comores, to overthrow the President.

What Capitaine Rubis may not have known, or may not have been certain about, is that between May 7 and May 15 Ollivier's potential mercenary venture had been called off – that is to say between the first and second round of the French Presidential Elections, when it had become obvious that President Mitterand's chosen successor Lionel Jospin was well and truly out of the running. In other words the change of the Presidential régime in France by election annulled plans for the change of Presidential régime by a subterfuge in the Comores. If one subscribes to the cock-up rather than to the conspiracy theory of history, then it seems probable that the wretched (and comparatively lowly) Rubis was warned there was going to be a *coup*, was later told the *coup* was cancelled, and was not therefore all that surprised – on the order, counter-order, disorder principle – to find that the *coup* was back on again but that Paris, typically enough, had simply forgotten to inform the man on the spot.

At any rate the Ollivier *coup* did not take place; and rather like René Dulac before him, rather like Servadac, this other potential rival to Bob Denard faded away from the mercenary scene; without, in Patrick Ollivier's case, ever really having had an opportunity to show his mettle.

Operation Azalée

President Chirac, it seemed, was by no means of the same bent as his predecessor President Mitterand. Despite the assurances on the Friday by his Prime Minister Alain Juppé that there would be no military intervention by France, by the Sunday French Hercules and Transail transport planes were flying detachments of France's special forces from Djibuti on the Red Sea into the vast island of Réunion and the little island of Mayotte.

On the Monday Prince Kemal Said went to the French Embassy in person, in his new glory as Co-President, to beg them to desist. On the Tuesday he went onto Radio Comores again to announce that the vast demonstration of support planned for Wednesday afternoon was being brought forward to 9 a.m. Wednesday morning. If successful, such a demonstration of popular support and approval should, the Co-Presidents and the mercenaries both thought, deter any French counter-invasion. Nevertheless, to be on the safe side, Bob Denard reinforced the defences around the Radio Station. But it was already too late. Offshore the patrol boat *La Rieuse* was patrolling the east coast, the patrol boat *La Boudeuse* was patrolling the north coast, and just over the horizon on the west coast the frigate *Floréal* was lurking with, on board, General Jean-Paul Dellenbach, commanding Operation Azalée.

At 23:00 hours that Tuesday evening, ten hours before the planned demonstration, the French counter-invasion was launched. Seaborne scouts from Marine

Commando Jaubert landed on the beaches opposite both Iconi and Hahaya airports. At 2 a.m. half a dozen Zodiacs landed more marine commandos plus men of the 1ᵉ RPIMA and 13ᵉ RDP - dragoon paras - at Iconi. Half an hour later three Pumas from Mayotte landed the operational headquarters of Lt Colonel Soum of the 1ᵉ RPIMA and his close protection squad on Hahaya airport itself. An hour later two more Pumas from the command frigate *Floréal* landed fifteen special anti-terrorist gendarmes of the GIGN at Iconi, to protect the French Embassy. At 5 p.m. two Transail from Réunion and Mayotte landed at Hahaya with the legionaries of the 2ᵉ REP on board. They quickly secured the airport perimeter. And finally at 5.30 p.m. just before dawn six more Transail debouched paras of the 2ᵉ RPIMA, infantry of the RIAOUM and gunners of the 2ᵉ RAMA. It was overkill. It was almost a text-book exercise. At Camp Kandani a distraught Bob Denard complained to deposed President Djohar: "First they send me here. Then they come to get me," as the planes flew overhead and the crackle of gun fire could be heard.

Just before dawn the two Christophes, woken by the sound of gunfire, roused their driver and drove out towards the French Embassy, towards Iconi. At a road block held by nervous Comorian soldiers they drove on, to turn a corner and be confronted by a long stretch of open road. From the other end they were fired upon. Their tyres were shot out. As they tried to make a run for it, Christophe Gautier, the reporter, was wounded by metal and glass splinters as the car blew up and by a bullet directly in his leg. His comrades dragged him out of the line of fire behind a nearby house; and there he was found, badly wounded, by a very threatening marine commando. Most of the day - once he had convinced his captors he was a journalist not a mercenary - he lay untreated bar a rough bandage in the French Embassy till, that evening, he was flown out to hospital at Réunion.

In the sporadic exchange of fire near Iconi Airport that early morning - though 'exchange' is perhaps the wrong word, it seems to have been entirely one-sided - the invading French forces shot dead four Comorians, and wounded a photographer, Patrick Durand of Agence Sigma. He was lucky. They killed his driver.

There were no real battles. How could thirty mercenaries and a few hundred very scared Comorians hold out against nearly a thousand heavily-armed professional French soldiers backed up by air support, armoured vehicles and artillery? But there had been a skirmish of sorts in the night outside Kandani Camp. Didier Grandière had been sent out on patrol. Two kilometres outside the Camp was a road block. He was ordered by radio to investigate. A rocket was fired at their vehicle, followed by a volley of shots. Once again the driver was instantly killed. Didier himself with seven bullets in him was left for dead by the roadside. He survived, though he had to spend one and a half years in hospital. In all there were reports of up to ten Comorians killed; with, on the French side, no casualties at all.

★   ★   ★

The wounding – the apparent death – of Grandière caused first anger, then consternation inside the mercenary camp. It looked as if the invading French forces were prepared to shoot to kill; whereas Denard was adamant that none of his men should fire on their fellow countrymen. As the morning wore on, both sides held their positions – the invaders occupying both airports and 'protecting' the Embassy, the mercenaries and their supporters entrenched at the Camp at Kandani.

But gradually anger gave way to apprehension. The mercenaries learnt that the invading French forces had been told they would find Moroccans leading the 'rebels'. Dominique Malacrino was not alone in being convinced that the French had orders simply to wipe out the mercenaries, to remove their embarrassing presence once and for all from the face of the earth. Up to now François Xavier Sidos' task had been, mainly, to write the speeches for Captain Combo. But he was also in charge of "public relations". And very wisely he suggested that the best protection for the mercenaries would be the journalists: that all the journalists and photographers on the island should be invited *inside* Kandani Camp, where by their presence alone they would form a *cordon sanitaire*. For the French military might happily massacre mercenaries, 'mistaking' them for Moroccans; but they would never do so in front of the eyes and cameras of the world's press.

Bob Denard was in radio contact with the French Embassy all afternoon. That night at 10 p.m. Colonel Soum came, by arrangement, under a sort of flag of truce, into Kandani Camp to 'rescue' President Djohar. Escorted back to the Embassy the liberated Djohar was informed by the Ambassador of France that his instructions were to send him, the President, to Réunion for medical treatment. Djohar protested. He simply wanted to be restored to power. France's Foreign Minister, Hervé de Charette, called from Paris. Djohar complained that he was not ill, that he was being deported. "You are still the President" replied Hervé de Charette, soothingly. But the French were adamant. "I understand," said Djohar to the Ambassador, Didier Ferrand. "You are sending me into exile, just as you did our last Sultan Said Ali." He was allowed to phone his son, and to bid his son accompany him. Djohar *Père et Fils* were flown by Puma from Iconi to Hahaya, by Transail from Hahaya, arriving at Réunion at two in the morning and being forced to spend three days, willy nilly, in hospital. Thereafter he was transferred for the next four months to a private house. But to the Comores the President – 'still' the President – was not allowed to return.

As for the Sultan's direct descendant, Prince Kemal Said was just coming to the end of his three days of ancestral glory as Co-President – the Monday, the Tuesday and the Wednesday. He had at least had that.

In the elections that were to follow once the dust had settled – in which President Djohar was not permitted to take part – Mohammed Taki was, at long last, after so many vicissitudes, elected President of the Comores. On the Grande Comore a small detachment of the Foreign Legion, a couple of hundred men, remained; stationed there after the rest of the French forces had been withdrawn.

★   ★   ★

Which happened soon enough. At midday on the Thursday Denard gave the orders for papers to be burnt and weapons to be destroyed. He assembled the journalists. He was looking businesslike that day rather than smart in khaki jacket, camouflage trousers, black headgear and sunglasses:

"I came here," he told them, "in the first place to liberate those to whom I had a debt of honour; and then to help restore political order in this country. I decided to mount the operation at the end of last year. I have no sleeping partner. This is a private operation and I financed it myself. It cost me ten million francs and this time I paid it all myself."

"I am sickened," he added, "by the intervention of France. I never believed France would mount an operation such as this. We are brothers in arms, soldiers on the same side." His bushy white moustache was a new feature, a boon to photographers. "I am sixty-seven," he continued, "and have nothing to lose. But the Comorian people deserve better. Now, however, I must yield to force."

To his men he issued orders: "The whole camp will be evacuated. I will leave first, flanked by my two adjutants. Then the rest will follow in groups of ten."

But the French were not about to allow Denard a dignified exit. At 2.30 they were in the camp, in force. Bob Denard was marched out, handcuffed to two rather abashed-looking gendarmes of the GIGN. He was flown first to Réunion, there interrogated, and then swiftly on a Transail back to the military base of Villacoublay in France. The red berets of Colonel Soum arrested the remaining mercenaries and any unwisely lingering Comorians. Half an hour after Denard's departure General Dellenbach arrived to take command in person of what hardly deserves the name of 'mopping-up' operations.

The mercenaries, some treated well, some treated roughly, were subsequently transferred to Réunion where they were held for a week, interrogated, then flown back to France.

The *Vulcain* was boarded and commandeered. Captain Faquet protested bitterly against an "act of piracy". Charlotte, shielded by journalists, nearly got away; but was held by Comorian gendarmes at Hahaya airport a few days later when she was on the verge of flying out.

This time Bob Denard had stayed in control of the Comores not for ten years, not for ten days even; but for exactly a week:- from the early hours of Wednesday 27 September when he and his thirty men had landed by Zodiac to the early hours of Wednesday 4 October when French special forces in overwhelming strength had 'invaded' by sea and by air. As Pascal Clin was later to put it, "*C'était une belle aventure. Je ne regrette rien*".

The End of Adventures

"Know that by adventure you will come to your kingdom, and by adventure you will hold your kingdom, and know that what adventure has given you, adventure will also take away. Therefore," prophesied Merlin to the young Arthur, "for all ages to come you will be named the King Adventurous."

It would be unseemly to compare Bob Denard to King Arthur;[2] except perhaps in this: that nobody could ever be sure, particularly in the Comores, that Bob Denard would not, like the King Arthur of legend, come again. Yet his life had been, if not "*une belle aventure*", at least far more adventurous than that of most mortal men. And this final *coup* of his had been, of all the *coups d'état* in this book (and possibly of most in the Twentieth Century), by far the most successful.

For with thirty-three men, in forty-eight hours, almost without bloodshed, almost without a shot fired, Bob Denard had toppled an unpopular régime, to great local popular rejoicing. In its place he had set up one that, as elections the following March were to show, was welcomed. The French were rid of President Djohar, thanks to Bob Denard; and had no intention whatsoever of allowing him back into power. They should, one feels, even if they were disinclined to allow the old mercenary to stay on in the islands, have given Denard at least a pat on the back - and, possibly, the *Légion d'Honneur* as well.

Instead, he (and, following him, Dominique Malacrino and Jean-Paul Guerrier) were whisked back into prison at *La Santé*. They were guilty of failing to observe the restrictions on their movements set by the *contrôle judiciaire*. Chantal Perdrix, as they might have foreseen, had been waiting for them, tongue metaphorically hanging out. And she even managed, within four weeks, to get herself a trip out to Réunion to interview ex-President Djohar and to see what further possible charges could be brought against 'her' trio.

They were kept in *La Santé* for no less than nine months for this comparatively pettifogging offence; and when, on 9 July 1996 the nine months were up Chantal Perdrix refused to release them. But a fortnight later she was overruled, and the trio were free men - though still of course under *contrôle judiciaire*.

Which Jean-Paul Guerrier did not respect. He vamoosed. So that when, just under three years later, Chantal finally had her way and the three were finally tried for complicity in the murder of President Abdallah before the *Cour d'Assizes* in Paris, 'Capitaine Siam' had to be tried in his absence.

The trial began on 4 May 1999 before a jury of four men and five women. It was odd that it went ahead at all, in the sense that the Abdallah family had withdrawn their *plainte* (lodged in 1990) in 1996 - reasonably enough, it might be thought, as Bob Denard and his men had in the interim liberated the late

---

[2] But see the present author's other classic *opus* "King Arthur and His Knights" (Oxford University Press).

President's twin sons from their horrid imprisonment. Of course this had nothing to do with his guilt or innocence, or that of Marques or of Siam. But the three had always stuck to the same story.

At the trial the ballistic experts contradicted themselves. A succession of aged witnesses - Maurice Delaunay now Mayor of Cannes, Maurice Robert now totally retired aged 80, General Jannou Lacaze, 75 - testified to Denard's services to the French Republic. As Denard himself put it, "*J'ai été un soldat, jamais un assassin*" - "I have been a soldier, never an assassin."

The *Avocat Général,* Philippe Bilger, asked for twelve to fifteen years' imprisonment; but had to admit that the version of events he put forward in his final speech was merely "plausible".

"Plausible!" retorted *Mâitre* Alexandre Varaut for the defence. "Plausible" was not enough to send his client, now aged 70, to die in prison. Denard was being defended by a father and son team. The father, *Mâitre* Jean-Marc Varaut, was the last to address the jury. He castigated the whole process of *instruction* (and by implication Chantal herself) as being chaotic and sinuous, pointed out that nothing at all had been said or alleged in the charges about the death of Sergeant-Chef Jaffar, and stressed that it had taken an unjust ten years to bring the matter to trial. "Hypotheses," he concluded, "are not sufficient for a conviction."

The jury after four hours' deliberation quite rightly agreed with the presumption of innocence. Bob Denard and Dominque Malacrino were acquitted; and walked from the *Palais de Justice* free men, to the applause of their relatives and the jeers and shouts of '*Assassins!*' from disappointed Comorians present. It was Wednesday 19 May 1999 - the trial had lasted just a fortnight. (And almost a year later Jean-Paul Guerrier too was acquitted in his absence.)

Bizarrely enough, only five days before the trial had began, there had been another *coup* in the Comores. This time it was Colonel Azali and the military who seized power. Mohammad Taki had died a few months earlier of a heart attack. His presidency had not been a success. Anjouan had declared independence, decided indeed that it wanted to return to French rule (like Mayotte) and President Taki's attempt to reconquer Anjouan *without* the help of mercenaries had ended in a disastrous military defeat. Not that President Chirac accepted Anjouan's desire to reintegrate *la metropole* - voluntary recolonization might have started off an embarrassing chain reaction throughout Africa. But Colonel Azali's *coup* (supported, it is said, by Captain Combo successfully reintegrated into the armed forces) was to lead to further *coups* by other Colonels on both Anjouan and Moheli. So that it is hard not to wonder whether the Comores might have been, if not a lot, at least a little better off should Bob Denard and his thirty-three have been permitted to stay on and in effect rule over those enchanting islands.

X

Bob Denard – Checkmate?

'Tis all a Chequer Board of Nights and Days.
Where Destiny with Men for Pieces Plays
Hither and Thither Moves, and Mates and Slays
And One by One Back in the Closet Lays

Edward Fitzgerald's *Omar Khayyam*

There was indeed talk of one more attempt by Bob to make a comeback. He, and Emmanuel Pochet, and one of the twins, Cheik Abdallah, had a meeting in Paris on 4 January 2002 with a right-wing Italian journalist, Franco Neruzzi, and there was talk of raising a group of Italian extreme right-wingers and former soldiers, at salaries of between 7,000 and 14,000 euros a month, to overthrow Colonel Azali. For the Colonel was about to organise popular elections to confirm himself in power; and certainly if Bob and Emmanuel and the rest felt that the elections might not be exactly free and fair, they had a point. When in April the results were declared, out of 56,256 votes cast on the Grande Comore Colonel Azali had obtained.... precisely 56,256.

But the meeting in Paris came to nothing; except great flurries in the Italian press and the courtrooms of Verona. Nor did a venture later that year in June when twelve French mercenaries were hired by one of the two rival Presidents of Madagascar – there was a Great Schism in Madagascar, rather like the Papal Schism of the Middle Ages – to train a crack battalion of locals to restore him to full power. The plane carrying the twelve , a Falcon 900 flying from Le Bourget, was stopped and turned back at Dar-es-Salaam on the request of the French authorities.

Inevitably there were rumours that these were Bob Denard's men; but it seems much more likely that they were now Dominique Malacrino's.

INTERLUDE IN THE IVORY COAST

For if there was any obvious successor to Bob Denard, it was 'Commandant Marques'. Dominique Malacrino was in his late forties by the year 2002; whereas Bob Denard was well into his seventies. He had a reputation, in mercenary circles, for efficiency and loyalty; and for both ruthlessness and discretion too. He did not have Denard's physical presence - he was a small man - but he had magnetism. When in the autumn of 2002 trouble, long brewing, blew up in the Ivory Coast, it is not surprising that President Laurent Gbagbo, feeling himself 'betrayed' by official France, turned to 'Commandant Marques'.

The Ivory Coast had been France's great success story in West Africa. It was prosperous, it was stable, it was awash with French businessmen and settlers and *coopérants*, it had a permanent French base at Port Bouar controlling the airport of the capital Abidjan. But cocoa prices collapsed, the economy collapsed, and by the time, in 1993, the old President, the former French senator, Félix Houphouet-Boigny, finally died, turmoil was likely to set in. Some say the funeral rites of *Le Vieux* at the vast cathedral he had had built at Yamoussoukro in the centre of his country, larger than St Peter's in Rome, marked the turning point of French influence in Africa. Possibly.

There were *coups,* popular uprisings, ethnic tensions; and on 19 September 2002 while the latest President, Gbagbo, was in Rome, a *coup* that failed. The Minister of the Interior was killed. General Guei, a former President thought to be behind the *coup*, was killed in his own house in Abidjan with nineteen members of his family. The *coup* having collapsed, the President returned, but the North rose in revolt. And the French, called on for aid, instead of suppressing the revolt in the North, set up a ceasefire line that effectively divided the country in two.

President Gbagbo was beside himself with fury. In October he enrolled 37 mercenaries under 'Commandant Marques' to train and command an elite unit of 105 of his own tribesmen. In December this group were ambushed in the West of the country by Liberians, and two of Malacrino's men were very badly wounded.

It seems that that marked the end of Marques' venture. The civil war in the Ivory Coast is still continuing nearly four years later as I write; and as I write there are reports of child soldiers being raised by Ivory Coast militia command-ers, recruited in Liberia for $300 a head, the unemployed of the Liberian civil wars[1] where, it is calculated, there were 12,000 child soldiers fighting (including 2,738 girls) valued above all for their ability to kill without asking questions. If these are to be the black mercenaries of future wars spreading all over West Africa, the future there looks grim indeed.

In between, in the years 2003 and 2004, there were South African and Bielorussian mercenaries hired by Laurent Gbagbo to replace the unsatisfactory French. One of those, based in South Africa, Richard Rouget, of dual French-South African nationality was, on 28 July 2003, the first man to be condemned in

South Africa under the new anti-mercenary laws[2] for "supplying mercenaries to the civil war in the Ivory Coast". Another, Karl Albert, a helicopter pilot, was the second - more heavily, not just given a suspended sentence like Richard Rouget, partly because he was a pure South African, and partly, I suspect, believe he had for many years previously worked for Executive Outcomes;[3] and so was singled out to be made an example of.

As for the Bielorussians, they (and other Slavs) were the crew of the two Suknoi 25 from Yamoussoukro that on 6 November 2004 bombed and rocketed a group of French 'peacekeeping' troops, killing nine. In retaliation President Chirac immediately ordered the Ivoirian air force to be destroyed - which was done, on the ground, within the hour. Next day fifteen Slav mercenaries were arrested by French forces as enormous anti-French riots broke out in the capital Abidjan.

The civil war, despite innumerable ceasefires and peace agreements, continues. No doubt it is only when it will be over that the true facts, and all the details, about the various groups of mercenaries involved will emerge. But that mercenaries, both European and African, have been involved and are continuing to be involved in the Ivory Coast civil war there can be little doubt.

The Trial of the Thirty

Never before had so many European mercenaries been gathered in the same courtroom. It was in the labyrinthine Palais de Justice, in the heart of Paris, five minutes' walk from Nôtre-Dame. One has to admire Chantal Perdrix for, if nothing else, her perseverance. Even before Denard and his adjutants came up for trial at the *Cour d'Assizes* she had been digging away at the latest *coup*, preparing another indictment.

But long before the new trial opened, Chantal had passed the *bâton* on to another *juge d'instruction*. All in all it took ten long years for the case to come to court; and when it came, it was on that same hoary old charge of *association des malfaiteurs* that Bob Denard had faced so many years previously after the Benin coup; and it was before that same hoary old court, the 14ᵉ *Chambre Correctionelle*. The great difference was that this time not just Bob Denard with one other was accused of evil-doing but the whole lot, all the mercenaries involved in Operation Kaskari, in the *coup* that had overthrown President Djohar in 1995.

The trial opened on Monday 20 February 2006. It is not quite accurate to say that 'all the mercenaries involved' were on trial. Firstly, much to the disappointment of the few journalists who did attend, neither Charlotte the cook nor Marie-Hélène the photographer were indicted. Not that that totally robbed the

---

[1] See Chapters Eleven, Thirteen and Sixteen for these wars.
[2] See Chapters Eleven, Twelve and Thirteen for these laws
[3] See Chapters Eleven, Twelve and Thirteen for Executive Outcomes

trial of glamour; there were any number of attractive young female *avocates* floating around the courtroom, including a beautiful blonde who turned out to be married (she kept quiet about it for as long as she could) to one of the accused, Francois Xavier Sidos.

The two engineers were not in the dock, either. Nor were the two Belgians, the elderly Le Bosco and the younger Pierre le Belge who had looked after President Djohar during his week's captivity in Kandani Camp. That the *procureur,* the prosecutor, explained, was his decision. Nor was the other foreigner, the mysterious disappearing Swede.

The *procureur,* by name Olivier Bray, was an intelligent, neurotic forty-something-year-old redhead, with a sharp face and the unappealing manner of a minor public school prefect. He had thirty names on his little list. But even of these thirty not all were in Court. Gerard Thiemmong and Captain Faquet of the *Vulcain* never put in an appearance - charges against them had, it seems, been dropped. Jean-Paul Guerrier was again *en fuite;* from him, M. Bray dramatically claimed, only "*silence radio*". But in fact he was known to be in Iraq. Jean-Philippe Lafont, a winegrower, was in prison already. And then the President of the Tribunal, a relaxed aristocratic figure, Thierry Dervernoux de Bonnefon, flanked by two inconspicuous female assessors, while running down the list, was told that two of those charged had in the meantime died. First Thierry Si Bong Chen Chung in June 2002; then François Robin, who had been with Chen Chung in Karen country, had on January 12 committed suicide. "*Ah bon,*" said *Monsieur le Président*, making a note.

But the most noticeable absentee was Bob Denard himself. His stout young lawyer, *Maître* Elie Hatem, waved a medical certificate. His client, alas, was suffering from Alzheimer's disease. His memory came in fits and starts only. He was in no physical or mental condition to attend the trial. So it was to be Hamlet without the Prince of Denmark. The thirty on trial in theory were thus reduced in practise to twenty-four. But it was still the largest number of mercenaries ever to face trial together anywhere in Europe since the Middle Ages - an historic occasion in its way.

*   *   *

The 14^e *Chambre Correctionelle* sat on the first floor of the *Palais de Justice* in an oak-panelled parquet-floored courtroom looking out over the Seine. Above the President and his two assessors stood a statue of Justice. To the right was the pulpit of the *procureur,* M. Bray, a lonely figure. In front of the President and *procureur* were the pews reserved for the accused and their milling black-robed white-cravatted lawyers; behind were seven rows of benches for the public, usually almost full, mainly with members of the Comorian community in Paris, beadily watched over - as were the accused - by a pair of standing gendarmes. Right in the front, almost under the nose of M. Bray, sat Dominique Malacrino, dark, a little hunched and ill-kempt, observant, largely silent. In the absence of Bob Denard he was the most important figure in the courtroom. It emerged that he was the son of an Italian immigrant father, one of eleven brothers and sisters, divorced from his Comorienne wife, apparently living in the countryside - no mention was made of his Ivory Coast venture - renovating a farmhouse. Didier Grandière was the most noticeable of the other mercenaries, for he sat always with his hand cupped to one ear. "Are you feeling better?" M. Bray was to ask him, with some attempt at sympathy, when the tale of his shooting was told. Yes, he was. But clearly the seven bullets had taken their toll.

The two other immediately noticeable mercenaries were the tubby almost cartoonish little person of Michel Gouge; and the grey-haired bespectacled pro-fessional figure of Francois-Xavier Sidos, often in consultation with his beautiful blonde *avocate*. The rest, at first, seemed a mixture of ordinary-looking men; some smartly dressed, others in sweaters and more casual clothes, with one longhaired almost *clochard* personage among them, distinctly out of place.

Under the French system the *Cour d'Assizes* tries serious crimes, with a jury. The *Chambres Correctionelles* are a rung lower down; the President and the two assessors judge the case but may only inflict penalties of up to ten years in prison. The procedure, to Anglo-Saxon eyes, is odd. There is very little calling of witnesses but a great deal of reading out by the President of sworn statements, a tedious procedure. Then, when the accused are hauled up, one by one, the President begins by summarising testimonials to their good character, and assessments by a professional psychologist, before going on to their personal circumstances and criminal records.

In fact hardly any of the accused had criminal records; except for Michel Gouge, for arms dealing, which he claimed to be all a mistake. As for the psychological assessments, they were almost invariably surprisingly favourable -well-balanced, normal, not aggressive, showing no particular pathology, above average intelligence, such were the phrases that were most often read out. Except for the *clochard,* the apparent tramp, Georges Cau. He was described as complex, immature and manipulative. Asked to comment, he retorted that the psychologist was *méchant* - malicious. But his was one of the most interesting statements. Most of the accused replied briefly and calmly and unemotionally to the President's and the *procureur's* questions. But Cau declared that he had always wanted to be a mercenary, that he had found the whole experience "too short, very complex, extremely interesting"; that he was a Catholic, that it had seemed to him 'cool'; and that he now intended to devote his life to animals.

The doctor, Olivier Frassnier, amazed the courtroom in a different sense when he revealed that he had not bothered to tell his wife and children where he was going. The only moment of humour in the whole trial came when Dominique Malacrino was being questioned by the President. Why had he not informed his *juge d'instruction* that he was planning to leave metropolitan France? "But I did," he replied. There was a pause. "After I had arrived in the Comores," he added with an almost straight face. Malacrino came across as surprisingly straightforward. Yes, he had been armed. Yes, he thought everyone on the *Vulcain* was well aware that they had enlisted for a military expedition.

These were two of the major points at issue. Time and again on the question of arms the mercenaries in the dock insisted that they had been armed only with light, sporting weapons; and furthermore that their ammunition had been blanks or wads, not live. The President was sceptical, the *procureur* pointed out that they all seemed to have agreed on a common story beforehand; and when gendarmes brought a case of arms solemnly into court under heavy guard and the mercenaries one by one denied recognising the weapons, he could barely contain his fury.

As for the question: had they known what they were doing? – here again many of them stuck to the line that they always believed, till they were well into the voyage and informed of the real objective, that they were going on an underwater treasure-hunt. Roger Fatah said he had been manipulated; Daniel Blairon that he had been totally deceived, ruined; Stephane Boyer that he regretted taking part in the affair; Didier Marinon, most vehement of all, that he had been ruined by Denard, who was greedy only for publicity and money. Gregory Zmora, more convincingly, admitted that he was bitter at the time: the bonus had not been paid, Denard had not said farewell properly, nor had he visited the wounded; but he, Zmora, felt no animosity now. His motives, he added, had been "money; and secondly a taste for adventure".

These were of course the foot soldiers, so to speak. Jean-Paul Guerrier, in his interrogation, was reported to have declared himself "very proud of what I have done"; and Francois-Xavier Sidos came out flatly with the statement that "Bob Denard is a great man". But the most measured verdict seems to have been that of Daniel Marteau. He half-echoed the words of Pascal Clin. "For me it was *une belle aventure*. But if it was to do again, I would not do it." Olivier Bray did not like Daniel Marteau. He referred to him in his summing-up without any real explanation as a "bad boy". He did not like Pascal Clin either. "Are you really Monsieur Clin?" he asked him – but failed to pursue this interesting line of thought, either.

★   ★   ★

The Court sat for three weeks; not every day and only in the afternoons – though occasionally the afternoons extended into the late evenings. On the Thursday of the first week deposed President Djohar died at his home at Mitsamiouli on the Grande Comore. It was an odd coincidence. He was of course by now aged ninety; and had never held power or office since his return from Réunion. His son was in Court, one of the very few witnesses to give evidence in person, a small quiet elderly man wearing British-style sports jacket and flannel trousers. And three or four Comorian lawyers were in court too, representing the *parti civile.* For under French law in a criminal prosecution the victims not only have a right to have their say in court but to claim damages from the accused - if, of course, the accused are found guilty. So the deposed President was represented by his lawyer; who on his death transferred his allegiance to the Djohar family. Captain - now Colonel and Chief of Staff - Soiliye, wounded in the leg at Radio Comores, was a second *parti civile.* And the third *parti civile* were the Comores themselves, now the Union of the Comores, on whose behalf spoke and pleaded and occasionally screamed and ranted as he strode around the courtroom a fierce, lean, bespectacled Saint-Just of a black lawyer, by far the most melodramatic of the twenty or thirty *avocats* who put in an appearance. (One, a heavy-set lawyer defending Gilles Rochard, simply declared that he was proud and honoured to shake his client's hand, proceeded to do so; and then, as if embarrassed by a fault of good manners, ambled round the courtroom shaking hands with all the mercenaries present - an unusual but rather effective line of defence.)

This was not the black Saint-Just's way. He railed, adapting De Gaulle's famous phrase, against *"un quarteron des mercenaires";* demanded to know why Bob Denard was being portrayed as almost a Christ-like figure; explained threateningly how merciful the Comores' authorities had acted in not insisting on a trial there since the penalty for waging war on the Comores was the death penalty; and referred elegiacally to the islands as beautiful, scented and peaceful - rather twisting Truth's tail with that last adjective. He shouted down various defence lawyers, and was in his turn booed and hooed by them in chorus. He was roused to an absolute paroxysm of rage when Denard's defence lawyer claimed that the Union of the Comores was a bogus federal state and so had no legal standing and therefore no right to the one symbolic euro of damages, plus the 700,000 very specific euros as criminal penalty it was claiming from his client. He interrupted the Defence's final speech, he demanded a right of reply, he screeched at the President; and the President, for once losing his temper, yelled back at him. It was a weird finish to the trial. Mercenaries and gendarmes alike looked on in bemused silence; till, asked for any final comments, a spokesman for all the mercenaries - it may have been Dessalles - said "I assume my responsibilities. But it's politics that will decide."

★   ★   ★

He was perfectly right, of course. All mercenary trials are political trials; though it is hard to see why this trial was brought at all, so many years after the event. Was it simply because in the course of their investigations the *gendarmerie* had accumulated, as Olivier Bray mentioned with admiration, three tons of paper-work (including the contents of Denard's dustbins) and this could not simply be written off as wasted effort? Was it a message from the French government to the Comorians and Africa in general that France would no longer tolerate mercenary activity? Had in fact the French intervention, Operation Azalée, been designed to distract attention from France's concurrent renewal of nuclear tests in the Pacific? And indeed in view of the horrid consequences for France's reputation of the *Rainbow Warrior* operation ten years earlier, when the DGSE had been directly involved, had the DGSE and the French State been behind Denard's *coup* the whole time? Using mercenaries who could be disowned rather than their own operatives – as was the case with the *Rainbow Warrior* – for whose wicked actions they could be held directly responsible? And then, treacherously, cast these mercenaries aside once the job – the removal from the political chessboard of President Djohar – had been done and their usefulness was over?

That of course was the real question at the heart of the trial. For if Denard's operation had been authorised, directly or indirectly, by the French state, then he and his men could hardly be said to be an association of wrongdoers. Arguments about this ranged back and forth and to and fro throughout the three weeks of the trial. At one point Saint-Just angrily asked Gilles Rochard if France and the Comores were at war. No, replied the accused; but he believed he had been acting in the interest of France.

Was he or was he not? Without Bob Denard there it was almost an insoluble question. Denard had never in so many words told his men that he had had the 'green light'; but he had often hinted that he had had the 'amber light'; and he had certainly from the *Vulcain* telephoned (presumably by satellite phone) Jacques Foccart and been telephoned by Maurice Robert. But what had they said to each other? As Denard's lawyer put it, this was largely a trial in which ghosts figured; for both Foccart and Robert and now Djohar too were dead; and even those who were alive, he complained, like Capitaine Rubis and General Germanos and the then Minister of Defence had refused to attend the trial, refused to give evidence, not replied to his request for information.

What is all this about 'green lights' and 'amber lights' and 'red lights'? demanded Saint-Just dismissively. Are we talking about a traffic accident here? And Olivier Bray reinforced the point when, in his final four-hour-long peroration, he claimed that the accused had held up a country in the same style as they might have held up a bank.

But Bray lost himself in a long, long, long account of how the *coup* might have been financed. Bob Denard had always, when interrogated, stuck to his story that he had financed the whole operation himself, and had had no backers. Untrue, cried Bray. It might have been the Israelis, it might have been South African hoteliers, there was talk of the Chinese mafia and of Japanese gambling interests. On the other hand it might very well have been dirty money laundered from the Spanish criminal Costas by one of Denard's more disreputable sons, Eric. "It's in the dossier," he kept repeating as he struggled on, trying to hold the Court's attention.

But that he only recovered when he came to the end of his oration; when he finally laid out what sentences he was asking for. All ears pricked, all glazed eyes refocused. He distinguished between younger men perhaps fascinated by adventure and easy money; and former members of what he maliciously and often referred to as the Pretorian (rather than the Presidential) Guard. For the rank and file he demanded suspended sentences of one year each for the youngest, and 2-3 years for the thirty-year-olds. For Lafont, already in prison, 3 years with two suspended; and for Gouge, in view of his previous criminal record, the same. For Malacrino, Sidos, Dessalles, Emmanuel Pochet, Fuhrman and Sanchez, 4 years, with half suspended - i.e. 2 years in jail. For Jean-Paul Guerrier, 5 years in prison backed up by an international arrest warrant; and for Bob Denard (who of course had already been sentenced to five years suspended on the same charge at the end of the Benin trial) 5 years in *prison ferme* this time round.

The President of the Tribunal banged his gavel. "Judgement on June 20," he announced.

★   ★   ★

This chapter is going to press before judgement. My personal opinion is that if anyone ought to have been on trial at all, it should logically have been the French Army, or that part of it that invaded the Comores in Operation Azalée; and there irresponsibly and unnecessarily shot dead, directly, several - possibly up to ten - Comorians. They were trigger-happy, and clearly encouraged by their commanders to be trigger-happy. Denard and his men were not.

Can Denard be sentenced to five more years in *La Santé*? He is at present living with Marie-Elise not down near Bordeaux but in the suburbs of Paris. *Mâitre* Elie Hatem, his lawyer, claims that his client is living only on his pension - as a former colonial marine long ago - of 250 euros a month (and that he himself was appointed to defend Denard by the State). If so, then it may well be true after all that Denard financed the final operation himself and lost all that remained of his fortune in doing so.

Perhaps all the same looking at his life as a whole, he has been despite its ending a fortunate mercenary leader. As one of his predecessors, one of the leaders of the mercenary *Grandes Compagnies* that pullulated in mediaeval France, the Bascot de Mauleon, told Froissart, the fascinated mediaeval chronicler:

> "I know of very few Companions bar myself who have not, somewhere or other, died a violent death."

And that Bob Denard has - so far at least - always avoided.

STOP PRESS

Judgement Day came on Tuesday 20 June 2006. It was swift but not brutal. The President of the Tribunal announced that all the accused had been found guilty; and then read out the sentences. Bob Denard was sentenced to five years imprisonment; but the sentence was suspended: Jean-Paul Guerrier, Dominique Malacrino, François Xavier Sidos, Jean-Claude Sanchez, Jean-Marie Dessalles, Emmanuel Pochet were all six condemned to three years; but the sentences were all suspended and (except in the case of Jean-Paul Guerrier) there was to be no entry in their criminal record. At the announcement the beautiful Madame Sidos' face crumpled up, and a slow tear trickled down her cheek. It seemed hard to understand why. Her husband would leave the court a free man, without a stain on his judicial record – surely a fine result from their point of view. But there would be a blemish on his character. The mercenaries had genuinely hoped, and half- expected, to be totally acquitted – to be found innocent.

The doctor was given 8 months; roly-poly Michel Gouge 30 months, Danny Forrer 12 months, the oddball Georges Cau 4 months, Olivier Feneteau, late of the *11 Choc*, 18 months as was the wounded Didier Grandière; whereas Roger Fatah, Serge Burie and Daniel Martau were completely let off. No explanation for these wide differences in sentence was offered; and in any case as all were suspended it hardly mattered. The Union of the Comores was awarded 1 euro symbolic damages and 20,000 euros compensation, to be paid by the accused jointly. The claims of Capitaine Soiliye were dismissed, those of the Djohar clan partly dismissed, partly adjourned. There was a faint air of anti-climax as the court, the gendarmes, the mercenaries, the lawyers and the television cameras dispersed. There had been neither applause nor jeers. Dominique Malacrino looked as downcast on leaving as he had on entering. Of Bob Denard there had been no sign. The whole trial had been something of a waste of time, effort and money.

And the President of the Tribunal obviously felt so too. In his short written judgement, he agreed that it was "impossible and unthinkable" that an operation that had lasted 131 days (from the purchase of the *Vulcain*) and had cost at least 10,000,000 francs, that had obligatorily involved "a whole cascade" of intermediaries and contacts should have been unknown to the secret services or to the *Cellule Africaine* of the Elysée Palace. "It is evident," ruled M. De Bonnefon, "therefore that the French Secret Services knew of the project of a coup d'état conceived by Robert DENARD, its preparation and its execution. It is equally clear that at the very least they did nothing to impede it and that they thus allowed it to be carried through to its conclusion."

The President, and the two assessors, reserved their harshest words not for any of the mercenaries but for the French armed forces. This part of the judgement is worth quoting extensively.

"On 4 October the French Army intervened. This was the beginning of operation AZALÉE that mobilised more than 1000 men...

"This intervention was particularly brutal since, although Robert DENARD had pledged not to resist nor to fire upon the French Army, the said French Army on several occasions opened fire without issuing warnings thereby causing several deaths among Comorian soldiers and civilians and many wounded including journalists present, notably Christophe GAUTIER, chief correspondent of VSD... Likewise, though he showed no signs of opening fire, Didier GRANDIÈRE was seriously wounded by a mortar shell and by a burst of five bullets.

"It seems furthermore that one had led these (French) soldiers to believe that they would be dealing with veritable terrorists of different origins, notably Lebanese, and it seems also, in view of several journalistic investigations included in this case's dossier and in view of several witness statements, that orders had been given that Robert DENARD and his men were to be actually eliminated, a project which aborted because of the unforeseen presence of journalists on the spot…"

Maybe the Bascot de Mauleon, quoted a couple of pages ago, had a point. Maybe Bob Denard came closer at that moment to a violent death than he had ever before come in his whole long life - and death, like so many mercenary leaders, at the hands of his own employers; or in this case putative employers (for the source of the funding, the President ruled, had despite all the efforts of the prosecution, remained totally obscure).

★   ★   ★

That said, read the last paragraph of the judgement again. Who was this anonymous "one" who had "led their (French) soldiers to believe they would be dealing with veritable terrorists"? "Orders were given" - but who precisely gave them? - "that Denard and his men were to be actually eliminated." Was it Colonel Soum of the red berets? Or the general commanding Operation Azalée from his frigate? Or possibly Colonel Kister at the French Embassy? Or behind him the French Secret Service?

This was in effect a murderous conspiracy that is still waiting to be elucidated; and one of particular interest - as they were the potential sacrificial victims on the altar of *Raison d'État* - to Bob Denard and his men. The judgement leaves the answer hanging. Could it indeed have been a collective decision of the French Cabinet? Or even - shades of *Murder in the Cathedral* here - of the President of France himself? Vital questions, still remaining to be answered…

Intermezzo

TWO CIVIL WARS

Yugoslavia and Angola

II

The Old Guard Fades, the Young Guard Advances

When and where do mercenaries appear? Traditionally in civil wars, in the break-up of great empires, when states fragment, when pretenders to power try to fight their way to the top. It was in these circumstances that they suddenly and unexpectedly appeared in the Congo in the nineteen-sixties.★ But it was also so over two thousand years earlier when Clearchus of Sparta and his Ten Thousand Greeks, perhaps the most famous mercenaries of all time, were hired to win a civil war in the Persian Empire; but lost and had to fight their way desperately out and home again to Greece after the treacherous killing of their leaders.★★

So *coups d'état,* sudden raids, rescue attempts are so to speak a sideline, a spin-off of normal mercenary activity; and though through force of circumstances this volume of mercenary history deals mainly with such events – and fascinating they are too – it would be extraordinary if there had been no contemporaneous civil wars in which mercenaries had taken part.

There were. And this chapter, this intermezzo, this interlude, will deal with two; the first a comparatively short but extremely shocking one, the second a vastly long affair that centred, unlike the first, on one man – Jonas Savimbi, and introduced, if only on the margin of events, one soon-to-be famous mercenary leader: Simon Mann.

CIVIL WAR: YUGOSLAVIA 1991 – 1995

There is a story that after the First World War, at the Versailles Peace Conference, the Great Powers were scratching their collective heads, utterly uncertain of what to do about the Balkans. So they called on an Oxford professor, a specialist in Serbo-Croat, to come up with a proposal. He did. They accepted it – and the Kingdom of the South Slavs, the State of Yugoslavia, was born. When a few years later the first series of civil wars, uprisings, assassinations and general mayhem that marked the history of the new State broke out, the great and the good of the world summoned Professor Seton-Watson back. What was his explanation? they demanded severely. The Professor shrugged his shoulders. "I made a mistake," he confessed.

Certainly when the Cold War came to a symbolic end with the fall of the Berlin Wall in 1989 and the subsequent collapse of the Soviet Union, no-one at the time seemed to remember the Seton-Watson legend nor to expect the break-up of the Federation of Yugoslavia, the Socialist Federal Republic of Yugoslavia as the Kingdom of the Serbs, the Croats and the Slovenes had, under Marshal Tito, become.

But break-up it did, most bloodily, in a series of confusing and dreadful little civil wars, where the ancient Kingdom of Serbia, plucky little Serbia of the First World War, heart of the Yugoslav resistance to the Nazis under Tito in the Second World War, tried to hold the Federation together by force of arms. And quickly the Serbs, formerly so admired, so heroic, became, at least in the eyes of the West, tyrants, oppressors, and the fomenters – after forty-five years of peace in Europe – of that unthinkable and totally unexpected calamity, an European War. Yugoslavia had indeed been a major mistake; and seventy years after its creation it was dissolving back into the six 'nations' from which it had been so artificially and so academically and so mistakenly formed.

Fortunately the civil wars in Yugoslavia did not spread. There was a risk that the Russians might become heavily involved on the side of their traditional allies, the Serbs; and as 'peace-keeping' forces from the West and East flew in, that there might be a dramatic clash between American and Russian troops. There was a risk that the conflict might involve in Slovenia the Italians, in Macedonia the Greeks. None of this happened. This new, totally unexpected European War was contained – basically limited to the central regions of Yugoslavia, to the three-way struggles between orthodox Serbia, catholic Croatia and muslim Bosnia-Herzogovina, three great chunks of adjoining territory, full of ancestral hatreds and passions that after forty-five years of being damped down – mainly thanks to Marshal Tito's firm dictatorship – had blown up, like volcanoes believed to be extinct but in fact only dormant, once again.

A New 'International' Brigade

The war really began in August 1991, weeks after Slovenia and Croatia had declared independence. The first mercenaries appeared on the Serb side as 'volunteers'. 'Captain Dragan' became a minor legend, apparently an Australian. But in fact he turned out to be, like others of his ilk, the son of immigrants to Australia from Yugoslavia, and there had been since the Second World War many of them. Dragan Yasiljokovic, alias Daniel Snedden, was known to the Melbourne police as a racketeer and pimp. Not all the 'volunteers' who went back to their ancestral Serbia from Australia fell into this sort of category; but the Serbs, who controlled the regular armed forces of Yugoslavia, soon realized they could do well enough without the marginal help of such 'volunteers'.

Croatia, Bosnia-Herzegovina and Serbia

It was a different story on the Croatian and Bosnian side. They were the under-dogs, and there was a distinctive sympathy throughout Western Europe for the underdogs. Indeed there were echoes – small echoes – of the wave of sympathy that had led to the formation of the International Brigade that had fought against Franco bravely, idealistically and unsuccessfully, in the Spanish Civil War of 1936-39.

An extraordinary boost to mercenary activity on the Croatian side was given precisely by a Spaniard, Eduardo Flores. This reporter for Barcelona's *La Vanguardia* did what Claud Cockburn and George Orwell and so many other English and French intellectuals had done in the Spanish Civil War: lain down their pens, and taken up guns. But Flores went even further. At Osijek in eastern Croatia he formed his own International Brigade and for some months his men dominated that front. Then, in January 1992, first a Swiss journalist, who had also apparently joined the Brigade, was murdered; next day, so was a British freelance photographer, Paul Jenks. Both were said to have quarrelled badly with Flores. The Croatians reacted; bad publicity and controversy they did not need. They first shifted and then apparently dissolved 'their' International Brigade.

Meanwhile, however, there was an extraordinary spate of interest in, and sym-pathy for, the Croatian cause in Britain. Extraordinary because Croatia had been on the 'wrong' side in the Second World War, a puppet Fascist state set up by

Mussolini and Hitler, and very Catholic to boot – not therefore of any natural appeal to the average Englishman. But: "I saw some stuff on the news about how Croatia is fighting for freedom, so I thought I'd come down and see what I could do to help," explained George Patterson, a 17-year-old who dropped out of school to join the Croatian National Guard. He was given one week's training with a Kalashnikov automatic rifle before being sent into action at Nostov. Danny Kington, 24, who at least was a former soldier, joined the same unit after seeing Serbian guerrillas on television "laughing like a bunch of savages" and firing mortars at a Catholic church "just for a bet".

Two years later, by early 1993, there was talk of "thousands" of British mercenaries in Croatia. Hundreds would be nearer the mark. They were, as always, a very mixed bunch, hanging around Zagreb, Croatia's capital, giving themselves military ranks to which they were not entitled (a 'Major Ward' kitted out in full Parachute Regiment uniform and cap badges was apparently merely a Territorial part-timer), joining odd Croatian militia groups, the HOS, the Black Legion and half-a-dozen others.

How did they get there? How were they recruited? Easy enough: this was not remotest Africa. Most of them simply bought train tickets to Zagreb. A few replied to ads in magazines like *Combat* or *Loot*. But it was all fairly disorganized, spontaneous – and, as always, stimulated more by idealism, or a desire for adventure, or the need to get away from home than any hopes of money or (despite the magazine's title) loot. Indeed conditions were spartan; most 'volunteers' got bed, meagre board, and a living allowance of about £20 a month. Unlike the Congo, there was no hope of 'liberating' banks. In fact 'mercenaries' they may well have been technically – undoubtedly were – but no-one could honestly say that their motivation was money.

By early 1993 the three competing armies were becoming much more professional. The Croatians had six well-organised brigades, each of 20,000 men, in the field, and were thought to be advised by Germans (traditional enough!). The Serbs had Russian advisers. The Bosnian Army, which had much improved, was rumoured (again traditionally enough for an offshoot of the Ottoman Empire) to have been retrained by Turks. There was becoming less and less need for odds and sods of mercenaries and volunteers. As the war concentrated on the struggle for Bosnia and the various bits and pieces of its territory, the most professional mercenary unit in the world, the Foreign Legion's 2ᵉ REP, guarded the airport at Sarajevo, Bosnia's capital, in – unusually for the Legion – a peace-keeping rather than war-fighting role.

Then an event occurred that virtually put an end to all this rather disjointed mercenary activity. On a cold Monday night in early February two British mercenaries, Ted Skinner and Derek Arnold, were found murdered near the town of Travnik. They had been abducted from their flat, taken to a small village, tortured; then, hands bound behind their backs, shot in the head and their bodies dumped.

The mysterious thing was they were in Bosnian territory, and working for the Bosnian commander in Travnik. So: who had executed them and why?

Gradually more became known about one of the two, Ted Skinner. Aged 38, he had left the family home at Wyndham Road, Chester twenty years earlier and emigrated to Australia. There he had served for eight years in the Royal Australian Regiment, becoming a sergeant. Back home by 1981, he had married, became a father, divorced – and was training guide-dogs for the blind before jumping at the chance to volunteer for Croatia. Back home again on leave he had boasted of shooting a young Serb gunman 'like a rabbit' – little wonder the Serbs had warned foreign mercenaries to leave or face execution – though to his parents, Ted and Joyce, he had claimed to be a lorry driver delivering humanitarian supplies.

In October 1992 he returned, but this time to help the Muslims. Apparently he claimed to have been a captain in the Argyll and Sutherland Highlanders. "They were very close to me in this command," said Colonel Ahmed Kulenovic, who commanded the Bosnian brigade in Travnik. "One had a medical training," (that must have been Foster) and the other, Ted, introduced himself as a former captain. "He was due to start training a new unit last Monday. He knew his job."

So what happened? Apparently Ted Skinner had made himself particularly helpful - after all, he himself was from Chester too - to Lt-Colonel Bob Stewart of the Cheshire Regiment, the British UN Force stationed only six miles away at Vitez. Now with the Muslim forces were a recently-arrived irregular brigade of *mujahideen,* veterans of the successful struggle against the Russians in Afghanistan. Had the two British mercenaries been passing information about these worrying newcomers on to 'Colonel Bob'? It is more than likely. As so often in mercenary history, bitter suspicion between two different rival groups of mercenaries - for the *mujahideen* were by definition in Bosnia mercenaries too – led to internecine killing. "There was obviously an easy relationship between Skinner and Colonel Bob," one newspaperman reported. Both the dead men "came here quite a bit and were very helpful with local knowledge," said a British officer at Vitez. "It was obviously a professional assassination," added Colonel Ahmed.

The bodies were flown home by the Foreign Office, who were unable, however, to trace any relatives of Derek Arnold. No-one was ever formally accused of, or prosecuted for, the double execution.

It had seemed inconceivable, after the Angolan tragedy,* that any Englishman or American with a minimum of common sense or any instinct for self-preservation would ever again become involved in any sort of mercenary activity. But nothing seems to put off would-be mercenaries – neither the danger of death in action, of execution by their own commanders, of treachery by their own allies or of severe punishment in the event of failure by the very instigators of their activity.

★   ★   ★

The war dragged on for two more years until the Dayton Peace Accords of November 1995 finally put an end to its tripartite horrors and left its signatories, President Slobodan Milosevic of Serbia, President Franjo Tudjman of Croatia and President Alija Izetbegovic of Bosnia-Herzegovina happily heading three new/old nations (though in the case of the first-named not long and happily) to add to the Concert of Europe. Like most European wars in the twentieth century it had lasted just over four years.

And, as in most European wars, since, indeed, the French Revolution of 1789, mercenaries had played only a minor part. Those that did appear had not seriously affected the outcome of the war, one way or another. Possibly the only exception were the *mujahideen* who had come to the aid of their beleaguered Muslim brothers of Bosnia. They were no doubt, most of them, idealists. But they were also, no doubt, paid. They were certainly fighting for a country that was not their own.

In the Spanish Civil War the International Brigade had also been, most of them, idealists. They had also, unarguably, been paid. Drawn from a dozen or more countries outside Spain, they were also fighting for a country, in their case the Spanish Republic, that was not their own. It may shake preconceived opinions to refer to the International Brigade as mercenaries; but by definition that is what they were: an organized, coherent, badly-paid group of fighting men employed in a civil war in a country that was not their own. And, by definition, the organised group that in the Yugoslav Civil War, most resembled the International Brigade was, it must be admitted, not the scattered individuals from other European countries but the *mujahideen* united by their muslim faith.

★   ★   ★

There was one further consequence of the Yugoslav war that could easily have been foreseen but which was not: and that was to throw onto the mercenary market, once the war had ended, any number of former fighters, Croats, Bosnians too, but mainly Serbs. The tale of how some of them, the most adventurous, or the most evasive, or possibly both, went out to the Congo to help Mobutu in his last and swiftest-moving civil war has already been told.★ Others joined the Foreign Legion. Others still went to Iraq – but that is another story, to be told (or, at least, to be examined and tentatively appraised, for this is, as I write, an ongoing affair) in the final chapter of this book.

II Civil War: Angola 1961 – 2002

Of all the civil wars in Africa that in Angola lasted, I believe, the longest. It began with uprisings against the Portuguese in 1961. It continued with the great struggle for power between the three rival factions, the FNLA, the MPLA, and

UNITA, when the Portuguese sailed away fourteen years later. And it went on when Holden Robert's FNLA was, despite Callan and the British mercenaries' best efforts,★ virtually wiped out.

And of all the revolutionary leaders in Africa Jonas Savimbi of UNITA was perhaps the most attractive - certainly the most recognisable. Burly, bearded, jovial, at ease with foreign correspondents, photographers, ambassadors and heads of state, almost always dressed in jungle fighting gear, recognized patriarch of the Ovimbundu tribes who dominated most of the rich plains of central Angola, he led his troops from the front. And he led them for almost forty years.

One could write a book about the rich life, varied fortunes and sad death of Jonas Savimbi; but that book is not this book. Though he, Jonas, will inevitably be the central figure of this demi-chapter, it is interesting to approach the immensely complex Angolan melodrama through the account, too, of a minor character, but one more directly relevant to the subject of this book, his fellow Ovimbundu tribesman, Daniel Chipenda.

DANIEL CHIPENDA AND JONAS SAVIMBI

Very biblical were the names of both. Jonas' father was head of a Protestant mission on the great Benguela Railway that cut the country almost neatly in two (he was also a stationmaster). Daniel's brother was a Pastor of the All African Council of Churches. Both were *assimilados*, that is to say educated and by this token admissible to Portuguese citizenship; and both crossed the ocean to study in Portugal. But both young men hated, if not all the Portuguese, at least the whole system of colonial rule.

They were just in their thirties when independence broke out all round. First the British, then the French, finally – reluctantly and chaotically – the Belgians freed their colonies in Africa. But the Portuguese had no intention of doing so. I remember well in Leo, capital of the Congo, in 1964 interviewing the Portuguese Consul-General. "We were in Africa a hundred years before you British," he table-thumped, "and be assured we will be in Africa a hundred years after you have left." He wasn't to prove exactly right. But certainly, by 1964, he could be proud enough that the Portuguese had suppressed first a 1961 uprising in Luanda, capital of Angola, and then a fierce revolt in the north, led by Holden Roberto of the Bakongo and his FNLA.

Jonas had arrived in Leo to join Holden Roberto as FNLA's secretary-general. But in 1964 he resigned, attacking its tribalism. For the great tribe of the Bakongo, who spread across the North of Angola into the Congo, considered themselves the natural rulers of the whole Congo basin; and indeed Holden Roberto was brother-in-law to the ruler of the Congo, General Mobutu.

Across the mighty River Congo lay Brazzaville – Brazza – capital of the tiny (compared to Mobutu's ex-Belgian Congo) ex-French Congo; and there Daniel

Chipenda had joined Holden Roberto's rival, the much more sophisticated poet-physician, Dr Agostinho Neto. Neto and his fellow intellectuals, many of them half Portuguese by blood, *mestizos,* led the MPLA. Jonas gravitated there. Indeed he was invited by Neto to become Secretary for Foreign Affairs of the MPLA. He refused.

Partly perhaps because he fell out with his fellow Ovimbundu, Daniel Chipenda. Chipenda was meant to be leading guerrilla attacks on the neighbouring Portuguese enclave of Cabinda. But Daniel was "ebullient, hard-drinking and a womaniser, notorious for his non-military exploits" and his hit-and-run raids were conducted with a miserable 5-10 guerrillas at a time. Jonas denounced Daniel to Neto. No wonder that in later years Chipenda was no fan of Savimbi's.

What a year that was, 1964! Che Guevara and Stokely Carmichael had arrived in Africa, followed by a thousand Cuban instructors to train both the Congo-Brazzaville army and the MPLA guerrillas. Jonas met Che in Algiers. But despite all the excitement, Jonas abandoned Agostinho Neto and the MPLA – too semi-white for his taste. He proceeded to, of all places, China; received $15,000 from the Chinese, and had them train his first followers – the "Chinese Eleven", the nucleus of the organisation he was about to set up on the borders of friendly Zambia, UNITA.

That of course meant a total break with Neto and the MPLA. Here is how Jonas Savimbi described the older man.:

> "Neto was made of cold but strong steel – cold but strong steel. He was not easy to bend. He was my adversary – I prefer not to call him an enemy – but he was a man of astounding intelligence and I respected him."

THE FIRST BLACK MERCENARIES

In the next ten years the three rival resistance movements made little headway against the Portuguese. Each had headquarters outside Angola – in Leo, Brazza, and Lusaka respectively – and each devoted an inordinate amount of energy to intriguing against and, where possible, eliminating each other.

Moreover, the Portuguese not only reinforced their troops with thousands of conscripts, they took into their pay what can only be described as the first real black mercenaries. These were the remains of the 8000-odd Katangese 'gendarmes' who had taken refuge in Angola, at the eastern end of the Benguela Railway, with Denard, Puren and Schramme in January 1963.★ Reinforced no doubt (if these had any instinct for self-preservation) by the 2-3000 who had pressed around Denard at the time of the "bicycle invasion" of Katanga in November 1967 demanding rifles to fight Mobutu. So there was in the north-east of Angola a strong force of mainly experienced Katangese fighters at least several thousand strong, living in exile, unable to return to their homeland, for briefly-independent Katanga had once again become part of Mobutu's Congo. Unfortunately there is no record of how and where and how effectively these black mercenaries were used; and no recognized leaders emerged from their ranks. But their 'natural' enemies were the Bakongo and Holden Roberto, the ally, protegé and relative of their oppressor Mobutu. One day perhaps their story will be told – it certainly had a dramatic sequence which is related in the previous volume – and one day it may well become obvious that these black mercenaries, the Katangese, were the forerunners of a new phenomenon in Africa.

For it would not be surprising to see in the next military generation the emergence of black mercenary leaders rising as it were from the ashes of the Denards and the Hoares – just as in medieval Italy the original leaders of the marauding Companies – French, German, Breton, Hungarian and English – were gradually replaced by the native Italian *condottieri*. These *condottieri* dominated Italian history for almost a century; and indeed even founded their own states.

Will history repeat itself? Will there ever be, in Africa, an Age of the Black Condottieri? Leading perhaps, as it did in Renaissance Italy, to the flowering of individual talent and creation of a new civilization? A fascinating question.... But beyond the scope of the present chapter. Back to Portuguese-ruled Angola.

THE 'CARNATION COUP'

No doubt about it, Angola was a backwater, and looked as if it was going to remain a backwater, as the Portuguese Consul-General had hopefully predicted, for many many decades to come.

Then suddenly, unexpectedly, almost totally out of the blue, came the eruption. The quiet lagoon exploded into violent life and even more violent death. The little fishes – Jonas and Daniel, Roberto and Neto – became big fishes; and sharks glided malevolently into the turbulent waters: Cubans, South Africans, Americans, Russians, the masters of the Cold War. For seventeen years, no less, Angola became the scene of an exceptionally fascinating military conflict; if only because it was the first and last time that white South Africa, the independent Republic of South Africa, went to war – and that, as the dice fell, on Jonas Savimbi's side; and Daniel Chipenda's too. Or rather Daniel on their's.

★   ★   ★

The eruption itself took place not in fact in Angola but in the mother-country, Portugal. On 25 April 1974 General Antonio Spinola seized power in Lisbon at the head of a left-wing Junta of National Salvation. The 'Carnation Coup' cost no lives. Within four weeks military operations in Angola were halted; within four months the right to independence was proclaimed. The anti-colonial forces had triumphed. The Portuguese oppressor was no more.

But *which* of the anti-colonial forces had triumphed? There lay the rub. Holden Roberto's FNLA? Jonas Savimbi's UNITA? Or Agostinho Neto's MPLA?

And if the MPLA seemed strongest in the capital, Luanda, it was in fact bitterly split into three competing factions: Neto's True MPLA, Andreade's Active Revolt, and Daniel Chipenda's Eastern Revolt. Briefly at the MPLA Congress at Brazza from August 31 to September 2 the three factions reunited, and Daniel became Vice-President. But some of *his* supporters had been viciously executed - their skulls cracked in wooden cages - by some of Neto's supporters in Zambia during the Congress; and understandably enough the factions fell apart again. Daniel led 2-3000 of his Chokwe and Mbundu guerrillas, the backbone of the Eastern Revolt, away from Brazza, across the River into Mobutu's Congo.

The Portuguese stayed on, rather pathetically, to attempt to hold the ring. Independence was scheduled for 11 November 1975. On 13 February 1975 Daniel's offices in Luanda - he was claiming now to be the Real MPLA - were attacked by Neto's men; fifteen of his followers were killed; and this time he broke away finally from the MPLA, taking his 3,000 men into Holden Roberto's ranks, to join the FNLA.

As for Jonas and UNITA, they concentrated in the Ovimbundu heartland, at Huambo, inland, on the Benguela Railway.

The South African Involvement

Angola is a vast country, bigger - just - than the four Provinces of South Africa put together. Under-populated, though, with perhaps 10 million inhabitants at the time of independence (about 40% of them Ovimbundu) as opposed to the 30 million-odd, black and white and coloured combined, of South Africa.

South West Africa is a vast country too, lieing just south of Angola, like Angola facing out across the Atlantic Ocean but even more under-populated, with only 1½ million inhabitants odd. It had been German South-West till the First World War (and the Germans had suppressed the great Herero Revolt of 1904-1907 with a cruelty and efficiency which the Portuguese might have envied). But since then it had become in effect white South Africa's Fifth Province. Down its desolate coast ran the barren Namib Desert. Inland lay the vast stretches of the Kalahari, home of Bushmen. Between the two lay the cultivatable plains, with in their centre the little German-style capital of Windhoek. To the south flowed the Orange River, border with South Africa proper. To the north stood the border with Angola. And in and around that northern border lay the lairs of SWAPO, South-West Africa's Liberation Movement - fortunately there was only one of them - led by Sam Nujoma. Sam was an Ovambo. The Ovambos were to the northern half of South West Africa what the Ovimbundu were to the central savannahs of Angola. When in 1966 Jonas Savimbi crossed back into Angola for the first time for eight years to found UNITA, he carried with him as a personal gift from Sam Nujoma his sidearm, a Tokarev pistol.

★   ★   ★

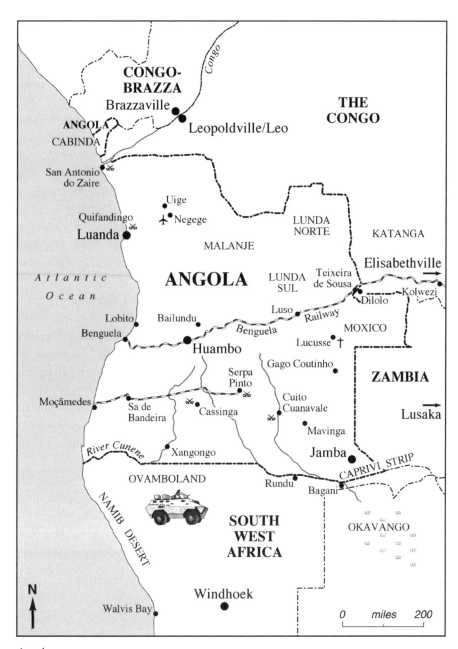

Angola

It is almost impossible now to imagine the appalled disgust with which white South Africa learnt that the Portuguese had decided to scarper from Angola and to hand over power to the blacks. It meant, inevitably, that unless South Africa took steps, SWAPO would have secure bases in Angola, instead of a few rough hideouts, and of course an immense boost in hopes and recruitment and, no doubt, weapons. But that disgust was nothing compared to the ultimate horror: the news, at first rumours only, then more and more certain, that the Cubans were coming!

For Fidel Castro – and what an extraordinary thing this was for a small island state on the other side of the Ocean to do – had decided to send an expeditionary force into Angola, to support Dr Agostinho Neto's MPLA and ensure that, on November 11, Independence Day, it was they, the Marxist-Leninist MPLA, that should seize power in Angola. And behind Fidel of course loomed the spectre of the Russians, and Communism, and the end of white rule and white capitalism not only in South West Africa, the next stepping stone after the 'liberation' of Angola, but in South Africa itself. Indeed the USSR freighter *Valery Mischlauk* had already unloaded, on the other side of Africa admittedly, at Dar-es-Salaam, no less than 785 tons of arms destined for SWAPO.

So the South African government decided that it should, that it must, that it would, halt the Cubans: and halt them not inside South West Africa but inside Angola. In strictly practicable terms it was decided that the South African Defence Force would invade Angola before Independence Day, before November 11; and seize at least the southern half of Angola, up to and beyond the Benguela Railway.

But in support of whom? Why, of Jonas Savimbi and UNITA. He might be black and not, in white South African eyes, very beautiful. But at least he spoke English, was, for a darkie, highly presentable; and above all Jonas was dogmatically anti-Russian, anti-Marxist.

As for Jonas – the greatest disgrace for any revolutionary black African leader was to accept aid from the white racist régime of Pretoria. He made up his mind to do it; but to keep it as hushed-up as possible. The South Africans agreed – 'Operation Savannah' was to be discreet, not last too long, be a warning shot across the Cubans' bows; and be limited to seizing as much 'traditional' UNITA – i.e. Ovimbundu – territory as possible before the symbolic date of November 11.

So, on 14 October 1975, three South African columns crossed the border from South West Africa into Angola. The 'invasion' had begun.

THE CIA TAKES A HAND

The United States was even more shaken up – if possible – than South Africa at the thought of its bogey-man Fidel Castro building himself a little Communist empire across the ocean in black Africa. But the American base of operations was

CIA headquarters at Leo, to the north of Angola; and thus they were backing Holden Roberto and the FNLA.

It is almost impossible to exaggerate the confusion and chaos that permeated Angola in those months and weeks preceding Independence. All three factions were fighting and killing each other in Luanda under the scared eyes of the Portuguese 'umpires'. In May the MPLA took over the Katangese, took them away from Portugal's payroll and onto its own, a useful body of mercenaries apparently 3,500 strong at the time. In August UNITA entered the civil war. On September 3 there docked at Brazza ships with a thousand Cubans aboard bound for Angola; and an air bridge was planned to raise Cuban numbers in Angola to 7,000 by December, to 12,000 by January.

Meanwhile the CIA armed and reinforced Holden Roberto and his men. The plan was for the FNLA to seize the capital Luanda before Independence Day, 11 November. On 10 November, the very day before, their forces had advanced to Quifandingo, only 20 miles north of the capital - 1,500 FNLA troops, 100 Portuguese settlers in Angola to back them up; and as allies two regular battalions of Mobutu's army. Offshore were yet more allies: the South African frigate *President Steyn* with, on shore, three South African artillery cannon and overhead - far too high overhead to be any use - three South African Mirage planes.

That day Holden Roberto's hopes of becoming the first President of Independent Angola were dashed for ever. That day the FNLA were virtually wiped out as an organised fighting force. In one hour the Cubans, well dug in, and well-armed, killed 800 FNLA, rocketed a dozen armoured cars and half a dozen jeeps, nearly captured a 26-man South African contingent (which escaped via the beach); and in effect triumphed totally under the eyes of CIA and South African military observers on the hills behind, overlooking what they came to christen Death Valley.

Next day Dr Agostinho Neto was proclaimed in Luanda President of the People's Democratic Republic of Angola - as the once-proud flag of Portugal was furled and the last Portuguese High Commissioner sailed sorrowfully away.

'OPERATION SAVANNAH'

Neto was lucky. For the South African columns in the south were racing ahead; and might just (but these were not their orders) have reached Luanda and placed Jonas Savimbi on the Presidential throne.

This despite the fact that it was a pretty amateurish invasion force. 'Zulu' Column on the coast consisted of seven South African officers, seven NCOs, and one Bushman battalion, zooming north in trucks, cars and landrovers. If readers look at the map, they will see the second smaller railway that stretches inland: - from Mocamedes to Sa de Bandeira to Serpa Pinto. Within a week of 'Zulu' Column's incursion Mocamedes and Sa de Bandeira were in UNITA's hands. As for Serpa Pinto, that was where the South Africans picked up Daniel Chipenda and what remained of his fighting forces.

What Daniel was doing down so far south I am not quite sure. Maybe Holden Roberto had sent him and his men down to raise the FNLA flag in the southern half of the country, an area where his group had no natural support at all. They were in a pretty bad way - unpaid, badly armed, "down and out" as the young South African officer who took them in hand put it, "a bunch of bank-robbers - they looked terrible". We do not know the name of the leader of 'Zulu' Column; he was known only as 'Rommel'. But we do know the name of the young South African officer who took the Chipenda semi-brigands in hand, rearmed and retrained them, added the best of them to 'Zulu' Column; and was eventually to give them a new and notorious insignia and to command them. His name was Jan Breytenbach; and he was to become Colonel commanding one of the most famous mercenary units of all time - No. 32 Battalion, the Buffalo Battalion.

So it came about that Daniel Chipenda's men, the Chokwe and the Mbundu (and probably by now some of his own Ovimbundu too), having been first the spearhead of the MPLA's Eastern Revolt, then the forces of the Real MPLA, then having entered the ranks of the FNLA, finally became white South Africa's most famous black mercenary force - white-officered admittedly, but always reckoned as 80% black and only 20% white. What a trajectory that was - more astounding even that that of the Katangese 'gendarmes' who had fought for an independent Katanga★ in the early Sixties, then for the Portuguese colonial forces, then for Portugal's one-time bitterest enemies, the MPLA - and were in a sense to redeem themselves by fighting again, though again hopelessly, for an independent Katanga - only to be routed, ironically enough, by France's elite mercenary force, Colonel Erulin's 2ᵉ REP of the Legion.★

★   ★   ★

Next month, in Huambo on the Benguela Railway, there was fighting between Daniel Chipenda's men - still officially part of the FNLA forces - and Jonas Savimbi's UNITA troops, with between 20 and 200 dead. So discipline and retraining had not by then got very far. That was on Christmas Eve 1975. And in any case by then the South African forces were on the verge of being pulled out.

For by then 'Zulu' Column, reinforced by a mortar group and by 20 of the splendidly mobile Eland armoured cars, had advanced north of the Benguela Railway; as had the inland 'Foxbat' Column led by 'Commandant Kaas'; while right in the interior 'X-ray' Column had taken Luso on the Railway, advanced north and at the 'Battle of Bridge 14' near Cela, at last encountered the Cubans. This time it was a decisive victory for the South Africans. 200 out of 1000 Cubans opposing them - perhaps one-third of the total Cuban force in Angola at the time - were killed there, plus the commander of the whole Expeditionary Force,

Commandant Raul Diaz Arguelles. That was in mid-December; and in a sense it was enough. 'Operation Savannah' had achieved its objective; the Cubans had been given a bloody nose. It was no part of the South African plan to occupy Angola permanently. It just remained to pull out with reasonable grace.

★   ★   ★

On January 16 1975 two South African generals flew to Cela where they met Holden Roberto and Daniel Chipenda - a Chipenda reduced to tears before them. Four days later Jonas Savimbi flew to Leo to meet General Vernon Walters, the CIA's Deputy Director. The message was basically the same; they, the Angolan Resistance, would be on their own, or almost. At the end of the month UNITA forces drove their 'allies', Chipenda's men, out of both Huambo and Serpa Pinto. They filtered across the border into South West Africa - the South Africans were still holding a buffer zone north of the border fifty miles deep for a few weeks more. And there, inside South West Africa, in the Caprivi Strip, the Buffalo Battalion was officially formed.

What exactly Daniel Chipenda's role now became is none too clear. Probably he was sidelined. Briefly the South Africans tried to form an "Anti-Communist Party of Southern Angola" from his supporters under the leadership of one of his lieutenants, Vita Kambuta. But Kambuta, flown to Leo to see Holden Roberto, deserted back to the now-triumphant MPLA. As for Daniel, he was to die many years later - on 28 February 1996 to be precise - in peaceful exile, in Cascais in Portugal. What Jonas, still fighting in Angola, thought of the unviolent, and unheroic death of his one-time enemy and potential rival is unknown. But Jonas was never, in the years to come, exactly at ease with the Buffalo Battalion - however many times the Buffalo Battalion was, directly or indirectly, to come riding to his rescue. Until, indeed, quite the contrary was to be the case.

BOB DENARD: MISSION IMPOSSIBLE

Despite the ghastly defeat at Quifandingo the CIA had not entirely despaired of Holden Roberto and the FNLA. They decided (and it was a fairly desperate resort) to boost his chances by hiring, via Mobutu and Leo, scores, hopefully hundreds, of British mercenaries to join and retrain the demoralised FNLA; and to keep the Cubans at bay in the interim. The story of 'Colonel Callan' and those desperate days in the north of Angola has already been told.★   By February 1976 *that* attempt had failed; and Holden Roberto - though of all the characters on the scene in 1975 he is the only one alive and well today in 2005 - was a force no longer to be reckoned with. The FNLA passed out of history.

And for a time it looked as if Jonas Savimbi and UNITA would go exactly the same way too. By now the Soviets were supplying millions of dollars' worth of arms and armaments to the MPLA and to the Cuban Expeditionary Force. There were T34 and T35 tanks, which even the reckless bravery of 'Colonel Callan' had only been able to halt temporarily as Cuban columns drove north to the Congo's borders. There were light amphibious tanks too, and missile-firing helicopters, and above all the multiple-barrelled 'Stalin's Organs' whose rockets had so demoralised the FNLA in 'Death Valley'.

As for the Americans, their aid to the FNLA and UNITA was on a much lower scale. They were hampered by the Clark Amendment, which forbade for the future any official aid at all. This did not however rule out the use of 'unofficial' CIA funds. Hence the meeting of General Vernon Walters with Jonas Savimbi in Leo. And hence the dispatch to Jonas' side of 25 French mercenaries at the end of January. Their task? To hold up the Cuban / MPLA advance now that the South Africans had pulled back to the border and were on the verge of pulling out altogether.

★   ★   ★

Bob Denard's involvement in the Cabinda affair has already been described. ★ That was pre-Independence, pre-11 November 1975; and when that came to an abrupt end, his ten men from Cabinda, under the command of René Dulac, *Le Grand,* 'retired' hastily to Leo.

A fortnight *after* Independence, that is to say when the CIA were beginning almost to despair of Holden Roberto and to consider supporting, at least in a minor way, Jonas Savimbi in his place, Bob Denard was summoned to Paris to meet, and negotiate with, a retired US Marine lieutenant-colonel working for the CIA. It was a tough negotiation. When it ended, Denard had obtained what he wanted: a guarantee of no less than $350,000 payable in advance to send twenty French mercenaries south to join Jonas Savimbi and UNITA on a five months' contract: there to train them on SAM 7 missiles to be used against the two squadrons of Russian MIGs reported to be based in Brazza and ready, it seemed, to intervene deep inside Angola to crush the last resistance to the MPLA and the Cubans.

In fact the final bill (including life insurance for the mercenaries) came to $425,000; and Bob sent out only fifteen, led by Freddie Thieleman and Le Bosco. But these were joined by the ten from Leo under René Dulac, so that he more than fulfilled his side of the contract. (An interesting sidelight is that in Leo the French - i.e. *Le Grand* - rejected as unsuitable material the three British mercenaries who had fled from Sao Salvador and taken refuge in John Simpson's room in the Intercontinental Hotel. John Simpson - this was his first 'mission' abroad for the BBC, long before he had become their world-famous Foreign Affairs chief correspondent, so his judgement may have been a little callow - considered the French to be of a much higher calibre than the British. *Le Grand* refused, typically, to give his name - and was known to Simpson only as 'Max'. He claimed to have been educated at a British public school. This sounds rather unlikely for René Dulac; but might possibly be true of Le Bosco, if Le Bosco was up at Leo briefly at the time. For Le Bosco was Belgian - not his real name either - and there were in the post-war days many Belgians, though very few French, at Downside, the famous Catholic Benedictine public school near Bath.)

★   ★   ★

Denard's men certainly transited via Leo; which ruled him personally out, for the ex-commander of Six Commando was still, for very obvious reasons,★ *persona non grata* with President Mobutu. They moved out into the field in the first week of February 1976 - to find UNITA's whole position on the verge of crumbling. The MPLA used helicopters to drop their Katangese mercenaries in UNITA's rear; and the terrifying 'Stalin's Organs' in front. Cuban tanks rolled into Huambo, Jonas' 'capital' on the 8th; MPLA forces took Lobito and Benguela at the coastal end of the Railway on the 10th. Further up the line, at Luso, Jonas was waiting desperately for four Israeli-piloted Mirage fighters based in Leo to swing into action; and for four French-manned missile-firing Alouette helicopters, also at Leo - whose HOT rockets would have wiped out the 'Stalin's Organs' that were so demoralising his men. Neither came. Nor - perhaps there was some sort of tacit bargain - did the two squadrons of Soviet MIGs in waiting at Brazza; at least not at this moment.

So, for a few nerve-wracking weeks, Denard's handful of men ranged up and down and near the Benguela Railway trying to hold up, to hold off, the Cuban columns with their Soviet tanks. The French did have issued to them some US Law anti-tank missiles; so the struggle was not totally one-sided.

But it was hopeless. Bob Denard finally flew out from Libreville to South Africa and then up to Rundu in the Caprivi Strip. By then things were pretty desperate. On March 13, if the story is true, the French mercenaries had shot down, by mistake , one of UNITA's own supply planes. Henri Alain, son of General Alain, who had been with Denard in 6 Commando and at Bukavu★ had been killed. Jonas and a few hundred followers had taken to the bush. Typhoid was rampant.

Bob Denard finally came face to face with Jonas Savimbi at Gago Coutinho, not far from the border with Zambia. He tried to persuade him to leave.

> "You cannot remain here," Bob told Jonas. "You have no chance whatsoever. If you stay you will be dead within two months.
>
> "If you come with us, it will be valuable to the West. We will arrange for you to stay in an African country until the situation changes. Then you can return to start your campaign again."

Savimbi refused. Not many African leaders in his position, strafed almost daily by Cuban-piloted MIG 21 fighter-bombers (which had indeed now entered the fray for the final 'kill'), would have done the same.

But Denard and his men, with considerable difficulty, were evacuated. As Bob said, *"Il aurait fallu être au moins deux cents cinquante. C'etait mission impossible"*.[1]

Henri Alain's body they found it impossible too to take with them. The general's son was buried where he had fallen; somewhere in the remote savannah of the Central Highlands.

★   ★   ★

That March UNITA columns, men, women and children 4,000 strong, moved out from Gago Coutinho into the surrounding forests; but heading west towards the interior, not east towards Zambia and safety.

That June 'Colonel Callan' and the British and American mercenaries captured in the North were tried by the People's Revolutionary Tribunal in Luanda; and on 10 July Costas Georgiou, the real name of 'Callan' himself, Andy MacKenzie, 'Brummy' Barker and Daniel Gearhart were shot at Grafanil military base outside Luanda by a firing squad of MPLA military police.

ACT THREE: THE LONG WAR 1977 - 1991

There is something almost Shakespearian about the Angolan Civil Wars. Envisaged as a historical tragedy of Five Acts, starting with the Rebellion against the Portuguese, continuing with the Imbroglio of Independence, it resolves into a long- simmering, violent, often heroic, certainly simplified, central act.

The Long War is a fascinating military study. It was fought almost entirely in the southern quarter of Angola. Basically the Cubans and the MPLA held the railway line Mocamedes - Sa de Bandeira - Serpa Pinto and, at the junction of two rivers, the stronghold of Cuito Cuanavale to the south east. In the quadrilateral south of the railway the South Africans fought SWAPO and, when necessary, the MPLA.

On the other side of the rivers, in the deep bush, Jonas Savimbi set up his extensive jungle base at Jamba, north of the Caprivi Strip, close to the border with Zambia. And from this base, for years, with varied success, UNITA battled the government forces - the MPLA and the Cubans. How Jonas survived, how King Hassan of Morocco allowed him to retrain his military cadres at Benguerir (almost in Bob Denard's Benin wake), how China, with American and South African connivance, delivered 600 tons of armaments to UNITA, how Dr Agostinho Neto, "Immortal Guide of the Angolan Revolution", nonetheless died a mortal's death on a visit to Moscow; and was succeeded as President of Angola

---

[1] "We should have had at least 250 men. It was mission impossible."

by the "strikingly handsome and highly articulate" José Eduardo Dos Santos, equipped both with a petroleum engineering degree and a Soviet wife, even how the Katangese (very possibly ill at ease with Cuban communists) were siphoned off back to the killing fields of Katanga★ - all that is another story.

The important thing to grasp is that Savimbi and UNITA survived; survived and indeed flourished.

Here is an elegant and reasonably objective description of Savimbi by the American diplomat Chester Crocker:

> "Jonas Savimbi had a world-class strategic mind…   It was difficult not to be impressed by this Angolan who combined the qualities of warlord, paramount chief, demagogue and statesman. His toughness and courage were as legendary as his ferocity towards those who crossed him. I respected Savimbi as a serious and capable person. Fluent in three African and four European languages and well schooled in modern history and world politics, Savimbi was more sophisticated in his grasp and judgements than his Western champions and most fellow African leaders."

If Savimbi is the Protagonist of this unfolding drama, such a character description explains much about his extraordinary success; and indeed, by implication, about his hubris, that was to lead to the peripateia of the 1992 elections and his eventual downfall. Sophistication, whether in Jonas or Oedipus, was a dubious blessing at best, a curse of the jealous gods at worst.

★   ★   ★

South Africa had a new Prime Minister, P.W. Botha, known as "the Old Crocodile"; who, wrote Chester Crocker, not entirely with admiration, "saw himself as the Charles de Gaulle of the Afrikaners' autonomous regional superpower". With a "hardline gynaecologist", Dr Willie Van Niekerk, as Administrator General in place at Windhoek, with General Magnus Malan as Minister of Defence, General Constant Viljoen as Army Chief, and General Jannie Geldenhuys, a "soldier's soldier" as Chief of Staff, with Armscor, South Africa's own armaments industry set up, funded and soon flourishing, white Boer-led South Africa set about repairing its awful error in having pulled out of Angola when, with a little more push, they might, in November 1975, have reached Luanda and imposed their will. Now the 2-3,000 Cubans were swelling towards 30,000…

South Africa reacted. The South West Africa Territorial Force -SWATF - was established, 20-25,000 strong: with the Bushman Battalion from West Caprivi as its original nucleus; basically trackers, split into companies of 100. To this was added a further Bushman battalion, two Ovambo battalions, one Kavango battalion, one Caprivi battalion and one Herero and Ovahumbo battalion. Then, as an eighth battalion, came Koevoets, the 'Crowbar' battalion, organised from scratch by South West African police officers – white police officers – of the Counter-Insurgency Unit with in its ranks 'turned' SWAPO deserters. This naturally, and quickly, became one of the most hated and aggressive SWATF units.

But none were as feared, none as militarily successful, as what now became under its proud new Colonel Jan Breytenbach the Buffalo Battalion. They were based in Bagani, in the Caprivi Strip; and on May 4 1978 the Buffalo Battalion carried out a daring airborne attack on the SWAPO base at Cassinga. Four Transail C160s and six Hercules C130s parachuted them in; and of the 2,000-odd SWAPO guerrillas based at 'Moscow' – as their camp was named – almost 600 were killed. Seeing that SWAPO forces were generally believed to number 8,000 at most, this was a devastating blow both in itself and to morale. "A jewel of military craftsmanship," General Geldenhuys ecstatically described it as. It certainly became controversial. For the 2,000 guerrillas had been living side by side like their women and children; and were those 600 dead all fighters and men?

This 'jewel', **Operation Reindeer,** was followed by **Operation Smokeshell** (1980) a scattered three-week-long ground battle (in which no Cubans were involved); **Operation Protea** (1981) a much more ambitious affair in which the South African Air Force attacked and destroyed Soviet-installed radar-stations and SAM-3 and SAM-6 missile sites, and South African ground forces captured one Soviet sergeant-major and killed two senior Red Army officers in 12 days of intense fighting (again no Cubans were involved); **Operation Super (1982)** a heliborne attack on a new SWAPO base; and **Operation Askari** (December 6 1983-January 31 1984), which involved 10,000 ground troops, waves of Mirage and Impala fighter bombers, which came up against tougher missile sites and better-managed armour – though 25 T54s were destroyed and a SAM-9 Missile System captured intact.

This was now becoming, as readers will have perceived, a serious large-scale war; and, on the back of the South African incursions, UNITA was doing very well, doubling the territory it controlled, establishing itself in Moxico and Malange Provinces, in Lunda Sud and Lunda Norte. A lull followed in 1984. In 1985 a South African commando unit was intercepted in May in Cabinda – its mission to sabotage the Gulf Oil installations there. Five of its members were killed, and its leader, Captain Wynard du Toit, captured. (He was later exchanged: but du Toit is a name for readers to remember.)

Almost in retaliation a large MPLA-Cuban offensive, backed by 1½ billion dollars of USSR aid and advisers, was launched against Jonas' base at Jamba; but blocked by UNITA and the South Africans. It was a precursor of an even vaster offensive two years later, Soviet-led by General Shagnovitch – there were now a thousand Red Army 'advisers' with the MPLA – that was smashed at the Battle of the Lomba River, largely by the 'new' South African artillery, the self-propelled 155mm guns that outranged both the USSR equipment, and incidentally, outranged too the best that the West could produce. Thousands of the government's best troops were pinned down and destroyed; and the assault ended in complete

Soviet humiliation. Triumphantly Jonas welcomed P.W. Botha (now President Botha under South Africa's new constitution), General Malan and General Geldenhuys at Jamba, his headquarters in the bush.

But the Cubans, who had taken no part in what they considered a misguided operation, now despatched 15,000 more troops to Angola and took over Cuito Cuanavale from the discredited Soviets and demoralised MPLA forces. By February 1988 thousands more Cubans moved into Cunene Province south of the Mocamedes Railway; the whole zone being placed under command of General Armando Ochoa Sanchez. Xangongo, forty miles from the Border, was upgraded as a massive airbase, defended by surface to air missiles, equipped with helicopter gun-ships and MIG 23s. Two hundred tanks moved south. From Havana Fidel Castro boasted of air superiority and warned South Africa of imminent defeat. In London Chester Crocker, desperately trying to arrange quadripartite peace deals on behalf of the State Department, regretted the "honour and pride of P.W. Botha and Fidel Castro, two highly-strung gentlemen" and described the situation as that of "two scorpions in a bottle", with neither daring to sting the other.

On June 8 General Geldenhuys put South Africa's territorial reserves on stand-by, the 140,000-strong Citizen Force, so serious did the threat seem. Three weeks later the stinging began in earnest; with bitter fighting near the Cunene Dam. There South Africa's heavy tanks, the Olifants - useless in the interior, too heavy on the bridges across the innumerable rivers and streams of the savannah - proved their worth, finally repulsing the last Cuban attack.

On the other flank, at the long-drawn-out Battle of Cuito Cuanavale, the Buffalo Battalion had its glory days. They led the fighting throughout the month of July. Neither side put forward its full strength; both sides claimed victory. But both in fact had drawn back from the brink of an out-and-out, Leipzig-style Battle of the Nations, with all its totally unpredictable consequences.

Peace followed, a peace of general psychological and indeed economic exhaustion:- the Accords of New York, the Tripartite Agreement, *Les Accords de Brazzaville.* Chester Crocker's exceptionally persevering diplomacy finally succeeded. Jonas Savimbi and Eduardo Dos Santos met at Mobutu's extraordinary Palace of Gbadolite. The Old Crocodile was replaced as President of South Africa by F.W. de Klerk. A treacherous 'Operation Final Assault' by the Soviets/MPLA against Jamba was foiled, just. Nelson Mandela was freed; and within weeks, on March 21 1990, South West Africa became an independent state, under the name of Namibia, with Sam Nujoma as the new nation's first President.[2]

The other half of the bargain followed a year later. A ceasefire in Angola between the MPLA and UNITA and, five weeks ahead of schedule, the final withdrawal to their tropical Caribbean island of the last of the no-doubt highly-relieved Cuban Expeditionary Force.

---

[2] Did Jonas Savimbi return the Tokarev pistol? Was he even invited to President Nujoma's Inauguration? Probably neither.

That was in the merry month of May 1991 – merrier than usual because the long, long war was over.

Deprived of their base in the Caprivi Strip, unwanted by either side in their native land, with no apparent war to fight or role to fill, the exiles of the Buffalo Battalion were pulled back, disconsolate, to remote barracks at Pomfret in the Republic of South Africa, mercenaries now further than ever from their home-lands and unlikely – so it seemed at the time – ever to return. But the strangest reversal of fate in fact awaited them.

Savimbi For President!

For eighteen long months peace reigned in the Republic of Angola. There were to be elections; that was part of the peace deal, and that was what Jonas had always demanded, had always been striving for. For none of the three rivals who had pro-claimed themselves Presidents of Angola on that far-off day of 11 November 1975 had in fact been elected by anyone other than their own Central Committees. Of the three one was dead (and his successor was a young, equally unelected figure) one was discredited and only one – Jonas himself – remained on the scene, in full and fine fettle. On September 21 1991 Jonas made a triumphant entry into Luanda, cheered on by masses of jubilant supporters. It looked as if he, repre-sentative of the largest tribal group in Angola by far, recognisable to all, known for his perseverance, a man whose face was familiar throughout the whole wide world, would at last attain that position for which his talents almost uniquely in Angola fitted him, of President of his country, elected by popular vote and popular acclaim. He himself, certainly, almost messianically, believed this to be his ineluctable destiny.

The elections were held a year later, on 29-30 September 1992. There were eleven presidential candidates. But only two of these were serious contenders: Savimbi and Dos Santos. However, as so often happens, particularly following a civil war and an externally-imposed peace, elections stirred up all the old hatreds, resentments and fears that had slumbered for over a year. The results were due to be declared on 17 October. But UNITA was convinced that the government – the MPLA – had shamelessly rigged the elections; and that their man would be cheated out of his rightful success and his deserved place as the new Head of State.

Had they? Had the MPLA rigged the elections? There was – and still is – enor-mous debate about this. UN observers declared them to be free and fair. But UN observers are notorious, at elections like these, for observing only what they wish to observe.

Between the date of the elections and the announcement of the results, in those intervening eighteen days, peace came to a sticky end. On 5 October UNITA withdrew its forces from the combined new 'united' army that was being set up. On 11 October heavy fighting broke out in Luanda. Jonas' nephew was killed; and so too was UNITA's deputy leader. On 13 October Pik Botha, South Africa's popular, bombastic Foreign Minister, flew out to Huambo to where Jonas had understandably pulled back, to plead with him to accept the election results, whatever they might be; and to warn him, no doubt, that should they turn out bad and should UNITA take up the armed struggle again, South Africa - a rapidly changing South Africa - would be in no position to give him further assistance.

On 17 October the results were declared: for Dos Santos 49.57% of the vote, for Savimbi 40.07%. Eduardo Dos Santos, not Jonas Savimbi, was therefore declared the truly elected President of the Democratic Republic of Angola.

Was this a fair result? Possibly. One theory is that the Ovimbundu of the cities, urbanized, no longer voted according to their tribal origins; and that Jonas had been wrong to assume their automatic support. But, whatever the truth of the matter, it was a shattering blow to a man who had expected to win and to a party that had hoped, at long last, to assume power.

In the last weeks of 1992, almost inevitably, conflicts between UNITA and the MPLA broke out in all the cities; and much more bitterly and viciously than ever before. Portugal sent ships and marines to evacuate the last of the Portuguese settlers - and there were still, amazingly, 40,000 of them who had stayed on - as urban chaos, hitherto avoided, ensued. By the turn of the year fighting had spread to 15 out of Angola's 18 provinces. And on 3 January 1993 President Dos Santos formally announced: "Angola is at war".

THE SECOND CIVIL WAR 1992 - 1994

This was to be a very different sort of war. Cuba was not involved, nor South Africa, nor Russia, nor America. In a sense it was a 'purer' civil war; and it rather looked as if, without Cuban support, the government, the MPLA, was, militarily speaking, a busted flush. In swift succession UNITA captured Uige one hundred and fifty miles north of Luanda (well outside its 'traditional' territory) and Negege, the strategic air base just south of Uige.

And then UNITA captured San Antonio do Zaire, right in the north, right on the southern shores of the Congo estuary. Readers of the second volume of this trilogy will remember how, 17 years earlier, on Saturday 7 February 1976, San Antonio had fallen to the Cuban tanks; and the unfortunate 'Brummy' Barker had been captured in his underpants as his three fellow British mercenaries (and the 16 wretched FNLA defenders) escaped across the Congo River to safety on the farther shore. Since then things had changed at San Antonio. Oil had been discovered offshore; and San Antonio was no longer a one-horse little town but the centre of operations of Canada-based Heritage Oil and Gas; and a most important source of revenue to the government in Luanda.

The government - the MPLA - squealed in protest (particularly when Gulf Oil began evacuating understandably nervous foreign workers from Cabinda to the north); and began referring wildly to white mercenaries from South Africa as being involved. But this was to attempt to raise, ridiculously and futilely, a bogeyman from the past. Jonas Savimbi was not like Holden Roberto; he had always detested the use of white mercenaries; and his one experience with a few of them, with Denard's group of 25 foisted upon him in his most desperate straits, had not been a happy experience. Never before and never after had he employed them, or considered employing them. And he did not do so at San Antonio. UNITA might ally with whites; just as it was originally trained by yellows. But, through and through, it remained a black, and often a very racist black, military force.

Enter The Eight Us Gernerlas

There now occurred the most extraordinary turning of metaphysical tables. Dos Santos, President of Angola, President of the MPLA, was president of a country and a party and a régime that had always condemned mercenaries, had set up a Popular Revolutionary Tribunal that had indeed condemned four to death, and an International Commission that had assembled Marxists from all corners of the globe to condemn the crime of *'mercenarismo'*. Yet now the situation that faced Dos Santos was this: he might have won, by fair means or foul, the recent elections. But the Second Civil War had well and truly begun; and though the government still held, just, the main towns (apart from Huambo), it looked very much as if their army was losing and as if Jonas Savimbi would before long be marching into the Presidential Palace in Luanda at the head of his victorious and exulting troops.

So what did Dos Santos do? Amazingly, he turned to the old enemies of his régime, the Americans, for help. This was perhaps not quite so extraordinary as it might seem at first; for there was, by now, a community of interests. Angola (including of course Cabinda, its original oil-rich enclave) was by now producing somewhere in the region of 900,000 barrels of oil a day; and of this a great deal was being supplied to the United States. Hence any interruption of supplies, and of existing contracts, injured the MPLA; but hurt America too.

So Dos Santos applied for aid in 'retraining' his army - the wavering MPLA Forces - not to the United States Government directly; but to MPRI - Military Professional Resources Inc - of Virginia.

MPRI had been set up in 1987/8 by eight retired American generals; of whom the moving spirit was Major General Vernon B. Lewis. Its executive director was four-star General Carl Vuono; and two of the others General Ed Soyster and General Frederic Kroesen, all with highly distinguished military careers behind them. It was based in Alexandria, just outside Washington D.C; it had, it claimed, 2,000 former US officers on its books; and it was, it boasted, "the greatest enterprise of military expertise in the world".

But what *was* MPRI, exactly? Hard to say. A powerful group of freelance mercenaries? Or a privatized sub-branch of the Department of Defence? MPRI was certainly at or about this time training the Croats (and supplying them with $1000 million-worth of military equipment a year). And they were to train the Croats so successfully that in August 1995 the Croat Army was to recapture Serb-held Krajina in a weekend. But at the same time they were quite clearly a channel for American military aid and most definitely an instrument of American foreign policy. For they **did** apparently sign a contract with Angola to retrain and re-equip the MPLA forces; but this contract was **revoked** by the Department of State's Office of Defence Trade Controls and its Bureau of Political-Military Affairs after reference to the Assistant Secretary of State. In other words the State Department had approved of MPRI's involvement with the (basically-Catholic anti-Communist) Croats; but subsequently vetoed its involvement with the still-officially-Marxist government of Angola.

And of course there may have been a slight residue of sentiment involved. For the United States via the CIA had encouraged and supported Jonas Savimbi and UNITA in its original struggle against the in their eyes unholy alliance of the local Marxists, the Cubans and the Soviets. They were abandoning him now. Like the United Nations, the United States formally condemned UNITA for relaunching the civil war; and Savimbi for refusing to accept the election results. But between official disapproval and active help in suppressing his movement and organising the military destruction of UNITA was a big, big difference and perhaps it was a matter of honour not to cross that line.

No such considerations of conscience applied, however, in the 'new' South Africa.

THE FOUNDING OF EXECUTIVE OUTCOMES

In 1989, in Pretoria, Eeben Barlow and Lafras Luitingh, with 24 other former SADF officers, founded Executive Outcomes. These were not retired generals, bigwigs like MPRI's founders. These were young men in their twenties or thirties whom the end of the long, long war in Angola and Namibia had left surplus to requirements, with military skills that there seemed little prospect of using in the direct service of their country. But by 1990, with the freeing of Nelson Mandela, everyone but the most blinkered Africaners could foresee the day when the ANC would take over the Republic; and then, with other black African countries opened up at last to all South African citizens, who was to say what opportunities might not arise in nations to the North - such as the vast and potentially vastly rich Congo?

So, from small beginnings, from a base at a small airport outside Johannesburg, Executive Outcomes gradually expanded; as a security firm; as a training outfit; in particular as a group that would send armed guards out to mines and oil installations.

And in 1989 too the Buffalo Battalion, withdrawn from Namibia, from its base in the Caprivi Strip, had been sent to Pomfret, a dreary little garrison town set on the edge of the Kalahari Desert, in the north of Cape Province, once the site of asbestos works, now disused, 100 miles away from the nearest neighbouring town. Pomfret was to become known, not affectionately, as the 'Mercenary Capital of South Africa'.

But the Buffalo Battalion was not disbanded, not quite yet. It was used, as mercenaries are always used, as the Foreign Legion was used in the Battle of the Kasbah in Algiers, for the dirty work of internal security that citizen soldiers find so repugnant. It was used, in those final long months of white rule, to keep a lid on the townships, to back up the armed police, to suppress riots. And of course as the blacks of the Buffalo Battalion spoke neither English nor Xhosa nor Zulu but only Portuguese and their own tribal languages, there could be no verbal appeals to them as 'comrades' by the rioters. They were a race apart, and they were hated. Back at Pomfret, though, in their dilapidated brick houses, lacking running water, they were isolated; but they were, at least a community, their wives and children, as always, with them. Inevitably many of their former white officers gravitated towards Executive Outcomes; and towards the similar little 'security' outfits that were springing up here and there as unemployed white officers and NCOs tried to recycle themselves in the business they knew best, or at least on its margins.

The Changing of the Guard

1993 was an extraordinarily significant year in modern mercenary history. In 1993 the first of the new mercenary leaders, the generation that was to supplant the Hoares and the Denards, appeared – and appeared on the scene in Angola. But the most extraordinary thing about this extraordinary succession is that these 'new' white mercenaries found themselves fighting on the side not of UNITA but of the MPLA; that is to say, on the side of the Marxist régime that professed to be horrified at the very thought of *'mercenarismo',* that crime against humanity and particularly, if their rhetoric is to be followed, against black humanity in Africa. Such a *volte-face* renders the humanist perhaps cynical, but the historian of mercenaries wryly content. Whenever mercenaries are really needed by states or insurrectionists, ideology tends to fly out of the window as opportunism seeps in.

To explain how this extraordinary new twist came about, we must leave Angola - with UNITA rampant in the North, threatening Cuito Cuanavale in the South, and fending off, successfully, the siege of its old 'capital', Huambo, in the Centre, on the Benguela Railway; with the North American oil companies attempting to exploit the oil fields off San Antonio and in Cabinda in turmoil and, worse still, losing revenue; and turn back a few years in time to a very different country and a totally different military atmosphere.

★   ★   ★

The Brigade - the Brigade of Guards - is, after the Household Cavalry, the smartest, best-turned-out, most effortlessly courageous, splendidly historic, beautifully disciplined collection of soldiers in the British Army. Its members guard, as their name implies, their Sovereign. They are based in the Capital, and at Windsor. Their officers are by tradition independently wealthy and drawn from the upper classes and the aristocracy. Within Her Majesty's Forces to be "in the Brigade" is to belong, almost, to a caste set apart: far superior, in any case, to such low forms of military life as members of the Parachute Regiment or of ordinary infantry regiments of the line.

Of the five Regiments of the Brigade the Coldstream and the Grenadiers consider themselves the superior. The Irish Guards, the Welsh Guards and the Scots Guards are all traditionally recruited from their respective Celtic countries. If any Guards Regiment were to be linked with modern mercenary history, one might have thought that, in view of their country's past traditions, in view of the 'Wild Geese'★★ it would be the Irish. Wrong. It was the Scots.

In 1979 in the Officers' Mess of the Scots Guards were four officers. The eldest and senior, Alastair Morrison, a Major, was to win the Military Cross in the Falklands three years later. Junior to him, just an Acting Major, was the Honourable Richard Bethell, son and heir of the 5ᵗʰ Lord Westbury, a Yorkshire peer. Two years his junior was Captain Simon Mann, second cousin to Sir Edward Mann, 3ʳᵈ Baronet of Billingford Hall in Norfolk; and below them a humble lieutenant, Tim Spicer, who had nevertheless won the Sword of Honour at Sandhurst.

These four officers were to serve together - and fight together - in Northern Ireland and the Falklands. That is not to say they were necessarily friends. Rivalries and enmities can flourish in even the most civilized of regiments. But, because of the disparity of their ages and ranks, they were not direct rivals. In any case it was only the youngest, Tim Spicer, who was to stay on for fifteen years more and rise steadily in rank. The rest - the senior three - had left the Regiment, the Brigade and the Army by the early eighties. They had reconverted to civilian, or rather to semi-military semi-civilian, life.

Alastair Morrison, the senior of the three, is also the least known. But it is said that it was Alastair Morrison who set the tone and direction for the next great wave of British mercenary activity. And it was his former fellow-officers of the Scots Guards who followed where he led.

★   ★   ★

The organisations they set up were more like David Stirling's Watchguard★ than John Banks' International Security Organisation Ltd or Security Advisory Services. But however high-faluting the titles, however glossy the brochures, they were all basically, like John Banks' dismal duo★, mercenary organisations. The great difference was in the veneer - much smoother in every sense of the word.

For these were organisations run, in the main, by former officers who had served their country honourably and not by disgraced troopers and dishonourably discharged NCOs. These were men who knew the ups and downs and twists and turns of the corridors of power; who were not on the margins of society; who had personal and family contacts with the high and mighty, indeed with the City as well as the Army and the Court. Not that these contacts always helped them. But they were there. It would be fair to describe them as the merchant venturers of the modern mercenary trade - in that sense, rather curiously, New Elizabethans emerging onto the world scene in the old age of their Monarch.

In 1988 Alastair Morrison and Richard Bethell, the two formers Majors, set up Defence Services Ltd - DSL. Exactly where they set up, exactly what services DSL offered, is a little obscure. Their organisation is said to have provided security guards for BP - British Petroleum - in Nigeria, tackled mine clearance for the United Nations in Bosnia and Croatia, trained Columbia's security services. None of these sounds improbable. But none of them led on to the enormous success and importance that attended Simon Mann's enterprise. That success and importance was due, of course, to Mann's talent and energy, training and perseverance - and indeed to his remarkable charm; but above all, I would say, to his personal connections with South Africa.

Simon Mann

Cricket was the great link with South Africa. Cricket - and love.

Sir Edward Mann, Simon's great grandfather, a wealthy brewer, became not only Mayor of Stepney by the City of London but also High Sheriff of Norfolk, and the first Baronet, with a seat at Thelvedon Hall. And also, equally importantly, a distinguished member of the MCC.

His second son, Francis Mann, even more distinguished, captained the MCC cricket team; and was a Captain too in the 1st Battalion, The Scots Guards in the Great War - twice wounded and thrice mentioned in dispatches.

At the end of which his son, George Mann, was born. George, most distinguished of all the Mann cricketers, captained the Eton Cricket Team in 1936. In 1938 and 1939 he won two Cricket Blues at Cambridge. He too joined The Scots Guards - this time for the Second World War - became a Major, one rank higher than his proud dad, and by repute "the best regimental officer in the British Army". After the war was won, he recovered from his wounds, helped no doubt by his legendary bravery (he had won both the D.S.O. and the M.C.); and went on, in 1947, to captain triumphantly England's Cricket Team that toured South Africa.

There, at Port Elizabeth, he scored as Captain a dashing Test Century; and a victory. Even more triumphantly on the voyage home he wooed and won a South African wife, Margaret - a successful shipboard romance.

They married in 1949. Their eldest child Simon was born on 26 January 1952; and he had of course via his mother a strong South African connection and many South African cousins; and via his father a name that reflected, in South African terms, glory long remembered. So that when he went back to South Africa...

★   ★   ★

First, however, a little more on Simon Mann's career and personality. Inevitably, like his father, he went to Eton; and almost as inevitably he went on to Sandhurst and, like his father and grandfather before him, into The Scots Guards.

It is always difficult to be sure exactly which regular officers applied for, and were seconded to, the SAS. But it seems that Alastair Morrison was; and it seems Simon Mann too, bored with regimental and ceremonial duties, transferred for a spell at least to the tougher world of the SAS. He married in 1977 – he was a Captain at the time – a very suitable bride, Jennifer Barham, whose family owned a celebrated garden at Rolvenden in Kent. They had two sons. Simon left the Army, still with the rank of Captain, in 1982. Their daughter Sophie was to be born three years later: and a year following that her mother and father divorced. Perhaps it had been too conventional a marriage, for, basically, an unconventional man.

For Simon Mann was always a bit of a buccaneer. He had not captained Eton's cricket team like his father, still less England's Test Match side. He could never have been described, as his father was, as "a charming gentlemanly figure from the old-world tradition of cricket". And those years after he had left the Army were difficult ones. The family brewery of Mann Crossman and Paulin Ltd on whose board his father and grandfather had both sat and for which his father George had worked for thirty years after the War, had been absorbed into the great Watney brewing empire (which thus became Watney Mann). So that, though money was plentiful, career opportunities and/or sinecures were not.

So Simon Mann drifted. He drifted into a job as salesman for computer security equipment at one stage; and then apparently into the bodyguard business, for rich Arabs with Scottish estates. When exactly he drifted out to South Africa is unclear. But it must have been well before 1993. For in early 1993 he was back in England, setting up the UK branch of Executive Outcomes, with the backing of Heritage Oil and Gas, in the name of Eeben Barlow and his wife Sue – whose address was given not as Pretoria, South Africa, but as Alton, Hampshire.

The Winning of the War

It was a year before this, in 1992, that Executive Outcome 'operatives' first appeared in Angola; and then they were hired not by the government but by the oil companies – to take over the maintenance services and recover any equipment that had fallen into the hands of 'brigands'. Of course by January 18 1993 it wasn't equipment that had fallen into the hands of 'brigands' - i.e. UNITA - at San Antonio; but the whole works, the whole installation.

From that date, therefore, the whole situation changed. From that date Executive Outcomes started working not just for Ranger Oil and Heritage Oil and Gulf Oil and the rest but also for the Angolan Government, the MPLA - though in a sense it came to much the same thing, for it was the oil revenues, whether via the companies or via the government, that paid their salaries. In mid-March fifty Executive Outcome mercenaries, in/with three ex-Soviet helicopters and supported offshore by the Angolan Navy, such as it was, attacked San Antonio and after a week's fighting recaptured the town and, presumably, the offshore oilfields with it. This was 'maintenance service' with a vengeance.

And it led, rapidly, to Executive Outcomes being given the contract to retrain the MPLA forces; and in particular to form 4,500 soldiers and 30 pilots whose special task would be to protect San Antonio and its 'black gold'. For Jonas did not take the loss of what might have become his greatest asset lightly. Six weeks later, in May, in four days of intensive fighting, UNITA recaptured San Antonio. And Mobutu's troops were said to be helping UNITA in Cabinda. In revenge, so to speak, the MPLA re-enlisted three brigades of Katangese from across the border, the *Forças Katangueses,* known as the *Tigres* - Mobutu's by now almost hereditary enemies, for these must have been the children of the Katangese whom he had crushed so brutally, with United Nations help★, in the early sixties.

It was a ding-dong war, this Second Civil War; and for most of 1993 it looked as if Jonas was winning. Though the world in general had him down now as a bad loser in a fair election and the United Nations decreed an oil and arms embargo against UNITA, the newly-independent Ukraine, overflowing with unwanted ex-Soviet equipment, supplied Savimbi with, allegedly, $50 million worth of armaments. He had to pay for them of course; but more and more now Jonas was using the dia-monds UNITA collected from the North of Angola to finance his war effort.

Then, in South Africa, a significant event occurred. Shortly before President de Klerk and Nelson Mandela jointly received the Nobel Peace Prize - that was in October 1993 - the Buffalo Battalion was finally disbanded. "This is a sad end for Buffalo," wrote one of its former officers, anonymously. "Whatever the politics and geopolitics of the time, they were a superb fighting force. They spearheaded operations deep into Angola. There were no saints in those wars."

Disbanded they may have been; but they stayed on in Pomfret, unemployed now - but desperate for employment. From this time I date the vast leap in Executive Outcome activities. Here was "a superb fighting force" of Angolans, stranded in South Africa, used to being commanded and led by white South African officers and NCOs. They knew the languages and the terrain of Angola. Of course Executive Outcomes recruited them; and of course, once again, they "spearheaded operations deep into Angola" - under a new leader, for at the same time Nick Van Den Bergh, a former SADF Lieutenant-Colonel took over as 'chief executive' of Executive Outcomes; seconded, it seems, by a certain Nick du Toit.

The actual incidents of the war that followed are relatively obscure. The world, generally, had lost interest in Angola and its endless conflicts. Without Russians and Cubans and the CIA and official South African forces it was now just another African civil war, dangerous and underreported. But the general outlines are clear. Executive Outcomes won a massive $40 million contract from the Angolan government, in effect to win the war. And in 1994, in effect, Executive Outcomes won the war. In August UNITA lost control of the diamond-mining areas in the north; in November it suffered a horrendous triple blow. San Antonio was recaptured; Uige, proclaimed his temporary capital by Jonas, was lost; and Huambo, pounded by artillery, finally fell. The Lusaka Peace Accords rapidly followed; though Jonas himself, much embittered, boycotted these. General de Matos, the MPLA's Chief of Staff, admitted that "hundreds" of South African mercenaries had been involved in the fighting.

Executive Outcomes, and its fortunes, and its manpower and above all its reputation were now expanding like a new solar system. "So successful has Executive Outcomes proved itself to be," reported South African Intelligence, almost starstruck, "that the OAU may be forced to... perhaps offer Executive Outcomes a contract for the management of peace-keeping operations continent-wide."

On the contrary, in the perhaps less awe-struck eyes of the British Defence Intelligence Staff, the group's "widespread activities" stretching across from Angola into neighbouring Zambia and the Congo, and, on the far side of the Congo, into Rwanda and Burundi were "a cause for concern". For:-

"It appears that the company and its associates are able to barter their services for a large share of an employing nation's natural resources and commodities."

Thus: "It has secured by military means key economic installations (diamonds, oil and other mineral resources) [and].... secured for itself substantial profits and disproportionate regional influence."

It sounds very much as if British government circles did not at all approve of Executive Outcomes' establishment in the United Kingdom, and of the rôle Simon Mann was playing in recruiting, however discreetly, at the British end of the operations. He was based at the time both in Britain and South Africa; but it is impossible to imagine that, with his SAS training and his hands-on quietly dashing character, he remained just a back-room boy. Certainly his contacts in South Africa in military and ex-military circles were extensive; and his future, and that of the mercenary company he and Eeben Barlow and Lafras Luitingh and Nick Van Den Bergh and Nick du Toit were running seemed to be enormously bright and profitable. Even the Defence Intelligence Staff were forced to admit, through clearly gritted teeth, that:

"On present showing Executive Outcomes will become ever richer and more potent, even to the extent of keeping military régimes in being..... Its influence in sub-Saharan Africa could become crucial."

THE UNEASY PEACE

That was, though, to reckon without the enormous changes in South Africa. Nelson Mandela was now President, with F.W. de Klerk and Thabo Mbeki as joint Vice-Presidents. The ANC was in power; and in Namibia even the disbanded Koevoets / Crowbar battalion, of SWAPO 'traitors', was being forgiven and reintegrated. Both sides in Angola had accepted the principle of quite a large UN Peacekeeping Force; and Jonas and President Dos Santos had meeting after meeting on neutral ground – in Lusaka in May, in Libreville in August, and in Brussels in September.

But Jonas' one overriding aim was to get rid of Executive Outcomes, the mercenary outfit that had in effect defeated him and his men, caused them to lose the Second Civil War, and robbed him of his second chance at the Presidency. He must have been even more embittered by the thought that so many Executive Outcome mercenaries had fought on his side against the MPLA and the Cubans in the Long War. Did it, incidentally, worry them? Probably not the blacks of the ex-Buffalo Battalion who were, after all, Daniel Chipenda's men originally and so had no affection at all for Jonas, purely an ally of circumstance. As for the white officers and NCOs, they no doubt eased their consciences by saying that, with the Cold War over, and the Russians and Cubans gone, the MPLA was Marxist only in name and in theory – and in any case its élite was as interested in petrol-dollars as they were themselves. Probably true enough; there were rumours that the élite in Luanda were pocketing $3 for every barrel of oil sold; and indeed President Dos Santos had built himself, outside Luanda, a miniature Versailles that rivalled Mobutu's Gbadolite: the Futungo Palace; from where, like Mobutu, he rarely emerged except under heavy guard.

Jonas was of course able to use the historic, and still official, MPLA detestation of mercenaries against these new hypocrites. He flew to Cape Town to see Nelson Mandela and Thabo Mbeki, to ask them, as a gesture of black African solidarity, to put a stop to Executive Outcomes activity. In New York the Security Council expressed its 'concern' over the slow (in fact non-existent) repatriation of mercenaries from Angola.

For by then, by 1996, with tension mounting in Angola, with the United Nations peacekeepers hard put to keep a peace continually being broken by minor clashes, with UNITA only notionally disarming and integrating, Executive Outcomes had secured contracts from Branch Energy, the holding company of Heritage Gas and Oil and its associate bodies, to protect not only the oil-fields of San Antonio but also the – vital to UNITA's finances – diamond mines of Lunda Norte. It is said the contract was for $100 million dollars a year; which sounds unbelievable.

It was enough in any case for Executive Outcomes to pay salaries of up to $13,000 a month (particularly for pilots) and to establish its own mechanized army and air force; which at its height comprised, on the ground, a fleet of 4 x 4s mounted with 30mm cannon, ex-Soviet BMP2 troop carriers and BTR60 amphibious vehicles; plus in the air M1 24 and M1 17 troop-carrying helicopters and M18 gun ships, MIG 23 and MIG 27 fighter-bombers, and two vast Boeing 727s bought from American Airlines. There had never before been any mercenary outfit equipped on anything like this scale.

★　　　★　　　★

However, the whole edifice was about to collapse. 1997 was a year of enormous trouble in both Congos, Brazza and Leo, with the MPLA and UNITA intervening on different sides. And, despite a so-called Government of National Unity and Reconciliation being formed in Angola, fighting spread from across the Congo borders back into Lunda Norte and the diamond fields. There, in June 1997 Executive Outcomes mercenaries for the last time held Savimbi's men at bay.

But Nelson, and Thabo Mbeki, the man who was to succeed him as President of South Africa, had listened to Jonas' pleas; and despite Nick Van Den Bergh's official representations before Parliamentary Committees in Pretoria, on May 20 1998 the Foreign Military Assistance Act became law in South Africa,

There can be no doubt that the Act, imposing penalties on all mercenary activity, recruitment, financing even, based in South Africa, was directly aimed at Executive Outcomes; and that it achieved its aim - its aim, and perhaps above all Jonas Savimbi's aim. With the full force of the State apparatus, military intelligence, police and justice, ready to crush it, Executive Outcomes could not survive. Its founders and leaders would have been mad to attempt to keep it in being. The company was wound up, dissolved, liquidated. The British side of the operation lingered on briefly as a shell. Its men, its mercenaries gradually quitted Angola - to return, in the case of what was once the Buffalo Battalion to the dismal bricks of Pomfret and renewed unemployment once again. Men like Eeben Barlow and Simon Mann no doubt 'retired' with regret; but patted themselves on the back for the vast amount of hay they had made while the mercenary sun shone; and after a well-earned period of rest and recuperation and Shangri-la turned their minds to possible future schemes that would not infringe, at least not too blatantly or obviously, the new laws - and for which the renewed chaos in the mighty Congo seemed to offer the best potential field of activity.

And meanwhile, in Angola, Jonas Savimbi, no doubt gloating to himself a very understandable gloat, had set about recapturing the diamond mines of Lunda Norte.

THE FINAL ACT: THE THIRD CIVIL WAR

It began in August 1998 with a massacre in Lunda Norte which each side blamed on the other; and it continued, sporadically and disjointedly, for 3½ years till the fatal day of Tuesday February 19 2002.

Jonas had started the third round with, reputedly, a vast war chest of $2 billion, obtained from the sale of diamonds, and an army of 15,000 men backed up by 10,000 auxiliaries. A curiously mixed force it was too, consisting basically of scattered UNITA forces, rearmed with Bulgarian weapons flown into a new base, at Bailundu north of Huambo; but reinforced by some of what had once been the fallen Mobutu's Presidential Guard; by some Serbian mercenaries who had gravitated to Mobutu's employment after the end of the Yugoslav Civil Wars; by some of the losers in the other Congolese conflict, in Brazzaville; and finally by some genocidal Hutu of the Interahamwe, chased right across the Congo by the vengeful Tutsi, and then out of Leo when Leo and Mobutu's régime had finally fallen. In other words a pretty unsavoury and incoherent mixture.

And on the MPLA side it was perhaps even more unsavoury and almost as incoherent. Executive Outcomes might have gone - and the last remnants are said to have been manoeuvred out by Hermann Cohen who manoeuvred back in MPRI - Military Professional Resources Inc of Virginia - with a contract to train two parachute brigades for the government. But there were also Brazilian jet fighters, with their pilots, Spanish counter-insurgency experts, all backed by vast oil revenues (as opposed to the "blood diamonds" of Savimbi, vividly condemned by the United Nations) till oil fell to $10 a barrel and, temporarily, the MPLA ran out of both steam and funds. Indeed by this time it might be said that the civil war had degenerated into a sordid battle to control the spoils of Angola.

But that is perhaps hardly fair to Jonas Savimbi. He was old now, in his late sixties, and still fighting in the bush. Abandoned by one faction of UNITA, abandoned too by his Western supporters and by most of his African fair-weather 'friends', despite the devastating loss of Jamba in early 2000, he struggled on gamely, the one African leader of presidential stature who, on and off, for forty years, had always led his men personally in the bush.

The end came on that fatal Tuesday in February 2002. Jonas was caught in camp at Lucusse, south east of Luso on the Railway, in the eastern province of Moxico - "surprised", it was said, "by Dos Santos' men". His death (and a fortnight later that of his deputy leader and successor, General Antonio Demba, reputedly of "acute diabetes") in effect brought to an end, at least for the years since then, the Angolan Civil Wars. On the Saturday his body, riddled with gunshot wounds, was shown on Angola TV. The corpse was buried, unceremoniously, in a shallow grave at Lucusse.

But was his death quite as simple as that? For countless years Jonas, carefully guarded, had lived as a guerrilla leader and yet had always avoided death. There is a tale that he was assassinated by a Mossad hit squad. But what the Israelis had against Savimbi, what they stood to gain by his death (unless - surely not! - Mossad was acting purely as hired assassins) is hard to see.

Did, on the other hand, Executive Outcomes play any part in it? Probably not.

But - there is a big but here - nine years earlier, in the course of the Second Civil War, three white South African mercenaries, wounded in the Angola fighting, were evacuated to a hospital in Windhoek, Namibia's capital.

The Afrikaans press revealed that the three were members of Executive Outcomes, hired by the Angolan Government, by Dos Santos and the MPLA, for a very special mission: to capture, or kill, Jonas Savimbi. Then they failed. But might Jonas' killing so many years later have been a last, magnificently successful, indeed winning stroke - before the drawing of stumps and close of play?

Book Two

GUINEAS GALORE

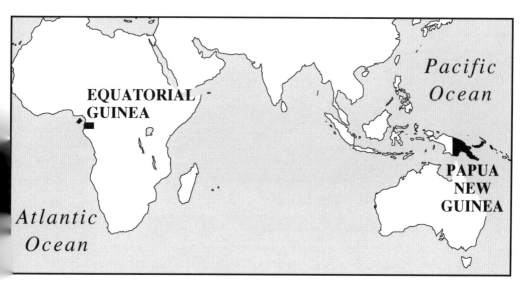

From The Pacific to the Atlantic

XII

Tim in the Coral Sea

The next story has a clean-cut hero, an almost irresistibly exotic setting, a series of hair breath escapes and adventures, a cast of swarthy or slinky villains each with style plus panache, and, most important of all, a happy ending - at least for the hero. All it lacks is a Snowy; though perhaps (who knows?) Tim took his black Labrador with him on the adventure trail.

The setting was, literally, at the other end of the earth: the Coral Sea, the Solomon Sea, the Bismarck Sea, the Banda Sea, the Torres Strait, the Gulf of Carpentras, Astrolabe Bay, St George's Channel - the names of the seas alone form a poetic litany. Add the clusters of islands: New Britain, New Ireland, New Hanover, the D'Entrecasteaux Archipelago, the Solomons themselves, the anthropologically famous Trobriands, and, northernmost of the Solomons, Bougainville, discovered in June 1768 by Count Louis Antoine Bougainville, on board his good ship *Boudeuse* in the course of his famous *Voyage Autour du Monde*.

And in the centre of all these little islands and small seas, lieing just to the north of the continent of Australia, emerges the vast, mountainous, forest-covered New Guinea, the second-largest island (after Greenland) in the world. "The Land of Ten Thousand Villages" they call it romantically. Less romantic - or more (it depends on your taste) - are the tribes of the interior: the Goilala, specialists in pay-back murders, the fearsome Orokaha of the coast, the Sefik who measure their prowess in human heads, and the Kuku-Kuku, cannibal killers clad in beaten bark, who live among their own dead. "New Guinea is unquestionably the most difficult country to govern in the world today," wrote Dr Margaret Mead in 1964. "There is nothing like it anywhere. It is an extremely difficult terrain. Transport is frightful.... in Papua New Guinea there are 700 different languages."

And what was true in 1964 seems to be as true forty years later. Picturesque tropical paradises can in fact be picturesque tropical hell-holes too. As I write these words, in the summer of 2005, Australian police have just been sent in to restore order in the capital, Port Moresby, where rape, murder and looting are everyday events, where walled compounds are protected by razor glass wire, and where "rascal gangs", far more sinister than their jolly name implies, terrorize the streets. Port Moresby is apparently, statistic for statistic, the murder capital of the whole wide world. And the interior is no better. In the spring of 2005 fighting was reported to have broken out in remote Chimbu province between 2000 rival warriors armed with bows and arrows and automatic weapons. Schools, clinics and hundred of homes were destroyed.

This was the land, this was the capital into which our hero and his men flew so light-heartedly in mid-March 1997.

★   ★   ★

I hope Tony Buckingham will not object if I picture him as Captain Haddock to Tim Spicer's Tintin. He is a big burly fellow, a rough diamond in every sense, not a sea-captain (and not black-bearded either) but a former North Sea diver. I imagine his vocabulary can be as pestiferous and fruity as the Captain's. But there the comparison ends. For Tony Buckingham has made an enormous fortune, and bought himself a Bentley, an estate in Hampshire, a house in The Vale, Chelsea. Diamond Works is his holding company in Canada; its subsidiary, Branch Energy, operates mines in Uganda and Sierra Leone - and in Angola too. Indeed he was involved with Simon Mann in setting up Executive Outcomes; in Hampshire he and the Manns are county neighbours.

But Tony Buckingham, unlike Captain Haddock, keeps very much in the background. All the more extraordinary that he went with Tim Spicer out to Australia, to the meeting in the coffee shop at the Hilton Hotel in Cairns, Queensland, where the adventure really began.

Perhaps not so extraordinary really. For, first of all, the meeting was secret; secondly it involved mines or rather one vast copper mine; and thirdly it looks very much as if Tim was Tony's protegé; as if indeed Buckingham had bankrolled Spicer. For in 1996 the offices of Tim Spicer's would-be mercenary outfit, Sandline International, were at Plaza 107, at the glass-fronted No 535 King's Road, Chelsea. And Plaza 107 was Tony Buckingham's London office headquarters.

Our new star, Tim Spicer, had had a much more successful Army career than Alastair Morrison or Richard Bethell or Simon Mann. He came from a military family; not, however, from as smart or wealthy a background as the others. Perhaps this was what made him all the more ambitious. His public school was respectable enough: Sherborne. But it was neither Harrow like Bethell nor Eton like Mann. He had knocked around the world for a couple of years after school; so he arrived older than most at Sandhurst. There his ambitions were rewarded: in 1976 he won the Sword of Honour as the best officer cadet of his intake. He joined the Brigade of Guards. He fought with his men at Tumbledown in the Falklands War; he was on the staff of General Sir Peter de la Billière in the First Iraqi War. By 1990 he had became one of no less than nine Lieutenant-Colonels in the Scots Guards. Two years later, moving up the scale, he commanded their Second Battalion, not without incident, on its always-stressful 'tour of duty' in Northern Ireland.

But then, rather suddenly and surprisingly, 'Colonel Tim' left the Army, and the Brigade, and the world he had known for almost twenty years. Perhaps he felt – there were still three Lieutenant-Colonels senior to him in the Scots Guards – that his prospects of promotion were blocked. Very likely – for there is no chance at all of making a fortune as a regular British Army officer – he wanted to earn a fair whack of 'wonga' before it was too late. So at first he headed for the City, joining the Foreign and Colonial Investment Group. But the City is no longer the conventional bowler-hatted repository it once was; and to have been a C.O. in the Brigade may well have been more a handicap than a help. After only a year Spicer got out.

It would be derogatory to call the little group of ex-Scots Guards Officers involved in the mercenary business a mafia, and too pompous on the other hand to refer to them as a club. Perhaps a band of brothers gives the best idea. For they knew each other pretty well, they had been through the same experiences together – even Simon Mann briefly rejoined the Army for the First Iraqi War – and though like all brothers they had their ins and outs and ups and downs, they stayed in pretty close contact; and, where they could, discreetly helped each other out. What is certainly true, truer of them than of previous mercenary leaders like Hoare and Denard or of course Callan, was that they were in it for what Simon Mann was so memorably to call the 'wonga', the money. Perhaps that was why it was the Scots Guards rather than the Welsh or Irish from whose ranks the new breed of mercenary leaders emerged. By tradition and reputation the Scots are, of all the inhabitants of the British Isles, by far the canniest when it comes to making money and by far the most mercenary (in a general sense this time) when it comes to pressing for payment of every penny they believe to be due to them. Tim Spicer may or may not have much Scots blood in his veins; but he had certainly imbibed this trait of the Scots character; as the sequel to his adventure will show.

By early 1996 when Tim Spicer had just set up his 'military consultancy' business in Chelsea, Alastair Morrison and Richard Bethell were deeply involved in negotiations that would lead, a year later, to the amalgamation of their organisation, DSL, with Armor Holdings, an American company specialising in manufacturing and distributing riot equipment. Armor Group was to be the result of this transatlantic merger. So they were pretty busy with high finance and long-winded legal negotiations, too busy, really, to get involved when approached for help by the Defence Minister of Papua New Guinea. So Alastair Morrison phoned the new boy on the block, his old fellow officer Tim Spicer, and – no doubt wanting to give Tim a helping hand – passed the business on to him. It was all a matter of helicopters, it seemed. And if Tim couldn't supply helicopters, he knew someone who certainly could: his almost exact contemporary, Simon Mann.

But it turned out to be about a good deal more than a couple of helicopters.

BRA

Her Sovereign Majesty Queen Elizabeth II, (to whom all Scots Guards officers owe their commission and have of course sworn an oath of loyalty) is not only Queen of the United Kingdom but also Queen of Australia, Queen of Papua New Guinea and indeed Queen of the Solomon Islands – over all of which outlandish continents and countries, now fully and theoretically equally independent, she reigns via her Governors-General or, in the case of the Solomon Islands, her Governor (who, since 1999, has been the Reverend Sir John Ini Lapli).

Unfortunately when the British, the Dutch and the Germans were milling around the South Pacific a hundred and fifty years ago and trying to decide amicably who should rule what, where and why, they detached the Island of Bougainville from the Solomon Islands to which ethnically and geographically it belonged; and lumped it in with the German possessions.

So by the beginning of the Twentieth Century the Dutch held half of the vast island of New Guinea (160,000 square miles) up to the 141st Meridian, a straight line on the map from North to South; the Germans had German New Guinea – Kaiser Wilhelms Land – including Bougainville to the North of the other half (93,000 square miles) – and the British ruled the 90,000 square miles of the rest, the other quarter, closest to Australia, the Protectorate of British New Guinea known as Papua; plus too the British Solomon Isles Protectorate way over to the right.

Times changed. The Germans were kicked out, almost amicably, during the First World War, and the Australians took over their territories and eventually, by agreement, British-ruled 'Papua' too. The Dutch were kicked out without any amicability at all after the Second World War, and the Indonesians took over their territory. But whereas Papua New Guinea – the Australian half – became independent in 1975 (and the Solomon Islands three years later) the Indonesians clung on like limpets to their half of New Guinea, West Irian. So that the vast island of New Guinea is still split down the middle, at the 141st Meridian. Indeed the Indonesian empire seems to have made a habit of holding on regardless to halves of island – half of the island of Timor too, and three-quarters of the island of Borneo. All very odd, historically. But irrelevant to our present story which concerns only Papua New Guinea, the independent half of the island, with its brilliant multi-coloured Bird of Paradise flag and its far tinier island dependency – despite all the vicissitudes of the past century, still attached to its big sister – Bougainville.

In many ways a great deal of trouble would have been spared if Bougainville had been properly annexed by its discoverer, Count Louis Antoine; and had remained French. It was a large island compared to many of the neighbouring Solomons, 130 miles long, and with 200,000 inhabitants equalling almost half the population of all the Solomons put together. But it was tiny compared to vast Papua New Guinea, with its four or five million people. For years and years

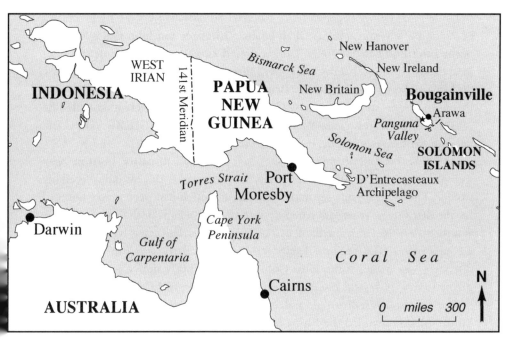

Papua New Guinea - and Bougainville

Bougainville was a sleepy backwater totally unimportant - except of course to its own inhabitants. And they, the Bougainvilleans, had not much time at all for the mainlanders. They are blue-black themselves, and they call the inhabitants of Port Moresby redskins, which is not meant, or taken, as a compliment. Also they are, most of them, Catholic; whereas Papua New Guinea is a pot-pourri of every variety of Christianity, paganism and cargo cults.

Deep in the interior of Bougainville lies the Panguna Valley, cut off by the Kron Prinz and the Kaiser mountain ranges. If only low-grade copper deposits had not been discovered there. But they were. And in the nineteen sixties Conzinc Rio Tinto of Australia, supported by New Broken Hill Consolidated Ltd, began to prospect. First 10,000, then 50,000 acres were opened up. It turned out that in the Panguna Valley Bougainville was sitting on a vast copper mine, with what was estimated to be the greatest reserves of copper in the whole world.

It was on 1 August 1969 that the first scrimmages between local tribes, who wanted no development and above all no loss of their ancestral lands, and the mining nabobs and their gangs took place at Rorovana in the Valley. By 1975 tempers were so inflamed that just before Papua New Guinea celebrated its independence and Sir John Guise (a quarter white, and a cricketer) became the first Governor General, five thousand people gathered in the little capital of Bougainville, Arawa, in its market square, to applaud as Bougainville declared its own separate independence and raised its own rather less glamorous blue, green and white flag.

Three years before independence Michael Somaré had been Chief Minister of Papua New Guinea, Julius Chan Finance Minister and John Guise Minister of the Interior. Their Sovereign Lady scattered knighthoods like confetti on her loyal Papuan leaders. Twenty years after Independence Sir John Guise had retired, Sir Michael Somaré born in New Britain, the Pango Party leader, was temporarily out of power, and under a new Governor General - strangely unknighted he (or she): Wima Korowa Paias Wingti - Sir Julius Chan GCMG, KBE and PC had become, for the second time, Prime Minister.

Sir Julius was one of the suave ones, half Chinese half native, born in New Ireland, educated across the Torres Straits in Queensland. But Sir Julius faced big trouble. The Bougainville separatist movement, which had been pretty nominal for the first fifteen years, had flared up into open rebellion in the past five. BRA was formed - the Bougainville Revolutionary Army; and what had been rather a comic opera UDI became deadly serious. Particularly when in 1995, a new discovery was made, of the Lihir Gold Field this time, a new Consortium was granted a new lease; and Bougainville elected a Transitional Government.

The ferociously tall tough and efficient-looking Brigadier General Jerry Singherok commanded the Papua New Guinea Defence Force. But it appears his troops were no match for the men (and women) of BRA. In June 1996 they launched a government offensive on Bougainville. It failed. BRA counter-attacked, much more successfully. These were not mock wars. They were conducted with all the traditional ferocity and violence of the region. Hundreds died on both sides, eventually thousands. Meanwhile the copper mines had closed down, and the goldfields lay unexploited - vast investments lost, capitalists and shareholders and management teams not exactly ruined - far from it - but indignant, frustrated, eager to recoup their losses.

No wonder Tony Buckingham, that mining operator, was interested. No wonder he had flown out with his protégé Tim Spicer to meet Brigadier General Singherok in the coffee shop at Cairns that Easter of 1996. The 'high concept' was, of course, the prising-open of that pearl of the Pacific, Bougainville, once again.

"PROJECT OYSTER"

"My name is Spicer - Tim Spicer," he could well have said. Certainly at the time Tim, though in his mid-forties, had all the boyish good looks of a James Bond; not unlike his almost exact contemporary Pierce Brosnan in fact, though lighter and slighter and much more obviously a gentleman. But just as crisp when necessary.

Unfortunately action did not proceed at the pace of a Bond movie. First of all Tim had to settle his 'consultancy fee'; and there was a little bit of haggling about that, with pompous references back to Sandline's 'financial director' (Captain Haddock?) before $250,000 was finally agreed on.

Then there was the question of helicopters. Like all army chiefs involved in trackless, jungly warfare, the Brigadier General and his boss, Mathias Ijape, the Minister of Defence (who had also come to the Cairns coffee shop) set almost magical faith in helicopters – and the Australian government had refused to let them have any.

What Tim promised he could get his hands on were two Russian models, the M.117, a troop carrier, and the smaller M.124, a gunship – one of each. "These helicopters look mean and are mean," Spicer was later to say. "They were intended to seize the psychological advantage from the enemy, to show them that the game was up." Weird really, when helicopters, as Afghanistan and Iraq (and countless Bond movies) have shown, are pretty easy targets for RPG shoulder-propelled missiles, and liable to blow up or crash with all hands aboard. Nevertheless that's what the US Army used, like swarms of bees in Vietnam. Not that that did them much good in the end. But it certainly established evident superiority in the air and *seemed* an undefeatable asset (as I remember personally, at the time of the Tet offensive).

Helicopters might look mean and be mean, but the trouble was that they look expensive and are expensive. Lots of toing and froing between the Cairns meeting and the end of 1996 went on; and in mid-summer Spicer, or more probably his "financial director", came up with a very interesting proposition. "We are proposing," he faxed from Chelsea to the Minister in Port Moresby, "that we form a joint venture with your government, ourselves and RTZ (Rio Tinto) to reopen and operate the Bougainville mine once recovered."

The wily Sir Julius Chan, the Prime Minister, was not too happy about all these goings on, and putatative deals. But the autumn of 1996 turned out to be a bad, bad season for him. The latest offensive in Bougainville went badly wrong, Sir Julius announced that he was "sick and tired of our boys coming home in body bags"; and then, on October 12, the premier of the Bougainville Transitional Government was shot dead in the south-west area of Bougainville while having dinner with his wife and children. "An act of madness," Sir Julius called it, and blamed BRA (with whom the dead man had broken two years earlier). But the area where the murder took place was under Defence Force control, so his own military were suspected – "our under-equipped under-trained and under-resourced security forces" Sir Julius called them. Tim Spicer was to put it more bluntly: "The PNG Defence Force had battlefield paralysis of the will."

So Sir Julius was won over to Tim's much more ambitions plans; which didn't just involve supplying helicopters but in "directing, participating in and conducting operations" to make BRA "militarily ineffective" – in simple language fighting and winning the war. Pretty ambitious for a barely budding mercenary operation, but no doubt Lt-Colonel Spicer felt that the Scots Guards versus BRA would turn out to be no match at all.

The only snag was that Tim was a Lt-Colonel no longer; he had no guardsmen to throw into the fray; and, come to that, he had no Russian helicopters either.

All he had, by early 1997, was a small office in Chelsea, large plans and -oh yes - a splendid contract finally signed and payment in advance of a very hefty slice of wonga into Sandline's Hong Kong bank account.

He also had of course his old chums. So naturally enough he turned to his far more experienced brother officer Simon Mann; and on February 25 Executive Outcomes was sub-contracted to provide the men, the equipment and the helicopters.

This was in 1997, at a time therefore of comparative peace and quiet in Angola; but two years before Executive Outcomes was wound up in South Africa. So there were plenty of mercenaries on the books and available at short notice. Nick Van Den Bergh, one of Executive Outcome's big wheels, took charge of raising 70 men for what Tim rather grandly christened the Combined Arms Training Team.

Exactly what part Simon Mann played in all this is rather obscure. Indeed exactly what the links between Executive Outcomes and Sandline International were is also rather obscure. They were not "one and the same company", Spicer was later to say, but they were "closely related". In any case Simon Mann never set foot in Papua New Guinea.

But Nick Van Den Bergh did. He, and Tim, and the 70 flew into Army barracks in mid-March, ninety minutes' flying time north of Port Moresby, to await the arrival of the two helicopters en route from the former Soviet Republic of Belarus. On Sunday 16 March Tim flew to the capital for a meeting with Brigadier General Singherok; and his adventures really began.

TROUBLE IN PORT MORESBY

First Tim had had a meeting with Sir Julius discussing "big-picture stuff". Then it was off, on that Sunday afternoon, from the Prime Minister's Office to army headquarters, Murray Barracks, a fifteen-minutes' drive away.

At Murray Barracks he was delayed outside Singherok's office, told to wait by a mere Colonel. "I'm expected by the General," he said, and marched straight in.

But inside the General's office there was no General. Instead, there were seven highly-overexcited armed men. One can picture Tim's open-mouthed amazement when he was told that an officers' coup was taking place, and his indignation when it was added that he personally was now under arrest. There was a bit of a scuffle. Rather naturally our hero came off the worse. His shoes were removed, the belt taken off his trousers; and, ignominiously clutching the said trousers to hold them up, he was bundled into a jeep, driven to the naval base, hustled out of the jeep and onto a landing craft - which then sailed two miles out to sea. "My mind was racing with all sorts of scenarios," he remembered. You can bet it was - and none of them likely to be very pleasant ones.

Sunday night, all Monday and Monday night Tim spent under guard two miles offshore. It wasn't till mid-day on the Tuesday that a dozen armed men drew alongside in a motor boat, and clambered aboard. They were led by one of the coup's ringleaders, Captain Belden Namah, clad in black vest, combat trousers and running shoes. Spicer was yelled at. He was ordered to walk to the end of the landing craft. This does not look good, he thought. Then he was blindfolded. Understandably he thought: this is the end.

And there, in that tight spot, let us temporarily leave our hero.

★   ★   ★

Coups are rather unusual in countries where Queen Elizabeth is Head of State, the officers have all sworn oaths of loyalty to her on receiving their commissions and there is a governor general to represent Her Majesty. I have never heard of any *coups d'état* in Australia or New Zealand; and there had certainly never been a coup plotted or executed before in Papua New Guinea, either. So rather than a bloody and brutal it was a confused and muddled affair, full of shouting and fury, signifying a great deal of trouble for both the Prime Minister and the General. And all caused - this is the quite extraordinary thing - by the hiring of mercenaries in the first place.

Most to blame is the Australian government. Of course there was unrest and mutterings among the junior army officers in Murray Barracks and elsewhere when rumours got out that white mercenaries were being hired to do *their* job - with the implication that they had proved quite incapable of doing it properly themselves. But it was the public declaration by John Howard, the right-wing Prime Minister of Australia, shortly before Spicer's men arrived that put the cat among the pigeons. The use of mercenaries, Howard declared, was "absolutely and completely unacceptable".

So Major Walter Enuma, leader of the seven who had pounced on Spicer at Murray Barracks, felt that he and his fellow-officers had, as it were, the go-ahead from their great and powerful neighbour, their former lords and masters, to get rid of these white intruders from the other side of the world; and that, in the beginning, was what the whole coup was about. As for the Brigadier General, he wasn't in on it. In fact when Spicer had asked where the General was that Sunday afternoon, he was told Singherok had been "taken care of".

But by Monday the Brigadier General, a born again Christian, had agreed to take charge of the coup, very possibly in order to prevent bloodshed. On the Monday therefore he went on the radio and, outrageously and unpredictably, called for the Prime Minister to resign.

Sir Julius was understandably miffed by all this. He had been none too keen on employing mercenaries in the first place, he had been persuaded to do so by both Brigadier General Singherok and his own Minister of Defence, Mathias Ijape. And now he'd got them, at great expense, into the country and almost ready to go into action against the blue-black rebels in Bougainville, here was his own Army Chief, instead of imposing discipline on a few rowdy officers, not only letting them get away with arresting 'his' new mercenary leader, an honoured guest, so to speak, who probably was utterly baffled by what was going on, but had also switched sides and loyalties and was now calling on him, the democratically-elected Prime Minister, to resign!

It was all too much. Sir Julius announced on the Tuesday not only that he had no intention of resigning but that Singherok was forthwith dismissed from all his commands.

Of course in cases like this it is easy enough for a politician to proclaim a general dismissed, far less easy actually to do anything about it. By Wednesday the situation was threatening to get totally out of hand…..

★   ★   ★

We left Tim standing, blindfolded, on Tuesday morning, at the end of his landing craft, two miles out at sea, surrounded by a dozen jabbering and aggressive soldiers, fearing the worst. A tight spot, indeed.

But the British public schoolboy has always been at his best in a tight spot. Tim was ordered down into the motor launch, which then zoomed away out over the Coral Sea. To a remote island, he wondered, where he could be shot out of hand and where no-one would ever know what had become of him. Then he felt the launch altering course. Peeking out from under his blindfold, he saw they were heading up a creek onto land.

There, hustled out, he was pushed into a red Toyota that, ironically was one of Sandline's own rented vehicles - now commandeered by the military - and driven to Tirama Barracks, ten miles from Port Moresby. He was locked into a room. "This is the end of the line for you," they told him.

Fortunately (how, one wonders, … and where?) Tim had managed to hide a knife on his person. Now or never was the moment to escape! He started cutting through the door. But he hadn't realized - he should have remembered the old army saying "Time spent in reconnaissance is never wasted" - that there was a sentry posted outside the room. The knife came through the door, the sentry spotted it, the door was flung open, a gun was put to Tim's head, there was more shouting and yelling; and the escape attempt ended up with Tim being thrown into a proper military jail, where he spent a wretched Tuesday night eaten alive by mosquitoes and very worried indeed about what his prospects might be. "Project Oyster" seemed to be closing down on him - and, he supposed, on his men. And what was his old chum and fellow officer Jerry Singherok doing about it?

★   ★   ★

The answer was: very little. For by Wednesday the Brigadier General had again lost control of the situation. It wasn't so much that Sir Julius had not resigned and that he himself had been dismissed. It was more that the whole affair was rapidly getting out of hand.

For outside Murray Barracks, as Wednesday wore on, thousands of civilians and soldiers were gathering to protest, to wave placards demanding "Sandline PISS OFF!" and to call for Sir Julius Chan's resignation. It was beginning to look like a popular uprising. No wonder there was trouble at Tirama Barracks too. They dragged Tim out of his cell, told him he was going to be thrown out of the country (which must have been a great relief, apart from the worry about the £250,000 in his 'safe house') and marched him to the barrack gates in his bare feet. But there Major Enuma and the leading rebel officers turned up to tell Tim he was going nowhere. He was punched, jabbed, yelled at. He announced that he was refusing to go back to his cell. NBG. Back to his cell he was frogmarched and the steel door clanged behind him.

Meanwhile as dusk fell on Port Moresby ten miles away, the situation in the capital began to deteriorate. Rioting broke out, then looting. Fortunately, as so often happens, the police force were better trained and disciplined than the mutinous soldiery. They were also loyal to the government - to Sir Julius. So, by the use of tear gas, they gradually got the situation under control.

On the Thursday morning Port Moresby awoke to a sense of devastation and a certain amount of taking of deep breaths. Everybody stepped back from the brink. Sir Julius announced that he was ending the contract with Sandline; and the Brigadier General, his dismissal apparently glossed over, was given the job of getting them out of the country.

Operation Rausim Quik it was called in the local pidgin English; and by Friday the 70 mercenaries under Nick Van Den Bergh, who had been waiting bewildered and semi-abandoned miles away in the jungle, were being flown out of Papua New Guinea, back home to South Africa. All still in one piece, slightly the richer in pocket but hardly back with a good exciting story to tell of their adventurous time Down Under.

All out but one. In the slightly calmer atmosphere of Thursday and Friday, and with the British High Commissioner Bob Low understandably making pressing enquiries into the whereabouts and safety of the now-notorious but missing-for-days British Subject, Colonel Spicer of Sandline fame, the police took charge. They first raided the rented house; and there found not Tim but a safe containing not only the £250,000 in banknotes but also a Russian Makarov 9mm pistol with 40 rounds of ammunition. Unlicensed!

So when the police extracted Tim from his hell hole in Tirama Barracks, which must have been most welcome, it was only to announce that he was being held and charged with a firearms offence, which must have been considerably less so. However a deal was struck. He would be allowed to reside at the British High Commission till his trial came up, provided his passport was surrendered. As for the £250,000 in cash, that would have to be held as evidence for the forthcoming Commission of Enquiry.

For the Prime Minister was determined both to clear his name and, even more important, to put his mutinous Brigadier General on the spot. And the best way to do that, he believed, was to bring all the details of the Sandline Contract (which he suspected had involved backhanders to Jerry Singherok) out into the open. And the best way to achieve that would be to set up an independent Commission of Enquiry at which the chief witness would inevitably have to be the mercenary leader, Sandline International's chief executive. And, of course, to achieve that, Tim Spicer had, by hook or by crook, to be kept in Papua New Guinea - but alive, well, and in one piece. Now that the mass of the mercenaries had been deported, the general fuss, Sir Julius calculated, would die down.

He calculated wrong. On the last day of that dramatic week, Saturday March 22, Major Walter Enuma declared himself to be commander of the armed forces - and gave Sir Julius till Tuesday to resign.

The weekend passed in feverish political activity. Papua New Guinea was a democracy, and none of the political parties were going to put up with mere Majors telling Prime Ministers, however detested or envied by other possible Prime Ministers, what to do. Nevertheless no-one wanted more riots and looting, and all the politicians had seen what influence the mutinous young officers had. So on Tuesday, Deadline Day, the House of Assembly obliged Major Enuma by calling a Vote of No Confidence in Sir Julius Chan as Prime Minister. Against all expectations he won the vote: by 58-39. The wily half-Chinaman had outmanoeuvred his opponents once more.

No, he had not. As soon as the results of the Vote became known, a thousand of the Major's troops surrounded the Parliament building. Though Chan himself managed to slip away via a side entrance, almost all the rest of the elected Members, 100 of them, were trapped inside overnight, without their pyjamas or sleeping bags.

Next day it was all over. Sir Julius Chan announced his resignation, his Minister of Defence Mathias Ijape announced his resignation, and the Deputy Prime Minister Chris Haveta announced his resignation. How bitterly all three must have regretted their decision ever to employ white mercenaries. Their contract with Sandline International had led them not to the crushing of the rebellion in Bougainville but to their own political graves.

THE END OF THE AFFAIR

For it did prove to be pretty well the end of the line for Sir Julius. After the Commission of Enquiry had reported he announced that it had vindicated him and that he was resuming office. But, two weeks later, at the General Election, he ignominiously lost his seat - that was on June 14, and Bill Skate became Prime Minister in his place.

As for Jerry Singherok, six weeks after that General Election, he was dismissed and charged with sedition. This time a new Brigadier General was officially appointed in his place. And when his trial eventually took place three years later, he was found guilty not indeed of sedition but on three counts of having accepted illegal payments - backhanders. So Sir Julius was belatedly vindicated, and the disgraced Jerry Singherok was barred for three years from holding public office.

The mutinous officers were not so lucky. Again three years later three of them including Captain Belden Namah were sentenced to long years in prison for mutiny. But for some reason not Major Walter Enuma. Even so Tim Spicer must have had a quiet chuckle when he learnt that the thug who had blindfolded him and nearly made him walk the plank had had his comeuppance.

For Tim himself had been released, and sent home on Tuesday April 8, 1997, with all the firearms charges dropped. But not before he had given evidence for three and a half days in the witness box before Mr Justice Warwick Andrew, presiding over the Commission of Enquiry.

Tim said, when pressed, that he did not know who the shareholders of Sandline were. Though Tony Buckingham was only, he claimed, "a friend who occasionally gives me advice", he had to admit that he had options on 10,000 shares in Diamond Works, Buckingham's holding company in Canada. So he did not come out of the Enquiry particularly well. But on the other hand out he came : "I am greatly relieved," he said. "Now I can go home."

And he came out a much, much wealthier mercenary, with wealth that a Mike Hoare or a Bob Denard or his fellow Regular Army officers still in the Scots Guards could only dream of: £18 million, no less, paid in advance into the Hong Kong bank account, in hand; and £18 million more, the second half of the payment, still owed.

Spicer was not the sort of chap to give up that amount of wonga. A year later, in June 1998, there was a Arbitration Hearing in Cairns: should Papua New Guinea honour the remainder of the contract? It should, was the ruling – and, incidentally, refund that £250,000 taken from the safe house and, incidentally, pay the 'consultancy fee' of $250,000 that had apparently never materialised.

Papua New Guinea appealed against the award. Queensland Supreme Court ruled that it had no jurisdiction to hear the appeal. And on May 1 1999 Radio Australia reported that the dispute had been settled. Sandline was to receive $13.3 million paid over the next twelve months in four instalments, plus ownership of all the military equipment sold to the Papua New Guinea government but never delivered - in particular therefore the two Russian helicopters, which had ended up in a sort of legal no-man's land, at a small airport near Darwin, and had presumably been rusting away there for over two years.

So Tim's three weeks may have been a pretty unpleasant experience, but they were certainly a profitable one. Indeed few three weeks in mercenary history throughout the ages can have brought in that amount of wonga for a campaign that was never fought.

And what of the people of Bougainville and of BRA?

Unstrafed by helicopters, unsubdued by mercenaries, they seem to have come out ahead of the whole show. At the beginning of the new millennium the Locoata Agreement was signed that set the little (comparatively speaking) island

on course for its own autonomous government with, later, a referendum to follow on the question of total independence.

  This despite the fact that the Solomon Islands had "betrayed" Bougainville by
earlier signing a Treaty recognizing Bougainville as an integral part of Papua New
Guinea. A "betrayal" of their own kith and kin that the Solomon Islanders paid
for by facing their own rebellion and potential coup in 2003. But Mr Howard
had learnt his lesson. An Australian 'peace-keeping' force landed 'to restore
order'. No white mercenaries this time; no would-be military strike by Sandline
International.

  Indeed by 2003 Sandline International had ceased to exist.

XIII

Diamonds and Chaos – The Respectable Mercenary

In joy and gladness with our hearts united
We'll shout the freedom of a land benighted
Long live Liberia, happy land
A home of glorious liberty, by God's command
Liberian National Anthem: The Chorus

In 1935, Graham Greene, not yet a famous novelist, and his cousin Barbara Greene walked across Liberia. It was not, in fact, a particularly exciting trip. They sailed out from Liverpool on an Elder Dempster packet, landed at Freetown, the Crown Colony of Sierra Leone, with its 40,000 native inhabitants, mainly English-speaking Creoles and the 120 Englishmen whom in Graham's view they so painfully aped, then went 'up the line' into the Protectorate where, Graham immediately noticed, the British Empire was as he expected it to be: at its best.

"The Englishmen here didn't talk about 'the bloody blacks' nor did they patronise or laugh at them; they had to deal with the real native, not the Creole, and the real native was someone to love and admire. The Englishmen here were of a finer, subtler type than on the Coast."

At Kailahun on the frontier they drank cocktails with the District Commissioner. Ahead of them lay the immense Liberian forest which covered most of the Liberian hinterland. Quite out of the blue on the first day of their march they found the President of Liberia, President Barclay, with a small escort in a village on their route. Barbara asked him whether his authority was the same as an American President's. More, he said in his strong American accent. "Once elected and in charge of the machine, why then, I'm boss of the whole show."

Quite obviously from their accounts neither Barbara nor Graham were able to take a black President at all seriously. President Barclay was the only black President in the whole wide world, and as head of the True Whig Party presided over a very bizarre little country indeed, a tiny offshoot of the United States on the wrong side of the Atlantic Ocean, complete with its own White House and even its own State Department. There was this difference: that it was entirely inhabited by negroes, and therefore in theory at least happily free from racial conflict.

Things however had not entirely worked out as planned. The freed negroes from America, settled by the anti-slavery societies, exploited "the natives" as ruthlessly as any white colonizers. Five years before the Greenes set foot in Liberia, the command of the Frontier Force, Liberia's army, 3000 strong, had passed into the hands of a mercenary adventurer, ex-US Army, a veteran of the Mexican Wars. His name was Colonel Elwood Davies, and he was rumoured to have swept down on the rebellious Krus of Old Sasstown, destroyed their villages, burnt their town and massacred 72 women and children.

But when Barbara and Graham came across him, at Tappee Ta in Grand Bassa Province, and invited him over to their tent he turned out to be very different from the black ogre of their imagination. "We want some whisky," Graham announced. "I always have a glass of Ovaltine at the end of a day's trek," explained the Colonel with a flash of his gold teeth. "But just tonight….." To Barbara he resembled with his neat pointed black beard a "handsome villain" in an old-fashioned play, tall, straight and good-looking in his clean, well-cut uniform. "No longer could I think of him as the cold-blooded murderer of women and children. His personality was too colourful, his gestures too theatrical."

He denied the massacres. He talked non-stop. He told them, with great charm, about Liberia.

"Liberia is a beautiful country. A beautiful country. I ought to know. I guess I've seen most of the world. But when I hear the young men of Monrovia saying that they want to see Europe or America, I say to them - see Liberia first. And I think that's a beautiful thought. See Liberia first. That's what I say. See Liberia first."

THE LAND BENIGHTED

The decades passed. President Barclay was succeeded by President Tubman, also of the True Whig Party. The settlers became known as the Americo-Liberians or Americos. In even tinier Sierra Leone, the Protectorate and the Crown Colony were merged, Independence was granted, the British left, and after a reasonable start under Sir Milton Margai, the first of a whole series of military coups took place. Early in the nineteen seventies Siaka Stevens declared a Republic, set himself up as President, and for 14 years established, with the backing of Lebanese merchants, a "veritable kleptocracy" that destroyed civil society.

The Mano River was the boundary separating the two small states. Corruption spread across the River. President Tolbert, also of the True Whig Party, succeeded President Tubman, and he and his cronies sold off, largely to American and Israeli interests, the natural resources of Liberia such as they were: concessions for vast tracts of mahogany logging, for rubber, sugar, rice, diamonds and iron. Then the unimaginable happened. Master Sergeant Samuel Doe, an illiterate 'native' of what was now the Armed Forces of Liberia, no longer the Frontier Force, marched into the White House with a dozen of his fellow Krahn tribesmen, eviscerated President Tolbert, tossed his body over the balcony; and next day publicly executed on the beach at Monrovia thirteen Cabinet Ministers plus the Chief Justice and the Major General in command of the late President's much-feared security guard. Fifteen telegraph poles were set up along the beach, the Ministers were stripped to their underwear before being tied to the poles, and then, as the drunken crowds of spectators laughed and jeered, to the music of juju and reggae, drunken soldiers poured more than five hundred rounds into their bodies as the vultures circled overhead and the yellow pie-dogs roamed hungrily around.

Those were the death knells not only of President Tolbert and his corrupt gang but of the True Whig Party and nearly 150 years of exploitive but reasonably stable rule by the Americo settlers over the native tribes of Colonel Elwood Davies' "beautiful country". It was a foretaste of even worse to come. No-one since that day in 1980, no successors of the Greenes, would ever have dreamt of attempting to trek peacefully through the dark and comparatively deserted Liberian forest. And massacres of women and children, destruction of whole villages, would become so commonplace as to defy description. Atrocity succeeded atrocity, horror piled on horror.

And yet at one stage there was hope. A man arose, Charles Taylor, a member of the Gio tribe but educated in Bentley College, Massachusetts, strikingly handsome, with immense energy, a large open face and intelligent eyes. Was he a revolutionary or a saviour? Hard to say. But anything seemed better than Master Sergeant Samuel Doe with his paranoia and secrecy, his ferocious temper, love of pornographic videos, his pet bonogo apes, and his mean vicious totally corrupt fellow thugs from the Krahn tribe.

In early December 1989 Charles Taylor led a small band of Libyan-trained Liberian exiles across the border from neighbouring Guinea into remote Nimba County. His second-in-command was a tall very dark well-spoken Mano tribesman, Prince Johnson by name. A second, larger invasion followed. There were, as always, rumours of white mercenaries being involved. There is a story that Nick du Toit, a bearded Afrikaner who had once commanded part of 32 Battalion was, then or later, one of Charles Taylor's "advisers". But what gave the invaders their edge was Charles Taylor's charismatic personality, his powers of leadership, and the juju charms, the special powers, the magic waters that protected his followers from bullets.

His powers of leadership however were not enough to keep his second-in-command loyal to him. Prince Johnson - Field Marshal Prince Johnson as he had now become - split away, after a quarrel over atrocities in the Bong Mines area. There were now three different tribal armies fighting in the hinterland; and in mid-August they were joined by a fourth, a so-called peacekeeping force of Ghanaians and above all Nigerians that indulged in as much generalized looting and killing as the other three.

These were the ghastly horrendous days of street-fighting in Monrovia with child soldiers boasting *noms-de-guerre* such as Demonology or Worse Than Death, wearing women's brightly coloured nightdresses and elegant hats, a nightmarish sight never seen before in Africa, a Clockwork Orange horror story magnified a thousand times over. And these were Charles Taylor's fighters too.

But it was Field Marshal Prince Johnson who finally trapped President Samuel Doe in the White House. A notorious video shows the final scenes as the former Master Sergeant, stripped and bound, cowers before the Field Marshal's feet. "I'm a humanitarian," says Prince Johnson. "Cut off one ear." It was sawn off. Prince Johnson held it above his mouth, dropped it in and proceeded to chew it. "No," pleaded the prisoner. "My penis. No, please, not my penis."

So ended Samuel Doe and the rule of the Krahns. But the Field Marshal did not take over. There were truces, ceasefires, negotiations, with the Nigerians holding the port and trying to hold the ring. Meanwhile Charles Taylor's army was spreading chaos elsewhere.

CIVIL WAR SPREADS TO SIERRA LEONE

Charles Taylor's vaulting ambition was to dominate the Mano River Basin. And what was so wrong with that? The Mano River divided two of the smallest West African countries: Liberia and Sierra Leone. Two very similar little countries, one American-speaking, one English-speaking, both dominated economically, socially and (till 1980) politically by the freed-slave caste in their respective capital cities of Monrovia and Freetown not far apart on the Atlantic Coast, both with hinterlands inhabited by fairly primitive tribesmen, often inter-related. So Charles Taylor's dream was to do away with the last vestiges of colonialism and imperialism, the ridiculously artificial boundaries imposed by the British, the French and the Americans and to unite Sierra Leone and Liberia. Under his own rule, of course.

The state that might have, could have, would have resulted would still have been smaller than neighbouring Guinea, the former French colony with its capital at Conakry also on the Atlantic Coast, but sweeping inland behind both Sierra Leone and Liberia. The combined population, though, of about seven million would have been roughly the same as that of Guinea; and indeed Charles Taylor may well have had a vision of incorporating Guinea too. For his tribe, the Gio, like so many tribes, spread across the borders of the three states. The snag was that, as inter-tribal fighting spread through Liberia, involving also the great trading tribe of the Mandingoes, on whose support Doe had relied, killings spread too into the hinterland of Guinea and Sierra Leone - made much worse when in April 1991, only months after Doe's death, Charles Taylor invaded Sierra Leone.

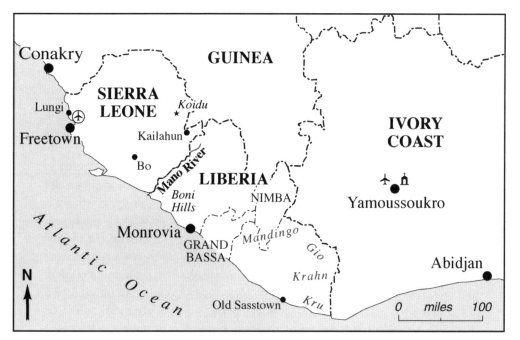

The Mano River Basin - Sierra Leone and Liberia (plus the Ivory Coast)

He used as his puppet and frontman a former corporal in the Sierra Leone army, Fodoy Sankoh by name; and Fodoy Sankoh's RUF (Revolutionary United Front) introduced into what had been the Protectorate in the good old days of civilized British rule the child soldiers, the killings, the mutilations, all the horrors that had begun in Liberia a couple of years earlier.

The difference, a vital difference, between Sierra Leone and Liberia was this: that Sierra Leone was diamond-rich, with the purest diamonds in the world, with alluvial diamonds too that could be scooped by the handful from certain river beds; and with one diamond mine in particular, Koidu, in the remote hinterland.

Koidu Mine was estimated to have reserves of four million carats, worth £200 a carat. The company leasing it was estimated to have spent £6 million in establishing the mine. And that company was Tony Buckingham's Diamond Works in which Tim Spicer had had those 10,000 share options.

★   ★   ★

President Momoh of Sierra Leone was a rather inept brigadier-general who had been selected by Siaka Stevens as his successor, and then elected. Incapable of running the country, he was incapable of running the armed forces. Unpaid, badly led, ill-equipped, the Sierra Leone army seemed to be yielding before the tribal boy soldiers of Sankoh and the RUF much as the armed forces of Liberia had failed to dominate Charles Taylor's and Prince Johnson's first rebel invasion.

But then there was a coup. Captain Valentine Strasser, with a group of young army officers, seized power in Freetown; and though Charles Taylor controlled by now about a fifth of the country, the advance of the RUF towards Freetown was halted, and both sides drew breath; while ex-President Momoh took refuge in neighbouring Guinea (soon to be joined by ex-Field Marshal Prince Johnson).

For though Charles Taylor was temporarily frustrated in Sierra Leone, he was moving closer and closer to supreme power in Liberia, concentrating on building up his resources. In these years his men took control of the whole export trade of Liberia, worth $400 million a year, with $75 million of that reputedly going to Charles Taylor personally. So that by 1994 he had built up a vast war-chest; and though he was not yet President of Liberia and "boss of the whole show" – that was to come three years later – he could afford to step up the static war in Sierra Leone.

So the rebels, the RUF, the fearsome ragged tribal soldiers who cut off fingers and feet and arms and brought gruesome Liberia into Sierra Leone, started closing on Freetown. This was when Captain Valentine Strasser, now President Strasser, started hiring mercenaries. In May 1995 he signed a contract with Executive Outcomes for an extraordinary twelve and a quarter million dollars a month, throwing in some mining concessions for good measure. In return Executive Outcomes supplied 285 mercenaries, paid from 15,000 to 18,000 dollars a month, whose first task was to halt the rebels outside Freetown. Then Executive Outcomes called in Gurkha Security Guards to help recapture Sierra Rutile Ltd's titanium mines in the east. No less than 58 Gurkhas were brought in, plus "crack troops" from neighbouring Guinea and Ukrainian pilots.

This was tough stuff. The number of mercenaries rose to about 500 over the next two years. Branch Energy and Sierra Rutile offered the equivalent of 15 million dollars more as an inducement to recapture and hold their mines. The rebels put a price of $2000 on the head of any South African captured alive – none, fortunately for themselves, appear to have been; though the head of Gurkha Security Guards, Robert MacKenzie, was caught and killed in an ambush. Night combats and helicopter-borne operations became the norm; and as the fame of Executive Outcomes spread the fortunes of its bosses – including of course that of Simon Mann – noticeably bounded.

This was indeed their heyday; active in Angola, probably active in the Congo, and now active in Sierra Leone too. But only just. By April 1995 Fodoy Sankoh's men and boys were advancing on Freetown. In January 1996, Valentine Strasser was overthrown by a fellow officer in a bloodless coup. And at this stage a new figure took a hand. Enter, Evelyn Waugh style, Peter Penfold.

OUR MAN IN – AND OUT OF – FREETOWN

"Some people would be absolutely beside themselves in a situation like this, I'd be talking to everyone I know – but he just stays calm and thinks things through."

This was his wife Celia speaking, who was studying theology in Oxford and had never set foot in Sierra Leone. She had met Peter Penfold when he was Deputy High Commissioner in Uganda and she was working at the World Bank. There they had seen out two coups before he was shifted as Governor to the peaceful and innocuous British Virgin Islands where she had married him. Now he was back in Africa - as Britain's High Commissioner in Sierra Leone. "People say he's cool in a crisis and I believe that is the best description of him."

This wifely discretion did not quite give the flavour of the man. For a Foreign Office diplomat Peter Penfold was something of an eccentric, somewhat flamboyant too - not just the cool crisp character Mrs Penfold pictured. He loved Africans, and they loved him. He had, at great personal risk, saved Henry Gombye's life - a BBC correspondent - in 1985 during General Tito Okello's coup in Kampala. He arrived in Freetown not by the conventional plane but by driving down from Dakar through the northern hinterland - to show it could be done. In Freetown he was famous for his crumpled linen suits and his battered Bentley. His hobby was mountaineering; his pride having been a Queen's Scout. He was determined to make his mark on Sierra Leone.

And so he did, by persuading the latest coup leader and his junta to resign and by organizing free elections only weeks after the coup. His candidate - Britain's candidate - was a Gray's Inn lawyer, a friend of Kofi Annan, the United Nations' boss, a respectable if colourless Moslem married, most unusually, to a Catholic and highly popular wife, Patricia. His name was Ahmed Tejan Kabbah. In March 1996 President Kabbah was democratically elected with 59.6% of the vote.

Yet in May 1997, on May 25 to be precise, the (comparatively) new President was overthrown, in another military coup, by Major Johnny Paul Koroma.

What had happened was that the Kabbah government had run out of money, or goodwill, to pay the Executive Outcomes mercenaries. Executive Outcomes, which had put an extra 150-200 mercenaries in the field and had regained control of the Kono diamond district, was owed up to $20 million. The contract - which after all had been arranged by Captain Valentine Strasser to bolster the disorganised government forces - was cancelled. "You won't last 90 days once we've gone," a white mercenary warned President Kabbah. And legend has it that he lasted only 89.

Charles Taylor may not have been behind Johnny Paul Koroma's coup, exactly. But he certainly was behind the alliance that Koroma and the armed forces, or what was left of them, formed with Sankoh's RUF, the rebels. His vast vision seemed to be coming true. He was about to be elected President of Liberia. Once he had been, his own men linked up with Johnny Paul's men and with the RUF; and, via the Boni Hills on Liberia's border, the Kono diamond district - and the Koidu diamond mine - were recaptured.

There was, in the days after the coup, something approaching chaos in Freetown. Peter Penfold entered legend, and won the gratitude of the terrified inhabitants of the capital, by ordering a rebel commander to stop the shelling of the Mama

Yoko Hotel where 800 civilians were sheltering. "I gave them ten minutes to stop shooting or I would advise the American government to send in troops," he said. "It was a total bluff." Robin Cook, Britain's Secretary of State for Foreign Affairs, publicly praised him as "a great credit to Britain and to the Foreign Office." And then, most unusually, Peter Penfold followed President Kebbah (whom Britain and the United States and the rest of the world still considered to be the legitimate President, no-one recognised Johnny Paul Koroma's coup) into exile in neighbouring Guinea, in its capital just up the coast, Conakry.

And there the disconsolate exiles might have stayed – had it not been for Tim Spicer.

Sandline Recidivus

It was only a year and a quarter since the fiasco in Papua New Guinea; and it might have been thought that Tim Spicer would be very wary indeed, after his bitter near-death experience in Port Moresby, of having anything at all to do with coups and plots and revolutions, and meetings with third-world leaders, and 'training' tribal armies, and perhaps above all in setting foot in anywhere called Guinea. But he was a mercenary, Sandline was still in business – indeed collecting its debts – this was his job, he had learnt from his past experiences, and though Sierra Leone was a hell hole, it was a hell hole where mercenaries had been very active indeed and where they knew the lie of the land.

So when a gentleman named Rakesh Saxena contacted him from Canada with a proposal to restore President Kabbah and an offer of $10 million to do so, Tim certainly didn't turn him down flat.

Who was Rakesh Saxena? It would be odd indeed if he were related to that Captain Umesh Saxena of Air India Flight 224 who had flown Mike Hoare and his men out of the Seychelles. He was an Indian certainly. He was a much much richer man than any airline pilot certainly. And he was in trouble certainly. He was accused of having defrauded the Bangkok Bank of Commerce of no less than $1.3 billion before, understandably, fleeing Thailand for Canada two years earlier. There the Mounties had arrested him, at lunch, with $100,000 lieing on the table beside him. He had been bailed, rearrested, bailed again. But it seems he know Khashoggi and Kabbah. It seems he had 'mining interests' in Sierra Leone. And it seems that he may have been a director of Diamond Works. Certainly Saxena and his eighty-odd companies were now based in Vancouver; where Tony Buckingham's company had its official home.

So it is not surprising that Kabbah's "minister of presidential affairs" wrote from Conakry to Rakesh Saxena only weeks after the coup that had driven him and his master into exile, asking him to finance a counter-coup. It is not surprising, either, that Saxena demanded from Kabbah a contract promising him mining concessions in Sierra Leone worth $150 million in return for his help. And it is not surprising that Tim Spicer slipped into *his* eventual contract a clause giving

Sandline, "the right to prospect for diamonds in certain areas of the country". What is a little surprising, however, is that Saxena turned to Sandline for military help rather than to the far more experienced Executive Outcomes.

Of course there was the problem that President Kabbah and the Sierra Leone government-in-exile still owed Executive Outcomes an enormous amount of money (which, as far as I know, was never paid). But there was the even greater problem that Executive Outcomes was, in South Africa at least, about to be wound up. For on 20 May 1998 President Nelson Mandela signed the Regulation of Foreign Military Assistance Act, an anti-mercenary act whose purpose was precisely to put an end to the activities of Executive Outcomes. It was a pretty tough Act. It was aimed at South African citizens, residents and foreigners who worked "from within the borders of the Republic", prohibiting them from "recruiting, using or training persons for or financing or engaging in mercenary activity"; and that included "any action aimed at overthrowing a government or undermining the constitutional order, sovereignty or territorial integrity of a state" or indeed – a catch-all clause, this – "any other action that has the result of furthering the military interests of a party to the armed conflict."

There had been consultations and preparatory committees leading up to this Act, and Nick Van Den Bergh had been one of those who had testified before such a committee, protesting that it would deprive him and many other former soldiers of the possibility of earning a living.[1] And indeed, had the Act been in force in 1997, (which it was not), he and his 70 men who flew out to Papua New Guinea could have been prosecuted, and fined or imprisoned, under its clauses.

It remained to be seen just how strictly the Foreign Military Assistance Act would be applied in South Africa. But of course right at the beginning Mandela's government would naturally have been on the *qui vive*, eager to make a few notorious examples. And for Mandela it was, so to speak, the crowning legal glory of his efforts to bring peace and harmony to all Africa. Next year he was to step down as President; to hand over to Thabo Mbeki.

As for Nick Van Den Bergh, as he slowly wound down Executive Outcomes' operations, he erected in his farm on the borders of Lesotho a granite monument inscribed with the names of the whites killed "on active service" with his mercenary outfit - more, I think, that the leaders of 5 Commando or 6 Commando or of course Callan's men in Angola had ever thought of doing.

★   ★   ★

---

[1] And also, arguably, of helping the good guys in Africa. A year later, in 1999 a year too late from Executive Outcomes' point of view, the Canadian General Ian Douglas published a study praising Executive Outcomes for bringing "stability" to Sierra Leone. "In an ideal world, of course," he added, " we would not need an organisation such as Executive Outcomes; but I am reluctant to say that they should abandon the scene simply because they are mercenaries." The UN Special Representative was even more flattering. "Their past is of little importance," he said, "compared to what they are achieving here and now."

In July 1997 Tim Spicer flew out to Conakry to prepare a 'feasibility study' for Saxena (fee: a modest $60,000 plus $10,000 expenses) and of course to meet President Kabbah and, incidentally, Peter Penfold. The plan was a grandiose one: 40-50,000 Kamajors would need equipping, supplying, training and leading. Once equipped, supplied, trained and led they would sweep Johnny Paul Koroma and Fodoy Sankoh's raggety-taggety soldiers and rebels away like chaff in the wind, and waft President Kabbah back to his rightful abode in State House, Freetown.

The whole world seemed to hate Johnny Paul Koroma and his tribal up-country regime. In October the United Nations passed a decree - Resolution 1132 - forbidding anyone from supplying arms to him or his supporters or indeed to Sierra Leone at all. That same month Tim Spicer and Eeben Barlow went to the State Department in Washington to obtain at least unofficial clearance for their plans. Then, most unusually, Tony Blair personally invited ex-President Kabbah to attend the Commonwealth Heads of State annual get-together, this time in Edinburgh. At the same time US Navy and Royal Navy ships took up position off Freetown.

In mid-January 1998 Tim Spicer had a meeting at the Foreign Office in Whitehall with Craig Murray, head of the FO's Equatorial Department. Ten days later Peter Penfold, on a visit to London, called in to see him at his offices in the King's Road. Meanwhile however there had been a most unfortunate development. The Nigerians had moved in. They had moved up the coast from their base in Monrovia's port, and in the name of peace-keeping had seized Lungi Airfield, across the river from the capital.

The British could of course work with the Nigerians, and with the comparatively well-trained Nigerian Army. The trouble was that Nigeria's President, General Abacha, was on the world's blacklist. He had very distinctly *not* been invited to the Commonwealth Heads of State conference; indeed Nigeria had, for human rights abuses, been suspended from membership of the Commonwealth. So the British were not particularly keen on letting the wicked General Abacha win the credit for restoring the good President Kabbah. Surreptitiously they backed Sandline.

Tim Spicer had to move fast. He had arranged his arms purchases in Bulgaria; and in early February had 35 tons of arms and ammunition flown in to Lungi Airfield, twenty miles from Freetown, on the other side of the river. He already had in place a small team of mercenaries designed to start training the Kamajors once the arms and ammunition had arrived. They had flown in on the M117 helicopter, the troop carrier, that had been salvaged from the Papua New Guinea affair and restored to Sandline in the final settlement. Their leader was a giant Fijian, known only as Fred. Fred had spent 22 years, he claimed, in the SAS - very possibly true, more and more Fijans were, and are, being recruited for the British Army, even though Her Majesty the Queen is no longer Head of State in Fiji; and the Fijians are therefore as much mercenaries serving a foreign power as Nepal's Gurkhas have always been.

Fred had been in Sierra Leone for several years, fighting for Executive Outcomes. The 'chopper pilot, Juba by name, was a South African, an Angola veteran. A silent Ethiopian engineer kept the M117 in the air. And Fred the Fijian was in close contact with Chief Hinge Norman, officially President Kabbah's Deputy Defence Minister, by position head and representative of the fearsome Kamajors.

To arm the Kamajors, or at least to begin arming and training them, the Antonov had flown in with 600 AK rifles, 30 light-machine-guns, 36 rocket-pro-pelled grenade launchers, and a million rounds of ammunition.

There were two snags: the first and probably the greatest was that Tim Spicer was not there in person. Of course it is perfectly understandable that he had decided not to put his head into the noose once more. After his arrest in Papua New Guinea he had learnt the old, old lesson that it is dangerous for a mer-cenary leader to expose himself in person, unless he has a very strong body of mercenaries with him. And he did not have a very strong body of mercenaries, because Saxena, owing to his "legal difficulties" in Canada, had not come up with anything like the $10 million dollars he had contracted to pay Sandline. Indeed probably only $1½ million ever changed hands.

The second snag, which Tim might have been able to sort out had he been on the spot, was that Lungi Airfield was controlled by the Nigerians. It was not therefore the wisest place to land a cargo of arms that was designed for another army. The Nigerians, from their experience in Liberia, knew all about the dangers of allowing rival militias to be armed with modern weapons. The trouble was that Tim had no choice. The only airfield in Sierra Leone capable of taking a heavy plane landing was, precisely, Lungi. And of course with the Nigerians appar-ently pleasantly co-operating with his helicopter and its crew, and, too, with a British frigate *H.M.S. Cornwall* lieing off-shore "in support", Tim had to believe all would go smoothly.

He was wrong. Not surprisingly the Nigerians impounded the whole weapons shipment. And probably they were, in the humanitarian sense, (though that is not of course why they did it), quite right to do so. For the Karamajors who, even comparatively underarmed and undertrained, did take part in the fighting that followed were described by the white mercenaries technically in control of them as "walking Christmas trees". They bedecked themselves with charms that could turn bullets to water, wore mirrors the size of ping-pong bats to dazzle and bewitch the enemy. "When I use this magic," one explained, "it brings the rebel to me, then I cut his throat. We fight in the name of Our Lord Jesus Christ." Or, as Fred the Fijian put it, "you get pretty superstitious in our line of work."

In the end - and the end came soon and suddenly - it was a combined opera-tion, launched on February 12, that drove Johnny Paul Koroma and his men out of a bruised and battered Freetown. The Nigerians of course with their 6000 men were the main striking force. But the Sandline helicopter ferried their commanding officers to and fro, across the bay from the port at Freetown to Lungi Airfield; and flew inland to rescue stranded Europeans and missionaries as the fighting spread, and flew for servicing out to the bay, to *H.M.S. Cornwall* whose commanding officer, Captain Anthony Dymock, helped out with his own smaller helicopter, a Sea King; and the Sandline helicopter force was instrumental, a little later on, in "liberating" the Koidu mine where the RUF had forced the locals to play the ghastly game of "rebel roulette" – selecting a piece of paper from piles strewn on the ground on which was written the name of the limb they were doomed to have chopped off.

On March 10 President Kabbah was welcomed back into 'his' capital by wildly cheering crowds of supporters. Riding alongside him in the open car, even more applauded, was the ruler of Nigeria, General Abacha – which from the point of view of Peter Penfold and Her Majesty's Government was the only fly in the ointment. But, all in all, it had been a very successful combined operation: by land (Nigerians) sea (Royal Navy) and air (Sandline). President Kabbah, the rightful President, out of power in May, had been restored the following March – with comparatively little final bloodshed, at least in the capital. It might have been thought – though there was still months, indeed years of mopping up in the hinterland to follow – that everyone involved would be rightly inclined to pat themselves, and each other, on the back.

ROWS – AND RESPECTABILITY

Instead, the most almighty row blew up. It blew up in England, it blew up – rather ridiculously, as they had never been used – about the arms shipment of 35 tons flown into Lungi Airfield; and it involved Tim Spicer and Sandline of course, but also Foreign Office officials, Ministers of State and Her Majesty's Secretary of State for Foreign Affairs, the Right Honourable Robin Cook, M.P.

What was at issue was this: had the shipment of arms been a breach of UN Resolution 1132; and, if so, had the British Government "illegally" connived at it? The real trouble was that Robin Cook on taking over as Foreign Secretary had proclaimed that Britain would in future follow an "ethical" foreign policy; and all his political opponents fastened on this unfortunate phrase, eager to bring him and, if possible, his political master Tony Blair, the Prime Minister, down. What particularly irked the Conservatives was the memory of how successfully Robin Cook when in opposition had savaged them over the arms-for-Iraq affair – in which he had made his name as a great and savage Parliamentary debater. Now the boot was on the other foot. There were questions in the House, parliamentary debates, committees, official enquiries and reams and reams of journalistic bombast. Names were named, obscure Foreign Office officials were given most unwelcome publicity, Ministry of Defence men were shamed, careers probably were ruined. It went on for months. But the Prime Minister survived, the chirpy, bearded little Foreign Secretary survived, at least for the time being, and two people particularly came out of it all smelling of roses.

One was Peter Penfold, whom the people of Freetown made their popular hero, holding mass demonstrations in his support when it looked as if the Foreign Office was about to make him the scapegoat for the whole affair, and in effect to sack him as High Commissioner. It is very rare indeed, to say the least, in former colonies of the British Empire to see an official representative of the former oppressive imperialist/colonialist régime cheered to the skies by the local population. It goes against all notions of political correctness. But that was what happened to Peter Penfold. That was his reward.

The other was Tim Spicer. When the heat was turned on Sandline and Customs and Excise National Investigation Service was ordered to investigate "a possible breach of UN Sanctions in relation to the shipment of small arms to Sierra Leone", his London lawyers, S.J. Berwin & Co, released a devastating letter sent to the Foreign Secretary earlier in which they listed all the Foreign Office and Defence personnel who had been briefed either by Tim Spicer or by Michael Grunberg, Sandline's 'consultant'; and, for good measure, threw in a list of State Department officials whom they were pretty sure had known all about the operation before it had ever begun. The Customs investigation was swiftly concluded and dropped, the media began taking Sandline's side, and eventually the whole affair petered out, despite the efforts of the Conservative opposition, foolish and perverse, to keep it alive and kicking. For, unlike the Papua New Guinea rebellion-suppression, the Sierra Leone president-restoration had been, all in all, a great triumph.

Except perhaps for Sandline financially. Tim Spicer may have covered his expenses, but I doubt very much whether he made any profit on the whole deal. But what he did achieve - and extraordinarily significant it was too - was to make his sort of mercenary activity respectable.

There was a leading article in *The Times* of 5 May 1998, headed 'Double Edged Sword' which it is worth quoting at length. "A whiff of hypocrisy," *The Times* noted, "hangs over the affair." For President Kabbah had been successfully restored, and the only sore point was that "Nigeria's disreputable military regime" had achieved this.

"This is a 'scandal' to be kept in perspective ..... Mercenaries have been used down the ages, often openly and effectively; the *condottieri* of Renaissance Italy were held in high respect. They could have a modern role. When national armies are being cut back and the public will not stand for casualties, the choice may be between limited privatisation of peacekeeping or no action at all. The manpower engaged in UN peacekeeping has been cut by 70% since its peak in 1994. The answer is not to criminalise operators who have skills the world needs but to develop a coherent framework."

This is quite extraordinary. In the very month in which mercenaries were being banned and threatened with jail in South Africa, they were given a semi-official seal of approval in Britain. "Operators who have skills the world needs" indeed!

The Scots Guards ex-officers network could have written that leading article themselves. A far cry indeed from the bloodstained "dogs of war" or "bunglers" image that had greeted the Papua New Guinea fiasco the year before.

And this was not a mere maverick Times Leader. Even more extraordinary was the letter that was printed in the same paper a fortnight later. It was signed by no less a person than the former Liberal Party leader, David Steel; and if there had been one political party that had invariably condemned mercenaries, particularly mercenaries in Africa, from the Nineteen Sixties onwards it had been Britain's Liberal Party.

Yet now: "In *The Times* leader of May 5th there was a sound call for a pragmatic assessment of mercenary forces," the ultra-politically-correct Lord Steel wrote. "I concur… We should not be so mealy-mouthed about privatized organisations which succeed where others fail but which (surprise, surprise) exist to make money."

Tim Spicer had, almost single-handed, made the mercenary trade respectable again.

XIV

Equatorial Guinea I –
The Forsyth Saga

All up and down the West Coast of Africa the Portuguese settled islands 500 years ago. Sugar was the crop they knew would bring in the great riches they were after, and sugar was what these little islands and archipelagos, once tamed, produced. But sugar plantations needed a vast number of workers, and all these islands were uninhabited – except one, Fernando Po. So the Portuguese settlers and overseers bought slaves and still more slaves from the great slave trading centres like Lagos (now the capital of Nigeria) where the slaves were sold.

They even had to buy slaves to work their plantations on populated Fernando Po, for the original inhabitants of Fernando Po, the Bubi, were no workers; whereas the mainland negroes were. The Spanish took over Fernando Po from the Portuguese; and founded a little city on its tip, Santa Isabel. But the British decided it would make a useful naval base; and Santa Isabel became, for a few years, Port Clarence; before we handed it back to the Spanish again.

Port Clarence or Santa Isabel, our man there governed it for the British and the Spanish, all 780 square miles of it, and from this island base became the first British Consul for the whole Bight of Benin. John Beecroft was his name. To Consul Beecroft the King of Lagos, deposed by his nephew and by the slavers, all his immediate family slaughtered, wrote an elegant appeal for help. "I need not tell you, Sir, what a sad calamity it is for a King to be reduced to my distressed circumstances." The King was given refuge at Port Clarence, *H.M.S. Bloodhound* and *H.M.S. Penelope* bombarded and destroyed the wicked nephew's magazine – it blew up – and the town of Lagos – it burnt down. More important, much more important, the Royal Navy by this gunboat aggression abolished slavery in the Bight of Benin. That was in December 1851. Meanwhile the population of Fernando Po was swelled by freed slaves liberated by the Royal Navy at sea – as was the population of Freetown, the Navy's other naval base out on the Atlantic Coast, far to the north. It was a pretty heroic episode. John Beecroft died on Fernando Po three years later. To stop slavery reviving [the distressed King, restored, was within months even more calamitously poisoned, poor fellow] we were obliged to annex Lagos. One thing led to another - in this case to our vastest and most populous colony in Africa, Nigeria.

Meanwhile the Spanish, not to be entirely left out, had seized a small rectangle of territory way down on the mainland, which they christened Rio Muni. Compared to the German Cameroons or to French Equatorial Africa, its neighbours, the Spanish-ruled enclave was just a pinprick; but it was still twelve times the size of the island of Fernando Po. All jungle, it was inhabited by the Fangs, as ferocious a tribe as their name implies. So Fernando Po and Rio Muni, very different, separated by hundreds of miles of ocean, were combined to form the weird little colony of Spanish Guinea.

There was already a French Guinea, which was pretty vast, and a Portuguese Guinea which was betwixt and between. It *is* confusing. None of them have anything at all to do with Papua New Guinea or with any of the Guyanas in South America. And with Independence came further changes of name: French Guinea became just Guinea - the country lapping around Sierra Leone and Liberia which has cropped up in the previous chapter but will not crop up in this. Portuguese Guinea to its north became Guinea-Bissau; and fortunately we can ignore coup-torn Guinea-Bissau. But little Spanish Guinea, both parts of it, became Equatorial Guinea. And Equatorial Guinea is the subject of this and succeeding chapters - and, oddly, the object of waves of successive mercenary *convoitise*.

FRANCISCO - AND FREDERICK

Francisco Nguema Macias at the age of 44 was elected first President of the independent Republic of Equatorial Guinea. And these were proper elections, with five candidates from different political parties, all organised by the Spanish. It was amazing, in a way, that Generalissimo Franco, the Caudillo of Spain, agreed to let this colony go when Dr Salazar in neighbouring Portugal was still clinging on to the Portuguese possessions in Africa. But probably the reason was that Spanish Guinea was small and worth little or nothing, cost more in running than it brought in profits. At any rate Nguema was elected President on September 29, Independence was celebrated on October 12, and Equatorial Guinea was admitted as the 126th Member of the United Nations on November 12.

This was all in the year of grace 1968. Just across the Bight of Benin Biafra's struggle for independence was reaching its first climax; and horrendous pictures of starving Biafran children were stirring pity and a desire to help throughout the Western world. That summer Red Cross aid flights used the little airport at Malabo (as Santa Isabel, once Port Clarence, had now been rechristened) as a staging post before flying into Biafra's shelled-out strafed air-strips until in the autumn Nguema's new independent government put a stop to them. "This change of policy," wrote Frederick Forsyth with furious indignation, "originated, apparently, on the night the Guinean Interior Minister turned up drunk at the airport with the Nigerian Consul."

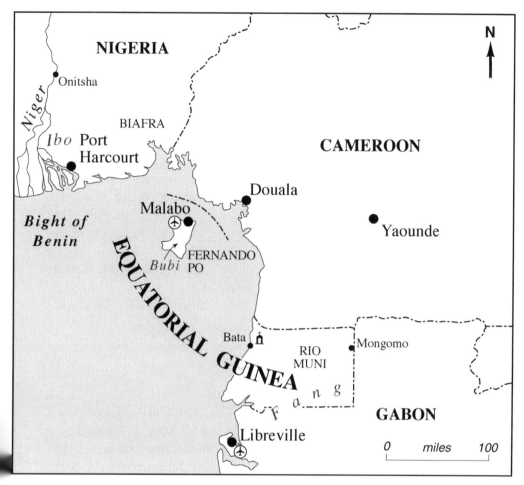

Equatorial Guinea and its Neighbours

Frederick Forsyth was in Biafra at the time. He had arrived early in 1968 and he left a year later, in February 1969, before the fall of Biafra, with most of a book written. It was his first book, a non-fiction book: and it was called *The Biafra Story*. Back in Europe he finished it, adding an Afterword in April and it was published in June as a Penguin Special (priced 30p or 6s!) very quickly. Here quoted from it (like the shorter quotation above) is his general view of white mercenaries at this period.

"Most have been revealed as little more than thugs in uniform and the riff-raff of the Congo did not even bother to come out to Biafra at all. Those who did fight at all fought with slightly greater technical know-how but no more courage or ferocity than the Biafran officers. The lack of contrast between the two is underlined by Major Williams, the one man who stuck by the Biafrans for twelve months of combat, and the only one who emerges as a figure really worth employing.

[And Forsyth concludes:]   Ironically the Biafran war story, far from consolidating
the position of the mercenary in Africa, has completely exploded the myth of the
Congo's 'White Giants'."

This must have injured the feelings of the mercenaries with whom Forsyth
had spent a lot of time during his year in Biafra. They liked him. He dined in
their Messes, he was their channel back to General Ojukwu, Biafra's President, he
coped with the front-line though he was not suicidally brave like Taffy Williams.
Whom, probably for that reason, he so much admired. "The trouble is," he would
say, "I've got a little picture in my mind of a factory where a little man is making
a bullet with 'Frederick Forsyth' marked on it, 'Frederick Forsyth' 'Frederick
Forsyth' ……" He never carried a gun. He never wore uniform. But he had
great charisma, he was very funny, a heavy smoker who drank 20-30 cups of coffee a day. He was welcome everywhere.

By the time he came to write his third famous thriller, *The Dogs of War,* Forsyth's
views had clearly changed. The book is dedicated:

> *For Giorgio, and Christian and Schlee*
> *And Big Marc and Black Johnny*
> *And the others in the unmarked graves*
> *At least we tried*

in a fashion that suggests the author now identifies himself with the 'White Giants'.
Giorgio is clearly the Italian Giorgio Norbiatto and Big Marc the Flamand Marc
Goosens. Black Johnnie was Johnnie Asamoya, an Ibo, brave, courageous and
able, second in command of the Guards Company. All three were killed in Biafra;
(Christian and Schlee are unknown to me). But in Forsyth's thriller 'Tiny Marc'
Vlaminck (who is killed in the final assault) is clearly modelled on Goosens; and
the Corsican Jean-Baptiste Langarotti (who survives) is equally clearly modelled
on Armand Ianarelli. As for Black Johnnie, "Johnny, a big grinning fighter who
had been promoted to captain," also dies in the final assault.

Forsyth did not make much money with *The Biafra Story,* though the first
printing sold out, as did a later updated version. He had by his idealistic, indignant resignation burnt his boats with his original employer, the BBC. Biafra had
collapsed, and there was no place for him in Africa; he was jobless and almost
penniless. Before joining the BBC in 1965 he had worked for Reuters in Paris,
and he decided to take a chance; to use his knowledge of France to write a novel,
a thriller based on an (only partly fictional) attempt to assassinate De Gaulle
ordered by the OAS.

The result was *The Day of the Jackal,* a long novel refused by many British publishers. Finally accepted, it became almost instantly a worldwide bestseller. With
this, and with his next German-based thriller, *The Odessa File,* Forsyth made a

great deal of money. For a period he went to live in Co Wicklow in Ireland (where writers pay no income tax), so he had even more at his disposal.

But he had never forgotten Biafra - as *The Dogs of War*, his third thriller, proves. Its prologue vividly describes Ojukwu's last flight out from Biafra on the Super Constellation, the 'grey ghost', and his farewells to 'his' faithful mercenaries led by the fictional Cat Shannon. And the story ends with Shannon double-crossing his capitalist employers and proposing to put Ojukwu (never named, merely described as 'the general') back in power on the imaginary island of Zangaro; and with a long heartfelt tirade by the hero Cat Shannon (in this instance clearly the author's mouth-piece) against British capitalists and against the British Foreign Office and against the suffering and starvation they had without conscience condoned in Biafra. There can be absolutely no doubt where, in Africa, the author's heart and sympathies continued to lie.

That is why it is not difficult to believe that *The Dogs of War*, Frederick Forsyth's third bestseller, is not so much fiction as 'faction'; indeed almost certainly the thinly disguised account of a mercenary coup planned and financed by Forsyth himself.

What was the target of that mercenary coup? President Nguema's Equatorial Guinea.

"THE DOGS OF WAR"

Read, or re-read, *The Dogs of War*. It tells the story of a successful coup by a handful of mercenaries who land by sea and in a swift night-attack storm the presidential palace of a dingy, corrupt, minor and imaginary West African republic called 'Zangaro'. The disappointing thing for many readers is that of the four hundred-odd pages only the last forty or so deal with the actual attack and battle. Elsewhere in the book there is very little blood and thunder. Indeed the whole central section, almost half the book, deals in meticulous detail and almost exclusively with the administrative side of setting up a mercenary coup.

If you want to know how to obtain an ex-user certificate for the purchase of arms, how to open a numbered bank account in Switzerland, how to set up a holding company in Luxembourg in order to disguise your vessel ownership, if you are vague about the uses of certified bank cheques, the techniques of freight clearance, or the rituals of French customs officers, here you will find, astonishingly authentic in detail, all the information you may need. It seems, on reading it, as if the author has been through the exact same process step by step himself and is far more interested in these mechanics than in the rather cursory sub-plots of Russian interference, rivalry between English and French mercenaries, and sex (a minimum) that are thrown in almost as a sop. For a best-selling thriller it is, if extremely authentic, almost rebarbatively technical.

And the reason for this is blindingly clear. It is an account, written after the event, of a coup plotted against Equatorial Guinea that never in the end took place. All the preparations were made, all the men and equipment were - almost - in place; but the final assault, the coup itself, never occurred. That is why the final forty pages are so cursory. They are fictional, and invented. The rest is fact, lightly fictionalized. Why, even the capital of 'Zangaro' is christened Clarence. Frederick Forsyth left clues galore for those who know where to look.

★   ★   ★

Only months after Independence things started to go very wrong in Equatorial Guinea. President Nguema was a Fang, a Fang from Mongomo deep in the hinterland; and the 'Mongomo clan' took over the government, and the National Guard. The Bubis of Fernando Po, a milder tribe, were ignored. So of course were the settled plantation workers, immigrants from Nigeria or rather, that part of Nigeria that had now become Biafra, Ibos and Catholics in the main, almost 20,000 of them. In February 1969 there were clashes with the former colonial power. Spanish troops briefly occupied the little airport at Malabo; and by March almost all the 7000 Spaniards who had stayed on after Independence had begun to leave; and the plantation-based economy (now exporting cocoa, not sugar) began to collapse.

Then came the first alleged coup: the first of so many alleged coups. One of the four rival presidential candidates, Atanasio Ndongo, was arrested and shot dead. Saturnino Ibongo, the country's man at the United Nations, was arrested at the airport and beaten to death. U Thanit, the United Nations' Secretary General, appealed to Generalissimo France to help restore order. But Franco, wisely enough, washed his hands of Equatorial Guinea. Virtual anarchy, the British Consul reported to the Foreign Office, spread throughout the island.

A year later, in January 1970, came the sudden collapse of Biafra. Frederick Forsyth was back in London, in Camden Town. His book, *The Biafra Story*, published a few months earlier was now of course wretchedly out of date. Its hero - his hero - was General Ojukwu. General Ojukwu was at least alive, safe and reasonably well - in exile. Then and there, with that quixotic fanaticism that so many Englishmen, from Byron onwards, have shown for the cause of an oppressed little country, Forsyth began plotting Ojukwu's return. For such a return, a safe base, a safe jumping-off point was needed.   And what better base than Fernando Po, a small island only 100 miles off the Biafran coast, where anarchy was breaking out?

"So who runs the show out there?" asks the wicked capitalist in *The Dogs of War*. "A man called Jean Kimba," replies his suave henchman. "Tough guy is he, this Kimba?"

"It's not that he's tough, sir. He's just downright mad. A raving megalomaniac and probably a paranoid to boot. He rules completely alone, surrounded by a small coterie of political yes-men. If they fall out with him, or arouse his suspicions in any way, they go into the cells of the old colonial police barracks. Rumour has it Kimba goes down there himself to supervise the torture session. He rules by a sort of mesmeric fear. The people think he has a powerful juju, or voodoo, or magic or whatever. He holds them in the most abject terror of him personally."

Frederick Forsyth had never met, and was never to meet, President Francisco Nguema personally; nor was he ever to set foot, yet, in Equatorial Guinea. But he gives a pretty accurate description of what the Fang President was to become in his description of 'Jean Kimba'. Except that Nguema's end was to be more macabre in real life than the rattle of machine-guns bullets from a mercenary's Schmeisser that ends President Kimba's life in *The Dogs of War*. As for the Fang, they become the brutal Vindu in the thriller; while the Bubi are the Caja. And the Ibo plantation workers, on whose help the mercenary hero, Cat Shannon, relies, are simply described as "black workers from elsewhere", "a third tribe, the most intelligent and hard working in the country." "They call them the Jews of Africa." And these , Cat Shannon tells the horrified suave sidekick, "will be the real power in this country from now on. Their country will be used as a base and a headquarters. From here the newly trained men will go back one day to avenge what was done to them. Maybe the general will come and set up residence here, in effect to rule it."

That was Frederick Forsyth's vision. It was an admirable, grandiose vision; and I believe he was, from the first, deadly serious about it.

Forsyth's Coup

Forsyth had kept in touch with one of the Biafran mercenaries to whom he refers but discreetly never names in *The Biafra Story*, one of the most experienced mercenaries in the world, Alexander Gay.

There was almost no mercenary venture in Africa in which Alexander Gay had not taken part - except, fortunately for him, Angola. He had enrolled in 52 Commando in the Congo under Peters and Gordon.★

He had known Hoare, Puren and Wicks.★

For his second contract he had joined 6 Commando under Denard; whom he much admired. Arrested with Ramon del Velasco in the north, he spent time in Mobutu's jail in Coquilhatville - only to be released and invited to join in suppressing Commandant Wauthier's rebellion.★

He refused; flew back to England; bored, contacted Maurice Lucien-Brun in Paris, flew back out to Leo, (where the unfortunate Ramon del Velasco, still in gaol, was to be killed by Mobutu together with RSM Sam Cassidy and other white mercenaries when the Mercenaries' Revolt broke out in the East) joined Denard again, together with a giant of a French ex-para named Biaunie. He followed Denard and Schramme on the Mercenaries' Revolt, fought through the siege of Bukavu, and was evacuated with Schramme's people across the Shangugu into Rwanda.★ From there, after a month's internment, he was flown out to Paris and liberty.

That had been in April 1968; and that would have been enough mercenary adventure and near-escapes for most men. But Alexander Gay, a Glaswegian and a well-educated man, had done his National Service in the Royal Signals and had been stationed in Nairobi, listening in with fascination - he of course spoke French, which was why he was given the job - to the radio traffic in the Congo; and seems to have had Africa and adventure in his blood.

Back in England with his old Congo mate Alan Carter, he was put in touch with the Welshman Taffy Williams, also an old Congo hand but one whom Alexander Gay had never come across. Taffy had already been in Biafra, recruited by Faulques - a Legion man through and through in spirit, though the Legion had apparently at one stage rejected him. When Faulques pulled out, Taffy, back in Europe, recruited via the Zambezi Club in Earl's Court both Alexander Gay, and a pleasant young Rhodesian, an explosives expert, Johnny Erasmus. They flew out from Lisbon to Biafra where 'Colonel' Steiner appointed Alexander Gay a Captain - his highest rank so far, he had been a corporal in the Royal Signals - and Taffy Williams his Brigade Major.

Alexander Gay was wounded at the battle of Kwala Junction★ where Black Johnnie was killed. Though evacuated to Paris, no sooner had they fixed him up at the American Hospital then he flew back to Africa, landing at Libreville in Gabon where he met the famous Colonel Le Braz, head of Omar Bongo's Presidential Guard - "a tanned hard-faced senior officer in tropical fawn uniform", veteran of Indochina and Algeria, who appears under his own name in the Prologue to *The Dogs of War*.

Back in Biafra Alexander Gay was given command of a Guards Brigade when Steiner upped his own command to a Division and, "stark raving mad", planned his never-to-happen attack on Lagos. All the same, when Steiner was disarmed and ignominiously sacked, Alexander Gay stuck with him.

Their next mercenary venture was, starting with Steiner's Catholic contacts in Cologne, in the Sudan.★ Gay was lucky to get out of the southern Sudan in one piece too. For Steiner, an ill man by this time - he had lost a lung in Biafra and had contracted TB - fell out with his follower, and asked 'General' Tafeng of the Anya-Nya to arrest Gay. Gay got out first; and by doing so avoided that more serious arrest that ended for ever Rolf Steiner's dreams of grandeur.

It was now 1970. Frederick Forsyth was in London, thinking about his plan, in contact with a disillusioned - and impoverished - Alexander Gay. Next year Gay got married. Armand Ianarelli came to his wedding, but Forsyth, though invited, did not.

They stayed in touch, though; and Alexander Gay, despite marriage, found it difficult to settle down. Just in case, he acquired two false passports (by something similar to the method Frederick Forsyth has the Jackal use in his first thriller. Interestingly enough, Gay learnt his method from another, earlier Sixties thriller, *The Dolly Dolly Spy*). He showed Frederick Forsyth too, with a 'live' model, how to build a trigger mechanism - the sort the Jackal had to construct in his (fictional) effort to kill De Gaulle. Restlessly, he moved to Brussels, first with this wife, then without her. He ran out of money.

So he was more than happy when Forsyth, now full of what Gay lacked, funds, approached him in early 1972. By then President Nguema was on the point of declaring himself President for Life, and was quarrelling bitterly with President Bongo of neighbouring, larger, Gabon, Le Braz' Gabon, over the possession of a small group of uninhabited islands. So the proposed coup was on: no longer a pipedream, for Forsyth had the money to fund it - and in Gay the man to manage it.

They met on the Continent. Could the plan work, asked Frederick Forsyth. And, if so, could you carry it out? Yes and yes, replied Alexander Gay's though the plan could go wrong and the whole concept, he thought, was dubious.

How dubious? That would depend. Obviously the first priority was a reconnaissance. That Alexander Gay offered to do in person; and Frederick Forsyth agreed to finance it.

Using his "Henry George Greaves" passport, Gay flew out to the Cameroons. Douala, the main coastal city and port of the Cameroons, is even closer to Malabo - less than a hundred miles of sea separate the two cities - than Port Harcourt in what had been Biafra. In the Cameroons 'Mr Greaves' obtained a tourist visa with some difficulty - money changed hands (as indeed it still does for those who want to obtain a visa nowadays: be prepared with plenty of dollars!) 'Mr Greaves' was - so well-prepared indeed that the Equatorial Guinea Consul, for whom a tourist was a rare bird, took him for an American. He flew in from Yaoundé, the capital of the Cameroons, to Malabo's small airport, handed over more dollars to the immigration and customs officials, and asked a taxi to take him to the best hotel - not much choice there, Malabo was a tiny run-down town, with an atmosphere of fear.

'Mr Greaves' stayed in Malabo almost a week, pretty conspicuous one might have thought as he was the one and only tourist on Fernando Po. Fortunately there was an American girl, a missionary, at the same hotel; so, once again, as so often in Africa's recent history, mercenaries and missionaries rubbed shoulders amicably.

In those few days he discovered the lay of the land. The Presidential Palace, formerly the Spanish Governor's *Residencia*, was an old colonial building of a certain grandeur overlooking the sea and Malabo's little harbour, guarded by an army camp below and by, Gay noted, new entrance gates. He suspected the soldiers slouching around had empty ammunition pouches, and at the price of a minor incident and a broken shoulder he confirmed this all-important fact. He took photos - that was a greater risk. But the hotel had sent a small boy to follow him around and dash back if he was arrested, so that they could get Consular help before he was beaten to death. He never got into the Presidential Palace, he never saw the President. But he saw enough to see that a swift sea-borne night attack on the harbour and the Palace could succeed.

Via the Cameroons he flew back to Europe and reported to the Coupmaster General. It could be done. Frederick Forsyth meanwhile had not been idle. He had arranged for 40 or 50 ex-Biafran soldiers to be on standby in Cotonou - not yet Bob Denard's target - the coastal capital of Benin, just up the Bight from Nigeria. We are now in the autumn of 1972. The coup was planned for January 1973.

Forsyth and Gay set themselves three tasks:-(a) to eliminate the President - that was to be Alexander Gay's personal responsibility (b) to seize and hold the town (c) to find, if possible, a political figure to front for them. The coup once achieved, they would fade quickly and discreetly away. There was no plan to stay on the island. As for the hinterland, Rio Muni, that could be totally ignored. It was no part of the plotters' plan to seize control of, or even to get remotely involved in, a rectangle of Fang-inhabited territory that was in any case hundreds of miles away.

It was now Alexander Gay's job to assemble the weapons, the boat, and the mercenaries.

Otto Schluyter of Hamburg was a licensed arms-dealer with whom Gay was in contact. He agreed to supply the AK 47s for the Biafran soldiers, with 330 rounds of ammunition per weapon; plus four light machine-guns, plus, most importantly, the two 60 mil. mortars with a thousand mortar bombs that would be used to shell the Presidential Palace and the army camp below it, and the two bazookas - RPGs - that would be needed for the final assault on the entrance gates and the Palace doors. Once the arms and ammunition and the rest of the equipment and of course the ten white mercenaries Forsyth and Gay had decided the operation would require were on board the ship, it would sail from the Canaries down the Atlantic Coast of Africa to Cotonou, there pick up the ex-Biafrans, strip, clean and fire all the weapons out at sea; and then sail to Malabo. The mother ship would remain anchored outside the little harbour while the three assault teams in the three Zodiacs with silenced outboard engines would set out under cover of night, land close to the army camp, set up the mortars and, hopefully cause total confusion, with the Army believing they were being shelled by the Palace and the Palace believing it was facing an Army coup.

The major worry was that Gay believed there were Central European body-guards, possibly KGB men, personally protecting the President. On the other hand if all went well, the assault teams would go in before midnight; and by first light have seized not only the Presidential Palace but the airport, the radio sta-tion, the main bank and - rather ambitiously - the Russian Embassy; which they would then proceed to offer, contents and all, to the Americans for the princely sum of a million dollars.

This of course assumed a certain amount of local support; and it was Forsyth's job to set about, via his Ibo contacts, arranging that. Gay had his moments of doubt – he suggested sub-contracting the whole operation to Bob Denard, only to be turned down flat. (In *The Dogs of War* there is a villainous French merce- nary "burly, with a down-turned moustache" named Charles Roux who "sneers" at the hero Cat Shannon, puts out a contract on him in Paris, and has to be dis- couraged, gruesomely, from foiling the whole plot.)

So Gay went ahead. He estimated the cost of his part of the operation at £50,000. His reward – and that of the other mercenaries – was to be a large lump sum on successful completion of the mission. Meanwhile he, and they, were to be paid six months' salary; and to stand by at one month's notice. These were gener- ous terms. Frederick Forsyth was not stinting on ' his' coup.

But all the same there was trouble assembling even such a small group of mer- cenaries. Armand Ianarelli, whom Gay particularly wanted, was not available. An advert in the *Daily Telegraph* asking for "Experienced ex-NCOs interested in overseas travel" brought only one reply, from Scott Sanderson, a former military policeman, who became Gay's bodyguard and assistant, travelled over with him to Guernsey, collected £30,000 in Guernsey banknotes, helped him buy fifty sets of army webbing in the East End, and then brought them over by van to Brussels. His job on the great night would be to stay on board the 'mother vessel' and keep the ship's crew in line.

There were difficulties in obtaining the right 'mother vessel' – a freighter, ideal, would have been just too expensive to purchase. And there were difficulties in getting the arms and ammunition delivered to Spain, despite Otto Schluyter's promises. For the arms, purchased from Omnipol, were being held in Ploetze on the Adriatic; and various plans had to be considered, for a rendezvous in mid- ocean or for picking them up directly from Yugoslavia. But Frederick Forsyth spoke fluent German; and, using the alias of Mr Van Cleef, sorted out problems by phone with Hamburg.

Meanwhile Gay had enlisted a Hungarian, Al Varga, sent to reconnoitre hotels in the south of Spain, a Smithfield porter named Ronald Gorman useful in load- ing the ship, and, most interesting of all, a former Congo mercenary named Alan Murphy.

Murphy had been an armourer in 5 Commando, a sergeant, a great sup- porter of Peters and one of Peters' mercenaries in Nigeria – on the opposite side, therefore, to Alexander Gay. But the two men got on when they eventually met. Murphy was a crack pistol shot, almost of Olympic Games standard, an arms freak and a body builder. He was small, narcissistic, unmarried, uninterested in women. He was a professional, and Gay planned to make him second-in-command of the assault force.

By early autumn Gay had found his boat at Fuengirola – the *Albatross*, a 64-foot converted fishing vessel, used by a British father-and-son outfit for currency smuggling. He chartered her for three months at £2000 a month. The arms transfer had been settled; and the crates were due to be loaded at Malaga just up the Costa del Sol ten days before Christmas.

The trouble was the men. They were assembled, waiting, in Marbella and Banus; and, understandably, with nothing else to do, drinking far too much. Nor did they look much like underwater archaeologists, the cover story.

Then things went wrong in Malaga. The Spanish official bribed by Otto Schluyter to allow the arms on board refused when faced with a dicey trawler with a bad local reputation rather than a proper freighter. The seven cases of whisky went on board alright, as did the 10,800 litres of diesel, and the one and a half tons of rice for the Biafran soldiers. Gay shifted the *Albatross* with the mercenaries on board to Gibraltar for Christmas, and then instructed it to proceed to Lanzarote in the Canary Isles. The revised plan was now to run the arms out in a motor boat and rendezvous with the *Albatross* off Tenerife before sailing on, as planned, to first Cotonou and then Malabo, and to triumph, wealth, success – or death.

So Gay flew to Hamburg, then Lisbon, taking with him as a go-fer a young French lad recommended by Biaunie. And this is where the whole story gets very obscure. In Lisbon he received a phone-call from Frederick Forsyth, calling off the whole operation. The Spanish police had got wind of the affair, and the *Albatross* was about to be raided at Lanzarote.

There is a suggestion – I personally find it impossible to credit – that Forsyth deliberately sabotaged his own operation. That, in other words, he had never really intended the coup to take place; but was using everybody at great expense (and the expenses had now doubled, to almost £100,000) to provide the factual, detailed background for a thriller. That, in other words, the whole thing had been a literary set-up from the beginning. The only argument I can see for this is that when *The Dogs of War* came out late in 1974, the following year, Forsyth made half a million pounds from it; so £100,000 would have been a good investment. But of course the whole idea is ridiculous: he could have easily written the book on imagination and research alone – after all no-one has ever suggested he hired a professional assassin to try and kill De Gaulle before writing *The Day of the Jackal*.

Also, and more importantly, it is all wrong psychologically. Anyone reading *The Dogs of War* can see how desperately its author would have wanted the coup to succeed. And this is particularly true if, as has been most convincingly suggested, Forsyth modelled his hero, Cat Shannon, not on Taffy Williams only but also on himself: for the 'Cat' was slight, Anglo-Irish, a chain smoker, a great coffee drinker, and very attractive indeed to women – all characteristics of his author – besides being totally devoted to Ojukwu and to the cause of Biafra.

Another suggestion is that Denard got to know of the operation; and, out of pique at not having been involved, sabotaged it. True, in *The Biafra Story* Taffy Williams' "assessment of most of the mercenaries, and particularly the French, is unprintable". True, *The Dogs of War* is vindictively anti-French, and might have been a literary revenge had Denard ruined its author's plan. But it seems inherently unlikely. Bob Denard had better things to do than to occupy himself with a possible coup in what was not even a French-speaking ex-colony. Though he may have learnt some lessons from its failure.

No, the most likely explanation is the only too obvious one: - that the Spanish police had got wind of something nefarious afoot on the Costa Del Sol, that the Spanish official who had accepted, for a consideration, Schluyter's end-user certificate - issued, stories differ, either by a Syrian or an Iraqi diplomat - had got the wind up; that the Spanish official all the same informed the Hamburg arms dealer that there would be a police raid on the boat; and that Schluyter warned 'Mr Van Cleef', who in his turn, and quite rightly, warned Alexander Gay.

Aftermath

Alexander Gay flew from Lisbon to Lanzarote, with a large sum in cash and his three passports - and of course his young French bodyguard. They booked into a hotel, then went out to the harbour and informed everybody that the operation was cancelled. As they were on board, port officials came out to search the boat; and back at the hotel the local *Policia* raided the hotel room, found £20,000 in the wall safe; and, understandably suspecting a drug operation, arrested Gay.

They were followed by an Anti-Terrorist unit of the Guardia Social from Madrid. No drugs had been found on the *Albatross*, but maps of Malabo and Fernando Po, and the military webbing. Alexander Gay trotted out a carefully-prepared cover story, about a German businessman with a daughter being held for ransom on the island. But the police worked it out. They even brought an ex-colonial Chief of Police of Santa Isabel to talk over his plans with Gay. And they told him that he and his men would be released without charge provided their own travel expenses from Madrid were covered. They even had a farewell 'celebratory' dinner on the island and gave Alexander Gay all his three passports back.

The men were sent home on a ship to Southampton - and disappeared from mercenary history: all except Alan Murphy. As for Alexander Gay, he flew to Paris, phoned Forsyth in London and demanded that the men be paid off in full as arranged. Forsyth agreed; and so Alexander Gay was paid off too, directly into his bank account in Switzerland with an extra one month's salary to boot. It may not have been much compared to the vast bonus he had hoped for; but it was a fair deal. And in any case Gay had always had his doubts as to whether the operation could succeed. He had felt it could go wrong, as so many night operations do, right at the beginning. Or, if successful, by dawn a neighbouring African State (Nigeria?) might immediately have intervened. So in a sense he was well out of it; skin in one piece and bank balance healthy.

But he still had, literally and metaphorically, trials to face. Metaphorically because his wife insisted that he settle down, take a steady job and break with his old chums like Armand Ianarelli. He travelled in Europe first for a year, before agreeing and settling down as a warehouseman, even though that first Christmas Alan Murphy came down to share festivities and memories with him.

Literally, because when he eventually returned to England, he flew into Birmingham and, having heard there was a warrant out, put himself into the hands of solicitors there. "I haven't found anyone who wants to arrest you yet," said the solicitor plaintively. It soon happened; an obscure affair of home-made explosives, an American Remington .45 and seven rounds of ammunition found in a hold-all in a left luggage locker in Victoria Station was one of the charges laid against him. Another was of "making a false statement to obtain a passport". The Catholic Church sent a supportive letter mentioning his help in Biafra. The Assistant Commissioner of Special Branch referred to useful information he had come up with. And Frederick Forsyth not only sent a character testimonial but stood bail. Though the judge in the Old Bailey slagged him off something cruel, Gay had pleaded guilty - he had no previous convictions, the testimonials clearly helped, and he was sentenced to eighteen months suspended on the explosives charge and a £500 fine for the undeniable passport offences.

But not a word of the foiled coup in Equatorial Guinea came out then. Not a suspicion was raised by the publication of *The Dogs of War*. It was not till Alan Murphy was charged, two years later, with touching up young kids in a Hackney swimming pool and police came to arrest him in his Goldsmith's Row bed-sitter that the whole story suddenly leaked. For Alan Murphy had kept not only a diary but documents; and these found their way from Special Branch to *The Sunday Times*.

Frederick Forsyth could have denied the story. But both then and thereafter he has always refused to comment. Alan Murphy might have confirmed it; but when police came to arrest him in March 1976 he opened fire on them with a .38 revolver. One constable was wounded on the stairway. An hour later, under siege, Alan Murphy shot himself through the heart.

So, with a bleak and seedy death, ended this tangled tale. If true, it is one of the most extraordinary stories of recent mercenary history, one of the most bizarre sequels to the Biafra war imaginable. Is it true? I cannot guarantee its truth; but it has been told, there is both internal and external evidence to support it; and personally I believe it to be far more likely to be true than not.

But there are a score of fascinating questions that remain. Above all, perhaps, did Ojukwu in exile in the Ivory Coast know anything of the proposed plan to restore him to an independent power base? If so, did he approve?

Only Frederick Forsyth can answer such questions.   But as he has always asserted that there is nothing to answer, it seems most doubtful whether he will ever do so.

XV

Equatorial Guinea II – Mann's Grand Plan?

Life is much stranger than fiction. So forget fiction, wrote Minette Marrin in *The Sunday Times*. "I don't know which part of this story is most implausible. It is high classical tragedy, it is Monty Python, it is pantomime, pathos and bathos all horribly entangled with a dazzling cast…..I keep wondering rather guiltily why I am enjoying the whole thing so much (and I am assuming that other people share my low tastes). It would be nice to be too high-minded for schadenfreude."

It's a morality tale, she added; and however jaded we imagine we are, most of us still long for morality tales. It is hard to disagree! That is what is ultimately so unsatisfactory about the first planned mercenary coup in Equatorial Guinea, as described in the last chapter. It is impossible to draw any moral conclusions from it at all. No-one got their come-uppance, neither plotters nor plotted-against, good did not triumph over evil, nor evil over good. It is like an unfinished story, a tale not rounded off.

Whereas this story, the story of the next two chapters - well, as regards that dazzling cast, let me quote Minette again. "We have Simon Mann, an Old Etonian mercenary and former SAS officer who smuggled a message from a filthy Zimbabwean jail demanding 'a large splodge of wonga' from Scratcher and Smelly and others to get him out. Both Smelly and Scratcher (and others) have an awful lot of wonga, as it appears to be called in this cautionary tale, although it is not an African word but a Romany term meaning moolah, dosh or loot…."

"Scratcher turned out to be Sir Mark Thatcher, wayward son of the legendary Margaret. He is now said to be extremely rich and lives … in great luxury in a millionaires' ghetto in South Africa. Curiously enough - so small is this weird world - none other than the son of the President of Equatorial Guinea, an exceptionally wretched country with huge oil reserves, is Scratcher's neighbour in this same ghetto.

"Smelly turns out to be Ely Calil, a friend of Scratcher as well as of Mann; he is an extremely rich and reclusive Lebanese entrepreneur and oil trader living in serious splendour in Chelsea… No self-respecting story-teller would dare to use the names Scratcher and Smelly. The connotations are too obvious for fiction – Scratcher for you-scratch-my-back and Smelly for stinking rich. Scratch and smell but don't scratch too deep."

And then Minette adds a word of warning that I, for my part, and before beginning the tale these chapters tell, must repeat. "This is a story bristling with 'allegedly' and 'reportedly' and assumptions of guilt by association." Many of the principal parties have totally denied having anything at all to do with a coup – including, in particularly, Ely Calil, Lord Archer, Greg Wales, others on the "Wonga List", most of the mercenaries imprisoned in Zimbabwe, the Armenians imprisoned in Malabo, Peter Mandelson, Severo Moto, and indeed Simon Mann himself. I am in two minds myself as to whether a coup was ever planned. On balance I think it was; and I will tell the tale as if I was sure of it, omitting the 'allegedly's and 'reportedly's from now on. But please, reader, remember: this may be as much a tale of fiction as was *The Dogs of War* – though it takes place in the same setting, a generation, thirty years, later.

The 'Freedom Coup'

At the end of the last chapter I mentioned a 'fascinating question': did General Ojukwu know of his planned restoration by Frederick Forsyth? Of course there is a corollary, a second, equally fascinating question. Did President Nguema know anything at all about his planned overthrow by Frederick Forsyth? Did he ever indeed read *The Dogs of War*?

Maybe not. He probably had little time for reading in 1974 when the thriller came out. For there had been a far more serious June coup attempt, atrociously suppressed. 118 political prisoners were killed, "tens of thousands" – a probable exaggeration – were said to have been massacred, and a quarter of the population driven into exile. This was the real start of five years of mad tyranny and paranoia. The following Christmas Nguema is said to have had 150 political prisoners shot in Malabo Stadium as loudspeakers played 'Those Were The Days, My Friend'. A Bubi Vice-President was found in his home, shot in the head. Everyone with spectacles was put on a death list. All the Ibo plantation workers were expelled. All boys between the ages of 7 to 14 were called up for forced labour service, and any head of family who refused to send his sons was shot. The final straw probably came in June 1978 when the President forcibly closed Bata Cathedral on the mainland and all other Catholic Churches. It does not do, as many small despots have found before Nguema, to assault the Catholic Church and the faith, however superstitious and syncretic, of the masses.

Teodoro Obiang Nguema Mbasogo was not only a Lieutenant Colonel, head of the National Guard and Deputy Defence Minister, but also and more importantly the President's nephew; and of course a member of the ruling Mongomo clan. Six of the members of the Guard had gone to his uncle the President and asked to be paid. Infuriated by their impertinence, the President had them shot.

Young Obiang - he was only 37 - led a coup, the so-called Freedom Coup of 3 August 1979 - the only successful coup, interestingly enough, of all Equatorial Guinea's coup-dotted history. Next day the churches were re-opened. Two weeks later the fleeing President was captured in the bush near Mongomo on the border with Gabon after a running series of skirmishes in Bata, 'capital' of Rio Muni on the mainland, and in the jungle hinterland. He was publicly tried, with six of his closest associates, by a "military and people's court" in an open-air cinema in Malabo. The accused were found guilty of treason, genocide, embezzlement and violation of human rights. On September 28 Obiang had his uncle, and the others, executed by firing squad - shades of that King of Lagos deposed by his own nephew two centuries before when Malabo was Port Clarence; though then a place of refuge rather than a mortuary. An opposition movement in Spain, where so many exiled groups had foregathered, claimed that Obiang had killed several of his own military colleagues before the 'Freedom Coup'; and denounced it as, simply, a 'Palace Revolution'.

What indeed was the difference between nephew and uncle? They were both Fangs, both from Mongomo, both despotic. But the younger man was - and is - more astute. He, Obiang, had to face his first coup attempt only eighteen months after his own Freedom Coup. It was probably the most nearly successful. Members of his own personal Presidential Guard, hired Moroccans, were shot down. Significant that they were Moroccans - a sign of the growing influence of France that was to culminate, years later, in French becoming an official language, and Equatorial Guinea abandoning its own currency to join the French CFA Zone: both much to the annoyance of the former Colonial rulers, the Spanish.

The Pope paid a brief visit to the restored flock, celebrated Mass, and gave his benediction. Later that year - 1982 - Obiang was elected President for seven years; and a political rival, Severo Moto, also a Fang but not from Mongomo, went into exile. There was a second coup attempt in 1983; a third coup attempt (followed by executions) in 1986; and a fourth coup attempt in August 1988 when Severo Moto had returned after six years in exile. Severo's right-hand-man was imprisoned for 17 years; and, wisely, Severo left for exile again - to form, in Madrid, another exile group in opposition.

The early 1990's saw three developments; first, a quarrel with Spain, that ended in the expulsion of the Consul General and the withdrawal of the two Spanish planes that linked the main and the smaller islands; secondly a quarrel with the Americans whose Ambassador received death threats. When the State Department was accused of using "witchcraft" and its man, John E. Bennett, of encouraging electoral boycotts by imbibing "traditional medicines", the USA closed down its embassy. A very weird, impoverished, little country was Equatorial Guinea, sliding inexorably downhill.

But all that was about to change. The third and by far the most important event was the discovery of off-shore oil - oilfields lieing under the ocean but within the territorial waters of Fernando Po (or Bioko, as the island had now been renamed). Mobil Oil revealed that by the end of 1996 its oilfield was producing 60,000 barrels a day. Vast American firms - Marathon, Exxon, Amerida Hess - staked claims and gradually moved in. At the time of writing production has gone up to around 350,000 barrels a day; and it is estimated it will rise to more than 500,000 barrels - or one barrel of oil a day for each and every inhabitant of the country.

"We shall be the Kuwait of Africa," proclaimed Obiang in 1996. Not exactly. Better in a way because the foreign presence is extraordinarily unobtrusive - all the activity takes place off-shore, out of sight and out of mind. Better for the United States because the oil can be shipped straight across the Atlantic without any interference from indignant and heavily-armed locals, as in the Rivers State of Nigeria or from neighbouring dictators, as in Kuwait itself. Better too because the oil levy taken out by the government - skimmed off from the top - is a tiny fraction of that which both the Angolan and the Nigerian governments demand and receive - only 20% as opposed to up to 74%. Better too for the President and the Mongomo clan because in such a small country there is more than enough in the skimmings to fill their accounts at Riggs Bank in Washington and elsewhere. But no better for the ordinary inhabitants of Equatorial Guinea, who barely see a dollar of the takings - Malabo must be the one capital in Africa that has not a single shop in it, and only two or three new buildings. It resembles a crumbling little Spanish provincial capital, where the only high-rise building is the Cathedral and the only elegant square is that separating the Cathedral from the Presidential Palace, formerly the Spanish Governor's Residencia. The whole place could certainly do with a whitewash, a coat of paint.

THE FAMILY MAN

In February 1996 Severo Moto and four other candidates withdrew at the last moment from Presidential Elections where Obiang, who had nastily labelled anyone who might vote against him "low-class", was re-elected for another seven years with 99% of the votes cast. Coup attempt No. 5 failed that summer, with various NCOs imprisoned or shot. Nothing daunted, back in exile, Severo tried again next year. This time he was arrested on the high seas with a cargo of arms by the Angolan authorities and deported back to Spain.

Understandably perhaps President Obiang had had enough of his fellow Fang - a larger, more jovial, more unctuous man than himself, one who had moreover trained in his youth for the priesthood. Severo and 12 others were tried in their absence for high treason, and sentenced, in his case, to 101 years (a miserable 30 only for the other 12). This was the third time he had been arrested and tried. The first had been two years' earlier, when he was actually on the island, for bribing a police officer and damaging the reputation of the Head of State - 2½ years. A few months later he was tried again for conspiracy in coup attempt No. 3 - 27 years. But then, unexpectedly, on the seventeenth anniversary of the Freedom Coup, he and all his co-conspirators had been pardoned. Obiang must, by 1997, have regretted that he had ever let his rival out of his clutches. That was the ingratitude that Presidential clemency brought!

1998 was a bad year in Equatorial Guinea. Fifteen Bubi leaders were tried and sentenced to death (later commuted). The Bubis in Madrid reported a "veritable genocide" on the island, and Amnesty International a hundred tortured and five killed. The year 2000 saw a number of ex-Ministers arrested. The year 2002 saw 68 opposition figures sentenced to 6-30 years for complicity in Coup No. 5. And one opposition journalist to 1 year for "libels and insult" against the Head of State. In December's Presidential Elections President Obiang was re-elected for a further seven years with, this time, an improved 99.5% of the vote - which (if he lives that long) will take him up to the year 2009; and no less than thirty years in power - much, much more than his unfortunate uncle.

But President Obiang may not live that long. He has cancer. He is ageing (so, come to that, is Severo Moto, now over sixty). He goes to Rabat in Morocco for treatment. He has two sons, Teodorin by his first wife Constantia, in February 2003 appointed Minister in control of oil and infrastructure, his father's favourite, something of a playboy, with his own - very popular - radio station, Radio Asonga. And Gabriel, by his second wife Cecilia who comes from the neighbouring ex-Portuguese islands of Sao Tomé e Principé, also subjected (though to a lesser extent) to coups, or alleged coups. Gabriel was at college in the United States, and is favoured by the Americans who - not before time - are reopening their embassy in Malabo.

He also has half-brothers: General Antonio, General Agustin, and General Armengol. General Armengol is (or was) Director of National Security and Chief of Police. It is therefore more than interesting that General Armengol is (or was) the major shareholder in the company that Nick du Toit set up in Malabo in 2003.

NICK DU TOIT

It was in early 2003 that Nick du Toit, and his camp-followers, arrived in Malabo. They say that Nick had once commanded the Buffalo Battalion. I am not sure about "commanded" but he had certainly been in it; and in the ten years since it had been officially disbanded he had been footloose, at a loose end in some ways, married, admittedly, to Belinda in Pretoria, with five youngish children there, but by nature an adventurer, a tall rangy Afrikaner who had certainly worked with and for Executive Outcomes, who had set up with Tai Minaar his own little mercenary outfit, Meteoric Tactical Solutions, MTS. Minaar had died mysteriously in September 2001, MTS had passed on to two other Afrikaners, Lourens 'Hecky'

Horn and Jacobus Carlse, and in 2002 Du Toit had certainly been in Liberia acting as a bodyguard/adviser to Charles Taylor. He was a man with contacts all over southern and central Africa, a licensed arms dealer too. But by 2003 he was in his late forties. My view is that he wanted to make money and settle down. A small inconspicuous comparatively peaceful – certainly compared to Liberia – and potentially extraordinarily rich African country: that might be the very place for him. With a few camp followers from the old days he came to Malabo, he looked around, he got the hang of the place; and he realised soon enough that for any business to get off the ground the ruling clan had to be cut in on the deal.

So by July 2003 he had set up, with General Armangol Ondo Nguema, the President's half-brother, as sleeping partner and the President's special adviser, Antonio Javier Nguema Nchama as a close associate, a company, Triple A Options, that was pretty well designed to do anything in or around Equatorial Guinea that might make money. Agriculture: that was one option – certainly the plantations were run down, almost totally abandoned and needed reviving. Shipping: that was another option, and there was trade to be done with boats to be bought or leased in Bata on the mainland. The third option was aviation; and this was where Antonio Javier came in. He was already the major shareholder in a local air transport business called Panac, run and set up by a German, Gerhard Eugen Metz. The German had hired Armenians – there were six of them in Malabo, and they had been, like so many of their fellow countrymen, all over Africa, hiring out their services – knowing little or nothing of the local language, Spanish, still less of local politics and intrigues. They were on the continent to make money and send it back to their benighted families at home. Of course being Armenians, brought up and educated in the USSR, their experience was with Soviet planes. Panac Cargo was authorised to have two: an Ilyushin 76 flown in from the Ukraine, an Antonov 12 from Russia.

And there let us leave Nick du Toit for the moment, trying to set up his businesses in Malabo, with bigshot local associates eager for their share of the takings, with a German associate and his Armenian flight crew; with a handful of his own fellow South Africans of various shades of colour; with vast opportunities to make money but too little capital to exploit them – and , of course with contacts all over Africa wondering what had become of old Nick, and what the old devil was up to these days.

MEMBERS OF THE CAST

It is a long time since we heard anything of Simon Mann. He of course knew Nick du Toit from the old days, and also Lourens 'Hecky' Horn and Jacobus Carlse, Nick's successors at MTS. But even before Executive Outcomes was wound up in South Africa in 1999, he had made enough money from all its enterprises in Angola and the Congo and Sierra Leone too to lead a much more relaxed life style with his second wife, Amanda. They bought – or rather the Guernsey company that Mann had set up bought – a Queen Anne house, Inchmery, set in 20 acres alongside the Beaulieu River in Hampshire – that was, in 1997, a fine home for the three children, his second batch, that Amanda, a tall steely young woman met at Christopher's in Covent Garden where she had been the launch manager, jovially nicknamed 'The Duchess', proceeded to present him with. But the couple kept on the South African home they leased at 88 Duckitt Avenue, Constantia, with its two swimming pools and array of garages and smart cars, Villa Musica.

It was an expensive lifestyle. Old George Mann, Simon's distinguished father, the England cricket captain and brewer, died at the age of 83 in August 2001; the Royal Family sent a representative to his memorial service in the Guards Chapel at Wellington Barracks. As the eldest of George's three sons, Simon no doubt inherited a certain amount. Next year he tried his hand at another career. He acted, rather well too, in the award-winning television drama-documentary "Bloody Sunday", playing the part of the 1st Paras Commander, Lt Colonel Derek Wilford, in the reconstruction of that so-called massacre in Londonderry thirty years before. "He is very English, a romantic," said Paul Greengrass, the director, "tremendously good company."

And of course it may have been his romantic side, his urge to try one last foray rather than the need for money that involved Simon Mann in mercenary adventures once again.

Money certainly came into it. Simon Mann had registered a company – another of those with meaningless names that give no clue as to what it is all about, like Executive Outcomes – in the British Virgin Isles. This one's title was Logo Logistics; and its bank account was in Guernsey. What seems certain is that, late in 2003, money went out from Guernsey to Malabo; from Logo Logistics to Triple Option A. And a lot of money too, either one million or two million dollars. In other words Simon Mann was investing heavily in his old buddy Nick du Toit's business ventures in Malabo, and in particular in "commercial security projects in West Africa" – which was rather an extension of Nick du Toit's original activities. But perhaps an inevitable one. For Nick's experience was all in 'security', his chief local partner was, after all, head of security in Equatorial Guinea, and clearly there were lots of non-sinister openings for security men in and around the island, even if only guarding the off-shore oil installations and the on-shore almost isolated camps where so many of the expatriate oil workers were housed. Some say President Obiang himself considered employing Nick directly. In a small world like Malabo this is more than possible. Certainly the government had white 'security advisers' hanging around – like a certain Johann Schmidt, a heavy-set South African with a limp apparently from a war wound in Angola, often to be seen in deep conversation with big black men in dark glasses in one of the handful of smartish hotels in Malabo, the Bahia. No-one much trusted him, or knew what he was really up to – one of those figures on the margin who like to create an aura of secrecy and self-importance around themselves.

And where did Simon Mann get all these millions of dollars from? This is where things become very complicated, and rather obscure. Apparently vast sums were moving in and out of Logo Logistics' bank account in Guernsey all through late 2003 and early 2004. And among those vast sums moving in the vastest had been $5 million from a group of Lebanese investors in Beirut - the Asian Trading and Investment Co SAL; for "unspecified projects".

Ely Calil has always maintained that he had nothing to do with this SAL; and indeed this may be one of those unfortunate cases of 'guilt by association'. All up and down the coast of West Africa Lebanese traders had settled in the old days of the British Empire; and the Calils had settled in Nigeria. Ely, their scion, had made his fortune in oil trading, moved to London, to a splendid home at 149 Old Church Street, Chelsea, married an American heiress Frances Condon in London in 1972, was said to have other homes in the Middle East and Nigeria and France as well as British citizenship and a Senegalese diplomatic passport. Ely Calil was no playboy. He *looks* rather like a playboy in the only photograph available of him, at his wedding over thirty years ago, handsome, dark, full-lipped, flashing (as one would expect given the occasion) a brilliant smile. But since then he had rather avoided publicity; except for some unwanted publicity in June 2002 when he was arrested by the French police in an obscure affair concerning illegal commissions paid to the Nigerian dictator, General Sami Abacha, by a subsidiary of the French oil giant Elf Aquitaine. Millions of dollars were involved, allegedly. All charges against him were subsequently dropped. But the episode does indicate that Ely Calil was still much involved in the oil business in West Africa; and in particular in the Bight of Benin.

Probably that was why he gave "modest" (his own phrase) financial support to Severo Moto. Severo Moto had by now formed his own "government-in-exile" in Madrid; and of course what was "modest" money by Ely Calil's standards may have seemed anything but modest to Severo. Certainly he, Severo, was pretty active at this time, in continual contact with the right-wing government in Spain of José Maria Aznar and even, in 2002, flying out to Washington, hiring a lobbying firm to represent him there, and setting up a meeting with Chris Snyder, a senior official in the African Bureau of the State Department.

We have to picture all these characters constantly flitting around: Nick du Toit to and fro from Equatorial Guinea to South Africa, Simon Mann from South Africa to Hampshire to Guernsey and (shortly) to Spain, Ely Calil all over the place making and investing his oil millions and Severo Moto, ever eager to return in triumph to his native land. Was he, Severo, behind the eventual coup plot? "Of course he was," said a Spanish commentator, Adolfo Marion. "He does nothing else. He makes a new attempt every six months." But he had no intention of setting foot in Malabo while the President was still there. Wisely. "Obiang wants me to go back to Equatorial Guinea and eat my testicles," he declared. "That's clear."

★   ★   ★

So here we have two sets of men: first the adventurers – Nick du Toit the Afrikaner and Simon Mann the Englishman; secondly the politician and his backer – Severo Moto the Guinean and Ely Calil the Lebanese. Who brought the quartet together? It seems to have been the fifth man: Greg Wales, a British accountant in his fifties, with what is vaguely described as "extensive interests" in Africa, including, of all unlikely places to have business interests in, Somalia. "Of course my name comes up," he was later to say, "because I have been in business with them. But it is a shock that anyone should assume I have anything to do with a coup."

Greg certainly knew Ely Calil; and indeed Peter Mandelson too who had rented one of Ely Calil's flats in Holland Park in 1999 (where Ely's actor son George also had a flat - the flat, given to him by his father, from which George's unfortunate girlfriend Laura Sadler had fallen to her death).

And Greg knew Simon Mann and Nick du Toit too. He had been a long time 'consultant' to Executive Outcomes; and he had set up Triple Options A for Nick in Malabo. He was in cahoots with both of them. "Simon had been thinking about buying an aircraft," he said, "because in theory you can do all sorts of things with one aircraft. You can run a bus service etc." He was also if not exactly in cahoots at least in contact with the Pentagon and the US Defence Department, whom he was later to warn, privately, that the situation in Equatorial Guinea was "dangerous". By this time Simon Mann was clearly thinking more of the etceteras than of running a bus service……

THE PLOT THICKENS

Whose idea was the plot? Extraordinarily difficult to say. In one sense of course it was Severo Moto's; he was, inevitably, the perpetual plotter. In another it was Ely Calil's. If he was giving financial support to Severo, which he was, it was not simply because he liked Severo's smile. He hoped for a return on his investment. He could only get a return on his investment if Severo returned to power; and that was certainly not going to be by a free and fair election. As an astute and extraordinarily successful businessman, Ely Calil could not but have welcomed a coup.

As for Nick du Toit, the idea must inevitably have occurred to him too. He was there, he had an organisation, he had a set-up, he knew the ropes; and though he may have had only the faintest notion who Severo Moto was, he must have known that there was a government-in-exile waiting in Madrid. And, government-in-exile or no government-in-exile, he must have been very well aware of the foetid 'family' atmosphere in Malabo, with the two rival sons and mothers, and the three powerful half-brothers, Generals Armengol, Antonio and Agustin. Indeed General Agustin, after an alleged 'suicide attempt', was dispatched to Spain that January of 2004 for 'medical treatment', escorted to the airport and put on the plane by General Armengol. The rumour was that the illness he had been suffering from was Presidential ambitions.

Of course in another sense the man responsible was President Obiang himself. If you seize power by a coup and keep yourself in power by continually suppressing coups - real or invented - every year or two, then no wonder, as Greg Wales was to put it, "Equatorial Guinea is the sort of place where if you don't hear a coup attempt is being planned, then there's something wrong".

Or one could argue that the whole idea was Frederick Forsyth's; and that it was Simon Mann who pulled it all together. For Simon Mann must have read *The Dogs of War*; and I would personally bet a large sum that he re-read it after he had flown out with Ely Calil to meet Severo Moto in Madrid early in 2004. "A good and honest man," Simon Mann described him as. This was a meeting where Mann was introduced to another exile, a General Sargosa (?) a former head of security in Malabo, who described in gruesome detail how he had been forced to watch while the President raped his wife. "They asked me," said Mann "if I could help escort Severo Moto home at a given moment when simultaneously there would be an uprising of military and civilians against Obiang. I agreed and I tried to help the cause."

I incline to believe that this was the original idea. But when, if ever, would this local uprising in Malabo occur? Simon Mann, with his quicksilver brain, must immediately have realized that, unlike Cat Shannon in *The Dogs of War* (or Frederick Forsyth and Alexander Gay in real life if he knew the background story, which he probably did not) any coup plotters this time would have a priceless asset in place in the form of men on the spot, experienced fighting men too, already by good fortune 'infiltrated' - that is to say, Nick du Toit and his followers. This 'asset' obviously doubled or trebled or quadrupled the chance of a successful coup; for mercenaries would not be landing or flying in blindly, they would have help, experienced and reliable help, already in place. And, better even than that, men on the spot with boats and planes and faces well-known to security officials and contacts with generals and special advisers: an instant fifth column.

All depended of course on Nick du Toit being won over; and he seems at first to have been hesitant, nervy, reluctant to get involved. Greg Wales phoned him; and they agreed to meet at the Sandton Sun Hotel in Johannesburg. At the first meeting the idea was planted. At the second meeting, four days later, Simon Mann appeared too; and the elements of a scheme were, over the next few days, worked out. Nick du Toit refused, on behalf of himself and his men, to take any armed part in the actual coup itself. But he, and his sidekick, Sergio Cardoso, would arrange to recruit fifty to sixty men, basically old Angola/Buffalo Battalion hands kicking their heels in the dusty wastes of Pomfret, give them a quick revival course of arms training at an old shooting range in disused mines to the south of Johannesburg, and put Simon Mann in touch with an arms dealer in Zimbabwe.

When it came to the actual coup, however, he and Sergio would be back in Malabo. They would act as guides and liaison but they would not, Nick insisted, carry weapons or take a direct part in any fighting or killing or arrests. His thinking was that, if everything went wrong, and the incoming mercenary force had to flee (rather like Denard at Cotonou), then he would not, literally or figuratively, have burnt his boats. Triple Options A could resume its normal business activities as if no coup attempt had ever taken place. An optimistic concept.

For his reward Du Toit was to get a million dollars, and command of the new Presidential Guard. Naturally, as soon as there was a new President, there would be a new Presidential Guard; and its commander would be an extraordinarily powerful personage on the island. And this was clearly a role that would suit Nick like a glove, much more than that of a local businessman - though the one did not rule out the other.

As for the new President, that would of course be Severo Moto. And the plan was, that as soon as the coup was successful, Severo Moto was to be flown in before dawn, together with his government-in-exile; so that Malabo would go to sleep one evening with President Obiang in charge and wake up next morning - if all went well - to find President Moto in control.

The reward for the coup plotters and the coup backers was to be $15 million guaranteed by the new President; and, rather more importantly in the longer term, control over the oil revenues, with Ely Calil becoming the chief oil broker for the new régime. That did not mean - that could not possibly have meant - that the new régime would annul the existing oil contracts. On the contrary at least tacit American approval was vital, and the hope was that the State Department would view a new régime - almost any new régime - as preferable to President Obiang's. Spain, and Spanish oil interests, might well get a look in later. But the $15 million dollars would come from the royalties already payable by Marathon, Exxon and the rest to the State.

For the moment, though, these millions of dollars were pie in the sky. What was needed was money to finance the coup, to buy arms, hire men, arrange transport, pay all the incidental costs and expenses. And this is where the famous Wonga List came in.

THE WONGA LIST

One needs to take the Wonga List with a pinch of salt. It 'emerged' from South African police sources who had apparently obtained it in their turn from young James Kershaw, Simon Mann's unofficial ADC in South Africa, whose job it was to chase up contributions from those who had agreed to invest in the coup, and to keep the books. When things had all gone wrong, the young man, only 23 or 24, was threatened with arrest unless, in the time-honoured phrase, he decided to assist the police with their enquiries. No doubt the police let him know fairly clearly what they would like to find out; and little James (who was whisked off pretty smartly into a witness protection scheme) did what he could to come up with what was wanted. Here, nonetheless, for what it is worth, is the list:

Name	Investment/Contribution
Ely Calil	$750,000
Karim Fallaha	$500,000
Greg Wales	$500,000
Simon Mann	$500,000
David Tremain	$500,000
Gary Hersham	$500,000
Gianfranco Cicogna	$500,000
Mark Thatcher	$275,000
J.H. Archer	$240,000

If however this is a complete fiction, it is a fairly clever one. It is not surprising that Ely Calil should have invested the most, being by far the richest. It may be perfectly true that he had nothing to do with the Asian Trading and Investment Company SAL; but his fellow Lebanese Karim Fallaha was a director. Nick du Toit at the second meeting at the Sandton Sun Hotel in Johannesburg had talked not only with Simon Mann but with a "tall quiet" Englishman named David who was also present. David Tremain was a South-African-based mining boss, who flew home from South Africa the very day after the plot was officially discovered. Gary Hersham is a Mayfair property dealer, who runs or ran an estate agency, Beauchamp, and who has admitted only to helping Simon Mann find a mortgage on his - actually probably his wife Amanda's - Notting Hill property. Gianfranco Cicogna, a South African television tycoon with a home in London, has agreed he was approached but "I did not really appreciate the grandeur of their ideas". Backed a coup? "Not really. I don't think it crossed my mind." And I must emphasise that everyone else on the list also denies investing in any such mischievous and madcap scheme - even if they had been offered the chance of trebling their money in a few weeks (provided of course everything went well).

Two names of course will particularly fascinate. Lord Archer, Jeffrey Howard Archer, famous novelist, famous party-giver, famous Conservative politician, famous near-Lord Mayor of London, famous ex-perjurer and ex-prisoner, strenuously denied via his London lawyers, Irwin Mitchell, that he had anything at all to do with any coup. When it was pointed out to him that $134,980, after bank charges, was paid into Logo Logistics bank account at the Royal Bank of Scotland, St Peter's Port, Guernsey by a J.H. Archer on 3 March 2004, Irwin Mitchell declared that "At no time has our client issued a cheque in the sums mentioned." When it was pointed out that it was a wire transfer not a cheque, "Lord Archer has made his statement and it does not amount to an acceptance that money was paid by Lord Archer into the account you mention." When it was further pointed out that Lord Archer was a "close friend" of Ely Calil and that there had been many phone calls from Calil's house to Archer's house in the weeks preceding the coup, including two calls on the significant date of January

3, the retort came that "Lord Archer was in Cambridge that day.....These two phone calls were between different family members."

Lord Archer's son, the Honourable James, has the same initials as his father. James, an Old Etonian, had made a lot of money in the City as a member of a flamboyant set of brokers known as the "Flaming Ferraris" before being banned from working there in 2001 as being "not a fit and proper" person for such activities. He was a friend to one of Ely Calil's sons. Could he have been the 'different family member' who made or received the phone calls? Could he have been the J.H. Archer involved? Or is this just another case, which one must always beware of, of 'guilt by association'?

Not that, it seems to me, there is any question of 'guilt' at all. For even if all these investors on the Wonga List had done what they were alleged to do, risked their money to assist in the overthrow of a hated and bloodstained despot, what moral code were they infringing? Presidents and Prime Ministers win praise from some, obloquy from others, for using the vast resources of great states to overthrow precisely a hated and bloodstained despot. 'Régime change' - if it is an acceptable aim and achievement in a major case, then any logic of moral philosophy must surely accept it as an acceptable aim and achievement in the case of a minor despot too.

SIR MARK THATCHER, SECOND BARONET

It strikes me as just too convenient for the South African police that Mark Thatcher's name appears on the Wonga List. The ANC had never forgotten that Mrs Thatcher had opposed Commonwealth sanctions against South Africa in what turned out to be the last years of apartheid; and Mark Thatcher was, notoriously, no-one's favourite except his mother's.

And possibly his wife Diane's. Mark had moved to America in 1984. There he had met, wooed and won Diane Burgdorf. "She's just an ordinary Texas millionairess", as her father Ted had rather fetchingly put it. But in fact she was rather extra-ordinary. A cheerleader and a blonde beauty pageant contestant, admittedly, but on the other side of the coin a committed Christian, educated at Bethany Lutheran College, Minnesota and at the Southern Methodist University in Dallas, Texas. She bore their grandmother two grandchildren, Michael and Amanda. And when the couple moved to South Africa in 1995/6, she ran prayer groups, and forgave her husband his possible infidelities with "the blonde in the pond" and one or two others.

The Thatchers bought a gabled house and settled down in Constantia, not far from the Manns. Simon and Mark were near contemporaries, Simon an Old Etonian, Mark an Old Harrovian. Mark, whose business career had been variegated, was reputed to be very rich (via those various commission deals that had brought him so bad a press when his mother was Prime Minster); and was interested in all sorts of business deals in Africa, including particularly – unfortunately for him – anything to do with helicopters. The Manns and the Thatchers moved inevitably in the same social circles in Cape Town. They were, if not close friends – too different in character and outlook, one would imagine, with a pretty long-established baronetcy in one family and a very nouveau one in the other – at least well-acquainted, and Simon and Mark had the occasional meal together.

As for Nick du Toit, he had met Mark Thatcher too and they had discussed a couple of old helicopters that Nick had under repair in Zambia. But, as often happens in these sort of negotiations, no eventual deal had been struck.

There were, however, three brothers, the Steyl brothers, whom Simon Mann knew well, who ran from Bethlehem in South Africa, four hours south of the capital, an air operation, Air Ambulance Africa, known by an odd but understandable coincidence as Triple A. With Crause Steyl Mark Thatcher signed a four-page contract by which he agreed to underwrite the charter of an Alouette III helicopter for six months. Triple A would share the revenue with him, and the cost would be $250,000 – almost exactly, readers will note, the amount Mark Thatcher is said to have contributed to the Wonga List.

The cost seems enormous; but Crause Steyl has explained that helicopters cost $600 an hour to run, with $5000 a month each for the pilots, and $10,000 a month for special insurance. Two points to note, which are not in Mark Thatcher's favour, are that the contract was signed on 4 January 2004, at the time when the preparations for the coup were about to become febrile, and that the eight African countries in which the helicopter could be used included Equatorial Guinea. One most important point to note, which is in his favour, is that the Alouette III is *not* – unlike Tim Spicer's M.117 and M.124 in Papua New Guinea – a military gunship or a troopcarrier. "I met Mark three or four times," Crause Steyl was to say later. "He was a partner in the venture. He put in about $250,000. The money was wired to my company in various instalments."

The difficulty with assuming that Mark Thatcher was therefore involved with the Equatorial Guinea coup is this (and it seems to me an insuperable one): – that there was absolutely no need at all for an Alouette III helicopter (or, come to that, any helicopter) at any stage of the planned operation. And if there was no role for the helicopter under-written by Mark Thatcher at any stage of the coup, then he was an innocent man, made an official scapegoat. That seems to me the only logical conclusion. More on which later.

THE FEBRUARY ATTEMPT

Mark Thatcher may have had wind of what was in the air. That is hardly a crime. So did many other people. Johann Schmidt had wind of something sinister afoot in Malabo, and sent e-mails to two M.I.6 "people I knew", to their "personal e-mail addresses" both in December and again in January, as also to an acquaintance at the State Department, Michael Westphal. These 'warnings' were later to cause embarrassment to Britain's Foreign Secretary, Jack Straw; for the Foreign Office had understandably, in view of the source they came from, reacted to them with indifference, particularly as the second e-mail predicted "simultaneous" coups in Sao Tomé e Princípe and Equatorial Guinea; which was palpable nonsense. But what was not nonsense was that "these actions are planned to take place in mid-March 2004". And not only Johann Schmidt but drinkers at The Bushlander - Die Bosvelder - a favourite pub with former military men at Centurion on the outskirts of Pretoria, were by now joking about "going fishing" or "exporting agricultural machinery" with or to old Nick's firm, Triple Options in Equatorial Guinea.

This may be, probably was, why Simon Mann decided to rush things forward. He realised that the cover story, of recruiting men for a typical Executive Outcomes job, guarding mines in The Congo, or Burundi, or even the Sudan, was wearing thin, because the recruiters were Nick du Toit and Sergio Cardoso, both of whom everyone knew were based in, associated with, heavily involved in Equatorial Guinea. The link was just too obvious. Therefore, if word was leaking out that something was due to happen in mid-March, better to catch everyone on the hop, and get it all over with before the end of February.

That seems the logical explanation for a still obscure little episode that occurred between February 17 and February 21.

★   ★   ★

Before that, earlier in February, Simon Mann and Nick du Toit had flown across to Zimbabwe to arrange for the purchase of arms. Zimbabwe desperately needed foreign currency, and the supplier was to be the state-run Zimbabwe Defence Industries, whose boss Colonel Tshinga Dube was personally known to an associate of Nick's, Henry Van der Westhuizen.

The cover story was to be the same: that the arms were being purchased to assure the protection of mines in the Congo; but not directly by Mann and du Toit. "We agreed to use a cover story," said du Toit later, "about supplying arms to a rebel general because that would be helpful to President Mugabe who had interests in the diamond mines there."

This fits in. It is pretty plausible. It is why the first plan was to fly the arms from Harare to Kolwezi in the Congo where they would be picked up on February 17 by Nick du Toit's Antonov, with the Armenian crew flying in from Malabo.

This was not a bad plan. But it went wrong. My guess is that it went wrong because it was Colonel Tshinga Dube's job to arrange for the arms to be flown to Kolwezi; and at the last minute he refused to do so unless he was paid in full in advance. While Mann, very understandably, refused to pay in advance until the arms were actually delivered. A classic stand-off.

So the Armenians were told to fly to Kolwezi to pick up crated 'merchandise'. They did so. They hung around Kolwezi waiting for a couple of days – they were used, after all, to delays and to hanging around obscure African airports – and when no 'merchandize' arrived, they were ordered back to Malabo. From their point of view just another odd job; and if time and money were wasted, it may have been their time but it was certainly not their money. It was to prove very bad cess for them all the same.

Crause Steyl meanwhile had picked up Severo Moto plus fellow exiles plus a handful of British and South African advisers from the hotel where they were waiting in the Canary Islands. He had flown them in a leased Beechcraft King Air 200 jet to Bamako airport in Mali where they were due to meet two mysterious fellow conspirators, two government ministers from Malabo – presumably with news of the proposed civil and military uprising against Obiang. But these two too failed to materialise. So back the whole group flew to their hotel in the Canaries, to await events.

★   ★   ★

This had all been a bit of a rush, and a bit of a fiasco – no more than that, because in any coup attempt (a historic example would be Colonel Claus von Stauffenberg's numerous attempts to assassinate Hitler) things are almost bound to go slightly or badly wrong. But it seems to me that it was now that Simon Mann decided to take everything into his own hands; to act swiftly and decisively, not to wait for any potential local uprising in Malabo, to have a precise and simple plan, to stick to it, to hope for that element of good luck without which no military operation can succeed, and to rush it through before mid-March when it looked as if the cat might be totally out of the bag.

THE BIG PICTURE, THE GRAND PLAN

Everything, clearly, depended on obtaining the weapons. Simon Mann decided he would only pay for these, or at least pay the final instalment of $100,000, when they were actually physically handed over to him. Where? In Zimbabwe. Where precisely in Zimbabwe? The obvious place was Harare airport. He would fly his own plane in, inspect the weapons, hand over the money, load and fly them out again.

Not on the Antonov however. Any more long-distance flights in and out of Equatorial Guinea would alert already edgy authorities. He needed his own plane. At the end of February with the Steyls' help he leased for $400,000 from a Kansas company, Dodson Aviation, a 40-year-old Boeing 727-100, formerly a US Coastguard plane, white, still with its US markings and its US number plate, N4610. Its engine was boosted so that it could use short runways. Its cargo hold was pres-

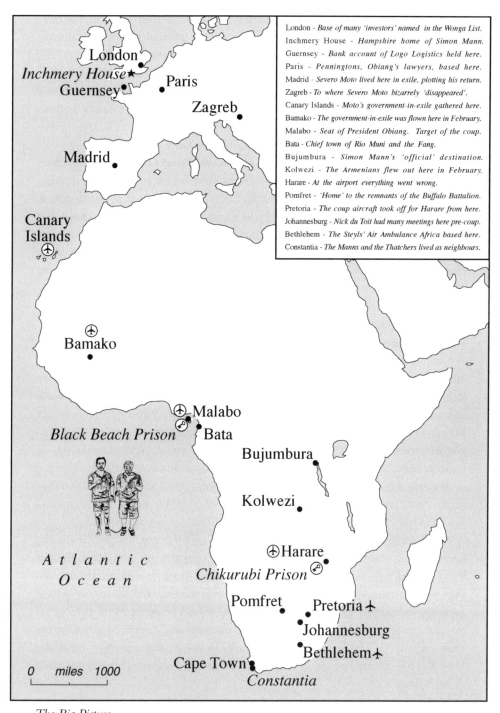

London - *Base of many 'investors' named in the Wonga List.*
Inchmery House - *Hampshire home of Simon Mann.*
Guernsey - *Bank account of Logo Logistics held here.*
Paris - *Penningtons, Obiang's lawyers, based here.*
Madrid - *Severo Moto lived here in exile, plotting his return.*
Zagreb - *To where Severo Moto bizarrely 'disappeared'.*
Canary Islands - *Moto's government-in-exile gathered here.*
Bamako - *The government-in-exile was flown here in February.*
Malabo - *Seat of President Obiang. Target of the coup.*
Bata - *Chief town of Rio Muni and the Fang.*
Bujumbura - *Simon Mann's 'official' destination.*
Kolwezi - *The Armenians flew out here in February.*
Harare - *At the airport everything went wrong.*
Pomfret - *'Home' to the remnants of the Buffalo Battalion.*
Pretoria - *The coup aircraft took off for Harare from here.*
Johannesburg - *Nick du Toit had many meetings here pre-coup.*
Bethlehem - *The Steyls' Air Ambulance Africa based here.*
Constantia - *The Manns and the Thatchers lived as neighbours.*

The Big Picture

surized, so that weapons could be extracted from storage during the flight. For crew he hired as pilots Niel Steyl, Crause Steyl's younger brother, and Hendrik Hamman from Namibia, with as flight engineer Ken Pain, an elderly 60.

There were a lot of weapons on order: 61 AK47s with 75,000 rounds of ammunition, 10 RPG Rocket launchers with 100 missiles, 20 light mortars with 800 60mm mortar bombs. Readers might compare this with what Frederick Forsyth had thought sufficient for his assault on the Presidential Palace in *The Dogs of War*. Obviously Mann was prepared, quite justifiably, for more of a battle.

The great question now for Simon Mann was how to get the arms and the men into Malabo. By land or by sea? Together or separately? He plumped for simplicity. Who could blame him? As he now had his own large plane in South Africa, he would put his men aboard there, fly to Zimbabwe, pick up the weapons, and fly on across the continent and the Bight of Benin to Malabo. Mercenaries and weapons would arrive together. But there would be no question, as with Mike Hoare and the Frothblowers in the Seychelles, of trying to smuggle the weapons in covertly. Unlike Mahé, Malabo airport was not in constant use, so that particular set of risks would not reoccur. It would be much more like Denard's airborne invasion of Cotonou - with the enormous difference that there would be assistance on the spot provided by Nick du Toit and his men.

Nick's men had a threefold role. The Boeing's arrival was planned for 2.30 a.m. on the night of Sunday March 7 when no other flights were expected and the little airport would be virtually deserted. Nick's first task was to drive out there an hour or two earlier, seize the control tower, change the radio frequency to 120 MHz - Boonzaier, 'Bones', one of Nick's men, would be in charge of the tower, and he would guide the incoming aircraft in and down. (Already that was an improvement on Bob Denard's scheme where the unknown aircraft had landed at dawn, and the whole operation had had to take place in daylight rather than in the early hours of the morning, under cover of darkness, when sentries and potential victims are, like Macbeth's Porter, and Duncan himself, least alert.)

Nick's second task, having secured the airport, set up a base, and got the Boeing safely landed, was to provide vehicles and guides for the incoming mercenaries. They would split into teams. One team, the base team, would secure the airport perimeter, and of course guard the Boeing, the essential means for getting away should everything go wrong. Two teams would be dropped off as "stopper groups", to set up road blocks designed to stave off any interference from army units encamped outside Malabo on the Luba Road. And two further teams, the most heavily-armed, would assault the Presidential Palace and the army camp down below.

Nick's third task, and a most vital one, was to make sure where President Obiang was sleeping that night. That was one of the major things that had gone wrong with Denard's attempt in Benin. President Kerekou had, most unusually, not been sleeping at the Presidential Palace that night; and as a result he went on the air when he should have been mortared to death at dawn; and thus virtually foiled the Cotonou coup by his voice alone.

In Malabo there was one man who always knew where Obiang was sleeping, the President's special adviser, Antonio Javier. And of course Nick knew Antonio Javier, his own business associate, very well. So Antonio Javier would be picked up from his home, and forced to lead the two teams to wherever, inside or outside the Presidential Palace - almost certainly inside - Obiang was sleeping that night. If Teodorin and General Armangol could be seized at the same time, so much the better. Clearly the amount of violence would depend a great deal on whether Antonio Javier could be persuaded to cooperate and to bluff his way in, plus escort. There was even some suggestion of a plan to wake the President up with the news that a special consignment of Toyotas had arrived unexpectedly at the airport as a gift to him from a fellow potentate, and he should get dressed and come out immediately to the airport to inspect them. That was clearly the best-case scenario; bluff and a sort of scurried, bustled arrest that would be carried out without any bloodshed at all. Hard to imagine that anyone really believed it would pass off so simply.

On the other hand, from the mercenaries' and from Simon Mann's point of view, obviously the less bloodshed there was the better. If President Obiang could be 'persuaded' out to the airport, then no sooner had Severo Moto been flown in - and the signal (like all communications) would be given to Crause Steyl, his pilot, by satellite phone - then, on the same plane, ex-President Obiang would be flown out in his turn to exile in Spain.

As for Nick du Toit, once he and his men had guided Mann's mercenaries to the various dropping-off points, their job was, by mutual agreement, over. They would simply drive to their respective homes in the various parts of Malabo and go to sleep like good citizens with easy consciences. They would not have handled a single weapon, still less fired a single shot. Whatever the outcome of the night's events, they would wake up in the morning apparently as ignorant and bemused as the normal citizens of Malabo.

Hopefully of course to hear a dawn broadcast by President Moto on the local radio and TV channels, announcing the good news that Obiang had fled the country (or been killed resisting arrest) and calling on his, Moto's, supporters and particularly the military to rally round to the new régime. It would have been a splendid Sunday. The new President might even have arranged for a *Te Deum* to be sung in the Cathedral.

★　　　　★　　　　★

What if, however, the citizenry had not rejoiced as planned and in particular the military had not rallied around? What if Malabo and the island had rallied to Severo, but Rio Muni and the hinterland had not? What if talk of mercenary coups had spread across the world's headlines and neighbouring Nigeria had growled menacingly?

This is where the tale of two Spanish frigates hovering in or near the Gulf of Guinea throughout late February and early March becomes plausible. There can be little doubt that Aznar's Spanish government would have preferred to see the pro-Spanish Severo in power rather than Obiang, so heavily influenced by, and prepared to be used by, the French. One can easily imagine an appeal by the new President to the Spanish government to help him in restoring order or preventing anarchy; and whether there were 500 Spanish marines aboard the frigates or 3000 *Guardia Civil* (as another, more unlikely rumour had it), the result of a swift appeal and a swift response would have been pretty much the same. 'Order,' the new order, would quickly have been established.

★   ★   ★

Where would Simon Mann and his mercenaries have been in all this? Very much keeping a low profile till the dust had settled, their money been paid - each black mercenary was to get £3,300 on successful completion of the operation - and their backers paid off. One may picture them skulking behind the closed gates of the Presidential Palace, doing everything to avoid journalists and cameras. But one may also picture them, or at any rate most of them, staying on. After all Nick du Toit might take over as Commander of the new Presidential Guard; but members of the Guard would, logically, best be men he knew, men on the spot, in other words former members of the Buffalo Battalion, men he had once commanded.

As for Simon Mann himself: - well, there is a fascinating document that could indicate his long-term plans. One has to be sceptical about it. It comes from "South African intelligence sources"; and its release was obviously designed to discredit Mann and the mercenaries. But that does not mean it is necessarily forged. Its language and tone is very British; and my guess - it is only a guess - is that it was written by young James Kershaw, Mann's personal assistant, possibly as his own independent project paper, but more likely because his boss had asked him to produce a plan for Equatorial Guinea's future.

In any case the actual plan, whoever produced it, is pretty grandiose. It envisages nothing less than the control of the whole state by the mercenaries - on the lines of Bob Denard's control of the Comores but on a far more ambitious scale. Rather more, indeed, on the lines of a Renaissance *condottiere* taking over an Italian city-state; or of Rajah Brooke - a comparison which might have appealed more to Simon Mann's romantic, imperial side - taking over Sarawak,

Not that there would be any direct takeover as such. The new President would remain in place, but strictly as a figurehead. Real power would be wielded by a yet-to-be-formed Bight of Benin Company.

The Company - interesting choice of initials - would have the sole right to make agreements or contracts with the new régime. The Company would control the recruitment and payment of government officials. The Company would take over State Oil and Economic Planning. The Company - for the new master would be a benevolent master - would create jobs and welfare programmes.

Perhaps over-ambitiously, the Company would insist on "sole right to have physical or other access" to the new President. For there was a danger that "once he has got the Presidency he will probably feel that he has got it mainly through his own efforts…. He may assume that whoever puts him in power can be a disposable syringe. He may…. regard us as a limitation on his doing and behaving as he wants (eg grabbing as much money as he can) and seek to be rid of us for his own reasons."

Quite so. This young Machiavelli suffers from no delusions as to the goodness of human nature once in power. As for 'E', the main backer, he "has been working on this for a long time; clearly he will have seen it [the coup, I imagine] as one where technicians execute the arrival plan and then he is in control. He may have an exaggerated view of his level of control over M."

So much for poor old 'E' and his illusions. As for 'us', so nicely sanitised as 'the technicians', "From our point of view he (Severo Moto) needs to achieve power by coup or putsch, not by public acclamation on return or by political dealing after it. We need to be fundamental to him in retaining it." And this we could best achieve, the writer adds, by a spot of delicate blackmail. "We must have the high moral ground. We must be in charge of the process of transparency, pursuing corruption." This process would "hopefully" provide "damaging information about M or at any rate some of his family or colleagues."

And in general it would be unwise to be too optimistic. "This is potentially a very lucrative game. We should expect bad behaviour; disloyalty; rampant individual greed; irrational behaviour ('kids in toyshop' type); back-stabbing…. and similar ungentlemanly activities."

★   ★   ★

What is one to make of this rather callow production? It was clearly written when the coup was in the air but long before it had taken place. One can picture Simon Mann picking it up, reading it with a wry grin, and tossing it aside. But it was imaginative. Certain ideas may well have clicked. The Bight of Benin Company - not a bad idea at all, both lucrative and benevolent. And, after all, the East India Company had had to start somewhere; and what was the Wonga List but a group of merchant adventurers in modern guise?

"I wouldn't think of myself as an Old Etonian success story," Simon Mann had once said. "I'm not a captain of industry or commanding officer of the Scots Guards." Not that that worried him, for "I don't get the feeling that anyone from Eton is keeping score". But perhaps now, in his early middle age, new vistas had opened: visions of greatness.

XVI

Equatorial Guinea III – Obiang Triumphans

In early March Simon Mann had been in Mali and the Cameroons. He flew to the eastern Congo and then, on Friday March 5, on to Harare. There he was joined by Nick du Toit's successors at Meteor Tactical Solutions, MTS, 'Hecky' Horn and Jacobus Carlse. Their job would be to check the arms and ammunition, make sure it was all present and correct, at Harare airport.

On the Canary Islands Crause Steyl was standing by with the King Air jet, ready to fly Severo Moto, his 'new' government, and his advisers in to Malabo as soon as the signal was given. It must have been a tense nail-biting wait for Severo, with the Presidency of his country at long last within his grasp - or almost.

In Malabo, on Saturday March 6, Nick du Toit briefed his three 'team leaders': Sergio Cardoso, his right-hand-man, who already knew everything, or almost everything; Marius Bonzaier, 'Bones', whose task it would be to talk the incoming plane safely down from the control tower at Malabo airport, and José Domingo, whose task it would be actually to seize the control tower. Nick himself, with Sergio, would be in charge of the ground vehicles, a minibus and two cars that would ferry the mercenaries to their respective dropping-off points - and, interestingly, would provide the incomers with little maps of Malabo photocopied from the local Pizza Parlour hand-out.

On Wonderboom airport, outside Pretoria, stood the Boeing 727, acquired only a week earlier, with its flight crew: Niel Crause and Hendrik Hammam, the co-pilots, Ken Pain the flight engineer.

On Sunday March 7, exactly as planned, the mercenaries assembled - sixty-four of them, mainly blacks but with a sprinkling of whites, by birth very mixed; 20 South Africans, 23 Angolans, 18 Namibians, 2 Congolese and 1 Zimbabwean; but all now with South African passports. All were unarmed, none were wearing uniform. They boarded the Boeing; and at about 4.30pm on that Sunday afternoon the Boeing took off. The operation to overthrow Obiang was at last under way.

Sunday Night: Harare and Malabo Airports

The Boeing's final destination, according to its flight plan, was Bujumbura, the capital of Burundi, to the east of the Congo. Its first port of call was Pietermaritzburg International Airport, to clear customs, a formality. Dusk was beginning to fall as it took off from Pietermaritzburg for the flight across the border into Zimbabwe.

At Harare airport Simon Mann was waiting in the early evening, with 'Hecky' Horn and Jacobus Carlse. They could breath a collective sigh of relief when at about 7.30 pm the Boeing touched down and taxied over to the civilian side for refuelling. Mann was in touch with the pilots, as he was with Malabo and indeed with the Canary Islands by satellite phone. First stage of the operation successfully accomplished. The team was on board, out of South Africa, ready for the long haul - the last stage. The plane was being refuelled. On board were two packets of money: $30,000 to pay for the landing fees, the refuelling and any additional unforeseen expenses; and $100,000, the second half of the payment for the arms. All that remained was to get the weapons and ammunition aboard, into the Boeing's hold, pay off Colonel Tshinga, then take off across the continent and the Bight of Benin. After which the only danger might be that the plan had been betrayed at the Malabo end; and that there would be a heavily-armed reception committee of Obiang's men waiting at Malabo airport instead of the friendly faces of Nick du Toit and his team. But that was always a risk in any armed raid, whether in time of peace or of war. It had been a risk on the Normandy beaches at D-Day. Eisenhower had decided to take it then. Mann *mutatis mutandis* would now.

Mann knew of course that there was also a risk at Harare. President Mugabe was a former terrorist leader, or freedom fighter, who had risked his life and his men's lives time and time again in the bitter struggle against the white settlers of Rhodesia. He particularly hated England, Englishmen, the former ruling classes, the former colonial power. He would crack down with great glee on any mercenary venture, particularly one led by a white upper-class Englishman, particularly one designed to overthrow a fellow black despot. Obiang of Equatorial Guinea might be small fry. But, if Obiang was successfully overthrown by a mercenary coup, might not Mugabe of Zimbabwe be next on the list?

On the other hand Zimbabwean troops had been heavily involved in the more recent bouts of civil wars in the Congo, and President Mugabe had interests, directly or indirectly, in the Kivu, Kasai and possibly Katanga mines. Executive Outcomes had protected these in the past, the Boeing was officially bound for that part of the world, that was where Colonel Tshinga had been informed it was heading for, the armament was not over-heavy in view of the Hutu and Banyamulenge threats in that part of the Congo - and in view of Zimbabwe's desperate economic plight, Zimbabwe Defence Industries needed all the hard currency it could earn. It would never be trusted again if it failed, even once, to supply the goods as agreed.

Niel Crause taxied the Boeing from the civil side of the airport over to the military side where the arms and ammunition were stored, under guard, ready for loading; and dowsed all the lights except the cockpit lights.

★   ★   ★

In Malabo at about 11 pm Nick du Toit and his men set out through the quiet dark streets of the little capital for the 3-mile drive to the almost-deserted airport. The Boeing was due to arrive two or three hours later; and it was vital to recce the airport and break into the control tower in plenty of time, with no last-minute rush.

Just as he was approaching the airport, Nick got a call on his satellite phone. It was crackly, difficult to pick up, barely audible, and Du Toit did not, at first, recognise Simon Mann's voice. But he finally got the message. It was brief, stark, without explanation. "It's necessary," said Mann, "to cancel the operation due to last-minute difficulties."

The call came through just as José Domingo and one of his team, George Allerson, were about to seize the control tower. Nick immediately phoned them, and the other vehicles in his little convoy. "I told them the operation had been cancelled and that they should take the vehicles back to our house. Afterwards, we all went to bed."

Perhaps Nick's people slept soundly that night, with the inevitable feelings of relief that a dangerous, if exciting, operation had been avoided; and that it had all been called off just in time before they had done anything irreversible or indeed finally committed themselves. For what in fact had they done? No damage at all to person or property. Looking at it objectively, they had simply driven out in convoy to Malabo airport late one Sunday night, then turned around, and come home again. They had carried no weapons or explosives. It was, in itself, a harmless, if pointless, little excursion.

★   ★   ★

Simon Mann deserves full marks for having made the call to Malabo. In the position in which he was in, it would have been only too easy to have concentrated on his own woes and to have omitted to warn off his associates, so many hundreds of miles, half a continent, away. Indeed by eleven o'clock that Sunday night it was extraordinarily lucky that he still had his satellite phone to hand at all.

Meanwhile in the Canary Isles Crause Steyl had received two text messages from his brother Niel. The first, ominous enough, read: "Simon is missing. I don't know what is happening." The next, four hours later, was shorter, abrupter and clearer: "Now they are arresting us."

★   ★   ★

What exactly the sequence of events was in those four hours at Harare airport, between 7.30pm when the Boeing landed and approximately 11.30 pm when Simon Mann with his phone call to Malabo finally halted the whole operation and Niel Crause with his phone message to his brother gave the bad news is still difficult to fathom.

Later on, with hindsight, there were to be all sorts of explanation. The coup had been rumbled, President Mugabe knew all about it, the South African police and/or intelligence service had warned their counterparts in Zimbabwe, ... British Intelligence, the CIA, the French... why, it had even been a put-up job by President Mbeki in the first place to give his good friend President Mugabe another propaganda weapon to use against the colonialist-imperialist British.

It is difficult to take any of this too seriously. If the coup was both known about in detail and, much more importantly, taken seriously on all sides, why were Nick du Toit and his men not immediately picked up at or en route to a heavily-guarded Malabo airport - as it undoubtedly would have been if President Obiang had had advance knowledge of the coup?

Personally my instinct is that there was a cock-up; that Colonel Tshinga and Zimbabwe Defence Industries intended to keep their part of the bargain and load up the arms and weapons, once paid for, as agreed. But that the Zimbabwean Customs and Immigrations officials at the airport had been kept in the dark. To them the Boeing looked suspicious - it still had US Coastguard markings on its side. They demanded to inspect the aircraft. Possibly they simply wanted to check the papers of the flight crew, which had been declared as being seven strong. But, finding only three in the cockpit, they had insisted on the rest of the plane being thrown open for inspection. And there they had found not an extra four men but, sitting silently in the dark, an extra, undeclared, sixty too many.

If this interpretation is correct, it is only too easy to picture hours of chaos at Harare airport as, in the night, different officials argued with each other, and Colonel Tshinga ordered armed soldiers to surround the Boeing, perhaps as much to keep Customs and Immigration out as to keep the sixty-plus merce-naries (about whose presence on board he may well have been totally ignorant - remember the arms and ammunitions were going into the plane's cargo hold, not its passenger compartment) in, and out of sight. As for *their* feelings, presum-ably once they were herded out of the plane and huddled together on the tarmac, surrounded by over-excited Zimbabwean soldiers, they must have realized that their excursion was off. Did they even know they were heading for Equatorial Guinea? Or did at any rate most of them still think they were bound for mine-guarding operations in the eastern Congo?

If I had been in Simon Mann's shoes at this particular juncture, I would have felt very inclined to back quietly away from the scene with Hecky and Jacobus and attempt to slip across the border by car or taxi before dawn. But Mann did not do so. Perhaps he was in no position to do so. He stayed with his men. And as the police took over from the military, impounded the plane, ferried the whole lot of them to jail, the story – in what must have been a very long night of interrogation indeed – began, inevitably, to come out.

Now Harare was not slow to communicate with Malabo. Nick du Toit and his men may have been sleeping the sleep of the just and the harmless but they were, next morning, rousted out of their homes by the police, their passports confiscated, and themselves arrested – eight South Africans in all. Later in the day, while they were peacefully sunning themselves on the beach, the six bewildered Armenians were picked up; and either with them or in between times, their German boss, the young Gerhard Eugen Merz.

BLACK BEACH, MALABO AND CHIKURUBI, HARARE

They were jailed in the notorious Black Beach prison, below the Presidential Palace but within sight of its balconies and terraces, where President Obiang could keep a beady eye on his 'favourite' prisoners. Soon enough, justly or unjustly, five Equatorial Guineans were added to the list, including Obiang's one-time genuine favourite, Antonio Javier, Nick's business associate and the man who reputedly knew precisely where the President was sleeping on any particular night.

At first Nick du Toit was optimistic. He appeared on local television that Thursday, flanked by armed soldiers, and confessed the plot, or at least a preliminary version of the plot: to kidnap Obiang and replace him by Severo Moto. He mentioned sixty mercenaries and, as backers, "some Americans" – was he still trying to protect Simon Mann? – and "a Lebanese". The Minister of Information, following him on TV, was more specific. He named Ely Calil, whom he called "the godfather of Severo Moto".

Ely Calil went to ground. In fact since the failure of the coup his whereabouts have remained obscure and understandably he has only issued statements through his lawyers. His son, George, was more open, more dismissive. "It's a great yarn. It sounds quite comical," he commented. "My father sounds more like a Bond villain every day."

Meanwhile, in prison in Malabo, Nick du Toit made a long signed statement. He thought he had a deal. He phoned – he was allowed to phone – his wife Belinda to say that he expected to be home the following weekend. Later, when he miserably realised that there was no deal, and that he and his men were to go on trial and would be tried with a whole panoply of charges – overthrowing the legitimate government of the Republic of Equatorial Guinea being almost the least of them – and that he Nick du Toit would personally be facing the death penalty, he retracted his confession. He was to say that he had been tortured, that it had been beaten out of him with sjamboks.

There may or may not be truth in this. What is certainly true is that the arrested German Gerhard Eugen Merz died nine days after his arrest. Of 'cerebral malaria', the prison authorities announced. Possibly - Black Beach prison was notoriously unhealthy, filthy, mosquito-infested. On the other hand the prison authorities may have tried but failed to beat a confession out of Merz; and possibly tried too hard.

In Zimbabwe meanwhile there were no television appearances of the mercenaries, no photos even. They were under lock and key in Chikurubi maximum security prison, on the outskirts of Harare. But Zimbabwean State Television *did* show the impounded Boeing and what had been found, passengers apart, aboard it: and a pretty unincriminating collection of objects these were. Walkie-talkies, satellite phones, bolt-cutters, axes, sledgehammers and what appeared to be a canister of riot control spray (ideal for immobilising a reluctant-to-be-kidnapped President?) - hardly the wherewithal for proving vicious intent and, arguably, all perfectly legitimate cargo in any case.

Simon Mann's name had leaked out by now, and the British press fastened eagerly on the Old Etonian with Scots Guards and brewing connections, printing photos of him in his boyhood at Eton and in his paratroop colonel acting role in the "Bloody Sunday" drama-documentary. But his name and Ely Calil's and of course Severo Moto's were the only names to have been named in connection with the coup at this point. Then either shortly before or shortly after his first court appearance Simon Mann wrote the famous letter from gaol, his *cri-de-coeur*, his appeal for help, that, so unfortunately for many, was to fall into the wrong hands, and from there into the public domain.

The letter was apparently smuggled out of Chikurubi Prison. Here is the text of all or at least most of it.

"It may be getting us out comes down to a large splodge of wonga! Of course investors did not think this would happen. Did I?

Do they think they can be part of something like this with only upside potential, no hardship or risk of it going wrong?

Please! It is essential that we get properly organized. Please trust and work with Alwyn and Jonathan and the others. They are getting frustrated that they cannot deal with Amanda or with James. Apparently they have been told they must deal with Rebecca and Nigel. This is fine in principle; but then they are told that Nigel and Rebecca are meeting on Tuesday etc etc.

Our situation is not good and it is very URGENT. They get no reply from Smelly and Scratcher; asked them to ring back after the Grand Prix race was over! This is not going well.

I must say once again: what will get us out is MAJOR CLOUT we need heavy influences of the sort that Rebecca, Smelly, Scratcher, Nigel, David Hart and it needs to be used, heavily and now.

Once we get into a real trial scenario we are f.....d. The opportunity lies in our own deportation from Z to SA. The window-dressing for this is that in SA we will face the Foreign Military Assistance Act. That will be fine. This will suit Z because they look good in SA. BUT it will only go with major influence being applied to BOTH simultaneously.

Cannot Amanda and/or Rebecca and (illegible name here) talk to (then with Alwyn in reserve). That way we can (illegible). We need to do so ASAP or else it will be too late.

Love to all

Simon Mann"

The letter is handwritten, on lined paper, in spidery handwriting in black ink. Whom exactly it is addressed to is not clear. It sounds like a Round Robin, to be passed around all Simon Mann's friends and family, and it sounds too as if it is not the first letter he had written from prison; and that he was being kept pretty well-informed (the Grand Prix touch, the Tuesday meeting difficulty) of what was going on, or not going on, in the outside world.

Amanda is clearly Simon Mann's wife. James is James Kershaw, his young assistant in South Africa. Alwyn is Alwyn Griebenow, a South African lawyer who was to act for 'Hecky' Horn and Jacobus Carlse, also of course jailed and facing charges alongside Simon Mann. Jonathan is Jonathan Samulenge, his upbeat, always optimistic, Zimbabwe lawyer. Rebecca is the almost obligatory mystery woman. David Hart is a fairly well-known Old Etonian, a middle-aged millionaire who in the 1980s was one of Margaret Thatcher's advisers and enforcers, in close contact too with Bill Casey, the then CIA boss , and is still linked nowadays with a number of defence contractors - unarguably a man of 'major clout'.

And of course - most famous of all since the letter, totally, unforgettably, notoriously so - Smelly and Scratcher are Ely Calil and Mark Thatcher; though both have, it must be said, denied it.

What Simon Mann dreaded - though he does not mention it in this letter, perhaps there was no need to as all were aware of it - was that he might be extradited to face trial in Equatorial Guinea. And there face the death penalty. For President Obiang and his Ministers were having a field day, legally. They had already announced that they would apply for Simon Mann's handover to themselves. They had already hired via their Paris Embassy (Equatorial Guinea has no Embassy in London) a British law firm named Penningtons to issue civil writs in the High Court against Ely Calil and others, and they were clearly determined to make a meal out of the failed coup attempt. Nobody had heard, so to speak, of Equatorial Guinea before; now the whole wide world would know of, and praise, this plucky little country. This plan would not in the end prove enormously successful.

For Simon Mann was not extradited to Equatorial Guinea; nor (at least at the time of writing) does he seem likely to be. As for his idea that it would be better to be deported from Z to SA, from Zimbabwe back to South Africa, there to face charges under the Foreign Military Assistance Act, that might well have seemed like an easy option *at the time*. For, since its coming into force in May 1998, there had only been, in those five years, a mere two prosecutions for mercenary activities under the Act. Both involved mercenaries who were employed by the President of the Ivory Coast, Laurent Gbagbo in the continuing civil war there that had really begun in 1999; and both were fined comparatively minor sums: 30,000 rand for Richard Rouget who had dual French/South African citizenship and thus more of an excuse, five times as much for Karl Albert the mercenary who had South African citizenship alone; and who had previously and notoriously worked for Executive Outcomes.

But that was not Simon Mann's immediate problem. On Tuesday March 23 after sixteen days of detention he and his fellow prisoners were all charged with conspiring to possess dangerous weapons, with acquiring firearms without a licence, with violating aviation control and immigration regulations. The court was convened in Chikurubi Prison itself, the very first time such a thing had happened. For on hearing that the prison authorities had only one lorry to take the men to the proper courtroom and that the military vehicles detailed to provide an escort kept breaking down, the Harare High Court had so ruled. Nevertheless the prisoners, like animals from Noah's Ark, two by two, were forced to jog across from one part of the prison to the other. And for the first time the world saw pictures of Simon Mann as he now was: a slight fit figure in khaki shirt and long shorts with a small grizzled beard, granny glasses and a mild slightly bemused air, shackled left wrist and left ankle to an older, dourer, sourer-looking white man, one of the ten white mercenaries charged.

They were all remanded in custody, not asked to plead.

THE TRIALS BEGIN

It seems that it was *after* rather than before this first appearance in court, probably on March 31, one week after, that Simon Mann smuggled out of jail his famous letter. How did he smuggle it out? Was it immediately intercepted? Or did it reach Amanda, Rebecca and all the rest only for the original to fall, much later, into official hands? One must suspect the latter. For it was among "documents seen by *The Observer*" in mid-July; which included also a signed confession (not of very much) by Mann. My guess is that young James Kershaw will have a lot of explaining of "ungentlemanly activities" to face if he ever meets a released Simon Mann again; and that South African intelligence continued, once they had Kershaw under control, to release to the press, at pretty carefully calculated intervals, documents that would badly damage the imprisoned mercenary's case.

Indeed these documents were "major clout", but from Simon Mann's point of view on the wrong side. On the 'right' side there was none; or what there was was ineffective. Instead of coordination of a defence there was, almost inevitably, dissipation of effort and mutual recrimination, even if only via the statements of 'friends'. Hilariously, for instance, one 'friend' of Ely Calil's announced that: "Ely does not consider himself a good friend of Simon Mann. Mann never called him Smelly to his face."

So Mann remained in his own fetid little cell in Chikurubi, 13 feet by 4½ feet, with, like his fellow prisoners, a bucket, often unemptied for days, for a latrine, a concrete floor and little to sleep on; while Du Toit, also in solitary confinement, faced even worse conditions in Black Beach jail, a big man, now gaunt, growing a God-the-Father-style long beard, fed on the occasional cup of rice or bread roll, in a slimy, dank, rat-infested cell. At least neither he nor his fellow prisoners were sent to Evinayong prison on the mainland, where local political prisoners so often ended up, forgotten.

They were far from forgotten. Lawyers now entered the scene in droves; and their fees for consultations, hearings, court appearances and the rest must have amounted, if bundled together, to an astronomic sum. For mass trials in Zimbabwe and Equatorial Guinea itself, charges in South Africa, actions in the Queen's Bench Division of the High Court in London, even legal hearings in Guernsey in the Channel Isles - all were coming up. In half a dozen countries and jurisdictions state counsel, defence counsel, barristers, solicitors, attorney-generals, prosecuting authorities, judges, magistrates, court officials, and policemen rubbed their collective hands together in anticipatory glee as they prepared, they too, for their fifteen minutes of notoriety and second-hand fame. President Obiang, in his almost insane desire for revenge, was creating a legal tidal wave of unforeseen, unpredictable proportions.

"Those behind the plot are nothing but bloodthirsty pirates and thieves," he declared. "They planned to kill me or abduct me and my government ministers and to bring in an enemy of the country. I intend to pursue all those who invested in the project through the courts in Britain and elsewhere, and by every means possible. This is where they should be brought to face consequences. Tell your British Government I want to see them in my country in my prisons." A little chilling. They would, Obiang added, be sentenced by his judges. But "if I were the judge, I would apply the maximum penalty - execution by firing squad."

Meanwhile in Paris, Henry Page, the Penningtons solicitor acting for the Equatorial Guinean Government, dotted the 'i's' and crossed the 't's'. "We intend to rigorously pursue all those who were behind the conspiracy to oust Obiang," he announced. "We are not looking for just the puppets but those who controlled the strings."

This was not good news for Smelly nor for Scratcher nor indeed for Greg Wales, whose name had by now been added to Obiang's black list. Ely Calil's lawyers, Bindman and Partners, issued a curt statement: "My client totally denies the allegations against him and will fully defend any legal process." Sir Mark Thatcher, wisely for the moment, lay low. Greg Wales, a blunter man, counterattacked. "What is going on here is an attempt by President Obiang to cling on to power," he declared.

On 21 July the first mass trial began, in the shed converted to a courtroom at Chikurubi Prison. 30 wives had come up from Pomfret hoping to see their men freed after over four months in jail. They were disappointed. The trial was adjourned for a week. On the 28 July Simon Mann pleaded guilty to attempting to procure weapons, anxious as Jonathan Samulenge, his lawyer, put it "not to waste the court's time", and the rest pleaded guilty to immigration and aviation offences but not to anything else. Except for 'Hecky' Horn and Jacobus Carlse who, like Simon Mann, had entered Zimbabwe perfectly legally and who pleaded innocent on all charges, guilty of none. Jonathan was optimistic. "The difference between buying and attempting to buy arms is like oil and water. I expect Mr Mann will get a small fine. If he does get a jail sentence it will be very short." The magistrate, Mishrod Guvamumbe, who was sitting alone, without a jury, prolonged the suspense by adjourning the trial for another month to consider his verdicts.

Two days before those verdicts were due, the scene shifted dramatically - south to Cape Town.

An Arrest in Cape Town

He must have been half expecting it. All South Africa was half expecting it. But it still came as a great shock to Sir Mark Thatcher when he was actually arrested, at 10 Dawn Avenue, his home in Constantia, at 7.20 am on the morning of Wednesday August 25. The Scorpions, a special 'elite' South African police unit, milked the arrest for all it was worth. "The Scorpions are a macho chest-thumping lot who like to see themselves in the G-Men mode" commented one 'friend' of Sir Mark. "They'll be loving this."

They arrested the former Prime Minister of Great Britain's son in his pyjamas. In his variegated life he had never been arrested before. He was charged of course with providing finance to a mercenary activity, an offence under Clause 2 of the Foreign Military Assistance Act. The Scorpions searched his house, went through all his papers, confiscated his computers. "Thatcher definitely knew the money was for a coup," declared their spokesman Sipho Nguema. "It is not a vague connection. He was a direct investor in a short-term project."

But despite Sipho's bluff - for that is all it turned out to be - the Scorpions found very little. There was no real paper trail connecting Mark Thatcher to the coup at all. All the same the charges had been filed, and an immense figure was set for bail, 2 million rand. The pretext for this was that Sir Mark had put, or was about to put, his house on the market; and so, by inference, was planning to flee the country. But seeing that his passport was confiscated, that he was ordered to report daily to nearby Wynberg Magistrates Court, and forbidden to travel outside Cape Province without written permission, it might have been thought that bail conditions were harsh enough for a man innocent till proved guilty, without demanding a vast sum in cash as well.

He himself made a dignified statement. "I am innocent of all charges against me. I have no involvement in an alleged coup in Equatorial Guinea and I reject all suggestions to the contrary." His South African lawyer was more outspoken. "A showboating exercise," he described it as, "designed to make a political point."

Nonetheless Equatorial Guinea wanted to extradite him. It looked like a steeplechase ahead, full of legal hurdles. The world's press were enjoying every minute of it, the future was bleak; and it is not surprising that his wife Diane decided that week-end to fly back to America and take the two Thatcher children, Michael aged 15 and Amanda aged 11 - old enough therefore to understand what was going on - with her. And the house was definitely put on the market. Mark Thatcher might be due for a long stay in Africa involuntarily; and if he were, he would need no home - a roof would be provided free over his head.

★   ★   ★

Meanwhile in Harare, two days after Sir Mark's arrest, the court reconvened and Mishrod the magistrate announced his verdict. The bulk of the mercenaries were found not guilty of the main charge of attempting to purchase firearms and intending to overthrow a legitimate government.

"The manner in which they were recruited arouses suspicion," Mishrod said. "However, the suspicion alone is not enough. The State failed to discharge its onus by proving the accused persons guilty beyond reasonable doubt."

As for Simon Mann, "The action by the accused amounts at most to attempting to purchase firearms" - which must have been a relief. "The accused," he announced (rather unnecessarily in view of Simon Mann's previous plea of guilty on this charge) "is found guilty."

The bulk of the mercenaries were not, however, released. They were guilty too - of the lesser immigration and aviation offences. Prolonging the suspense once more, Mishrod adjourned the court for two weeks to give him time to ponder the sentences.

Jonathan Samulenge was still upbeat. On the eve Simon Mann had been "in a very positive state of mind". "Very surprised" to hear of Mark Thatcher's arrest, and "naturally concerned as any friend would be." Post-verdict:- "We expect he will be given a short prison sentence or even a small fine when sentencing is handed down on September 10."

Poor Jonathan. Mishrod was to have a nasty little shock in store for him.

MEANWHILE IN MALABO

Meanwhile in Malabo the mass trial – much less of a mass there, only nineteen in the dock as opposed to nearly seventy in Harare – had been proceeding by fits and starts. The trouble was that Western journalists were not as amenable as President Obiang and his jovial Minister of Information, Don Alfonso, were used to journalists being. They came, they hung around – and only too often they left after a few days, not to write the required articles about the evil-doing of Nick du Toit and his wicked band but, instead, to publish distinctly unfavourable articles about conditions in Equatorial Guinea, poverty, corruption, torture – from the Government's point of view, all sorts of uncalled-for and unnecessary topics. Worse still, the worldwide publicity appeared to have sparked a Senatorial investigation in Washington into the misappropriation by Obiang and his clan of no less than $35,000,000 paid into their accounts in Riggs Bank, also in Washington.

Then, on the Monday following the guilty findings in Harare, things took a turn for the worse actually during the trial. It was being held in one of the handful of modern buildings in Malabo, the Banapa International Conference Centre on the little capital's outskirts, not a converted shed as in Harare, but a beautiful vast airy porticoed centre, with tended gardens, air-conditioning and comfortable seats in the auditorium. It was conducted, of course, in Spanish; and there was no simultaneous translation via headphones. So most of the accused and most of the many journalists and embassy and Amnesty observers and the like had very little notion of what was going on.

But they certainly understood, and reacted, and reported what was going on when Sergio Cardoso boldly and – one would guess, thinking of the likely repercussions back in Black Beach – almost insanely spoke out.

"This is the first time I have seen a person questioned," he said, "and taken to the torture room at the same time. I want to emphasise the person who tortured me is here in court. He was there when I was being questioned. If I am lying, let me show the Court who it was. I have the scars and I can show them."

The snag with the language barrier was that it could work both ways. Just as the accused did not speak Spanish, so the judges and the prosecution did not speak English. In other words Cardoso got all this out, in open court, and put on record by the international press before the authorities really understood what was going on. No wonder the trial was halted and, next day, adjourned for a month in order (one imagines) that the accused should have the time thoroughly to learn the lesson as to what sort of defence they might, and what sort of defence they might not, be wise to offer in open court.

★   ★   ★

On the very same day back in South Africa 'Hecky' Horn and Jacobus Carlse, freed just before the weekend in Harare and cleared of all charges, were in court again. Alwyn Griebenow had flown them out of Zimbabwe; but he had had to warn them that as soon as they landed in South Africa, they would be re-arrested: this time on charges of contravening the Foreign Military Assistance Act. And there was a third, much more important figure charged with them - Crause Steyl of Triple A of Bethlehem, Air Ambulance Africa, a share in whose helicopter venture Mark Thatcher had financed.

They all pleaded guilty to contravening the Act. They were given hefty suspended prison sentences, and equally hefty immediate ones if they did not pay up the fines. They paid up, immediately. The fines were not peanuts; but they were certainly preferable to years in jail: 75,000 rand for 33-year-old 'Hecky' Horn, 75,000 rand for his senior 40-year-old Jacobus Carlse, and a fairly whopping 200,000 rand for the middle Steyl brother, Crause.

But it was all a set-up, a plea bargain. The Youth League of the ANC went somewhat over the top, denouncing the bargain as "an abomination and a miscarriage of justice." Alwyn Griebenow, their lawyer, was quite open about it: "We did indeed make a plea bargain with the State," he said. "They do want us to testify and we said we would be willing to do that. We do not have a problem with that."

Testify against whom? Sir Mark Thatcher, of course. The 'get Thatcher' movement was raising up a head of steam in South Africa. Crause Steyl was the vital witness, indeed the only real witness now that the hoped-for paper-trail/computer-trail had proved a dead end; and if, as one story goes, Crause only agreed to testify against Sir Mark to help save his younger brother Niel from a stiff sentence up in Harare rather than to save his own skin in South Africa, why, that is an admirable example of fraternal feelings. Even though, either way, it does lead to some doubts as to whether Crause's eventual tale might not be doctored to suit the case for the prosecution.

The next day Mrs Thatcher - Lady Thatcher as she now was, a shaken widow since the death of her husband Sir Denis the previous year - had taken a hand. She no longer had major political clout but she did have money. And on September 1, the day after his wife and children had flown out, leaving Mark Thatcher to face the music alone under what was in effect house arrest, it was his mother who, apparently, came up with his bail money. Of her twin children Mark rather than Carol had always been the favourite. And, apparently too, rumours of his vast fortune had been wildly exaggerated - which is very believable indeed.

Mark had been much less favoured by his father Denis, himself a very successful business man, who deprecatingly would refer to him as "the boy". And he was no favourite at all of the press. He did give one interview while on bail to the American magazine *Vanity Fair*. "Thank God my father isn't alive to see this," he said wholeheartedly; and he added that, after this, he would find it hard to find another career, being "like a corpse floating down the Colorado River."

That remark, widely quoted, merely reinforced Sir Mark's distrust of journalists. "Like a cork floating down the Colorado River," was what he had actually said. An easy mistake to make from the recording journalist's point of view. But of course there is all the difference in the world between a corpse that can only sink and disintegrate, and a cork that will continue, whatever the tsunamis, to bob up again and again.

SEPTEMBER 10 – SENTENCES IN HARARE

On Friday, September 10 the accused in Chikurubi Prison appeared for sentencing. It was a bitter day for them. As in the Seychelles, in the High Court at Victoria, the trial appears to have been conducted fairly and with courtesy, without ranting and with attention to legal argument. But as in Angola, in the People's Court at Luanda, the sentences on the mercenaries seemed to bear little or no relation to the actual nature of the offences; indeed to be entirely political. The judiciary may still preserve the forms of independence from the executive in Zimbabwe. That is amazing enough, encouraging too. Mishrod Guvamumbe had rejected various of the prosecution's claims, shown himself to be a fair-minded even-handed magistrate. But when it came to sentencing, I doubt very much whether the choice was his.

Most of the mercenaries had expected to be released. What had they been found guilty of? Immigration offences. But they had no desire, any of them, to set foot on Zimbabwe soil; nor had they even done so until they had been bundled at gunpoint, unwillingly, out onto the tarmac. The prosecution had asked for 12-18 months' imprisonment for what had been, at most, administrative offences. They had already been on remand in Chikurubi for over 5 months. They were sentenced to 12 months, almost all of them; the 2 pilots to 18 months.

As for their leader, "The accused was the author of the whole transaction" the magistrate declaimed. Fair enough. "He was caught trying to take firearms out of the country." Fair enough. The offences were "well-planned and well-executed, and that must be reflected in the sentence."

Here one fails to follow Mishrod's logic. Was he saying that if things had been badly planned and ineptly carried out, the offence would have been less? Or was he simply trying to spare Simon Mann's feelings by adding a kind of judicial pat on the back - double-edged though the phrasing may have been?

At any rate Simon Mann was not let off with a fine, or a short spell in prison. He was sent down for seven years. As he left the courtroom, understandably grim-faced, he gave a defiant two-fingered salute to observers - a gesture that appealed.

Jonathan Samulenge, optimism all gone, said he thought the sentence "excessive. And it induces a sense of shock." However, his client, he added, would not appeal.

The Boeing 707, and the two packets of dollars aboard it (and presumably the can of anti-riot spray too) were declared forfeited to the State of Zimbabwe.

NOVEMBER 26 – SENTENCES IN MALABO

The only surprising thing in Malabo was that the authorities shied away from adding Gerhard Eugen Metz, post-mortem, to the list of the accused. Otherwise everyone who was anyone in the whole affair, present or absent, seemed to be technically on trial. The *Fiscal*, the Public Prosecutor, asked for the death penalty for Don Nicholas du Toit, present, and Don Severo Moto, absent. Also added to the list were Mark Thatcher, David Hart, Nigel Morgan, Gianfranco Cicogna, a whole batch of Equatorial Guinean exiles, rather oddly Tony Buckingham (if I heard his name correctly) and a string of others whose names I failed to catch.

It was almost 2 o'clock on Friday 26 November when eight cars and two trucks, amid a blazing of sirens, drew to a halt in front of the Banapa Conference Centre. About thirty armed soldiers jumped out, and the nineteen prisoners, shackled and handcuffed, shuffled into the *Sala de Paz*, the Hall of Peace, to hear their fates. Nick du Toit managed a wan smile for his wife Belinda who had been in Malabo for a few days waiting for this fateful day, with Georgia, 'Bones' wife, staying quietly out of sight in one of Malabo's cheaper little hotels.

In the capital itself there was no atmosphere of crisis or tension or even excitement. The thing had been dragging on too long for the ordinary citizen to remain even remotely interested. Besides, what had actually happened in Malabo? Nothing. True, President Mugabe had paid a State Visit earlier in the month of November and had been hailed as the Saviour of Equatorial Guinea. But what most people remembered about the solemn cavalcade through the streets of Malabo was that President Obiang's car had been booed by a group of school children; and, according to some reports, had even had stones thrown at it.

The President had returned to Malabo from a visit abroad two days before the sentences were due to be pronounced. But he did not grace the *Sala de Paz* with his presence, at least not in person. A portrait of him overlooked the scene – quite a discreet portrait, to be fair. At 2.15 beneath the portrait the judges took their seats – the *Presidente del Tribunal* and his two assessors – all three in dark suits. Heavily-armed soldiers filled the back row of the hall. It was about a fifth full with perhaps a hundred people there in all. The soldiers' rubber boots squeaked. The prisoners' chains, as they rose, tinkled. Tension visibly mounted.

There was no delay. In rapid Spanish the President of the Tribunal proceeded to read out the sentences. For Don Severo Moto not the death sentence but 25 years of strict prison on one charge, another 25 years of strict prison on the second charge, 13 years of ordinary prison on the third charge; and a fine of 2000 millions of CFA francs. For four of his associates, also fortunately for themselves, like Moto, not present, 20 years and a day, 20 years and a day, 12 years and a day, 12 years and a day – plus a fine of 1000 million each "to indemnify the State".

Don Nicholas du Toit, if he was following all this, must have been breathing a sigh of relief. It was not a day for death penalties. He was given 21 years strict prison, plus 13 years ordinary prison plus a fine of 1300 million.

Then his four 'team leaders' were sentenced: Sergio Cardoso, 'Bones', George Allerson and José Domingo. 12 years and a day strict prison, 5 years ordinary prison, and a 200 million fine each.

Now came a really astounding set of sentences. The Armenians might have expected to be acquitted – especially in view of the fact that an official delegation from the Republic of Armenia had come to Malabo to plead their cause, and was in court. Instead, Ashot Karapetyan, their chief, was sentenced to 12 years and a day plus 12 years and a day plus 50 millions. The other five got off with 7 years plus 7 years plus 25 millions. Their lawyer, afterwards, was explosively, understandably indignant. "Where was the proof?" he kept asking, "Where was the evidence?"

The Equatorial Guineans in court escaped lightly, with what seems almost like a rap across the knuckles by comparison to their fellow accused: 1 year 4 months and 1 day each, plus 25 millions – and, surprisingly, no longer a sentence nor heavier a fine for Antonio Javier than for the others.

Both planes belonging to Triple A Options and to Panac, the late Gerhard Eugen Metz's company, were confiscated: the Antonov and the Ilyushin.

But really by far the most extraordinary thing, by far – to be cynical – the cleverest thing that the Equatorial Guinean authorities arranged (apart from not imposing the death penalty) was the total acquittal of three of the eight South Africans. Mark Schmidt, who had been a lodger with the Bonzaiers, left the *Sala de Paz* a free man, and so did Joao Ribeiro and Abel Agusto, plus, interestingly, one, and only one, of the local men accused, Anecleto Oyono Nchama.

The whole thing was over by 2.35 pm. As for Mark Thatcher and the others also accused but absent, no sentences were pronounced. They were *identificados*, identified, the President declared, in a somewhat sinister, almost Orwellian touch. Their names would remain on the books, awaiting their future arrival.

The Nigerian Consul, a splendid figure in a startling white suit, arrived at Banapa Conference Centre just as the trial was over.

JANUARY 12, 2005 – SENTENCE IN CAPE TOWN

Margaret Thatcher spent Christmas and the New Year with her lonely son in Cape Town. He still had to report to the local police station every day, he still could not travel outside Cape Province, he still had his passport confiscated.

He was still faced, too, with the horrendous prospect of being extradited to Malabo. But that had somewhat receded since, after great protesting by his own lawyers, Equatorial Guinea had won the right to question him publicly in court in South Africa.

Mark Thatcher finally appeared in the High Court in Cape Town on Wednesday, January 12. The hearing lasted less than ten minutes. "Do you understand the charge sheet against you?" asked Mr Justice Molala. "Yes." "Do you admit all the allegations on the charge sheet?" "Yes." In a statement agreed between the prosecution and the defence he admitted chartering an Aloutte III helicopter, he admitted five separate meetings with Simon Mann, he admitted that before making the payments "the accused began to doubt Mann's true intentions and suspected that Mann might be planning to become involved in mercenary activity in the West Africa region. Despite his misgivings," the document continued, "the accused decided to invest money in the charter of the helicopter. In fact Mann did intend to use the helicopter in mercenary activity." "He nevertheless fulfilled his agreement," the 'confession' concluded,... "he should have exercised more caution."

It was, in fact, another plea bargain. Mr Justice Molala imposed a fine of 3,000,000 rand – which, readers will note, is no less than fifteen times as much as the maximum fine ever previously imposed for any breach of the Foreign Military Assistance Act; and specified that it must be paid within seven days on pain of five years' imprisonment.

It was paid, presumably by Sir Mark's lawyers, on the spot. And that very night, his passport restored, the man who had now admitted his guilt in court was out on a British Airways flight back to London.

Through gritted teeth Sipho Nguema, the Scorpions' spokesman, declared: "Mr Mark Thatcher has agreed to cooperate fully with the investigation, so we are happy."

★   ★   ★

The quite extraordinary thing is that Mark Thatcher, though free and out of the country and really with no inducement ever to set foot in South Africa again, came back voluntarily and of his own free will five weeks later. It must have been part of the plea bargain that he would return. But how on earth, had he failed to do so, would the South African authorities have enforced his appearance back at Wynberg Magistrates Court, outside Cape Town? And, from his own point of view, was there not a great risk that, whatever the agreement officially made , he might, once back in South Africa, again be re-arrested and possibly deported to Equatorial Guinea?

At any rate back he came, and on February 18 faced his longest bout of public questioning yet. These were weird proceedings. The *Fiscal* had submitted 43 written questions; but José Olo Obongo had not come over to ask them himself in person. Instead, a South African woman magistrate, Helen Alman, put them to Sir Mark on Obongo's behalf, misspellings and odd grammar all religiously included.

Asked about Simon Francis Maan, "On the assumption that we're talking about Simon Mann, spelt M-a-nn, our last meeting was in February 2004 at a restaurant in Johannesburg." Yes, he had discussed Equatorial Guinea with Mann twice, "in the context of the West African region." His reaction to the news of Mann's arrest? "Curiosity as to the reason for his detention."

As for "Lord Jeffrey Archers," "I know no Jeffrey Archers with an 's'. I do know Lord Jeffrey Archer whom I have known since the mid-1980s. I have not met him in the last three or four years."

As for "Scratcher", no, said Sir Mark, that was not his nickname. (To which, in the famous phrase of Mandy Rice-Davies, one might retort: "Well, he would say that, wouldn't he?")

Some of the questions were astute, others irrelevant, others completely incomprehensible. For Mark Thatcher it was a nerve-wracking experience. But for Obongo and Obiang and Equatorial Guinea in general it was a near disaster: they emerged as something of a legal laughing-stock, internationally.

Sir Mark, no doubt much relieved, flew back to London unimpeded. He had kept his part of the plea bargain. But his real punishment still awaited him. It was not totally unexpected. But it was totally unjust. There is an American law that restricts the issue of visas to foreigners with criminal records. It is part of the panoply of U.S. anti-communist and now anti-terrorist laws. It can be applied with discretion.

Mark Thatcher had just acquired a criminal record, at least theoretically, at least in strict law, though it was only in South Africa. Nevertheless the US authorities, heavy-handed or vindictive or eager to curry favour with President Obiang, or all three, in early April refused to renew his expired US visa. So Sir Mark was in effect forbidden to join his wife and children in the United States. It seems almost incredible when one considers the whole circumstances of how he was, in effect, blackmailed by the South African authorities to make a 'confession' if he ever wanted to get his passport back again. And yet having 'confessed' and having at long last obtained his passport back, he was out of Africa in one piece only to find that this 'confession', this plea of guilty extracted from him by force of circumstances, was used by the American authorities to prevent him from making use of his passport for the main reason for which he had (in my view) 'confessed' to a crime that all the indications are he had never committed; that is to say in order to obtain freedom of movement for himself and to join his wife and children in a free country.

He issued a dignified statement, saying that he intended to make his family home, in the circumstances, in Europe. Various press reports hinted that the marriage was coming apart. But the Thatchers spent a week together in France in early 2005. "Diane is loyal," said a 'family friend', "and her strong religious conviction makes her determined to keep the family together." Their children, however, are continuing to be educated in the junior Lady Thatcher's - and God's - own country.

RIPPLES

The single most dramatic event that followed, in the spring of 2005, is that Severo Moto suddenly went missing from his home in Madrid. Kidnapped by mercenaries acting for Obiang? About to launch another more successful coup? Assassinated? Unfortunately for the Spanish press, which went to town on the story, none of these. He turned up three weeks later in, of all places, Zagreb, capital of Croatia. He claimed, extravagantly, that the new, left-wing Spanish government had had plans to kill him. "As an opposition leader and the most popular politician in my country, I became an obstacle to Spain's (oil) deal with Obiang and so they want to remove me." Later things were patched up, and Severo Moto is, it seems, back in Madrid, with his status as a political refugee confirmed. President Obiang probably much regrets that the Spanish government failed in their alleged intentions.

Meanwhile President Obiang's other legal actions seem to have become bogged down in procedural difficulties. A delegation of Ministers, including the *Fiscal*, came to London to persuade - order? - Her Majesty's Government to mount a prosecution against a List of Eight. They were seen by Chris Mullin, a junior Minister of State at the Foreign Office, informed that HMG "can't tell the police who and what to investigate," complained that they had been "treated with contempt". They retaliated, on their return to Malabo, by accusing the Foreign Secretary, Jack Straw, of having known all about the coup well in advance and induced Johann Schmidt to come up with his story of e-mails to important British officials in December 2003 and January 2004 - to diplomats at the High Commission in South Africa, the authorities in Equatorial Guinea announced. (What they failed to make totally clear was that the National Security Officer in Malabo had detained Johann shortly before he was released and made his statement.) He later amended it to say his reports had been sent to Secret Intelligence Service Officers whom he knew - at their home addresses. The point here perhaps being that no journalist would expect him to name the names of these men; whereas they could have checked whether his story was admitted or denied if British diplomats in Pretoria had been the alleged recipients.

At any rate there was a tremendous hoo-ha in the British Press - this was at the end of November 2004 - led, inevitably, by *The Observer*, with front-page headlines and, interspersed with the news story, comments about the Foreign Secretary's "clear obligations under international law". "Charges that Britain knew in advance of the plot and failed to warn Obiang's government could not be graver," trumpeted a Special Report. For Her Majesty's Government Baroness Symons, a rather more senior Minister of State at the Foreign Office than Chris Mullin, retorted robustly, and perfectly accurately, that while most governments, HMG's included, deprecated coups, "governments are under no legal obligation to pass on information they may receive about such possible action". Perfectly accurately at least as regards the second half of these remarks. The Baroness' statement came, admittedly, after President Obiang had really gone too far. He was now threatening to instigate a lawsuit against Her Majesty's Secretary of State for Foreign Affairs in the International Court of Justice at The Hague. But, like all the other legal actions instigated by Obiang outside Africa, this one too seems to have become bogged down; not to have progressed. Penningtons, the firm of British solicitors who were with such wholehearted enthusiasm acting on behalf of the despot's government, were making themselves extremely unpopular on their home territory and elsewhere. Henry Page, their man in Paris, was publicly rebuked in a Guernsey Court - where he was trying to obtain the right for Obiang to have access to Simon Mann's Logo Logistics bank account - by the presiding judge. Page, a member of a family closely connected with the Foreign Office, had apparently barged into Simon Mann's prison cell at Chikurubi in order to try and extract a confession. "I was extremely distressed, disoriented and extremely vulnerable. My physical and mental condition would clearly have been apparent to Mr Page," went Simon Mann's written statement. Henry Page denied it was so. The judge did not appear to believe him. "What on earth Mr Page thought he was doing I don't know," he commented. Whatever the rights and wrongs of the incident, a complaint was made to the Law Society in London of undue pressure, and both Penningtons and Henry Page's reputation suffered. Why they ever consented to take on the ill-reputed dictator of a small African country as a client and then issue public statement after public statement supporting his case is something of a mystery. Fat fees do not entirely compensate for damaged reputations.

Another person whose reputation was, in his case, most unjustly attacked was the vulnerable Labour politician, now a European Commissioner, Peter Mandelson. A scatter-gun scatter-brained journalist named Rod Liddle tried to smear him in a series of hysterical articles in the normally unhysterical right-wing London weekly, *The Spectator*.

Admittedly Liddle attacked everyone; he attacked the "venal, vicious and incompetent" Obiang and his "idiot son". He attacked Jack Straw as a "master of dissimulation, … sharp practice, underhand dealing… and every other stratagem of concealment and deceit" and demanded, *à la Observer*, to know "why did Britain not at once comply with her obligations and warn Equatorial Guinea?" He attacked Ely Calil for renting a flat to Peter Mandelson in the distant past, for not being in London to answer his questions, for being "somewhat dubious", for being "ectoplasmic", for fleeing the country, for having been an adviser to Jeffrey Archer.

He attacked Peter Mandelson for having rented the said flat from Ely Calil, for being a mate of Ely Calil's, for refusing to reply to a list of written questions sent by Liddle to his office in Brussels, and because "You just knew he had to be involved somewhere along the line, didn't you?" He reported, apparently with the utmost seriousness, "For the first time we can reveal that the South African

Police, the elite 'Scorpions' unit, most definitely wish to interview Mr Mandelson, and will be making contact."

And then, in his final piece, having smeared Peter Mandelson by association, he seemed, with far more justification, to attack himself (and by implication *The Observer*): "Increasingly these days we call our politicians to account on technicalities.…We jubilantly assert that our Foreign Secretary looks as if he's flouted international law over Equatorial Guinea; he really should have told Mr Obiang what was going on. And so we go for him because we can, because on this minor and most insignificant of points he is clearly vulnerable."

Quite so. But if he really felt that why on earth did he do it?

★   ★   ★

Simon Mann, it will be remembered, had decided not to appeal against his seven years' sentence. But when in October 2004 Amanda gave birth to her third child, Arthur, he changed his mind. Discreetly, without publicity, but unsurprisingly it was learnt in the New Year that his sentence had been reduced to four years. Jonathan even hoped that there might be a presidential pardon on the occasion of the March 2005 elections, as was the custom. There was not.

But on May 15 sixty two of his fellow prisoners were finally released. Two could not be because they had died in jail. One, with tuberculosis, stayed behind in Harare. Their families had been waiting for over a week at Beit Bridge, the border crossing into South Africa. Their release had been repeatedly announced, then delayed by Zimbabwean officials. The sixty one who finally crossed had a bleak future facing them. "I can confirm," said a spokesman for the South African Ministry of Defence, Sam Mkhwanzi, "that Pomfret is to be destroyed." It had been a bleak home; with its 700 lean-to shacks, run-down school and handful of shops. But it had been home all the same.

Mann's family had arranged for each of the imprisoned mercenaries, or their families, to be paid £500 each, as some sort of consolation no doubt for the failure of the coup and their long imprisonment. It was perhaps only a gesture; but it was an expensive gesture when added to Simon Mann's already pretty vast financial losses; and no other mercenary, as far as I know, has ever done anything like it.

Understandably there was not much gratitude from the families. To take a perhaps typical case: Eduardo Tchimuishi, an Angolan by birth, had joined the SADF at the age of 20, served as a South African soldier for 29 years; and in the Buffalo Battalion for 18. He was 49 years old. His wife, three sons, five daughters and six infant grandchildren lived in Pomfret. "They shouldn't have given him seven years," his wife Bibiana said of Mann after the sentences in Harare were announced, "they should have given him the death penalty."

REFLECTIONS

On Mark Thatcher. Two columnists in *The Independent on Sunday* reflected on Mark Thatcher's role in the same issue.

"Few people remember now," wrote the first, "the details of his alleged role in securing contracts in the Middle East – it was never proved that he did anything illegal – but the impression remains that he exploited his mother's position for personal advantage." As for Equatorial Guinea, "we may not be able to follow every twist of the (alleged) plot but we are reminded that top Tories used to hang out with some rather questionable people."

The second columnist was blunter. "The…. aspect of the Thatcher affair that intrigues me is the African response. You can be car-jacked and murdered in South Africa without anyone taking much notice or you can embezzle money for years (if you are a top person) before the police take action; if you are Winnie Mandela you get nothing more serious than a rap over the knuckles for appalling crimes. But now, suddenly, the police have moved with alacrity to pin something on Mark Thatcher."

I have made no secret in this volume of my opinion that the South African system of justice, operating as it does without a jury, is flawed; is in fact unjust. Whether white-run or black-run appears to make not the slightest difference in principle. Mark Thatcher may indeed have mixed with rather questionable people. But he had never done anything illegal. I do not believe that this time he did anything illegal. He was charged, should have had the charges withdrawn, was accused on the basis of Crause Steyl's story when Crause Steyl had every motive to state what the authorities wished him to state in order, basically, to save himself from prison. Then he was put in the position where he either faced a series of trials dragging on possibly for years *à la Bleak House* or was offered the chance of getting his passport back on condition that he 'confessed' and paid in effect a monstrously large wodge of ransom money to the South African government in order to redeem his passport. As he said on the steps of the courthouse, "There is no price too high for me to pay to be reunited with my family. I am sure all of you who are husbands and fathers will understand."

But the price was far too high. Compare the size of his fine – 3,000,000 rand – not only with other fines for 'real' mercenaries under the Foreign Military Assistance Act – 30,000 to at most 200,000 rand – but also with what Mike Hoare hoped to make if the Seychelles coup had been successful: 100,000 rand. Even had Mark Thatcher been totally guilty as charged – of helping to finance a helicopter for a mercenary operation (a helicopter that never in fact left South Africa) – the fine would still be utterly out of proportion for what would have been merely an ancillary part of the operation.

Now look at his agreed 'confession' again. It is quite carefully worded. He 'doubted' he 'suspected', he had 'misgivings', he should have shown 'more caution'. And suddenly in the middle of all this it is boldly stated, without details or any evidence at all, "In fact Mann did intend to use the helicopter for mercenary activity." But where exactly? At what point of the operation? Why? To what purpose?

Mark Thatcher in my view was punished, and punished with vindictive severity, not because of what he did but because of who he was, and what he represented.

On Severo Moto. Having already been sentenced in his absence to 101 years' imprisonment for high treason seven years earlier, it is doubtful that Severo Moto was particularly worried by having another 63 years added on top of that. The same goes, *mutatis mutandis*, for his colleagues in exile. As for the fines of 2000 million CFA and downwards, it seems unlikely that those sums will ever reach the Equatorial Guinea Treasury - particularly since Severo Moto, I have been told, has barely two cents to rub together.

On the Armenians in Malabo. An enormous and barely comprehensible jail sentence. For doing precisely what?

On the accusations against the British Government and the Foreign Secretary. All seem based on the very dubious evidence of Johann Schmidt, who like Crause Steyl, had every inducement to come up with the story, and details, that in his case the Equatorial Guinean government wished him to come up with.

On the mercenaries in general. Here was a coup in which not a single person was killed, not a single person was wounded, no-one (except the mercenaries themselves after their arrests) was so much as scratched. No property was damaged. No disorders occurred, no aircraft was hijacked, no airport had its orderly function disrupted.

Not a shot was fired in anger. Indeed not a single mercenary ever so much as held a single weapon in his hands - the ones in Harare because they were arrested before any weapons passed into their possession; the ones in Malabo because that was part of their deal - insisted on by themselves.

In fact as a coup it was a non-event. It was as much as non-event as Frederick Forsyth and Alexander Gay's planned coup against the same target - the President of Equatorial Guinea - a generation earlier. Nothing in the end happened.

Except of course, that in the second case a lot of men, black and white, spent a lot of time in insalubrious prisons; that a lot of their backers lost a lot of money; and a lot of lawyers made a lot of money.

On Simon Mann and Nick du Toit. Had the coup been successful, had they succeeded in overthrowing President Obiang, would it have been a good thing for the world in general and Equatorial Guinea in particular? Probably - though by no means certainly.

Who faces the bleaker future? Nick du Toit and his fellow prisoners in Black Beach. "Many are extremely weak because of torture and ill-treatment and because of chronic illnesses," said a spokesman for Amnesty International in mid-2005. "Unless immediate action is taken, many of those detained there will die."

But despite the substantial cut in his sentence, the prospects for Simon Mann are not good, either. If, on release, he is sent back to South Africa - he has dual South African and British citizenship - will he not be immediately arrested, charged and prosecuted under the Foreign Military Assistance Act? He is now in his fifties. Under a white régime the book was thrown at Mike Hoare - ten years imprisonment for a minor offence - though he was in his sixties. Under a black régime how likely is it that Simon Mann will be allowed to fade peacefully away? Yet there is something resilient about Simon Mann, something of the prisoner of the Chateau d'If, something that makes one almost hope that he will emerge years later with totally changed fortunes, to, like the Count of Monte Cristo, wreak a fitting revenge on his persecutors.

Epilogue

CONDOTTIERI OF THE TWENTY-FIRST CENTURY

Iraq and Afghanistan

XVII

Aegis In Iraq

Aegis: Protection: in Greek mythology a shield belonging to Zeus or Pallas Athene.
Olive: Peace; of which the olive-leaf or branch was in Greek times the emblem.
Erinys: In Greek mythology a Fury.

Words are important. Terms are important. Titles are important. Take the Italian title *condottiere:* it glows with a haze of military romanticism. But in actual fact it was, by origin, down-to-earth. A *condottiere* was simply a military man who signed a *condotta* - a contract - with his employer. He was a military contractor. Curious, then, that the term of "military contractor" came back into use in Iraq and Afghanistan in this present century. Consider, for example, the following passage written by Rory Stewart, Governor (temporarily) of the remote Iraqi province of Dhi Qar in the aftermath of an attack by the Sadr militia on the Coalition Provisional Authority's headquarters in Nasiriyah in May 2004.

"I spent the morning with the Control Risks Group teams [his bodyguards] destroying all the paperwork and piling up the computer equipment and putting incendiary grenades next to it, ready for the moment when the site was finally abandoned… Just before the truck arrived, one of the CRG men came up to me and thanked me for 'real leadership', but they were the heroes. They had manned the machine guns on the roof, kept the enemy heads down, monitored the incoming fire and made suggestions about patrols and air support. Through all of this they had been in their element; considered, rational, matter-of-fact. Between them they had a couple of hundred years military experience." [There were six of them led by a Geoff Mabberly, "recently retired after twenty-two years in the British infantry", so some must have been considerably older¹] "and they knew far more than I did. I only had to smile, look calm, gather them every half-hour and listen, clarify, summarize and send their views to Baghdad. A little later, I heard a Canadian General

---

¹ By no means impossible. Jesse Gentry and Henry A. Doll, two "contractors" employed by the US company Dyncorp and killed in a convoy on the Tikrit-Baghdad Road, were retired police

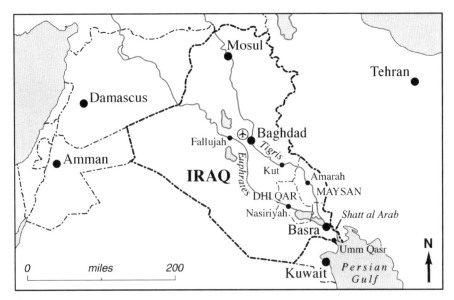

Iraq

say military contractors were mercenaries whose loyalty could not be relied on. I told him these contractors had risked their lives manning guns that soldiers had abandoned. A hundred of them could have brought order back to the province."

   The soldiers who had abandoned their guns, whom Rory Stewart was so justifiably angry about, were regular soldiers of the regular Italian Army, stationed at an army camp nearby, with orders to defend the civilian Coalition Headquarters. When summoned their Quick Reaction Force took *seven hours* to arrive. Rory Stewart, a Foreign Office man who writes in a restrained prose, makes it clear that this was far from the only case where mercenaries proved much more reliable than supposedly professional regular soldiers. In Kut, in the neighbouring province, "where Mark Etherington, who had flown into Iraq with me, was the Coalition Governor", the compound had also been attacked by militia from the Sadr movement. "The Ukrainian soldiers protecting him tried to run away and he had to order his bodyguard team to drive their armoured vehicles across the exit to stop the Ukrainians from escaping. His bodyguards kept up steady defensive fire for hours while Baghdad struggled to respond. When a helicopter gunship arrived, Mark was able to extract his team to the military base."

   There can be no doubt where Stewart's sympathies lie. Yet at the head of one of his chapters he quotes – he is fond of quoting him – Machiavelli's famous condemnation of mercenaries from Chapter 12 of *The Prince*:

---

officers aged, respectively, 61 and 56. Tak, an ex-SAS Fijian ambushed in a lone Landrover on the Kuwait border in November 2003, killed all three of his ambushers. He was 58. And two years later, aged 60, he went on a PMC training course to acquire a now-obligatory diploma…

"Mercenaries and auxiliaries are useless and dangerous... for they are disunited, ambitious, undisciplined and treacherous... weak and cowardly when they are met by determined enemies, they have no fear of God and do not maintain commitments with men."

Quoted tongue-in-cheek, no doubt; for those who were "weak and cowardly", who did not "maintain commitments with men" were the regulars, not the "military contractors" (as indeed was true of Machiavelli's contemporaries too: his views were totally biased by his own ambitions for his native city, Florence★★).

But what were mercenaries doing in Iraq at all? Why on earth were they needed when there were so many scores of thousands of regular troops in the country? What were they there **for**?

A fascinating question: to attempt to answer which it is necessary to go back a little in time.

THE DOWNWARD SLIDE OF TIM SPICER

We left Tim Spicer six years (and three chapters) ago recovering from the Sandline/ Sierra Leone affair. How had he been faring in the meantime? The short answer is: none too brilliantly. He was reduced to what that experienced and caustic investigative journalist, Duncan Campbell, called the role of "a relatively minor player" on the fringes of the mercenary business and sinking rapidly into obscurity.

He resigned from Sandline in 1999, created a new company, Crisis and Risk Management, in May 2000 (a week later the United Kingdom branch of Executive Outcomes was dissolved) and changed its name to Strategic Consultancy International in April 2001. But whatever the name was, no business came Tim Spicer's way - except perhaps in Nepal and that (if indeed it was more than a rumour) was not at all successful: training the Royal Nepalese Army to defeat the Maoist rebels which, as all the world now knows, it has singularly failed to do.

Next he launched Trident Maritime, its operating address next door to his then home in Cheval Place, Kensington, with a "global operational presence" - Tim, both chairman and chief executive officer, was always a dab hand with the big phrases - that seemed to consist of a slick web-site, a P.R. 'vice-president of marketing' and a tie-in with a professor of electrical engineering at the University of Maryland, by name Gilmer Blankenship (shades of John Buchan here - did Professor Blankenship suffer from duo-denal dyspepsia, one wonders, like Richard Hannay's wise old American mentor, John S. Blenkiron of Boston, Mass?)

Trident at least won a contract. On 24 July 2001[2] Tamil Tigers launched a devastating attack against Bandaranaike International Airport in the capital, Colombo,

---

[2] Note the date. Six weeks *before* terrorist attacks became of worldwide importance.

destroying on the ground about $500 million worth of civilian and military air-craft. Lloyds of London insisted, if they were to carry on insuring Ceylon's trade, that the government must commission a full security review of all its airports and seaports.

This was interesting. This was 'security consultancy' in a big way. On Lloyd's recommendation Trident Maritime was given the job. Spicer and a team of fifteen went out: men such as Hal Doyne-Ditmus, ex MI5, John Wilson a "methods of entry" expert, Tom Lockhart a "technical surveillance expert" and Mike Coldrick, a highly-decorated bomb disposal expert. "You tend to know who's who," Spicer told Duncan Campbell. "There is an informal network of people who know each other and have worked with you or have served together in the armed forces."

Recommendations were made. But 2002 turned out to be a bad year all round for Tim Spicer. First, in February, there was a ceasefire in Sri Lanka that led Lloyds of London to drop its $50 million surcharge, the motive behind the whole affair. Then Sandline Consultancy, an offshoot that Tim had kept going, was dissolved by official order for failing to file accounts; and Strategic Consulting International went off the air - its website was closed down. Finally in the autumn Trident itself disappeared. "It has closed," said Professor Blankenship. "We've had to stop the operation in the last couple of weeks… It wasn't managed particularly well - that's pretty much why the company failed."

Who would have thought, given this fairly dismal record, that Tim Spicer would ever triumphantly rise again like a phoenix from the ashes?

'Private Military Companies' - Birth of a Euphemism

Certainly not Duncan Campbell. He was writing at the end of October 2002; and quite clearly he considers Spicer to be an interesting case-study but a spent force. What he, Duncan Campbell, had however put his finger on - and what I do not think anyone else had preceded him in doing - was the extraordinarily interesting fact that Tim Spicer had introduced, and successfully introduced, an entirely new phrase and behind the phrase, an entirely new concept into the English language. That phrase was "private military company" - PMC.

Perhaps not so much introduced as popularised. Duncan Campbell traces it way back to a lunch that Simon Mann and Tony Buckingham invited Tim Spicer to, in Chelsea in October 1996. It was to discuss the 'rebranding' of Executive Outcomes which, all agreed, "carried a lot of political baggage". The actual term had apparently first been used in writing a year earlier by Agence France Presse in a report describing how four mercenaries captured by UNITA in Northern Angola were working for the "private military company Executive Outcomes".

It was not used again, in the English language press, till 1997 when a pub-lic relations firm, Pearson's, was hired to put the best gloss possible on Tim and Sandline's fiasco in Papua New Guinea. "I am not entirely sure where it (the term private military company) came from," said Sara Pearson. "It started to creep into the vocabulary… At the very beginning in the Papua New Guinea incident it was still 'dogs of war'. Then it became 'mercenaries' and then subsequent to the Sierra Leone business the words 'private military company' crept into the vernacular."

Around this time the phrase began to be used by charities working abroad – NGOs such as Oxfam or Medécins sans Frontières. In places like Liberia and Sierra Leone they found it was too dangerous to rely on local guides and translators only. They needed – these and other NGOs were top-heavy bureaucracies by now – armed guards, and armed guards they could rely on, not just local tough boys. But for Oxfam or Medécins sans Frontières to hire mercenaries as bodyguards and to be reported as doing so seemed extraordinarily distasteful. "People came up with this term as a brand new idea," said a specialist conflict and peace researcher. "It was trying to find a word that gave them some respectability – a cleaner term."

"To be honest," said Tim Spicer when the question was put to him, "I don't really care who coined it. It either came from somebody or it came from us. It's a good term. I'm happy to take the credit if you want to say I invented it."

Invented it or not, he certainly made use of it from then on. Why? Because, as Sara Pearson succinctly put it: "It certainly took a lot of the emotion out of the situation." Not much later, on March 28, 1998 the Institute of Strategic Studies in London held a conference on "private armies and military intervention". Most speakers referred to "mercenary companies", "military companies", or, traditionally enough, "private armies". Not Tim Spicer. To the general surprise he turned up and spoke at the Conference, arguing in favour of "Private Military Companies"; and the very same day Sandline published a four-page "white paper" entitled "Private Military Companies – Independent or Regulated?"

From that day onwards the term began to gain general acceptance. Next year, as the parliamentary enquiry into the 'illegal' arms shipment to Sierra Leone drew to its close, Tim Spicer circulated an open letter to newspapers and members of Parliament drawing the contrast between 'modern' Private Military Companies and 'old-style' mercenary bands. By February 2002 when the British government finally produced a green paper on the whole subject, it was entitled not *"Mercenaries: Options for Regulation"* but *"Private Military Companies: Options for Regulation"*. The term – which took a little longer to catch on in America than it had originally done in England (indeed American officials prefer the term Private Security Companies – PSCs – which sounds a mite more restricted in scope) is now normal government-speak as well as military-speak. It has in a way been Tim Spicer's greatest triumph; and in its way it is typical of the man. Unlike his predecessors, unlike Mike Hoare, unlike Bob Denard, unlike his contemporary Simon Mann, Spicer has understood the importance of words, of terms, of titles. He had already contributed, indirectly, to making the concept of 'mercenaries' respectable again, by his skilful use of lawyers and public relations people, as was emphasised at the end of Chapter 13, in the context of the Sandline/Sierra Leone furore. He had now gone better still, far better. He had, if not invented, at least introduced and was to popularise a new term for mercenary companies, a new set of initials – PMC (or PSC) – that had not only taken, as Ms Pearson had put it, the emotion out of the situation, but pretty nearly the sting out of the tail, the prejudice out of the concept. In effect Tim Spicer had not only, after 225-odd years★★, made mercenaries respectable again. He had effectively by sleight of tongue, by use of a new term, neutralised the whole concept.

Spicer's Upward Spiral

And of course that was not all he had done. He had made himself more than respectable – he had made himself a respected authority. When another conference, this time organised by the Royal United Services Institute, was held a few years later (on 6 December 2004 to be precise) at Oxford University, its title was "Private Military Companies in the Current Global Order", its subject "How and Why PMCs are playing such an important role in the world's conflicts", its attendance a couple of hundred government and military officials, academics, mercenaries and journalists all sitting comfortably side by side in the fairly hallowed surroundings of Rhodes House – and the principal address was given by "Lieutenant Colonel Tim Spicer, Chief Executive Officer and chairman, AEGIS Defence Services Limited".

Here was another example of the importance of terms and titles, of Tim's impressive innovating ability. Aegis – his new mercenary company, his new PMC – what an inspired choice that title was! Where Denard and Hoare had been content with 5 Commando and 6 Commando and Presidential Guards and, in Hoare's case, an over-jokey Frothblowers, Spicer had already shown talent with the title Sandline (drawing a *ne plus ultra* line in the sand was presumably the thought behind it), had taken a step towards classical mythology with the somewhat humdrum Trident – of Poseidon, Lord of the Sea – and had now gone distinctly upmarket with the far classier Aegis – of Zeus, Father of Gods and Men.

These are not trivial points. When Sir John Hawkwood in the late Middle Ages christened his mercenary gang the White Company or Albert Stertz his the Company of the Rose, their titles echoed through all the Western world. Simon Mann had stuck with the banal, uninspiring Executive Outcomes and was (at the time of this Rhodes House Conference) possibly toying with the Bight of Benin Company. The Americans tended to stick with their more practical titles of the DynCorp/ArmorGroup variety (though there were also BlackWater and Janusian, the origins of which titles I do not know – perhaps geographical rather than mythological?) But it was the British who eventually followed Spicer's inspired lead with titles for their mercenary outfits like Olive and Erinys. Not all of them - the early PMCs stuck with Global Risk Strategies, Control Risks and even, in the case of that other Scots Guards mercenary leader, Richard Bethell (now, following the death of his father, the 6th Lord Westbury), the totally anodyne Hart Group.

Frederick Forsyth was, as a romantic and military-minded literary man, clearly attracted by the title of Aegis, and its resonance, as much as by the capabilities of Tim Spicer and his prospects. Was he a personal chum of Tim's? Presumably he must have been, otherwise he would not have been let in - as he was - on the ground floor. Of the original £100 share issue in Aegis, Frederick Forsyth took up £4 - one twenty-fifth of the capital - and no doubt invested a good deal more than the nominal £4. "Usually, I lose money," said Forsyth. Not this time. "It has certainly been one of my better flutters," he added. He could chortle that again. For in March 2004, eight months before the Rhodes House Conference, in exactly the same month in which Simon Mann was risking his all and aiming at a great fortune in Equatorial Guinea, Tim Spicer was on Aegis' behalf signing a mercenary contract - a *condotta* of the twenty-first century - for almost **three hundred million dollars**: probably the most magnificent and profitable *condotta,* all things compared, ever signed by any mercenary leader in history.

So that at the Rhodes House Conference in December the Wheel of Fortune had indeed turned full circle - both for Simon Mann, rotting away in Chikurubi jail, and for Tim Spicer, among all those academics, officials and journalists gathered to listen to his keynote address, almost certainly by far and away the richest man in the room - quite probably worth as much as all the other participants at the Conference lumped together. As they knew; for this miraboulous mouth-watering contract was in these circles at least common knowledge. The irony must have brought a pained grimace to the face in particular of one of these journalists present; for there, in Lieutenant-Colonel Spicer, Chairman and Chief Executive's audience, was sitting Duncan Campbell, who had so justifiably - but so erroneously - two years earlier labelled Tim Spicer a "relatively minor player". The moral (if there is a moral)? Never dismiss a mercenary leader as down and done for till he is stone dead. They are a resilient breed; and to them the title story of Frederick Forsyth's book of short stories *No Comebacks*[3] most certainly does not apply.

AEGIS - AND BLACK WATER: COUSINS UNDER THE SKIN

The precise sum that Aegis was awarded in March 2004 was $292,500,000 for a contract of three years' duration. The contract was, broadly, for providing 'security

---

[3] Well worth reading in the present author's (undoubtedly biased) view for the episode in the title story when the hero/villain wishing to employ a mercenary turns to the present author's past works as his guide - a literary compliment of sorts, if a somewhat back-handed one!

services' in Iraq; and in particular for coordinating the services of other 'contractors'. For Aegis, and Tim Spicer, were by no means the only mercenary company hired by the main mercenary employer, the US Department of Defence; nor indeed the first. That honour seems to have been obtained by BlackWater.

BlackWater, like so many of the American private military companies, had been set up in the period 1996/7 when, with the Cold War over, the United States, the United Kingdom and of course Russia, their former enemy, the ex-Union of Soviet Socialist Republics, were reducing their official armed forces drastically. When official armed forces are cut, unofficial or semi-official groups tend to spring up, if only to give employment to the suddenly unemployed; and this seems particularly to be the case in free-market economies such as the United States. Most of the new groups like the Vinnell Corporation, like Military Professional Resources Inc, the eight generals' brainchild, like DynCorp too, sprang up in Virginia, close to Washington and the Pentagon. BlackWater by contrast had its base in North Carolina. It was set up by Gary Jackson, a former Navy Seal, twenty-five miles south of the naval base of Norfolk. And what it specialised in was training. It trained marines for the US Navy. And this was what the other groups did too: they trained.[4]

★   ★   ★

Were they mercenary companies strictly speaking? This is where definitions get tricky. The vast American corporations like Bechtel and Halliburton and Kellogg Brown and Root - KBR - that built American bases in the Middle East and supplied American forces with food and equipment and planned and administered the renovation of hospitals and the oil industry, that in a word took charge of logistics - in Iraq, in the bases from which Iraq was supplied in Kuwait and the Gulf and also, though to a lesser degree, in Afghanistan - can hardly be called mercenaries. They won enormous, hallucinatory contracts from the United States Government and the United States military; but basically they were American civilian contractors working for the American authorities. True, as the Iraqi insurgency gained in strength from mid-2003 onwards and renovation became both more difficult and more dangerous, they had to protect their works and they had to protect their workers and they had to protect their executives. So they in their turn hired private security firms - they spread the manna.

And so, more amazingly, did the public authorities. BlackWater was the first into Baghdad, in early April 2003. They were hired as a protection force by the State Department. They provided bodyguards for Paul Bremer, the Proconsul;

---

[4] The Vinnell Corporation, for example, had signed a contract for $163 million to train the Saudi Arabian National Guard, 75,000 men strong. It was to go on to train the (new) Iraqi National Guard - one day perhaps the Iraqi Army revived.

and pretty much for all the American officials based in what became the Green Zone, the 'safe' zone of Baghdad; and particularly when these same officials travelled out of it. They had their own MH-6 helicopters, and their Mamba and Saxon armoured vehicles. By mid-July 2004 BlackWater had 450 men in and around Baghdad.

But were they mercenaries? Strictly speaking, not quite. They were soldiers, almost undeniably; they were working for money, totally undeniably. But they were not serving "a foreign power". They were Americans, working for and paid by the United States. So, technically speaking, they were in a different category from Aegis. For Spicer's men were hired not by the United Kingdom – which would have made them military sub-contractors – but by the United States, a country not their own. Therefore they were by strict definition mercenaries. All most confusing. Though more confusing in theory than in practise.

★   ★   ★

For all these "military contractors" – one can see the usefulness of the term now, for it covers both mercenaries strictly speaking and those of the same ilk working directly for (and paid by) their own country – were birds of the same feather, doing pretty much the same sort of job. They did it in different ways of course, different styles. BlackWater was noticeably gung-ho; and they paid a terrible price for it when at Fallujah, in the notoriously dangerous 'Sunni Triangle' two of their 4 x 4s were caught by insurgents, separated from the military food convoy BlackWater had been escorting up the highway, and destroyed. The four men in the vehicles – one ex-Delta-Force, three ex-Rangers – were killed; and, in a scene that shocked the world with its savagery, two of their mutilated, burnt and blackened bodies were suspended from a bridge straddling the Euphrates. Most shocking of all was the way the crowds of Iraqis, in apparent ecstasy, rejoiced. That 'incident' occurred on 31 March 2004. Four days later US Marines stormed Fallujah and avenged their wretched deaths. For the links between BlackWater and the Marines were understandably close, as BlackWater had trained so many of their men. This is a case where the regular forces and the supplementary 'contractors' worked well together, almost in osmosis. It was not always so. The British regular forces, unlike the Americans, detested the mercenaries of Aegis, though they shared the same base camp at Basra. And though too most of the mercenaries of Aegis were, like their mercenary chief Tim Spicer, former members of, precisely, the British armed forces.

Partly this was due to understandable envy. The mercenaries of Aegis were paid far better – perhaps three or four times better – than the average British soldier in Iraq. But then the same was true of BlackWater; the men of BlackWater were paid three or four times better than the average US GI in Iraq. The difference of course, as has just been pointed out, was that the US 'military contractors' had

had very close working relationships with the US armed forces before they ever set foot in Iraq; as trainers or as suppliers or as base-builders. Whereas the British 'military contractors' had had nothing at all to do with the British armed forces before they appeared on the scene as, in the eyes of British regulars, over-paid interlopers. Even their officers were treated as pariahs in the messes of Basra. (And for the historian of mercenaries there is nothing in the least unusual in this: mercenaries are invariably, when allied to regular forces, treated with distrust and distaste by the latter – as Xenophon and Clearchus and the Ten Thousand had found out so painfully in Persia over two thousand years earlier★★ and as indeed Tim Spicer and Nick Van Den Bergh and their Seventy had discovered far more recently in Papua New Guinea..)

How Aegis Won Its Contract – despite DynCorp

It was probably the slaughter of the BlackWater 'contractors' that speeded up the signing of the US Department of Defence contract with Aegis. For it proved the need for a certain coordination, at the very least a sharing of information, between the numerous private military companies that were, by the spring of 2004, a year after the fall of Baghdad and the collapse of Saddam Hussein's régime, operating in a slightly helter-skelter fashion all over occupied Iraq. For some, like BlackWater, were escorting convoys and US bigwigs, contracted both by the Department of Defence and the State Department. Others, like Olive Security, had been hired by the giant Bechtel to guard its reconstruction projects all over the country including the security – and running – of the port of Umm Qasr on the Shatt-al-Arab. Erinys was protecting pipe-lines and oil wells and (rather amazingly) a US Corps of Engineers division. Global Risks was providing bodyguards – perhaps the most dangerous task of all – for members of the Iraqi government. Control Risks Group was hired by the Foreign Office and the Department of International Development to protect their visiting and permanent officials and buildings. And so on and so forth. What was lacking was any overall coordination; and it was that that in the spring of 2004, with the Coalition Provisional Authority about to hand over power, at least officially, to the Iraqi government, Tim Spicer and Aegis had won the contract to supply.

How did he win it? By technical know-how? Improbable, though of course technical know-how had to be there. My view is that, whereas all the other PMC leaders and founders were, probably by their own deliberate choice, shadowy figures, Tim Spicer alone was not. Of all the mercenary leaders since Mike Hoare he is the only one – or at least the only one both sane and presentable (unlike, for instance, a Rolf Steiner★) – who has actively sought publicity, who has learnt how to handle it, who has used it for his own ends and who has profited by it. For why on earth should the US Department of Defence have awarded the almost-unknown, certainly track-record-less, Aegis that enormous $292.5 million contract when there were five other companies in the running? Mainly, no doubt, because Tim Spicer was both presentable and by then a well-known public figure and speaker in the military-academic transatlantic world; indeed an authority. It helped of course that he was British, had commanded a Guards Regiment, and had probably submitted a lower quotation for the 'job' than rival American companies that, it had again and again become clear, were recklessly inflating their costs and going wildly over-budget, so great and tempting were the showers of gold being scattered by the US government all over Iraq.

One of the rival companies, however, bitterly protested. This was DynCorp of Virginia. DynCorp, like so many of these companies had started off as a maintenance and engineering outfit, keeping US helicopters up and flying in the first Iraq War. Then it had won contracts, said to be worth $48 million each, to set up and maintain two Gulf bases, one in Qatar, one in Kuwait. It was to expand into US embassies' protection, and into training the new police forces being set up under US auspices in both Afghanistan and Iraq. It was a vigorous and, as its name implies, a dynamic component of the expanding American worldwide military power; and it did not see why it should be done out of a fantastically lucrative contract by a small limey rival.[5]

So in effect DynCorp mounted a dirty-tricks campaign in an attempt to have the Aegis contract revoked and its Chief Executive discredited. It dug into Tim Spicer's past. It came up with the Sierra Leone 'scandal' and the Papua New Guinea 'fiasco'. But in the first case Tim Spicer had been effective, in the second honest. DynCorp delved deeper.

★   ★   ★

In the autumn of 1992 Lieutenant Colonel Spicer had been commanding the Second Battalion, Scots Guards on one of its periodic tours of duty in Northern Ireland. In September two of his men, Guardsman Wright and Guardsman Fisher, were out on patrol in the North Lodge area of North Belfast. They stopped and searched Peter McBride, an 18-year-old teenager. As he turned away, they shot and killed him, claiming later that they suspected he was going to throw a coffee-jar bomb at them.

Colonel Spicer stuck by his men. He believed their story, interviewed them with the RSM and Company Commander, wanted to get them back out on patrol again before they lost their nerve. "Both men were clearly in shock," he later said, "They were young – Wright just 19 and Fisher 24 – and had not been in this sort of situa-

---

[5.] DynCorp appears to have been well compensated for whatever it missed out on in Iraq. By early 2005 it was, for a contract of $200 million, retraining – a thankless task indeed – a new and hopefully reformed and "human-rights conscious" Liberian army 4000 strong under the aegis of Andy Michels of the State Department, Head of Team for Reform of Security in Monrovia.

tion before. Both were upset and it was common sense to get them back out there doing their jobs…You have to do it before your nerve goes forever."

Instead, the RUC - the Royal Ulster Constabulary - interrogated them. They were subsequently tried for murder. The judge, unlike their Colonel, did not believe their story. They were convicted, sentenced to life imprisonment, lost an appeal in 1995 but were released (as of course were many IRA convicted murderers) in the general settlement three years later.

This was the 'scandal' that DynCorp and a group of Democratic Senators headed by Ted Kennedy and loudly supported by Father Sean McManus of the Irish National Caucus in Washington D.C. raked up in an attempt to discredit Tim Spicer. Whatever opinion readers may have of the tragedies and killings that were almost daily occurrences on the streets of Belfast, it is hard to blame a commanding officer for supporting his own men.

At any rate, on 13 September 2004, the US Government Accountability Office rejected the DynCorp protest on technical grounds and confirmed the award of the contract "pursuant to Solicitation No W91150-04-R-0005" to "Mr Spicer" and "Aegis Defence Services Limited". If nothing else, the episode indicates how ferocious was the rivalry between the different mercenary companies and how little love was lost between them. It reminds one of nothing so much as the rivalry between the early *condottieri* in late mediaeval Italy for the rich contracts being offered by Pisa and Siena and Florence.★★ Similar was the atmosphere, similar the reactions in Washington, Baghdad and indeed Kabul nearly seven centuries later.

Aegis immediately set to work on the task for which it had primarily been contracted: coordinating the defence and protection in particular of civilian companies for the Reconstruction Operations Centre in Baghdad and its five regional headquarters throughout Iraq. This involved a highly technical newly developed system called Tapestry, and the setting up of transponders with panic buttons attached on all civilian vehicles (including protection vehicles of other PMCs) at use in reconstruction projects in Iraq. It involved coordination, diplomacy - and the setting up, too, of Aegis bases at Baghdad, Basra, Mosul, Ramadi and Tikrit. It involved, therefore, a great expansion in manpower

THE NEW 'MILITARY CONTRACTORS' - MEN, MOTIVES AND RECRUITMENT

The figures that follow may surprise. By 2005 there were, it was calculated, 135,000 US regular soldiers and marines in Iraq, 9000 British troops (basically stationed in the South, in Basra and the surrounding provinces) and 15,000 of all the other Coalition Forces combined: Poles, Ukrainians, Italians, Australians and so forth. *But* there were also between 20,000 and 30,000 mercenaries or semi-mercenaries, no less, 'belonging' to between 20 and 40 mercenary or semi-mercenary outfits of all shapes and sizes - private military companies, PMCs. *Therefore* these mercenary/

semi-mercenary groups, taken together, were the second most powerful military force in Iraq, numerically speaking, after the United States regulars. They had become immensely significant - a modern mercenary army.

★   ★   ★

Who were the men who worked for all these private military companies? As the opening paragraphs of this chapter imply and as history dictates, they were, like Hawkwood's men in the White Company, like Stertz's men in the Company of the Rose, almost all former professional soldiers - in many cases with much, much more experience than the regular Coalition Forces.

Consider, for example, Aegis. By 2005 Tim Spicer had 945 employees on his payroll in Iraq; pretty much comparable to what Sir John Hawkwood had had in Italy. Of these a large number - 244 - were locals: bottle-washers, guides, interpreters and so on, Iraqis in the case of Spicer, Italians in the case of Hawkwood; and in the case of Aegis another 126 were "Third Country Nationals" - mainly Indians (including some Gurkhas) who took charge of the cleaning, the catering and, especially in the case of the Gurkhas, guard duties too. That left 554, of whom a good quarter (including the handful of women) were admin and secretarial.

The vast majority of these were (as in the case of the White Company) British - 423 to be precise. The next largest contingent were white South Africans. But, as Flaubert puts it in his great mercenary-revolt novel *Salammbo*: "there were men there from all the nations in the world" - in Aegis' case from Australia and Canada and America, from New Zealand and Norway, from Columbia in South America and the Lebanon in the Middle East, from Belgium and France and Holland, from Sweden and Denmark, Poland and Germany, and even a single stray warrior from the homeland of the sagas, Iceland - a far cry indeed from those days with Trident Maritime when Tim Spicer could lay his hands only on fifteen Englishmen of his own sort.

He himself was based in London, with offices at 118 Piccadilly, from where he ran what was now a multi-national operation of extreme complexity, with only occasional visits to the field, to 'his' men and centre of operations in Basra.

As for 'his' men and the reasons for their joining:- first and foremost was the money, their pay, and the fact that, unlike so many other mercenaries, they knew that they could count on it. This pay was often exaggerated. It varied enormously with rank and responsibilities. On average it was £200-£250 a day. As for leave, the rotation was roughly 8 weeks on, 2 weeks off. As for contracts, Aegis offered its employees a one-year contract; which was longer than most other mercenary companies offered. But on the other hand if the mercenary wanted to break the contract there was nothing to stop him. He simply upped sticks and left. There could be no crime of 'desertion' in a mercenary force as there is in a regular army; and that, of course, together with the pay, was another major attraction.

★   ★   ★

There were said to be only 200 French mercenaries in Iraq - Aegis only had 2 in its ranks - but one of them, one who gave a fascinating though anonymous interview in 2006, may well have been Jean-Paul Guerrier, 'Capitaine Siam', absent *-en fuite* - from the Trial of the Thirty in Paris in the spring of that year. This mercenary had served several years in the French army, in an elite unit (not - for once - the Foreign Legion).

"For my first mission," he explained, "I was recruited by a head-hunter who had heard of me from a third party. In this job you have to be known, and have a fat address book. It's a small world, 90% dominated by the Anglo-Saxons and the French are not particularly welcome there. But keep your head down, do your job, and doors will always be open. You can even at this stage make contact via chat-rooms on the internet. 'So and so is recruiting...'; 'I am at such and such a place...'; 'X is looking for people'."

"The recruiter contacted me in the first place. Once we'd agreed on terms and conditions, he sent me the contract over the internet. I confirmed my agreement, and received a return air-ticket to Amman. It may seem surprising; but there was no face-to-face interview. In Amman we were met by an agent for the company who took care of all the formalities - customs, hotel, etcetera. Once in Iraq we slept in air-conditioned tents till hotel rooms were found" - it sounds as if this was in the Green Zone in Baghdad - "one room shared by two of us. I was in a team escorting an American admiral. Imagine his surprise when he found a *frenchie* at his side. Apart from two South Africans the rest of the bodyguard group were Americans. I was gunner/driver, paid $10,000 a month, all expenses covered - except for the occasional Whopper at Big Burger. The equipment was all American: Glock 17 and M4s, bullet-proof vests, light armoured vehicles. Danger? Danger was everywhere, even in the Green Zone. But the risks are those that come with the job. If you don't like them, you are free to leave at any moment. Every morning there is a brief mortar attack. Then, on the road, particularly to the airport, there are ambushes, explosions, the whole works.... And, believe me, they get better from day to day. There's a convoy, US army or private military, every five minutes, and all they have to do is watch and learn from their mistakes. As for the Iraqis, they have a lot to put up with - especially those who live in the Red Zone. What the future of Iraq will be I have no idea. But there will be plenty of work to come in the private sector."

WEAPONS AND TACTICS.

A word about weapons and tactics. Rory Stewart describes, with a slightly ironic touch, how a 'contractor', "six foot four and his chest so broad that at first I thought he was wearing body armour under his T-shirt" stood "with a beer-can in one fist" and declaimed:

"Right, I'm going up to Majar now. I'll tab it myself. All I need is to strap on an M4, a Glock, an M72, A2, an L2, a twelve-bore and a Minimi."

The M4, explains a British 'military contractor', John Geddes, in *his* book, (the only book written - so far as I know - by a mercenary in Iraq) is "standard GI weaponry, compact and very accurate". The Minimi, a light machine-gun, "really can pour out a tremendous weight of fire"; and most British 'contractors' now carry them, as well as a Glock or Beretta pistol "for personal protection". As for the rest of the alphabet soup of weapons, Geddes and the thirty-plus fellow mercenaries mainly ex-SAS who arrived in Iraq, he claims, with the first wave of invaders (on a six-week recce mission to spy out the land for future reconstruction projects) much preferred sturdy ex-Soviet kit like AK 47s, PKM machine-guns, light RPK-74 machine guns, PP Sh-41 submachine-guns, huge 50 cal. Dushkas and the Dragonov sniper rifle "simply because you never know when you're going to have to take a long shot". All these were dished out to this first group - they had driven up from Kuwait in seven landrovers, unarmed - by friendly US officers from the vast stockpiles of Iraqi weapons captured when Baghdad had fallen to the Coalition forces. And for those first six weeks the men on this mission could, for the first and last time, drive round the whole of Iraq freely, welcomed and unattacked.

This situation of course - the honeymoon period - did not last much beyond the summer of 2003. From that time on escorts had to be provided and, as Rory Stewart says, "Two armoured vehicles and a bodyguard of four was now" - he was talking of September 2003 when he first flew in - "the minimum requirement for moving a civilian safely from the airport. The vehicles cost about $170,000 apiece, and the men were paid about $500 a day."

These would have been Control Risks Group 'contractors', and their contract - they were a long-established and rather more discreet and conventional security company than most - with the Foreign Office and with Britain's Department of International Development was worth £23.5 million. The group Geddes came in with was probably (it remains anonymous in his book) Global Risk Strategies, that had employed only two people - its two founders, one of whom was Charlie Andrews, an ex-Royal Marines Officer - before the take-over of Afghanistan. When Kabul fell to the Northern Alliance in November 2001 - almost eighteen months before the fall of Baghdad - Global Risk were given a contract to distribute new Afghan banknotes all over that turbulent land. They performed so successfully that they were eventually given the same task - and many more too - in Iraq. Where by the autumn of 2004 they had an estimated 1200 mercenaries on their payroll, mainly Gurkhas and Fijians. But in those first days, after the six weeks initial recce, they had to hand over to ArmorGroup - much to the annoyance of Geddes and his buddies, bundled out of Iraq, back to Kuwait and the UK.

Geddes, according to his own account, was back within a week, acting as escort/bodyguard to various TV camera crews and, for a dangerous period, as a Lone Ranger, a freelance. He spent eighteen months in Iraq in all, and was followed by his own son Kurt, also like himself an ex-Para. So not all mercenaries who were there in Iraq were employed by PMCs; though the vast majority certainly were. Nor were all recruited by word of mouth or the internet. Former SAS (and presumably Paras too) handed their details to a regimental 'resettlement officer' with a request to "push my details around the security companies".

Nor did they all drive, like Rory Stewart's escorts, $170,000 vehicles. Indeed, if Geddes is to be believed, many of the British mercenaries preferred to blend into the local scenery by arranging convoys of clapped-out cars and vans and lorries with good engines but ruined exteriors; and despised the abrasive tactics of firms such as BlackWater who relied on speed and firepower rather than guile and deceit, drove at high speed in conspicuously armoured vehicles, ready to force any local Iraqis off the road - thereby making themselves not only detested but a highly visible target for ambushes. Giving all due allowance for sour grapes and poor relation syndrome, a story of Bungo, Geddes' friend, who "spotted a big column of Yank PMC vehicles coming towards us when suddenly they were firing at us out of the blue" has the ring of truth about it. Apparently the trigger-happy American gunmen claimed to have mistaken the Union Jack for the Iraqi flag. "Some of those rednecks live in a parallel universe," a very shaken Bungo commented to Geddes. "Bungo was lucky to survive that encounter," wrote his friend. "He flies the Stars and Stripes now but still reckons the Americans are more dangerous than the insurgency."

OLIVE AND ERINYS

Olive Security, rather like Global Risks, was set up as a two-man company in 2001. Its founder was Jonathan Allum, an ex-Parachute Regiment Officer. It was running at an annual loss of £60,000 when it was hired by 'unembedded' British TV crews for protection during the invasion of Iraq; and in particular covered Sky News while Sky News was covering the fall of Baghdad. From the time it impressed Bechtel it never looked back. By 2005 it had 500 staff in Iraq, a turnover of £60 million a year, contracts with twenty other US and British companies involved in reconstruction work, and a growing, glowing reputation. Indeed it was named "Consultancy Firm of the Year," no less, in Southern Iraq.

Its success and reputation are due not only to what it does but to whom it employs - and of course to the extent to which it lives up to its peace-enforcing rather than war-fighting title. For it recruits not Fijians or Gurkhas, not tough NCOs from the Paras or SAS but former Army Officers aged between 25-50 who have done at least two tours of duty in a hot-spot - e.g. in Afghanistan, Yugoslavia, Sierra Leone or indeed in Iraq itself. And presumably in Northern Ireland too – though shades of the Black and Tans, themselves mainly if not entirely ex-officers from the First World War army, must be lurking in the collective memory here: and that as a warning rather than an example.

Their 'Operations Deployment Manager' is a former Welsh Guards officer, Simon Treadgold. Harry Legge-Bourke used to work for them, brother of Tiggy Legge-Bourke, former nanny to Princes William and Harry; as did her husband Charles Pettifer, himself once an officer in the Coldstream Guards. Intriguingly, their board of consultants has been joined in early 2006 not only by Lieutenant General Sir Cedric Delves, a former commanding officer of the SAS (who was awarded the DSO for gallantry in the Falklands) but also by Major General Arthur Denaro, a close personal friend and walking companion of the Prince of Wales, former polo-playing coach of Prince Harry, former commandant of the Royal Military Academy at Sandhurst, where both Princes have been trained, and former commanding officer of the Queen's Royal Irish Hussars in the first Iraqi War. In other words Olive Security has a kudos, a respectability, a sense of almost having been dubbed - to exaggerate slightly - *By Appointment Purveyors of Mercenaries* that Aegis, with its slightly dicey pre-history, can only envy.

★   ★   ★

Erinys International is in many ways a complete contrast to Olive Security. To take numbers first: it employed in mid-2004 no less than 6,500 men, due to rise - apparently - to 14,500. These were mainly Arabs, commanded and trained by white South Africans; recruited by the Erinys office in Baghdad or in neighbouring Amman; and their main task was to protect 140 oil wells in almost the same number of square kilometres; for $50 million dollars a year (annual contract renewed in early May 2004); rising - understandably if the numbers indeed rose by the proportion proposed - to $70 million a year. And it was never a two-man band or a small operation to start with. Erinys was set up largely if not entirely with Arab capital invested by a pair of Jordanian brothers, Abdul and Huda Farouki, established in the United States, whose construction companies had received many million dollars in loans from Ahmed Chalabi's Amman-based Petra Bank before it collapsed in 1989.

So this was big business; and not only big business but big politics too. For another director of Erinys was Faisal Daghestani, credited with establishing Ahmed Chalabi's political party, the Iraqi National Congress. So - again exaggerating - it would be possible to label Erinys as being, potentially at least, Chalabi's political militia rather than a simple PMC. And the title Erinys - Fury - was as justified, in an opposite sense, as the title Olive seems to have been: for, unlike most PMCs, Erinys was also liable to undertake "freelance" work for the Department of Defence of an "offensive nature".

Whole books will one day be written about these various and varied companies, their scope, backgrounds, achievements, rise and possibly subsequent fall. All that can be done in this chapter, written while the Iraqi Insurgency seems to be veering not towards settlement but towards civil war, is to give some indication of the fascinating, possibly frightening, complexities involved in this whole tangled business.

Certainly in Eriny's case there were multiple layers of much complexity. For, Arabs and Iraqi politicians and oilwells apart, the British too were distinctly involved at the administrative if not at the financial level. Alastair Morrison, of the original quartet of Scots Guards officers, was one of Erinys' bosses till he resigned – or was forced out – in March 2004, just two months before Erinys' contract was renewed. Apparently there were "strong personal antagonisms" with the fellow-Briton who was, or became, the Group Managing Director, Jonathan Garrett – despite the fact that Jonathan Garrett was an Old Boy of DSL - Defense Systems Limited - the company Alastair Morrison and Richard Bethell had jointly set up together before it was merged with Armor Holdings to form ArmorGroup. Wheels within wheels, one imagines, and plenty of difficulties over money and its destination, to say nothing of politics and its desires.

Indeed the whole history of Erinys seems to have been one of almost continual upset; for the October previously its chairman Sean Clery had resigned when he discovered that Erinys was involved in "downstream security operations" - whatever that may mean. Most interesting here is the fact that Clery was a South African former diplomat and intelligence officer; and certainly Erinys recruited widely among white South Africans.[6]

★   ★   ★

Indeed white South Africans formed an enormous proportion of the mercenaries in Iraq; with estimates of their total number ranging between 1400 and 5-10,000. It even happened that dozens of regular army officers from the SADF (now the SANDF - the South African army) accumulated leave in order to 'moonlight' in Iraq; as was revealed in April 2005 when a military court in Pretoria fined Lt Colonel Gus Maartens £180 for "breaches of military discipline" - including being absent without leave: in Iraq.

Despite attempts to tighten up the Foreign Military Assistance Act the lure is, for many white South Africans, just too powerful. Take the case of Deon Gouws, hired by Erinys, who flew out with seventeen of his compatriots on 8 January 2004. He was a former policeman, who had worked for the notorious Vlakplaas unit, who had appeared before the Truth and Reconciliation Commission, had been forgiven his brutal violence, but, at the age of 43, was retired, living on a

---

[6] As did our old acquaintances 'Hecky' Horn and Jacobus Carlse of MTS - Meteoric Tactical Services - for a comparatively meagre escort contract of $250,000; no doubt *before* their arrest at Harare Airport.

pension of only 5000 rand a month. In Iraq he was offered well over ten times that amount – and this still came cheap to the employers when compared to the cost of a British or American 'contractor'. "They know we're good at this sort of work," explained Gouws; and when quizzed about South Africa's anti-mercenary laws: "I'm not a mercenary," he replied. "I wasn't there to take part in the fighting. We were just paid to protect people." A point of view, certainly. But Erinys subsequently removed from its Internet site all references to its South Africa contacts. Nevertheless Aegis in mid-2005 had on its payroll in Basra no less than 53 South Africans – the largest contingent after the 423 British.

And there were not only white South Africans being lined up. There was talk at one stage of no less than 10,000 black East Africans being recruited by Askar Security Services of Uganda, (though as far as I know that has come to nothing – as yet.)   The white South Africans for their part were in general much disliked by their fellow mercenaries – Afrikaners almost entirely, chippy, introspective, racist (though that must have been confusingly complicated in Iraq) and sexist too; not impressed by the 'Baghdad Babes', the team of six British gunwomen, mainly ex-Metropolitan police, who did a man's job out there. "Some of those South Africans just make it their business to get on your wrong side," commented Penny, the original Babe (per Geddes, a leggy six-foot blonde), "they're a cussed lot."

Casualties – and Expectations

Cursed certainly in the case of Deon Gouws. Twenty days after arriving in Baghdad an ambulance loaded with explosives blew up the Hotel Shaheen where he and five of his fellow 'contractors' were lodged. His room-mate was killed instantly. He himself lost his right arm and his left eye; and was evacuated to Germany. Back in Johannesburg "This war is not our war," he declared. "There you're a target every second. It's a hell. To go out there is madness." But every day he received phone calls from people wanting to enlist. "They only have one objective. It's money, money, always money."

Heinrich Visagie, formerly of the Special Task Force, another police unit with a reputation for brutality, was killed at Fallujah on 7 April 2004, aged 29. That was only days after the notorious killing of the BlackWater four. Four Gurkhas working for Global Risk Strategies were killed by a mortar bomb exploding in the Green Zone on 26 November that same year. On 28 May 2005 a 44-year-old Japanese, Akihito Saito, who – most unusually for a Jap – had served in the Foreign Legion, and was working for an (unidentified) British PMC, was kidnapped by the terrorist group Ansar Al-Sunna and, after four weeks' captivity, macabrely executed on video. All in all it is thought that about three hundred 'military contractors' have been killed in Iraq, and many hundreds more wounded. And not only in Iraq. On 9 October 2005 four British 'contractors' were blown up and badly injured in Kandahar by a suicide bomber – at the time a new phenomenon in Afghanistan – while escorting a Foreign Office official to that southern city from the capital, Kabul. For, though to a lesser extent, almost all the major PMCs have carved out a role in Afghanistan too.

In such circumstances the odd 'unfortunate incident' is bound to occur. What is surprising is that there have not been more of them. Certain of the notorious interrogators at Abu Gharib prison were 'contractors'. More seriously, in December 2005 certain 'video nasties' were posted on the internet, apparently showing 'contractors' along the airport route opening fire at random on Iraqi motorists – and it was alleged that these were Aegis' men; an allegation immediately denied by Aegis. An anonymous source at Aegis claimed that the videos – all short, some showing a return of fire only when fired upon – were probably posted by a disgruntled former employee, sacked for being unprofessional. Calls for an official enquiry petered out; though the new Iraqi government brought in rules imposing licences upon PMCs and weapon-carrying 'contractors'. But there have been no allegations – as yet – of massacres by mercenaries, or mass murders, or revenge killings, or even of summary executions. Which is, to say the least, surprising. For in situations like Iraq such rumours, true or false, are only too easily set up and spread.

★   ★   ★

Ten miles outside Amman in Jordan lies the small impoverished settlement of Zarqa. There, born into a poor family of seven sisters and two brothers, Abu Musad began his almost-forty years of life on this earth, in 1967. As a youth he went out to Afghanistan, to fight against the Russians. "He represents a superhero for the tribe," said a cousin of his. "He is a source of pride and honour. They are proud they produced the historical hero, the saviour. We wish we had ten Zarqawis."

Not everyone agreed with Al Zarqawi's desire to establish the Rule of God on earth. "He was more extreme than Bin Laden. He used to say Bin Laden was too tolerant." Not everyone included the Hashemite Kingdom of Jordan which imprisoned Abu Musad for seven years, from 1992-1999. In prison be became a real hero, a real leader to his fellow prisoners. "He was always serious. He doesn't chat. He moves people, captures their hearts." He went back to Afghanistan; then, in 2002, on to Iraq.

Not the Coalition Provisional Authority, either, who after the capture of Saddam Hussein saw Abu Musad al Zarqawi as the greatest single threat to their rule in Iraq, particularly ih the Sunni Triangle. They put a price on his head of no less than $25 million. And to win that reward, that blood-money, became something of an obsession among the mercenaries in Iraq. Understandably so. It was a unique opportunity to gain fabulous wealth – better than looting a bank in the Congo or even a diamond mine in Sierra Leone – with all the kudos of performing an act of great public benefit (excepting of course the point of view of many

Sunnis) and becoming a kind of popular hero forever (except of course to those just mentioned).

So all sorts of plots and projects were aired and formed – some based on totally false rumours such as that Abu Musad al Zarqawi was one-legged. Which he was not. As was conclusively proved when in the spring of 2006 he was apparently betrayed by some of his fellow insurgents who revealed his presence in a remote farmhouse to the official American forces. They bombed the farmhouse, killed al Zarqawi, and thus foiled the hopes and plans of tens of thousands of mercenaries.

For whom all that remains, in this sphere, is to head for Waziristan and seek the head of Osama bin Laden himself, the greatest mercenary prize still available at the time of writing – if indeed bin Laden is (a) in Waziristan (b) still in the land of the living. In this respect at least Iraq has proved a disappointment to the latest generation of condottieri.

THE BONANZA – THE REASON WHY

But in almost every other respect Iraq has proved an enormous boon, a land of opportunity, an almost bottomless Ali Baba treasure cave for the mercenaries of this new century. And an unexpected, unhoped-for one, almost a heaven-sent bolt from the blue. For put it this way: if the invasion of Iraq – and the subsequent insurgency – had *not* occurred, what future, if any, would there have been for Tim Spicer and his ilk? Would Aegis not have gone the way of Trident Maritime and Sandline and indeed Executive Outcomes? Would the unlucky Frederick Forsyth have seen yet another of his investments peter out?

Probably. For who would ever have imagined that the invasion of a comparatively second-class Middle Eastern country would have involved not only a prolonged occupation by an enormous American army, plus its allies, but also by an ever-expanding army of mercenaries too? If such a question had been put in those terms to either military experts or political commentators or both, before the invasion of Iraq, it is hard to imagine that a single one of them would have forecast what in fact has actually followed. Indeed not one – at least as regards the expanding use of mercenaries – ever did.

Which brings us back to the questions posed towards the beginning of this chapter. What were mercenaries doing in Iraq at all? Why were they needed? What were they there **for**?

★ ★ ★

There is a theory, an overall view, that is gradually gaining favour. I do not subscribe to it myself but I may very well be wrong. It is this:- that Iraq is a gigantic military experiment in which the West, and particularly the United States, are testing out the idea of replacing their regular ground troops with – over the long run – hired military companies. In other words what we are now seeing in Iraq is the (moderately discreet) beginning of an enormous military change. In future mercenary companies will be keeping the peace and fighting our wars for us (and, by extension, for the United Nations too) all over the globe.

The arguments in favour of this theory are, basically, three. The first, rather surprisingly, is a matter of money. Contrary to what seems to be obvious commonsense, it is less expensive to hire mercenaries than to keep a regular army in being. True, mercenaries may earn three or four times as much as an average (Western) soldier. But the savings, enormous savings, lie in the welfare benefits that mercenaries neither claim nor expect. Apparently it now costs no less than $112,000 a year simply to keep a G.I. in the field – largely due to improved health care and benefits. Then there is the training, plus the barracks, the pensions, the welfare of families and all the rest of the paraphernalia. Plus the fact that an Army has to stay in being whether a war is being fought or not. Hire a mercenary army and you – the State – can more or less forget about welfare benefits or pensions or families or indeed training. And when the war for which the mercenaries are hired is over, they can be paid off and dismissed. Mercenary armies are – at least as far as the Western world is concerned – cheaper: an economy.

The second argument – and this is undoubtedly true and always has been – is that mercenaries are expendable. US soldiers or British soldiers are killed say in Iraq or Afghanistan; there is inevitably a fuss, or, at the least, notice taken in the media. Body counts are added up, weeping relatives are filmed, corpses are flown home and solemnly buried, posthumous honours are awarded. A mercenary is killed – and there is none of this. Like poor Fred in the famous rhyme, he was alive and is dead; there's now no more to be said. It may be heartless. But it is, and always will be, true.

The third argument is less specific, broader. It is this: that armies are changing rapidly, that in prosperous states of the Western world – particularly in those where conscription has never been the norm, like the United States and the United Kingdom – fewer and fewer young men are volunteering for the armed forces, or at least for the poor bloody infantry as opposed to the specialist arms. Already in the British Army it is calculated that about one tenth of those serving are foreigners, not British citizens at all (largely Fijians and West Indians from the Caribbean Islands). Being foreigners serving a state that is not their own, they are by definition mercenaries. In other words Her Majesty's Government is already employing large members of mercenaries as regular troops, though attempting to disguise the fact – and certainly mitigating the impression[7] – by scattering these mercenaries here and there among different regiments and battalions rather than allowing them to group together in their own special units.

---

[7] Which may account for the cool reception given by the Army authorities to the Prince of Wales' recent suggestion that a turbaned Sikh battalion should be recruited and formed – in line though that is with the British Indian Army tradition in the days of the Empire. .

But what if this trend continues? What if HMG one day finds itself recruiting not 10% but 40%, 50%, 60% or 70% of its infantry abroad? Then it will in effect have a regular army of mercenaries - no doubt British-officered and commanded, but a mercenary army all the same. What then, the argument might go, is the difference between employing full-time an army of mercenaries and hiring, as and when occasion demands, different, smaller mercenary bands, mostly also British-officered? In principle it is impossible to see much real difference; in practice the latter would certainly cost less and give - probably - as good value for much less money.

And, furthermore, it does seem to be the way things are now developing, certainly in the United Kingdom, if not yet - not as openly at least - in the United States. For regulars, particularly from the elite fighting units like the Paras and the SAS, are haemorrhaging away from the British Army to join the ranks of the private military companies and treble or quadruple the money they earn. So much so that in the spring of 2006 an Army source admitted: "We're losing far too many high-quality troops to private military contractors. So they're being offered a kind of gap year if they fancy going off for a while to make more money." After which they are being allowed to come back and take up regimental life as before without, it appears, any downgrading in rank. But how many will actually re-enlist after having tasted the comparative freedom and certainly much higher pay of companies such as Aegis or Olive or the rest?

Not, the historian should note, that this is a new phenomenon. The Royal Navy had much the same problem three hundred years ago when privateers at sea on the Spanish Main played the same role then that private military companies on land are playing now in the Middle East.

"The privateers which are commissioned by the government," complained Admiral Whetstone in the West Indies, with more vehemence and less tolerance than his anonymous British Army successor now- the year then was 1702 - "have slockstered away many of our men, notwithstanding we use all the care we can to prevent it."

Nonetheless the Royal Navy survived then; and no doubt the British Army will survive its present 'slockstering' now.

★ ★ ★

But what is certainly true is that mercenaries in Iraq have been taking over, in one form or another, many of the duties that traditionally would have been performed by regular ground troops; that they are, in their role as auxiliaries, much appreciated by the various colonels and generals of the Coalition forces if only because they permit the said colonels and generals not to disperse their own regular troops on minor but essential military duties; that they are fighting and dying in proportionate numbers to the regulars; that they have proved their worth militarily; and indeed that it is perfectly possible to imagine a situation where the regular Coalition forces will gradually be withdrawn but the PMCs, the mercenaries, will stay on to became the military backbone of the régime in Iraq and of the West's interest in that country; and indeed possibly – though at the moment it seems less likely – in Afghanistan too.

THE FUTURE

Prophecy in mercenary matters is always dangerous – even that very tentative prophecy above.

Nevertheless there is one forecast that should be made, one question that should be posed (even if no attempt is made here to answer it) at the end of a chapter that has certainly not told a coherent story – as most previous chapters have done – but has, hopefully, daubed in a colourful, if necessarily patchy, picture. It is a question that Departments of Defence and State Departments and Foreign Offices should certainly be scratching their wise old heads over. The question is this: what is to become of all these thousands of 'military contractors' and their leaders, the new *condottieri*, when the Iraq episode finally comes to an end?

For if there is one lesson that mercenary history teaches – and this is a forecast I will certainly venture – it is that large and powerful mercenary forces do not simply fade away with a bow and a smile and a graceful wave of the hand when their regular employment comes to an end.

Take, for instance, the famous case of the 1er REP of the Foreign Legion, so often referred to in the course of this book. When in April 1961 the Regiment was, following the (failed) *Coup of the Four Generals* in Algeria, solemnly paraded and ignominiously disbanded and its barracks at Zeralda blown up,* no doubt De Gaulle thought that that was the end of the matter. So it was, in one sense; for the 1er REP was never reformed, and does not now exist. But the ex-members of this Regiment spread out, maintained contact, and became not only the nucleus of the OAS, France's own anti-Gaullist Secret Army, but also of all modern mercenaries in Africa throughout the Sixties. They most certainly did not simply fade away.

Some of course, like Sir John Hawkwood of the White Company, may go on to an honoured retirement, with a famous commemorative fresco painted on the inside of the Duomo, commissioned by the grateful city fathers of Florence, and buried, by special request of the King of England, back in the family tomb at Sible Hedingham in Essex.

But others, like Hawkwood's predecessor Fra Moriale of the Great Company, more typically go on to sow confusion and spread panic among the states that once employed them. Fra Moriale indeed aimed at establishing his power over a whole peninsula – in his case, the peninsula of Italy. He nearly succeeded. In fact he failed; and was beheaded by the then dictator of Rome, Cola Di Rienzo. One might call him the Simon Mann of his day, particularly if Simon Mann passes from the dungeons of the tyrant Mugabe into the execution chambers of the tyrant Obiang - as is still very possible.

Following the same conceit: Tim Spicer, Colonel Tim Spicer, now shows signs of becoming the John Hawkwood of the twenty-first century and can perhaps hope for commemorative paintings too (though hardly in Baghdad's mosques) - and who knows? - even a knighthood in the future as well as his present immense riches. But does he, one cannot help wondering, ever spare a thought for his wretched fellow Scots Guards officer languishing miserably in Chikurubi as he himself might have been languishing still in Port Moresby's prison if all had gone even more wrong than it actually did in Papua New Guinea? Is there solidarity among mercenaries? Does it ever cross Tim Spicer's mind that he might use his new-found power, or wealth, or both, to extract his old comrade Simon Mann from that miserable imprisonment in Zimbabwe?

Now *that*, should it ever be the case, would open - and deserve - a new chapter (in both senses) in mercenary history.

Books – A Short Selection with Acknowledgements

SAMANTHA WEINBERG, *Last of the Pirates : The Search for Bob Denard* (Jonathan Cape, 1994).

A splendid book, describing this young journalist's quest that led her to the Comores - as well as to Paris and South Africa; to which I gratefully acknowledge a great debt for both information and insights.

PIERRE LUNEL, *Bob Denard: Le Roi de Fortune* (Editions 1, 1991).

A massive volume, the nearest thing to an 'official' biography of Denard; to which I also owe a great debt.

PATRICK OLLIVIER: *Soldat de Fortune* (Editions Gérard de Villiers, 1990).

A memoir, well-written and particularly interesting on his time as a mercenary with Grey's Scouts in Rhodesia. A little sketchier on the Comores and Chad; but again I would like to acknowledge my debt to this account.

PIERRE PÉAN, *Affaires Africaines* (Editions Fayard, 1983)

This book caused an immense controversy when it came out in France over twenty years ago, consisting as it does largely of a documented attack on France's ally, President Bongo of Gabon. It describes Bongo's Presidential Guard in great detail; and Bob Denard is here one of the major villains of the piece.

Its author's account of the attempted mercenary coup at Cotonou is largely taken from documents first published in full by the excellent and always well-informed progressive journal *Afrique-Asia*.

STEPHEN SMITH and ANTOINE GLASER, *Ces Messieurs d'Afrique* (Calmann Levy 1982).

An *exposé* of personages involved in French/African affairs; including chapters on Paul Barril, Jean-Yves Ollivier and Jean-Christophe Mitterand, the late President's son.

MIKE HOARE, *Three Years with Sylvia* (Robert Hale, 1971).
Hoare's sailing book is written in a relaxed and open style; very enjoyable reading, and I would like to acknowledge my debt to it.

MIKE HOARE, *The Seychelles Affair* (Bantam Press, 1986).
Disappointing - except for the account of the author's time in jail when the writing is vivid, the emotions still raw, the impression painful.

FRED BRIDGLAND, *Jonas Savimbi - A Key to Africa* (Mainstream Publishing, Edinburgh 1986)
A long and detailed book by a well-known journalist, generally - but not invariably - favourable to Jonas. Again I would like to acknowledge my debt to this fascinating account (which of course finishes with high hopes, many years before its subject's death).

CHESTER CROCKER, *High Noon in Southern Africa* (W.W. Norton & Co., 1993)
A witty and extremely well-written account by a US diplomat of his unrelenting drive to obtain peace in Angola - and send the Cubans home.

STEPHEN ELLIS, *The Mask of Anarchy - The destruction of Liberia and the Religious Dimension of an African Civil War* (Hurst & Co., London, 1999).
A really excellent academic book, the reputation of which is growing year by year since its publication.

RUSSELL BANKS, *The Darling* (Harper Collins, US, 2004)
A splendidly picturesque and vivid novel, now published in many countries, set mainly in Liberia - which contains a vivid and seemingly accurate portrayal of Charles Taylor and his life.

FREDERICK FORSYTH, *The Biafra Story* (Penguin, 1969)
The famous thriller-writer's first book was published as a Penguin Special in 1969 before the fall of Biafra and reissued in 1976. It is a personalised non-fiction account of the civil war in Nigeria from, as the title implies, the Biafran point of view.

FREDERICK FORSYTH, *The Dogs of War* (Hutchinsons 1974; Corgi paperback edition 1975, many times reprinted)
Forsyth's great mercenary thriller, "fictional"; but only too clearly based on Equatorial Guinea. (See Chapter 14).

FREDERICK FORSYTH, *No Comebacks* (Corgi paperback edition, 1982, 1983)

Ten short stories; of the first, the title story, the protagonist is Calvi, a Corsican mercenary. A personal reference will strike readers of the present book.

MINETTE WALTERS, *The Devil's Feathers*　(Macmillan 2005).

One of her thriller-novels with the greatest potential, alas not fully exploited. Listed here (a) because her thrillers always entrance the present author (b) her villain in this one is a psychopath of a mercenary; and the best scenes in the book feature him in Sierra Leone which (unlike the main portion, set in the sinister English countryside as usual) are intensely believable.

RORY STEWART, *Occupational Hazards - My Time Governing in Iraq* (Picador / Pan Macmillan 2006).

JOHN GEDDES, *Highway to Hell* (Century 2006).

Both the above very recent autobiographical memoirs deal with Iraq, are referred to in the final chapter; and I would like to acknowledge my debt to both authors and publishers.

As I would also to many, many journalists, reporters and foreign correspondents and to their newspapers and magazines; too many to list; but I would make particular mention here, and particularly acknowledge my debt to, two almost indispensable, highly informative reviews published respectively in London and Paris, *Africa Confidential* and *Lettre de l'Océan Indién*.

The Mercenary Trilogy
Volumes I and II

Most wars have been fought by, or with, mercenary forces. The purpose of **The Mercenary Trilogy** is therefore *neither* to attempt the almost impossible task of writing the entire worldwide history of mercenary soldiering - for that would be very little less than a history of warfare in general and would need twenty volumes, not three - *nor* to provide a potted history which would simply be a roll call of names, dates, forces, armaments, battles and campaigns. A pretty dull three volumes these would make.

No. The purpose of these three books is to give an overview of the most interesting periods in mercenary history, with particular reference to the twentieth and twenty-first centuries - modern times.

★   ★   ★

Each volume stands by itself. Each is a narrative. Each tells a number of closely or loosely-related stories.

About the present, the third volume, *Hired Guns and Coups d'Etat 1976-2006,* I need only say that, despite its title, it covers certain civil wars as well as the *coups d'état* that are its main topic.

The second volume, *'Mad Dogs' and Mercenaries 1960-1997,* slightly overlaps - insofar as it carries the history of the Congo through to the overthrow of Mobutu. Its main protagonists are 'Mad Mike' Hoare and Bob Denard, both of whom appear in - indeed dominate - the first half of the current volume.

The first volume, *The Wolves of War 400 B.C. - 1800 A.D.*, deals with the Free Companies, the Condottieri and the ferocious Swiss; but ranges backward to the famous Ten Thousand, whose exploits in Persia kick-started mercenary history in the ancient world, and forward to the Hessians on whom the eighteenth-century British so mistakenly counted to quash the American Revolution.

THE WOLVES OF WAR

MERCENARIES: 400 BC TO 1800 AD

ANTHONY MOCKLER

This is the first Volume of the Mercenary Trilogy by Anthony Mockler, the world's leading authority on mercenary soldiers.

There is a pattern to mercenary history, that repeats itself from ancient to mediaeval to renaissance times; and the 'thread' is this:-

A mercenary should never, ever, totally trust his employers, still less his employers' allies. This first becomes apparent with the famous epic of the Ten Thousand, whose mercenary leaders were so treacherously killed by their Persian allies; and continues throughout the history of the Free Companies in the Middle Ages, so beloved of Froissart; and of the Condottieri of the Renaissance, their Italian successors – it was a great mistake as a mercenary leader to take service with Cesare Borgia. But employers too would be wrong to trust brutal mercenaries such as the Swiss mountaineers (now sanitized as the Papal Guard) or ineffectual mercenaries like the beautifully-turned-out Hessians whom George III and his generals relied on so expensively and so erroneously to give the American rebels a severe drubbing. Then came the French Revolution – which virtually, but not entirely, put an end to mercenary soldiering in the sacred name of nationalism and revolutionary ideals.

★   ★   ★

To order *The Wolves of War* visit www.huntermackay.com or write to:

Hunter Mackay
140 Upper Road
Oxford
OX1 5LW

Hunter Mackay (Scotland)
The Guynd
By Arbroath
Angus

ISBN 0-947907-05-X
ISBN 978-0-947907-05-1

This is the second Volume of the
Mercenary Trilogy by Anthony Mockler,
the world's leading authority on mercenary
soldiers.

When mercenaries suddenly reappeared
in the Congo in 1960, like evil genii
released from some anachronistic, distaste-
fully mediaeval, bottle, there was a storm
of protest, a genuine cry of horror, and
inevitable confusion of roles. 'That mad
bloodhound Hoare' East Germany's Radio
described 'Mad Mike' as; and it is from this
(and of course the famous Noel Coward
ditty) that the second volume takes it title.

It traces the origins of the modern mercenary to that most famous mercenary
force of all time, the French Foreign Legion; and goes on to describe in particular
the Civil Wars in the Congo (where so many of the original mercenary leaders
were formerly Foreign Legion paratroops) right up to the fall of Mobutu. But it
covers also the civil wars in Biafra, in the Sudan and in the Yemen where mercenaries (including Bob Denard) played dramatic though less decisive roles. Above
all it tells the full story of the extraordinary Mercenaries' Revolt led by 'Black
Jack' Schramme.

★   ★   ★

To order '*Mad Dogs' and Mercenaries* visit www.huntermackay.com or write to:

Hunter Mackay   Hunter Mackay (Scotland)
140 Upper Road   The Guynd
Oxford   By Arbroath,
OX1 5LW   Angus

ISBN 0-947907-06-8
ISBN 978-0-947907-06-8

Index